Marketing Management

AN OVERVIEW

DALE M. LEWISON
THE UNIVERSITY OF AKRON

THE DRYDEN PRESS
HARCOURT BRACE COLLEGE PUBLISHERS

Fort Worth Philadelphia San Diego New York Orlando Austin San Antonio
Toronto Montreal London Sydney Tokyo

To the other three... Gary, Regina, and Rebecca

EXECUTIVE EDITOR	*Lyn Hastert Maize*
ASSOCIATE EDITOR	*Paul Stewart*
PROJECT EDITOR	*Kathryn Stewart*
PRODUCTION MANAGER	*Jessica Wyatt*
PRODUCT MANAGER	*Lisé Johnson*
ART DIRECTOR	*Scott Baker*
ART & LITERARY RIGHTS EDITOR	*Annette Coolidge*
ELECTRONIC PUBLISHING COORDINATOR	*Kathi Embry*
COPY EDITOR	*Sheryl Nelson*
PROOFREADER	*Kay Kaylor*
CRITICAL READER	*Milt Silver*
INDEXER	*Sylvia Coates*
TEXT TYPE	*10/12 Palatino*

Copyright © 1996 by Harcourt Brace & Company

All rights reserved. No part of this publication may be reproduced or transmitted in any form or by any means, electronic or mechanical, including photocopy, recording, or any information storage and retrieval system, without permission in writing from the publisher.

Requests for permission to make copies of any part of the work should be mailed to: Permissions Department, Harcourt Brace & Company, 6277 Sea Harbor Drive, Orlando, FL 32887-6777.

Address for Editorial Correspondence
The Dryden Press, 301 Commerce Street, Suite 3700, Fort Worth, TX 76102

Address for Orders
The Dryden Press, 6277 Sea Harbor Drive, Orlando, FL 32887
1-800-782-4479, or 1-800-433-0001 (in Florida)

ISBN: 0-03-098153-0

Library of Congress Catalog Card Number: 95-70434

Printed in the United States of America
5 6 7 8 9 0 1 2 3 4 090 9 8 7 6 5 4 3 2 1

The Dryden Press
Harcourt Brace College Publishers

The Dryden Press Series in Marketing

Avila, Williams, Ingram, and LaForge
The Professional Selling Skills Workbook

Bateson
Managing Services Marketing: Text and Readings
Third Edition

Blackwell, Blackwell, and Talarzyk
Contemporary Cases in Consumer Behavior
Fourth Edition

Boone and Kurtz
Contemporary Marketing Plus
Eighth Edition

Churchill
Basic Marketing Research
Third Edition

Churchill
Marketing Research: Methodological Foundations
Sixth Edition

Czinkota and Ronkainen
Global Marketing

Czinkota and Ronkainen
International Marketing
Fourth Edition

Czinkota and Ronkainen
International Marketing Strategy: Environmental Assessment and Entry Strategies

Dickson
Marketing Management

Engel, Blackwell, and Miniard
Consumer Behavior
Eighth Edition

Futrell
Sales Management
Fourth Edition

Grover
Theory & Simulation of Market-Focused Management

Ghosh
Retail Management
Second Edition

Hassan and Blackwell
Global Marketing: Managerial Dimensions and Cases

Hutt and Speh
Business Marketing Management: A Strategic View of Industrial and Organizational Markets
Fifth Edition

Ingram and LaForge
Sales Management: Analysis and Decision Making
Second Edition

Lewison
Marketing Management: An Overview

Lindgren and Shimp
Marketing: An Interactive Learning System

Krugman, Reid, Dunn, and Barban
Advertising: Its Role in Modern Marketing
Eighth Edition

Oberhaus, Ratliffe, and Stauble
Professional Selling: A Relationship Process
Second Edition

Parente, Vanden Bergh, Barban, and Marra
Advertising Campaign Strategy: A Guide to Marketing Communication Plans

Rachman
Marketing Today
Third Edition

Rosenbloom
Marketing Channels: A Management View
Fifth Edition

Schaffer
Applying Marketing Principles Software

Schellinck and Maddox
Marketing Research: A Computer-Assisted Approach

Schnaars
MICROSIM
Marketing simulation available for IBM PC and Apple

Schuster and Copeland
Global Business: Planning for Sales and Negotiations

Shimp
Promotion Management and Marketing Communications
Third Edition

Talarzyk
Cases and Exercises in Marketing

Terpstra and Sarathy
International Marketing
Sixth Edition

Weitz and Wensley
Readings in Strategic Marketing Analysis, Planning, and Implementation

Zikmund
Exploring Marketing Research
Fifth Edition

Harcourt Brace College Outline Series

Peterson
Principles of Marketing

PREFACE

Marketing Management: An Overview presents complete yet concise coverage of the essential marketing concepts, processes, strategies, and tactics most commonly used by the marketing manager. By striking a balance between the theory and practice of marketing, this textbook is equally suitable for use as an instructional tool within an academic classroom setting and as a general reference book within the practical business world. For the classroom situation—where students need a common knowledge base of marketing management fundamentals—this textbook offers a clear and succinct overview of the field of marketing management and serves as an appropriate

- primary text selection for the undergraduate marketing management course
- primary text selection for professional development seminars and continuing education in marketing and marketing management
- supplementary text selection for undergraduate marketing management case or problems courses in which the instructor prefers to select his or her own cases, projects, games, or other pedagogical teaching methods
- supplementary text selection for graduate marketing management case or problems courses in which the instructor prefers to select his or her own class materials and employ his or her own teaching methods

Both the content and organization of this textbook support its versatility and multipurpose character. The text offers a breadth of coverage and a depth of coverage that are consistent with the needs of a wide range of adopters. All key marketing topics are discussed with an appropriate level of detail and supported by practical examples and illustrations. The organization provides a very systematic and logical presentation of the marketing management function.

Part I and Chapter 1 introduce the field of marketing and establish the organizational framework used throughout the text. The decidedly management character of the text is confirmed in Part II with an extensive discussion of both the business and marketing planning processes. Each planning level is reviewed starting with the strategic business plan in Chapter 2, continuing with the strategic marketing plan in Chapter 3 and the annual marketing plan in Chapter 4, and concluding with a discussion of the marketing information system in Chapter 5.

Assessing various types of marketing situations is highlighted in Part III. The processes of analyzing environments (Chapter 6), consumers (Chapter 7), competitors (Chapter 8), and markets (Chapter 9) are identified and described in Part III. The four basic marketing mix decisions are previewed in Part IV. Product, distribution, promotion, and price decisions are discussed in Chapters 10, 11, 12, and 13, respectively. The implementation and control of the marketing mix is the focus of Part V and Chapter 14. The special requirements associated with services marketing, nonprofit marketing, and international marketing are examined in Part VI and Chapter 15.

SUPPLEMENTS

The Dryden Press will provide complimentary supplements or supplement packages to those adopters qualified under our adoption policy. Please contact your sales representative to learn how you may qualify. If as an adopter or potential user you receive supplements you do not need, please return them to your sales representative or send them to:

Attn: Returns Department
Troy Warehouse
465 South Lincoln Drive
Troy, MO 63379

ACKNOWLEDGMENTS

The author would like to acknowledge the contributions and suggestions of my students, colleagues, editors, and reviewers. For their support and encouragement, special appreciation goes to Steve Hallam, Dean of the College of Business Administration, James Inman, Associate Dean, and my colleagues in the Marketing Department at The University of Akron. A special thanks goes to Karen Nelsen for her administrative and production assistance, to my graduate assistant Tom Sherer for his editorial and research assistance, to Dr. Paulette Polley for co-authoring Chapter 15, and to Gary White for co-authoring the three appendices. Additionally, I would like to thank the many editors at The Dryden Press for their contributions and all their hard work. Especially, Kathryn Stewart, project editor; Jessica Wyatt, production manager; Scott Baker, art director; and Kathi Embry, electronic publishing coordinator. Also I would like to thank Lyn Hastert Maize, now executive editor, who originally signed this project, Jim Lizotte, acquisitions editor, Paul Stewart, associate editor, who saw the project through to completion, and Lisé W. Johnson, executive product manager. Finally I am indebted to the following reviewers for their valuable suggestions: William T. Faranda, University of Virginia; Sharon Thach, Tennessee State University; and Fred Trawick, University of Alabama at Birmingham.

Brief Table of Contents

Preface

Part I – Marketing Management   1

Chapter 1   Marketing Management   3

Part II – Marketing Planning   23

Chapter 2   The Strategic Business Plan   25
Chapter 3   The Strategic Marketing Plan   46
Chapter 4   The Annual Marketing Plan   63
Chapter 5   The Marketing Information System   80

Part III – Marketing Situations   105

Chapter 6   Environmental Analysis   107
Chapter 7   Consumer Analysis   133
Chapter 8   Competitor Analysis   163
Chapter 9   Market Analysis   190

Part IV – Marketing Decisions   217

Chapter 10   Product Decisions   219
Chapter 11   Distribution Decisions   258
Chapter 12   Promotion Decisions   294
Chapter 13   Pricing Decisions   334

Part V – Marketing Actions   355

Chapter 14   Implementing and Controlling the Marketing Effort   356

Part VI – Marketing Issues   373

Chapter 15   Service, Nonprofit, and International Marketing   375

Appendices

Appendix A   A Business Student's Guide to Library Resources   409
Appendix B   A Business Student's Guide to Professional and Trade Associations   427
Appendix C   A Business Student's Guide to Case Analysis   438

Credits   449

Index   451

Contents

PREFACE ... v

Part I – Marketing Management   1

CHAPTER 1   MARKETING MANAGEMENT ... 3
  Introduction ... 4
  Marketing Definitions ... 4
   The Marketing Function ... 6
   The Management Process ... 6
   Marketing Activities ... 8
   Facilitating Activities ... 8
   The Exchange Process ... 10
   The Consumption Process ... 13
  Marketing Perspectives ... 14
   Marketing Eras ... 14
   Marketing Philosophies ... 15
  A Planning Model ... 19
   Levels of Planning ... 19
   Types of Planning ... 21
   Stages in the Planning Process ... 21
  Concluding Remarks ... 21

Part II – Marketing Planning   23

CHAPTER 2   THE STRATEGIC BUSINESS PLAN ... 25
  Introduction ... 26
  The Strategic Business Plan ... 26
  Organizational Mission ... 26
   Mission Statement ... 27
   Scope Statement ... 27
   Value Statement ... 29
   Vision Statement ... 29
  Portfolio Analysis ... 30
   Boston Consulting Group's Matrix ... 31

	General Electric's Business Screen	33
	Profit-Impact-of-Market Strategy Program	35
	Business Opportunities	37
	Growth Opportunities	37
	Restructuring Opportunities	41
	Concluding Remarks	43
CHAPTER 3	THE STRATEGIC MARKETING PLAN	46
	Introduction	47
	The Strategic Marketing Plan	47
	Marketing Goals	48
	SWOT Analysis	49
	Internal Organizational Scan	50
	External Environmental Scan	52
	SWOT Matrix	53
	Marketing Strategies	55
	Differentiating Strategies	56
	Positioning Strategies	59
	Concluding Remarks	61
CHAPTER 4	THE ANNUAL MARKETING PLAN	63
	Introduction	64
	The Annual Marketing Plan	64
	Title Page	64
	Table of Contents	65
	Executive Summary	65
	Marketing Objectives	66
	Situation Analysis	66
	Marketing Programs	66
	Marketing Actions	66
	Marketing Issues	66
	Reference Sources	66
	Marketing Objectives	67
	Market Objectives	67
	Financial Objectives	70
	Societal Objectives	72
	Situation Analysis	72
	Corporate Review	73
	Environmental Analysis	73
	Consumer Analysis	74
	Competitor Analysis	74
	Market Analysis	74

	Marketing Programs	75
	Product Decisions	75
	Distribution Decisions	76
	Promotion Decisions	77
	Price Decisions	78
	Concluding Remarks	78
CHAPTER 5	THE MARKETING INFORMATION SYSTEM	80
	Introduction	81
	The Marketing Information System	81
	Stage 1: Locating Information	81
	Stage 2: Gathering Information	83
	Stage 3: Processing Information	84
	Stage 4: Utilizing Information	85
	Marketing Intelligence	86
	Library Sources	86
	Government Sources	86
	Association Sources	87
	Commercial Sources	88
	Marketing Research	89
	Step 1: Problem Definition	92
	Step 2: Hypothesis Formulation	93
	Step 3: Research Design	93
	Step 4: Data Collection	94
	Records Search	102
	Analytical Models	102
	Concluding Remarks	104

Part III – Marketing Situations 105

CHAPTER 6	ENVIRONMENTAL ANALYSIS	107
	Introduction	108
	Population and Demographic Trends	110
	Population Growth	111
	Demographic Trends	111
	Economic and Competitive Forces	115
	Economic Systems	115
	Economic Conditions	116
	Economic Issues	117
	Competitive Market Structures	118
	Social and Cultural Influences	119
	The Social Agenda	119

	The Cultural Agenda	121
	Political and Legal Issues	125
	The Political System	126
	The Legal System	126
	Scientific and Technological Advances	128
	Concluding Remarks	130
Chapter 7	**Consumer Analysis**	**133**
	Introduction	134
	Consumer Buying Behavior	134
	Consumer Buying Behavior Model	134
	Consumer Buying Decision Process	134
	Psychological Influences	139
	Personal Influences	144
	Social Influences	147
	Situational Influences	152
	Organizational Buying Behavior	152
	Organizational Buying Model	154
	Organizational Markets	154
	Organizational Buying	157
	Concluding Remarks	161
Chapter 8	**Competitor Analysis**	**163**
	Introduction	164
	Competitive Analysis Model	164
	Competitor Identification	165
	Levels of Competition	166
	Forms of Competition	168
	Competitor Intelligence	171
	Competitor Relations	176
	Competitive Advantages	177
	Cost Leadership	178
	Differentiation	180
	Focus	180
	Competitive Strategies	181
	Attack Strategies	181
	Defense Strategies	184
	Concluding Remarks	187
Chapter 9	**Market Analysis**	**190**
	Introduction	191
	Market Analysis	191
	Defining a Market	191

Analyzing a Market	194
Market Segmentation	195
Step 1: Identifying Market Segments	195
Step 2: Profiling Market Segments	204
Step 3: Evaluating Market Segments	206
Market Targeting	207
Step 4: Selecting Market Segments	207
Step 5: Targeting Market Segments	209
Market Positioning	212
Step 6: Developing Positioning Strategies	213
Step 7: Tailoring Marketing Mixes	213
Concluding Remarks	213

Part IV – Marketing Decisions 217

CHAPTER 10 PRODUCT DECISIONS 219

Introduction	220
Product Concepts	220
Total-Product Concept	220
Product-Mix Concept	223
Product Life Cycles	225
Product Classification	228
Consumer Products	228
Organizational Products	231
Product Management	231
Product-Item Management	231
Product-Line Management	240
Product-Mix Management	242
New Product Management	245
Product Development Process	245
Product Adoption Process	251
Product Diffusion Process	253
Concluding Remarks	255

CHAPTER 11 DISTRIBUTION DECISIONS 258

Introduction	259
Marketing Channels	259
Channel Systems: An Intercompany Network	259
Channel Institutions: The Marketing Team	261
Channel Interactions: A Cooperative Effort	261
Channel Flows: A Distributive Pathway	262
The Design of Marketing Channels	265

	Recognizing Distribution Needs	265
	Establishing Distribution Objectives	267
	Identifying Distribution Alternatives	268
	Evaluating Distribution Alternatives	273
	Selecting Distribution Alternatives	279
	The Management of Marketing Channels	281
	Channel Conflict	282
	Channel Control	285
	Channel Cooperation	288
	Concluding Remarks	292
CHAPTER 12	**PROMOTION DECISIONS**	**294**
	Introduction	295
	The Marketing Communications Process	296
	The Basic Communication Model	296
	The AIDA and Hierarchy of Effects Models	297
	The Marketing Communications Mix	299
	Individual Marketing Communications Mix Components	299
	Integrative Marketing Communications	301
	The Promotion Management Process	302
	Review Annual Marketing Plan	302
	Establish Promotion Objectives	303
	Organize Promotion Campaign	303
	Prepare Promotion Budget	305
	Implement Promotion Campaign	305
	The Advertising Component	305
	Types of Advertising	305
	The Creative Advertising Campaign	308
	Advertising Management	316
	The Personal Selling Component	317
	Types of Personal Selling	317
	The Personal Selling Process	318
	Sales Management	323
	The Direct-Marketing Component	327
	Direct-Mail Marketing	327
	Mail-Order Marketing	328
	Direct-Response Marketing	329
	The Sales Promotion Component	330
	Concluding Remarks	330
CHAPTER 13	**PRICING DECISIONS**	**334**

Introduction	335
Pricing Perspectives	336
Price and the Exchange Process	336
Price and the Value Concept	336
Pricing Determinants	338
Demand Characteristics	338
Cost Structures	338
Customer Expectations	339
Competitive Conditions	339
Legal Constraints	340
Pricing Objectives	341
Competition-Based Objectives	341
Sales-Oriented Objectives	342
Profit-Directed Objectives	342
Pricing Methods	342
Cost-Based Pricing	343
Profit-Based Pricing	345
Customer-Based Pricing	345
Competition-Based Pricing	345
Vendor-Based Pricing	346
Pricing Strategies	346
Differential Pricing	346
Competitive Pricing	349
Geographic Pricing	350
Product-Line Pricing	350
Psychological Pricing	351
Promotional Pricing	352
Concluding Remarks	353

Part V – Marketing Actions 355

CHAPTER 14 IMPLEMENTING AND CONTROLLING THE MARKETING EFFORT 356

Introduction	357
Marketing Management Process Revisited	357
Implementing	357
Organizing the Marketing Effort	358
Executing the Marketing Effort	365
Controlling	367
Monitoring the Marketing Effort	368
Modifying the Marketing Effort	370
Concluding Remarks	371

Part VI – Marketing Issues   373

Chapter 15	Service, Nonprofit, and International Marketing	375
	Introduction	376
	Service Marketing	376
	Nature of Service Marketing	377
	Strategies for Service Marketers	379
	Nonprofit Marketing	386
	Nature of Nonprofit Marketing	386
	Forms of Nonprofit Marketing	386
	International Marketing	388
	Motivation for Marketing Abroad	388
	Deterrents to International Marketing	390
	Cultural and Social Influences	391
	Political and Legal Influences	394
	Economic Integration	396
	International Marketing Mix	400
	Concluding Remarks	406
Appendix A	A Business Student's Guide to Library Resources	409
	Introduction	409
	Finding Books	410
	Finding Journal Articles	412
	The Reference Department	414
	Government Documents	415
	Audiovisual Materials	417
	Business Information Sources	417
	Locating Materials Outside of the College or University Library	424
Appendix B	A Business Student's Guide to Professional and Trade Associations	427
Appendix C	A Business Student's Guide to Case Analysis	438
	Introduction	438
	Case Analysis	439
	Case Analysis Procedures	439
	Case Analysis Structure	439
	Case Analysis Pitfalls	445
	Concluding Remarks	447
Credits		449
Index		451

MARKETING MANAGEMENT

CHAPTER 1   MARKETING MANAGEMENT

Marketing Management

Chapter Outline

- **Introduction**
- **Marketing Definitions**
    - The Marketing Function
    - The Management Process
    - Marketing Activities
    - Facilitating Activities
    - The Exchange Process
    - The Consumption Process
- **Marketing Perspectives**
    - Marketing Eras
    - Marketing Philosophies
- **A Planning Model**
    - Levels of Planning
    - Types of Planning
    - Stages in the Planning Process
- **Concluding Remarks**

Introduction

This text focuses on marketing and the management of marketing activities and presents a general survey of the basic principles and concepts of marketing together with those strategies and tactics that marketing managers employ to gain a sustainable competitive advantage within selected markets. Effective decision making and problem solving are explored through illustrations and examples of marketing applications used by today's successful marketing executive. The intent of this text is to provide the reader with a basic foundation of marketing knowledge and an overview of marketing management.

A visual representation of the structure and content of the text is presented in Figure 1-1. As shown, Part I provides an overview of marketing management and the issues faced by the marketing manager. Part II discusses marketing planning and examines the planning process at three different levels within an organization—the strategic business plan (Chapter 2), the strategic marketing plan (Chapter 3), and the annual marketing plan (Chapter 4). Chapter 5 outlines the basic marketing information system needed in developing both strategic and operational marketing plans.

Marketing managers must deal with and adjust to many different, largely uncontrollable marketing situations. Part III identifies and describes the process of analyzing environments (Chapter 6), consumers (Chapter 7), competitors (Chapter 8), and markets (Chapter 9). With the development of marketing plans and the analysis of marketing situations, management is then in a position to make intelligent decisions regarding the four essential elements of the marketing mix. Part IV is a preview of marketing decisions relative to the firm's products (Chapter 10), distribution systems (Chapter 11), promotions (Chapter 12), and prices (Chapter 13).

Part V deals with the marketing actions of implementing and controlling the marketing effort (Chapter 14). In Part VI, the unique issues dealing with the marketing of services and international marketing (Chapter 15) are identified and discussed.

The purpose of Chapter 1 is to characterize the field of marketing and summarize the situations faced by the marketing manager. First, key marketing definitions are presented, followed by a close examination of the basic components of the marketing management process. Next, various historical viewpoints of marketing are reviewed from the perspectives of marketing eras and marketing philosophies. Finally, a strategic planning model is presented and used as an organizational framework for Part II.

Marketing Definitions

Marketing is one of the functional areas of business. Together with such functions as production, finance, human resources, accounting, and

FIGURE 1-1

AN OVERVIEW OF THE TEXT

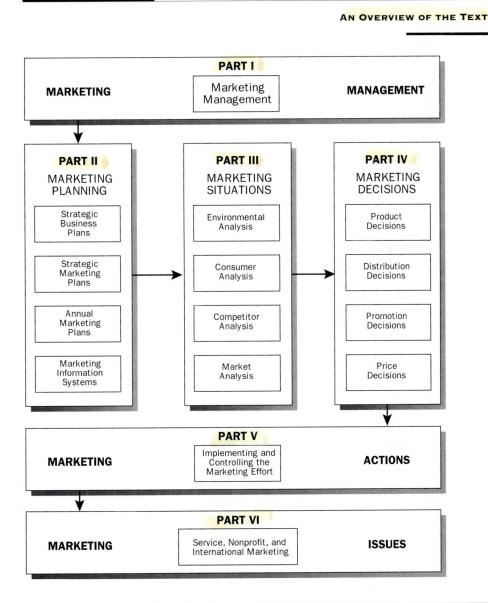

research and development, the marketing function plays an important and vital role in determining the success of any organization. The importance of marketing lies in the fact that it encompasses a wide range of activities that are directed at connecting the firm with those individuals or organizations who comprise the firm's markets. "In the market-driven company, every important judgment managers make must be based on current, complete, and correct information about the market, including assessments of both customers and competitors."[1]

THE MARKETING FUNCTION

What is the marketing function? "There is no agreement on a definition of marketing. A shelffull of textbooks on the subject produces a shelffull of differences."[2] Perhaps the most commonly accepted definition of marketing is the description offered by the American Marketing Association:

> **Marketing** is the process of planning and executing the conception, pricing, promotion, and distribution of ideas, goods, and services to create exchanges that will satisfy individual and organizational objectives.

Effective management of this exchange process provides the focal point for the following definition of marketing management:

> **Marketing management** is the process of managing marketing activities in order to facilitate the exchange process between individual and organizational consumers.

As illustrated in Figure 1-2, the key conceptual point of our definition of marketing management is that it is a *management process* directed at enhancing both *marketing activities* and *facilitating activities* in order to promote both the *exchange and consumption processes*.

THE MANAGEMENT PROCESS

Marketing management, part of the managerial process, concerns itself with the effective and efficient attainment of organizational aspirations and purposes (such as missions, goals, and objectives). **Effectiveness** is the degree to which an organization achieves a defined aspiration while **efficiency** is the amount of resources used by the organization in attaining that purpose. In the case of a marketing organization, effective and efficient marketing management consists of promoting desirable exchange relationships and consumption patterns while minimizing the cost of marketing and facilitating activities. A high-performance marketing organization is one that has achieved its aspirations in an efficient and effective manner.

Effective and efficient management is the result of careful and logical thoughts and actions. Marketing managers achieve their stated purposes through the three steps of planning, implementing, and controlling. Figure 1-3 illustrates the relationship of these three steps.

FIGURE 1-2

A Definition of Marketing Management

❑ *Planning*—concerns

1. *defining* where the marketing organization wants to be in the future (mission statements, goals, and objectives).

2. *deciding* how to get there (strategies, tactics, and courses of action).

❑ *Implementing*—deals with

1. *organizing* how tasks are assigned, people are grouped, and resources are allocated.

2. *leading* employees by inspiring and motivating them to make a significant contribution to the organization's aspirations.

❑ *Controlling*—includes

1. *monitoring* the performance of employees and organizational units relative to established plans.

2. *reacting* by either rewarding effective and efficient performance or by taking corrective action in cases where performance levels are not consistent with established plans.

FIGURE 1-3

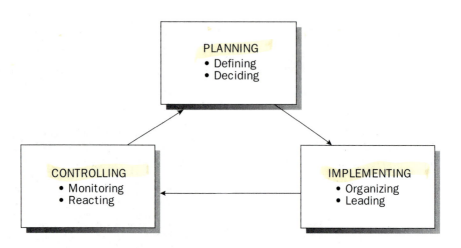

THE MANAGEMENT PROCESS

MARKETING ACTIVITIES

As suggested by the definitions of marketing and marketing management, the marketing function incorporates a diverse and complex set of activities designed to promote exchanges between an organization and its consuming public and to advance the demand and consumption of the organization's outputs. Traditionally, marketing activities are classified into the following four general marketing functions:

1. Creating products
2. Distributing products
3. Promoting products
4. Pricing products

A **product** is a generic term used in identifying what is being marketed; it can be a tangible good or an intangible service or idea. This combination of activities or functions is often referred to as the **marketing mix** or the **four Ps of marketing** (product, place, promotion, and price). While the four chapters presented in Part IV will discuss each of these activities in depth, Figure 1-4 outlines the basic decisions of each element of the marketing mix.

FACILITATING ACTIVITIES

Financing, informing, consulting, risktaking, and grading are activities that further the exchange process and assist the marketing manager to develop and implement a successful marketing mix.

FIGURE 1-4

MARKETING MIX DECISIONS

Marketing Mix	Product Mix	Price Mix	Distribution Mix	Mass Communication Mix	Personal Communication Mix	Publicity Mix
Basic Mix	Basic Product Mix	Basic Price Mix	Basic Distribution Mix	Basic Mass Communication Mix	Basic Personal Communication Mix	Basic Publicity Mix
	Instruments that mainly aim at the satisfaction of the prospective exchange party's needs.	Instruments that mainly fix the size and the way of payment exchanged for the goods or services.	Instruments that mainly determine the intensity and manner of how the goods will be made available.	Nonpersonal communication efforts that mainly aim at announcing the offer or maintaining awareness and knowledge about it: evoking or maintaining favorable feelings and removing barriers to wanting.	Personal communication efforts that mainly aim at announcing the offer or maintaining awareness and knowledge about it: evoking or maintaining favorable feelings and removing barriers to wanting.	Efforts that aim at inciting third parties (persons and authorities) to favorable communication about the offer.
	e.g.: product characteristics, options, assortment, brand name, packaging, quantity, factory guarantee.	e.g.: list price, usual terms of payment, usual payment, usual discounts, terms of credit, long-term savings campaigns.	e.g.: different types of distribution channels, density of the distribution system, trade relation mix (policy of margins, terms of delivery, etc.), merchandising advice.	e.g.: theme-advertising in various media, permanent exhibitions, certain forms of sponsoring.	e.g.: amount and type of selling, personal remunerations.	e.g.: press bulletins, press conferences, tours by journalists.

SOURCE: Adapted from Walter Van Waterschoot and Christophe Van den Bulte, "The 4P Classification of the Marketing Mix Revisited," *Journal of Marketing*, Vol. 56, No. 4 (October 1992), 90.

Inventory **financing** is one way a member of a marketing system (such as a manufacturer) might provide credit to another member (such as a retailer). Long- and short-term loans for capital equipment and physical facilities are another means by which the exchange process can be facilitated through financial transactions. Consumer credit, such as credit cards and charge accounts, allows the final consumer to finance purchases until the needed resources can be found.

Informing involves gathering, analyzing, and disseminating useful information to facilitate the decision-making process of producers, distributors, retailers, and consumers. External marketing intelligence and research, together with internal record searching and analytical models, are the key components of a marketing information system. A host of consulting services offer advice on a wide range of problems. Some of the more common consulting services are in accounting, advertising, business logistics, buyer behavior, financial management, human resource management, information systems, inventory management, legal issues, location analysis, market analysis, and sales forecasting.

Risk taking refers to a wide range of activities that involve taking action now in anticipation of future rewards. From the manufacturer who develops and markets a new product to the retailer who creates and sells a new assortment of merchandise, risk taking is essential if new opportunities are to be developed and realized. Some organizations facilitate the exchange process by reducing the risks of doing business, e.g., insurance companies and security firms.

Grading is the standardization of product quality (such as grades of beef) and quantity (standard sizes and weights). Grading activities greatly enhance the exchange process by giving buyers and sellers a base or reference point by which direct comparison of different products can be made. Comparisons help to reduce some of the risks associated with the exchange process.

THE EXCHANGE PROCESS

The focal point of marketing management is the exchange process. **Exchange** can be described as a process in which two or more individual consumers or business organizations give and receive something of value. As suggested by this definition, the prerequisites for exchange are two interested parties that have something of value to exchange and are able to communicate with one another. Furthermore, exchange is a voluntary process in which both parties are free to accept or reject any offer. Exchanges occur most frequently when both parties perceive the process as a win-win situation; that is, each benefits by being better off than before the exchange. As illustrated in Figure 1-5, the exchange process includes consumers who have needs, desires, and demands that they want satisfied and marketers who offer products (goods, services, and ideas) intended to provide consumer satisfaction. The exchange process occurs when an actual transaction takes place. A **transaction** is an agreement between a consumer and a marketer to exchange something of value under certain terms and conditions. The most common forms of transactions are **monetary transactions** (money for products) and **barter transactions** (products for products).

CONSUMERS: NEEDS, WANTS, AND DEMANDS Consumers have needs and desires, which translate into demands that they want fulfilled. A

MARKETING DEFINITIONS

▪ FIGURE 1–5

THE EXCHANGE PROCESS

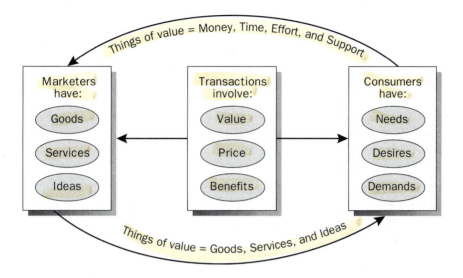

need is an essential physiological or psychological requirement necessary to the general physical and mental welfare of the consumer. Food, shelter, sleep, clothing, and safety are basic needs shared by all consumers. For a business, needs are essential resources required to successfully accomplish the company's mission. **Desires** are wants that are more akin to wishes. In the case of the individual consumer, desires are conscious impulses to attain objects or experiences that promise enjoyment. For a business, any optional products that enhance the efficiency and effectiveness of operations could be considered objects of desire. Desires differ from needs in that they are less essential for the well-being of the individual consumer or organization. For example, A.T. Cross Co., makers of sleek and thin gold-filled and sterling-silver pens, missed the opportunity to move into the luxury pen market because the firm failed to appreciate consumers' desire for fat pens of different shapes and styles, such as Mont blanc.[3] For a need or desire to become a demand the individual or organizational consumer must have the willingness and the ability to enter into the exchange process.

Demands are needs or desires supported by the ability and willingness to buy. The **ability to buy** is the financial resources, such as income, credit, and assets, available to the individual or organizational consumer for engaging in exchange transactions. **Willingness to buy** is determined by the belief that the transaction offers something of value to the consumer. As shown in Figure 1-5, consumers who have needs and desires will provide things of value (money, support, or time) in exchange for valuable things (products). For any exchange relationship, market potential is defined by the total number of consumers who have both the ability and willingness to enter into meaningful transactions.

MARKETERS: GOODS, SERVICES, AND IDEAS Products, in the form of goods, services, and ideas, are things of value that marketers bring to the exchange process (see Figure 1-5). **Goods** are tangible items defined by their size, shape, and weight together with their chemical or biological makeup. The value of goods can be judged by seeing, touching, smelling, hearing, or tasting them. **Services** are largely intangible activities that typically involve the application of human skills within a consumer problem-solving context. Problem-solving services can be personal, financial, medical, legal, or recreational. **Ideas** are concepts and ways of thinking about a particular event or situation. As highly intangible products, ideas are often extensions of the opinions, attitudes, interests, and beliefs of the individual or organization marketing the idea. Political, social, cultural, and religious ideas are examples of conceptual thinking that are marketed to mass audiences on a regular basis.

TRANSACTIONS: VALUE, PRICE, AND BENEFITS If the exchange of "something of value" is the essential ingredient of a transaction, what, then, is value? **Value** is the interactive and changing transactional relationship between price paid and benefit received. While this price/benefit ratio has different meanings during different transactions, in the end, value is simply giving consumers expected benefits at a price they feel is fair. A key responsibility of marketing management is to determine how much value consumers place on the benefits they receive from a given product and then establish prices that are consistent with that value assessment.

Price is the expression of the value placed on a product by a marketer and accepted or rejected by a consumer. The right price is one that completes the exchange process by allowing the marketer to profit in some way while providing the consumer with value satisfaction before, during, and after the exchange. While monetary expressions of price are most common, price can also be expressed in terms of time, effort, support, and other tangible and intangible contributions.

Benefits are positive product attributes consumers think are important and useful. Cobra Golf specializes in irons with oversize heads and graphite shafts, clubs that help most people knock a ball farther and straighter than conventional clubs.[4] Benefits are most often expressed in terms of a product's utility and quality. **Product utility** is its inherent ability to satisfy a consumer's needs and desires; that is, what the product does for the consumer. The Franklin Quest Co. sells day planners that are something more than just fancy calendars. The firm's product lines are part of an integrated time management system that assists the consumer in managing and controlling time and daily activities.[5] Marketing managers enhance product benefits by adding form, time, place, and possession utilities. **Form utility** is the functional benefit derived from good product design and enhanced product features. It involves both the functional and psychological satisfaction the consumer receives from the physical characteristics of the product, or a good's shape, function, or style. **Time utility** is the benefit of providing the product to the consumer when needed; it is the satisfaction that consumers receive from having a product available at the appropriate time. **Place utility** is created by making products available where consumers want them. The key benefit affiliated with time and place utility is customer convenience. **Possession utility** is the satisfaction the consumer derives from owning, using, and having the product. By taking title to a product, the consumer assumes control of that product and its legitimate usage rights.

Product quality is the second element that determines the potential value of a product to a particular consumer; it is best described as how well a product lives up to the performance expectations of the consumer. The two central questions relative to value concerns are " Do expected benefits equal realized benefits?" and "Is the consumer's perceived value from the exchange process enhanced?" The quality of goods might be described in terms of the utilitarian benefits that are associated with good materials and superior workmanship. Ermenegildo Zegna, the Italian manufacturer of fine menswear, has built its reputation by offering classic tailoring of rich and supple fabrics, with an obsessive attention to detail. "The wool in Zegna's new top-of-the-line fabric is spun into strands so fine that one kilogram of them stretches 150,000 meters. Buttons on Zegna's most expensive jackets are handsewn. Before leaving the factory, Zegna's suit jackets are handpressed."[6] In contrast, the bulk of today's affordable leather jackets are made of pigskin or goatskin, which are cheaper than lambskin or calfskin but tend not to be as thick, supple, or luxurious.[7] A description of service quality, on the other hand, could include the number and types of services offered, the terms and conditions under which services are provided, the manner in which services are performed, and the way consumers are treated, assisted, and served. For example, UPS, a company that built its business by stressing unconditional prompt delivery is now giving its drivers free time to talk with customers with the goal of developing closer customer relationships.[8] Idea quality might be judged on the basis of its originality, conformity, or clarity as seen by the consumer.

THE CONSUMPTION PROCESS

The final key concept in our definition of marketing management is that the end result of the exchange process is consumption wherein a product is used. Who does the consuming? Consumers are typically classified as either individual consumers or business organizations. The **individual consumer** is the ultimate consumer who buys products for personal or household use. **Organizational consumers** are business and nonprofit organizations that purchase products either for (1) use in producing other products, (2) operating an organization, or (3) resale to other consumers. Organizational consumers are subclassified into business organizations (manufacturers, wholesalers, or retailers), which engage in the exchange process for the purpose of making a profit, and nonprofit organizations (universities, governmental agencies, or charitable organizations), which are seeking some nonprofit social mission. The aim of effective and efficient marketing management is greater consumption by the targeted consumer groups. Chapter 7 further explores the distinction between individual and organizational consumers.

Marketing Perspectives

The arts and sciences of marketing have steadily developed as market economies have become predominant within the world economic order. In this section we examine both the historical growth of marketing (marketing eras) and some of the more established philosophies that impact current marketing practices.

Marketing Eras

Since the latter half of the nineteenth century, the focus of American business has changed from the production-oriented strategies of the industrial revolution to the marketing-focused strategies of today. Marketing scholars depict the development of marketing as three distinct and successive eras: production, sales, and marketing.

Production Era During the production era manufacturers focused on production and operations; marketing was viewed as something to do after the goods had been produced. Production era managers assumed that consumers would buy goods that were reasonably priced and well-made. Marketing was not part of management's vocabulary; the firm's sales force was simply viewed as an extension of the manufacturing function. Faster and more efficient production techniques were the principal competitive strategies embraced by management. The production era dominated the American scene from the late 1800s to the late 1920s. Production-oriented operations succeeded during this time frame because consumer demand for most products often exceeded supply. Even wholesalers and retailers were more operations oriented than consumer focused. The Great Depression of the early 1930s brought an end to this supply-side business philosophy.

SALES ERA The sales-orientation era extended from the mid-1930s into the 1950s. "Ask not what consumers want; sell them what you have" was the underlying philosophy during this era. During the sales era companies competed by relying on their sales organization, which was expected to sell whatever products the firm produced or stocked. Personal selling and advertising became the cornerstone of the firm's effort to convince the consumer to select its products from a rather competitive selection of products. The aggressive "hard sell" and the slick "ad campaign" were used to achieve sales goals. The principal strategy of the time was to push the product through channels of distribution by relying on a strong selling effort at all levels (wholesale and retail) within the distribution channel. It was probably during this time that sales acquired some of its unsavory reputation as an aggressive profession.

MARKETING ERA With the advent of more educated consumers and the development of a more competitive marketplace, sales and marketing entered a new consumer-oriented era. This third era began in the 1950s with a commitment to giving consumers what they wanted and not trying to sell the consumer something just because it had already been produced. This market orientation was the natural response to a marketplace that had changed into a **buyer's market** where supply exceeded demand. To catch the consumer's attention and to gain the consumer's patronage, marketers first had to identify consumer needs and wants and then develop products and marketing programs to meet those needs. It was during this era that many top managers adopted the idea that "companies survive and prosper by being better than the competition at providing what people want and need."[9] The marketing era continues today with the prevalence of several consumer-oriented philosophies. For example, at Goodyear Tire & Rubber Co., senior management requires that marketing provide engineering with information on what consumers want based on extensive market research. Armed with that type of information, Goodyear engineers were able to develop the successful *Aquatred* tire that met consumers' need for a high-performance, wet weather tire.[10]

MARKETING PHILOSOPHIES

Business organizations are often guided by underlying convictions or philosophies that assist managers in the decision-making process. One such philosophy is the marketing concept. The following discussion is a description of the development of the marketing concept and how it has helped to shape the thinking of generations of marketing managers.

TRADITIONAL MARKETING CONCEPT Traditionally, the **marketing concept** has been described as the philosophical viewpoint that the overall goal of every business organization should be *customer satisfaction* at a *fair profit*. The adoption of the marketing concept was the acceptance of a way of thinking about how a business should operate. It reflected the willingness to recognize and understand the consumer's needs and wants and a willingness to adjust any of the marketing mix elements (product, price, place, and promotion) to satisfy those needs and wants. The marketing concept stressed keying supply to demand rather than demand to supply.

CONTEMPORARY MARKETING CONCEPT A more contemporary and extensive view of the marketing concept, proposed by Frederick E. Webster, Jr., suggests that marketing's job is to provide information to decision makers throughout the organization and to develop programs that respond to changing customer needs and preferences. As Webster wrote:

> To survive in the future, every business will have to be customer-focused, market-driven, global in scope, and flexible in its ability to deliver superior value to customers whose preferences and expectations change continuously as they are exposed to new product offerings and communications about them.[11]

The new marketing concept requires the organization to be *market-driven* and not just *customer-driven*. As described by Webster, while customer orientation is still a primary goal, it is not enough. "Being market-driven means understanding how customer needs and company capabilities intersect in a competitive context because all of these factors converge to form the customer's definition of value."[12] In becoming a market-driven organization, Webster offers the following fifteen guidelines:

1. Create customer focus throughout the business.
2. Listen to the customers as individuals.
3. Define and nurture distinctive competencies.
4. Define marketing as market intelligence.
5. Target customers precisely.
6. Manage for profitability, not sales volume.
7. Make customer value the guiding star.
8. Let the customer define quality.
9. Measure and manage customer expectations.
10. Build customer relationships and loyalty.
11. Define the business as a service business.
12. Commit to continuous improvement and innovation.
13. Manage organizational culture along with strategy and structure.

14. Grow with partners and strategic alliances.

15. Destroy marketing bureaucracy.[13]

This expanded view of the marketing concept dictates hands-on involvement by management at all levels within the organization and in all functional areas of the business. It represents a commitment by the organization and its strategic partners to develop and deliver superior value to customers. The new marketing concept requires that everyone put the customer first. It "is more than a philosophy; it's a way of doing business."[14]

RELATIONSHIP MARKETING   A logical extension of the marketing concept is **relationship marketing**—the operational philosophy that all marketing activities be directed at establishing, developing, and maintaining successful relational exchanges. While relationship marketing has historically been viewed as the partnership between an organization and its customers, most marketers today take the broader view in which relationship marketing includes the creation of win-win relational exchanges between the organization and all of its strategic partners.[15] Figure 1-6 identifies the four categories of relational exchanges and describes some of the specific relationships that must be built and nurtured among exchange partners.

MARKETING NETWORKS   Marketing partnerships develop into **marketing networks,** defined as:

> a group of independently owned and managed firms that agree to be partners rather than adversaries. Because each partner's individual success is tied to the success of the overall network, the firms pursue common goals. They engage in cooperative behaviors and coordinate activities in such areas as marketing, production, finance, purchasing, and research and development.[16]

As global competition intensifies, organizations "must court allies to promote their own survival and prosperity ... These alliances give rise to what we now refer to as 'strategic network competition' and also give new meaning to the concept of relationship marketing."[17]

RETENTION MARKETING   Perhaps the final development of the marketing concept is a successful program in which the customer becomes a long-term strategic business asset. **Retention marketing** involves finding and holding onto customers and employees over time and developing customer and employee loyalty.[18] The logic of a retention marketing program lies in the fact that it costs five times as much to attract one new customer as it does to retain an existing one.[19] Equally costly is the recruitment and training of new employees. Loyalty-based management, which focuses on customer and employee retention to enhance profitability, has

FIGURE 1-6

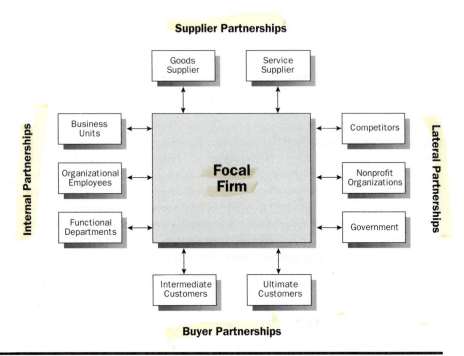

THE FOUR CATEGORIES OF RELATIONAL EXCHANGES

SOURCE: Adapted from Shelby D. Hunt and Robert M. Morgan, "Relationship Marketing in the Era of Network Competitions," *Marketing Management*, Vol. 3, No. 1 (1994), 22.

as its goal "zero defections."[20] Loyal, satisfied customers have proven to be more profitable over time. Loyal, satisfied employees have proven to be more productive over time. Retention marketing recognizes loyal customers and employees as business assets that can provide significant returns on the organization's investment of time, money, and effort.[21] This fact brings us full-circle back to the original idea expressed in the traditional marketing concept that every business is entitled to a fair return on its investment and effort. Without profits the firm could not survive to satisfy anyone's needs.

SOCIETAL MARKETING CONCEPT With the adoption of the marketing concept by both business and nonbusiness organizations, the need to broaden the marketing concept became apparent. The **societal marketing concept** is the philosophy that an organization's marketing efforts should satisfy customers' needs while meeting the firm's financial objectives and serving the best interests of society. The well-being of society is the social responsibility that each marketer must recognize and support. In addition to customers, organizations have publics or stakeholders they are obligated to consider when engaging in marketing activities. Socially responsible marketing managers accept the obligation to consider operating efficiencies, financial returns, customer satisfaction, and societal well-being as equally important in evaluating the organization's performance. According to Dan Cordtz:

> Some 90 percent of the nation's largest corporations have now adopted written codes of ethics that prescribe what is and isn't acceptable in their day-to-day operations.[22]

A PLANNING MODEL

As previously defined, planning is the process of defining where the organization wants to go and deciding how to get there. Planning forces the marketing manager to think critically about the organization and its future; it is a systematic approach to anticipating changes, charting future actions, coordinating effective responses, and meeting stated goals and objectives. The planning process has been conceptualized and described in a variety of ways, depending on the author's purposes. To facilitate the reader's comprehension of this text's approach to planning, Figure 1-7 presents a three-dimensional view of planning based on (1) levels of planning, (2) types of planning, and (3) stages in the planning process.

LEVELS OF PLANNING

Planning occurs at several different levels within the organization. **Business planning** is corporate level planning conducted at organization headquarters by top management (such as the chief executive officer, president, vice president of marketing); it is directed at developing an overall plan for the entire organization. Planning at the corporate level is strategic in nature and is directed at establishing the organization's mission, analyzing the organization's portfolio of businesses, and identifying potential business opportunities (see Figure 1-7). Chapter 2 presents an in-depth discussion of the *strategic business plan*.

Divisional planning involves developing a course of action for each of the organization's strategic business units (SBUs)—a business division with a clearly identifiable marketing strategy that targets a market segment (customer focus) within a defined competitive environment (market position). Goldstar, the South Korean electrical appliances and consumer electronics conglomerate, is organized around the following four SBUs:

1. Home appliances
2. Television sets

FIGURE 1-7

A Planning Model

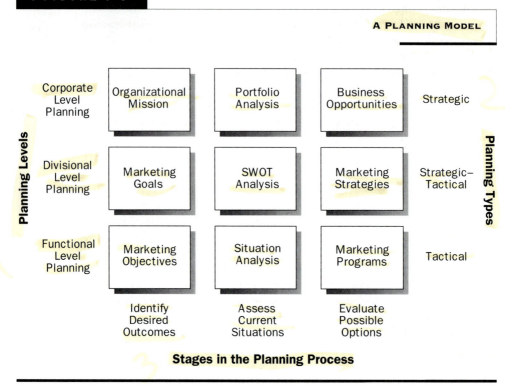

Stages in the Planning Process

---

3. Audio/video products

4. Computer and office automation equipment[23]

Strategic planning is carried out at this level by divisional officers and managers who attempt to translate the organization's mission into goals for each SBU. Strategic marketing management consists of defining marketing goals, conducting an analysis of the strengths, weaknesses, opportunities, and threats (SWOT), and investigating new marketing strategies (see Figure 1-7). Some initial efforts at tactical planning also take place at the division planning level. Chapter 3 outlines the pertinent issues in developing the strategic marketing plan.

Functional planning is directed at developing operational plans that specify actions needed to transform business and divisional strategic plans into tactical plans. At this operational level, each of the functional areas of business (such as production, finance, and marketing) requires tactical plans that are both executable and controllable, as well as consistent with the corporate mission and divisional goals. For the marketing manager, the functional planning process entails the delineation of marketing objectives, the completion of a situation analysis, and the creation of a marketing program (see Figure 1-7). The annual marketing plan is discussed further in Chapter 4.

TYPES OF PLANNING

Strategic planning involves the long-term, broad-based intentions of the organization that unfold over a period of time; it is a multifaceted outline of what the organization hopes to accomplish now and in the future. Strategic planning addresses long-term needs and provides direction for the actions undertaken at the corporate and divisional level of the organization (see Figure 1-7). A **strategy** is a specific plan of action directed at achieving a desired outcome.

A logical extension of strategic planning is **tactical planning**—the process of planning short-term, focused, and functionally based activities that are designed to implement various aspects of the organization's strategic plan. A **tactic** describes what needs to be done and what steps should be taken to execute a strategy. As shown in Figure 1-7, tactical planning is conducted by middle managers, who are responsible for functional plans. Tactical marketing plans are directed at achieving specific marketing objectives, adapting to specific marketing situations, and creating specific customer-oriented marketing programs.

STAGES IN THE PLANNING PROCESS

Figure 1-7 identifies relationships among the three basic stages of the planning process, the types of planning, and the levels of planning. The three stages are:

1. Identifying desired outcomes (organizational mission, business goals, and marketing objectives)

2. Assessing current situations (portfolio analysis, SWOT analysis, and situation analysis)

3. Evaluating possible options (business opportunities, marketing strategies, and marketing programs)

CONCLUDING REMARKS

Marketing and marketing management are well-developed business disciplines that play a crucial role in the success of most organizations. Their pivotal role lies in the fact that the marketing function provides the interface between organizations and their consumers. Now that we have reviewed the fundamental natures of marketing and marketing management and having previewed the essential elements of the planning process, the next four chapters offer a more substantial dialogue on marketing planning and the information systems needed to support that planning process.

Endnotes

1. Frederick E. Webster, Jr., "Executing the New Marketing Concept," *Marketing Management*, Vol. 3, No. 1 (1994), 11.

2. Richard S. Tedlow and Geoffrey Jones, *The Rise and Fall of Mass Marketing* (London: Routledge, 1993), 1.

3. Michael Schuman, "Thin Is Out, Fat Is In," *Forbes* (May 9, 1995), 92.

4. Damon Darlin, "Borrow From Thy Neighbor," *Forbes* (November 7, 1995), 214.

5. Amy Feldman, "We'll Make You Scary," *Forbes* (February 14, 1995), 96.

6. Joshua Levine, "Armani's Counterpoint," *Forbes* (July 4, 1994), 122.

7. Teri Agins, "As Leather Gets Cheaper, It Loses Its Cool," *Wall Street Journal* (December 20, 1994), B1.

8. David Greising, "Quality, How to Make It Pay," *Business Week* (August 8, 1994), 57.

9. Geoffrey Randell, *Effective Marketing* (London: Routledge, 1994), 2.

10. Seth Lubove, "The Last Bastion," *Forbes* (February 14, 1995), 56.

11. Frederick E. Webster, Jr., "Defining the New Marketing Concept," *Marketing Management*, Vol. 2, No. 4 (1994), 23.

12. Frederick E. Webster, Jr., "Executing the New Marketing Concept," 9.

13. Ibid., 10.

14. Ibid., 16.

15. See Shelby D. Hunt and Robert M. Morgan, "Relationship Marketing in the Era of Network Competition," *Marketing Management*, Vol. 3, No. 1 (1994), 19–28. Also see Robert M. Morgan and Shelby D. Hunt, "The Commitment-Trust Theory of Relationship Marketing," *Journal of Marketing* (July 1994).

16. Ibid., 22.

17. Ibid., 20.

18. See *Seeking Customers*, Benson P. Shapiro and John J. Sviokla, eds. (Boston: Harvard Business School, 1993). Also see *Keeping Customers*, edited by Benson P. Shapiro and John J. Sviokla (Boston: Harvard Business School Publishing Corporation, 1993).

19. See Daniel P. Finkelman, "Crossing the Zone of Indifference," *Marketing Management*, Vol. 2, No. 3 (1993), 22–31

20. Frederick F. Reichheld, "Loyalty and the Renaissance of Marketing," *MarketingManagement*, Vol. 2, No. 4 (1994) 10. Also see Sreekanth Sampathkurmaran, "Migration Analysis Helps Stop Customer Attrition," *Marketing News* (August 29, 1994), 18.

21. Don E. Schultz, "Maybe It's Time to Think of Customers as Assets," *Marketing News* (January 2, 1995), 30.

22. Dan Cordtz, "Ethicsplosion!" *Financial World* (Fall 1994), 58.

23. Laxmi Nakarmi, "Goldstar Is Burning Bright," *Business Week* (September 26, 1994), 130.

MARKETING PLANNING

CHAPTER 2 THE STRATEGIC BUSINESS PLAN

CHAPTER 3 THE STRATEGIC MARKETING PLAN

CHAPTER 4 THE ANNUAL MARKETING PLAN

CHAPTER 5 THE MARKETING INFORMATION SYSTEM

THE STRATEGIC BUSINESS PLAN

CHAPTER OUTLINE

- INTRODUCTION
- THE STRATEGIC BUSINESS PLAN
- ORGANIZATIONAL MISSION
    - MISSION STATEMENT
    - SCOPE STATEMENT
    - VALUE STATEMENT
    - VISION STATEMENT
- PORTFOLIO ANALYSIS
    - BOSTON CONSULTING GROUP'S MATRIX
    - GENERAL ELECTRIC'S BUSINESS SCREEN
    - PROFIT-IMPACT-OF-MARKET STRATEGY PROGRAM
- BUSINESS OPPORTUNITIES
    - GROWTH OPPORTUNITIES
    - RESTRUCTURING OPPORTUNITIES
- CONCLUDING REMARKS

Introduction

The three levels of planning start with the most generalized plan formulated at the highest levels within the organization—the strategic business plan. It progresses in Chapters 3 and 4 to more specific plans developed at lower management levels, or the strategic and annual marketing plans. Each of the three levels of plans will be examined in terms of the three-stage planning process. The stages are identifying desired outcomes, assessing current situations, and evaluating possible options. The structure of this and the two subsequent chapters corresponds to this framework.

The Strategic Business Plan

The **strategic business plan** is a corporate-level plan developed by top management to lay out the general, long-term intentions and direction of the organization. As a broad statement based on experience, intuition, and analytical judgment, the strategic business plan determines the nature, scope, and tone of the organization and provides the general framework for how management intends to make the entire organization successful. Corporate strategic business planners are also responsible for allocating resources among various operational or legal business entities within the organization. This allocation process is based on top management's assessments of how the organization can find the best match between its human, financial, and physical resources and the opportunities and threats within its environment. Identification of the best strategic fit between resources and environment is an essential outcome of any successful strategic business plan.

The three stages of the strategic business plan are illustrated in Figure 2-1. In stage one, corporate planners use the organizational mission to identify desired outcomes for the entire organization. Stage two focuses on portfolio analysis. One of several different portfolio analyses can be conducted to assess the organization's current situation. Finally, stage three deals with the issue of evaluating possible options by exploring one or more different business opportunities. The remainder of this chapter examines each of these three stages in greater depth.

Organizational Mission

An organization's mission is an expression of its purpose; it tells what the organization hopes to accomplish and how it plans to achieve this goal. This expression of purpose provides management with a clear sense of direction.

FIGURE 2-1

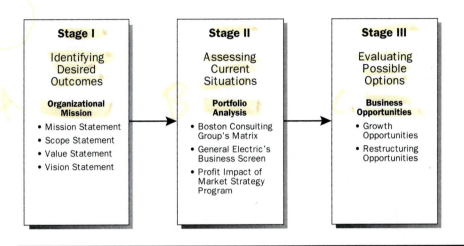

THE STRATEGIC BUSINESS PLAN

MISSION STATEMENT

In verbalizing the organization's overall mission, strategic planners use a broad and comprehensive declaration called a **mission statement**—a universal yet meaningful expression of the organization's intended operational scope, its sense of social responsibility, and its intended future directions.

Jack Smith, CEO of General Motors, described his organization's mission as simply being the world leader in transportation products and services.[1] To support and enhance the mission statement, management often develops shorter, more pointed expressions of its aims and intentions. These more limited accounts of the organization's mission are commonly referred to by such terms as *scope statements*, *value statements*, and *vision statements*.

SCOPE STATEMENT

A mission **scope statement** is an assertion of the organization's basic operational scope that distinguishes it from other businesses and organizations. It identifies and defines both the business and customer domains in which the organization operates or plans to operate. As Figure 2-2 illustrates, the scope statement answers the first three basic business domain questions. What is our business? What will our business be? What should our business be? The scope statement also answers the following customer-domain questions: Who is our customer? Who will our customer be? and Who

FIGURE 2-2

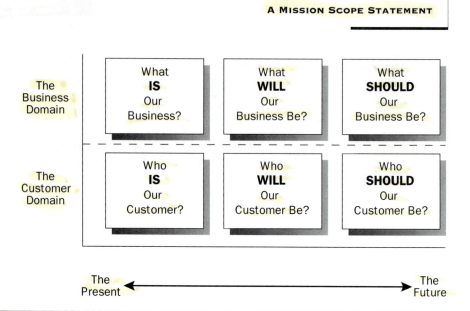

A MISSION SCOPE STATEMENT

should our customer be? In answering these questions, strategic planners investigate and delineate the organization's following scopes:

- *Customer scope*—the types and numbers of final and organizational consumers and consumer markets that the firm is willing to consider and serve.
- *Market scope*—the location and extent of the geographic markets and submarkets that the organization is capable of identifying and developing.
- *Industry scope*—the category and variety of industries and businesses that the organization is willing to develop or acquire.
- *Product scope*—the width and depth of the product lines and items that the organization is willing to develop/buy, support/stock, and sell/merchandise.
- *Competitive scope*—the type and degree of competition that the organization is willing to challenge or accept.
- *Channel scope*—the nature and number of supplier and customer relationships that the organization is willing to develop, maintain, and enhance.
- *Environmental scope*—the type and number of environmental opportunities or threats that the organization is capable of dealing with in an effective and efficient manner.

- *Competencies scope*—the type and number of distinctive competencies or relative advantages the organization enjoys over its competitors.

- *Managerial scope*—the preferences and expertise of the organization's cadre of managers.

A good mission scope statement acts as the general control system by forcing the organization to define its purpose and follow its intended directions.

VALUE STATEMENT

A mission **value statement** identifies the organization's responsibilities toward the people with whom it interacts and the way the organization intends to fulfill its unique role in society. A statement of the organization's values might reaffirm its commitment to:

- *Customers*—by offering better products and services than competitive institutions.

- *Communities*—by assuming a role as a socially responsible organization. Coors Brewing has pledged to spend $40 million on funding for literacy organizations and public-service ads on literacy.[2]

- *Shareholders*—by providing a superior return on their investment.

- *Employees*—by providing rewarding career opportunities. Levi Strauss strives to make all employees feel as if they are an integral part of the making and selling of blue jeans by making sure all views on all issues are heard and respected.[3]

- *Channels partners*—by dealing in a cooperative spirit and a fair manner. Chrysler Corp. rewards suppliers' cost-cutting efforts by helping suppliers shrink inventories, banish waste, and by standardizing component parts.[4]

Value statements set the ethical tone of the operational policies, which direct and guide the actions of the organization. One writer suggests that ethical business practices might be described as maximizing long-term owner value while respecting distributive justice (rewards are proportional to contributions) and ordinary decency (honesty and fairness).[5]

VISION STATEMENT

Finally, the mission's **vision statement** provides a general blueprint for accomplishing the organization's purposes; it provides management at all levels with a general sense of how the organization plans to create new customers and satisfy existing customers. Organizational survival necessitates that management teams develop and retain a strong, viable customer base; hence, a need exists to develop mission statements that provide a vision of how customers are to be served. Michael Treacy and Fred Wiersema suggest that organizations achieve success by focusing on one of three different means of providing superior customer value. An organization's vision might be articulated as the pursuit of one of these distinct customer value disciplines.[6]

- *Operational excellence*—organizations that provide middle-of-the-market products at the best price with the least inconvenience. The guiding vision is to provide the customer with a low-price or hassle-free service or both through efficient distribution systems, strong centralized control, a high level of employee empowerment, standardized operating procedures, and a conforming corporate culture. Wal-Mart and Dell Computer epitomize the operational-excellence approach to creating customer value.

- *Product leadership*—organizations that offer products that push performance boundaries through innovation and new product development. The organization's vision is to offer the best products available by nurturing new ideas within a loose-knit organizational structure whose corporate culture encourages experimentation. Johnson & Johnson's product leadership in the medical equipment field and Nike's style and technology leadership role in athletic wear are both excellent examples of the product-leadership vision.

- *Customer intimacy*—organizations that focus on delivering what specific customers want by cultivating close customer relationships. The organization's vision is to satisfy unique, individual customer needs by gaining intimate knowledge of the customers and providing solutions to their problems. This visionary approach attempts to achieve optimum results by empowering the employees who deal directly with the customer, by stressing the need for maintaining customer loyalty, and by creating a corporate culture that is highly adaptive to customer concerns. Cable and Wireless's relentless pursuit of close relationships with small-business customers for long-distance telephone services is one example of a firm that seeks intimate relations with its customers.

The vision statement also provides an insight into what the organization is trying to become over the longterm; as such, it tends to be a prophecy of those achievements that management hopes will materialize in the future (such as market share, growth potential, or profitability).

PORTFOLIO ANALYSIS

An **organization portfolio** is the collection of strategic business units (SBUs) held and managed by the organization. SBUs typically operate as separate business units with their own strategic thrust and unique roles within the mission of the organization. Pepsi Co, Pizza Hut, KFC, Taco Bell, and Frito-Lay are key SBUs of PepsiCo, Inc.'s organization portfolio.[7] **Portfolio analysis** is the process by which corporate management assesses an SBU's current situation (where it is now) in order to suggest possible courses of action for the future (where it wants to be). By providing insights into how each SBU is contributing to the organization's mission, portfolio analysis allows top management to better access its total collection of businesses, allocate resources more effectively among various SBUs based on their needs and performance characteristics, and refine judgments as to future roles of each SBU within the organization's portfolio of businesses.

The two most common approaches to portfolio analysis are the industry-growth/market-share matrix developed by the Boston Consulting Group (BCG) and the industry-attractiveness/business-strengths approach developed at General Electric (see Figure 2-1). While not strictly a portfolio analysis approach, the Strategic Planning Institute's profit-impact-of-market strategy is an alternative approach to assessing current situations that provides individual corporate planners with valuable performance information on various business units.

BOSTON CONSULTING GROUP'S MATRIX

The Boston Consulting Group's portfolio analysis approach allows an organization to classify and evaluate each SBU with respect to the annualized industry growth rate of similar businesses within the SBU's market and the SBU's market share relative to the major competitors within the industry. As illustrated in the industry-growth/market-share matrix in Figure 2-3, the industry growth rate is shown on the vertical axis while the horizontal axis delineates market share. To facilitate the strategic planner's evaluation of each SBU's past performances and future prospects, the growth/share matrix is divided into four quadrants that classify the organization's SBUs as one of four different types of businesses: stars, cash cows, question marks, or dogs (see Figure 2-3).

Stars are SBUs that have a high market share within a high-growth industry. As market leaders within their respective industries, stars are heavy cash users and require considerable financial, marketing, and operational support in order to take advantage of their leadership positions and to meet the demands of a growth industry. Stars offer an organization the best potential for future growth and profits. **Cash cows** are SBUs with a high market share within a low-growth industry; that is, market leaders within less desirable markets. As suggested by the name, cash cows play a key role within an organization's portfolio by providing a positive cash flow that is sufficient to support the expansion of stars and question marks. For example, Tandy, the Fort Worth-based electronics and computer company, needs Radio Shack to keep churning out profits to finance high-profile, new retailing ventures that it is pinning its future on, such as Incredible Universe and Computer City Superstore.[8]

FIGURE 2-3

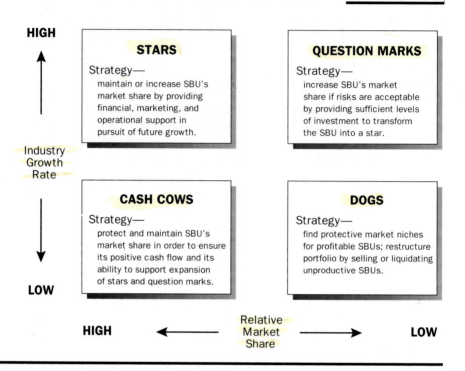

BCG's INDUSTRY-GROWTH/MARKET-SHARE MATRIX

SBUs with a low market share within a high-growth industry are classified as **question marks.** These high-risk SBUs offer considerable growth potential but require greater amounts of support in order to compete effectively with stronger competitors in highly competitive industries. If the organization elects to support a question mark, the goal becomes one of moving that SBU into the star status, where it can repay the organization for its investment. **Dogs** are SBUs with a low market share in a low-growth industry. While some dogs can be modestly productive by generating a small but acceptable positive cash flow, most dogs have dim prospects for the future and are prime candidates for divestiture. Dogs that have found a protected market niche within a low-growth industry are often maintained so long as they retain a positive cash flow. Unproductive dogs with their vulnerable positions within no-growth industries often become "cash traps" and appear to be lost causes. In the declining U.S. cigarette market, American Brands unloaded its collection of shopworn brands like Lucky Strike, Pall Mall, and Tarelton after failing to find a suitable market niche for them.[9]

From a strategic planning perspective, a well-balanced and healthy organizational portfolio will have some cash cows that are capable of providing investment capital now and in the future, stars that have excellent prospects for market-share growth and high-profit performance, and question marks that offer prospects for new business developments. The size and vulnerability of the organization's overall collection of businesses and of each of the SBUs within the collection are important indicators of the health and viability of the organization.

GENERAL ELECTRIC'S BUSINESS SCREEN

General Electric's business screen is a means for senior executives to evaluate SBUs on the basis of the attractiveness of the particular industry in which the SBU operates and the comparable business strengths of the SBU relative to competing business formats. The GE screen is designed to evaluate the overall desirability of an industry currently being serviced by one of the organization's SBUs and ascertain the SBU's relative ability to compete within that industry. In using the GE portfolio approach, planners construct a nine-cell matrix similar to the one shown in Figure 2-4. The GE model plots industry attractiveness (high, medium, low) on the horizontal axis and the business strengths (weak, medium, strong) on the vertical axis. The multidimensional character of each axis can be characterized as follows:

❏ *Industry attractiveness*—the overall desirability of an industry to

1. Support the organization as measured by such factors as total market size and market growth rate
2. Generate acceptable profits as measured by historic profit margins and competitive intensity
3. Permit efficient low-cost operations as measured by economies of scale and productivity efficiencies
4. Offer a friendly operating environment as measured by social and political expectations, and legal and environmental regulations, as well as economic and inflationary pressures

❏ *Business strengths*—the relative business strengths of the organization in terms of

1. Existing market share and market share growth rate
2. Selection and uniqueness of product offering
3. Efficiency and productivity of the business logistics system
4. Number and quality of services offered
5. Reach and effectiveness of customer communications
6. Image and reputation of the organization

FIGURE 2-4

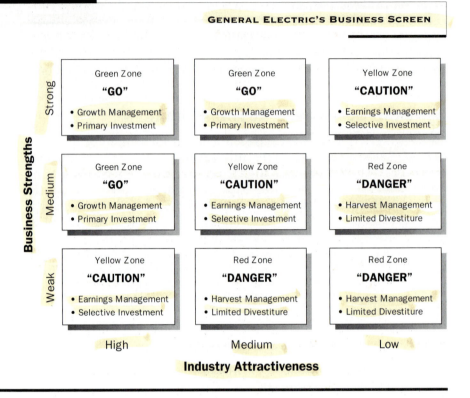

7. Talents and strengths of the management team
8. Technologies and systems that support the decision-making process

Each of the various industry-attractiveness and business-strengths factors can be quantified using rating scales and be weighted as to their importance.

Figure 2-4 shows that the nine cells of the matrix fall into three general action zones—green, yellow, and red. The three upper left-hand cells make-up the **green zone—growth and primary investment**—in which an organization's SBU is judged to be relatively strong within a highly attractive industry. This zone represents the best opportunity for existing operating units' continued growth and for future investment in expanding operations. Key green zone strategies include the protection and intensification of these businesses through continuing investment and enhancement of competitive business strengths. The **yellow zone—earnings management and selective investment**—consists of the three middle diagonal cells of the GE matrix. "Caution" is the watchword for developing strategies and taking actions for the SBUs classified as yellow. Careful management of existing SBUs for cash generation and selective investment in those SBUs that have some business strengths and that compete in moderately attractive industries are the fundamental strategies for the yellow zone. The **red zone—harvest management and limited divestiture—** is the "danger zone"; the three lower right-hand cells of the matrix involve SBUs that have few if any business strengths and are associated with unattractive industries. SBUs occupying these cells are often milked (harvested) of their cash to support the organization's development of other more promising businesses. Those SBUs not having a positive cash flow are prime candidates for liquidation.

PROFIT-IMPACT-OF-MARKET STRATEGY PROGRAM

An alternative to or variation of portfolio analysis is the program known as the **profit-impact-of-market strategy (PIMS)**, a database containing facts about 3,000 strategic business units. Developed by the Strategic Planning Institute, it provides member organizations with information on how well similar organizations have performed under similar marketplace conditions and identifies general principles that appear linked to success or failure of organizations under given market conditions and competitive circumstances. PIMS is different from traditional portfolio methods of assessing current situations in that it takes a much more comprehensive view of the factors that determine the success or failure of organizations, and it provides a wealth of knowledge on the real-world business experiences of its clients. PIMS not only helps managers assess their current situations, but it also provides planners with insights on why certain SBUs are performing in a certain way.

The diagnostic and prescriptive information found within the PIMS data bank provides the user with both a performance assessment and a strategy formulation capability. The data bank is based on information obtained from participating organizations and covers about one hundred different items ranging from conditions of the business environment to the structure of the production process. Figure 2-5 outlines the building blocks of the PIMS data bank.

The PIMS program has identified the following key generalizations about organizational and strategic business unit success:

❏ Organizations that have larger market shares tend to be more profitable. (This generalization is often disputed by some strategic planners.)

❏ Organizations that offer products with a higher perceived quality tend to be more profitable.

❏ Organizations that require a higher level of investment tend to be less profitable.

❏ Organizations that have lower cost structures tend to be more profitable.

FIGURE 2-5

PIMS DATA BANK ITEMS

CHARACTERISTICS OF THE BUSINESS ENVIRONMENT
- Long-run growth rate of the market
- Short-run growth rate of the market
- Rate of inflation of selling price levels
- Number and size of customers
- Purchase frequency and magnitude

COMPETITIVE POSITION OF THE BUSINESS
- Share of the served market
- Share relative to that of largest competitors
- Product quality relative to that of competitors
- Prices relative to those of competitors
- Pay scales relative to those of competitors
- Marketing efforts relative to those of competitors
- Pattern of marketing segmentation
- Rate of new product introductions

STRUCTURE OF THE PRODUCTION PROCESS
- Capital intensity (degree of automation, etc.)
- Degree of vertical integration
- Capacity utilization
- Productivity of capital equipment
- Productivity of people
- Inventory levels

DISCRETIONARY BUDGET ALLOCATIONS
- R&D budgets
- Advertising and promotion budgets
- Sales force expenditures

STRATEGIC MOVES
- Patterns of change in the controllable elements above

OPERATING RESULTS
- Profitability results
- Cash flow results
- Growth results

SOURCE: Strategic Planning Institute (Cambridge, MA).

BUSINESS OPPORTUNITIES

❑ Organizations that are in mature and stable markets can affect profitability in a positive manner by using a vertical integration strategy.

❑ Organizations that have higher labor productivity (value added per employee) tend to be more profitable.

By comparing the relative performances and positions of the organization's SBUs using the PIMS data bank, the strategic business planner has a real-world benchmark on which to assess the current situation and to evaluate the future direction of each strategic business unit within the organization's portfolio.

BUSINESS OPPORTUNITIES

The third stage of the strategic business plan involves evaluating possible strategic options; that is, the identification and assessment of potential business opportunities. While portfolio analysis (stage two) considers the questions of "What is our business?" and "What will our business be?" this final business planning stage takes up the issue of "What should our business be?" This stage of the business plan is devoted to finding one or more ways of bridging the strategic gap between current and desired performance of the organization's business portfolio by taking advantage of business opportunities for better growth and improved performance. Growth and restructuring are the primary business opportunities that might be available to the organization or to one of its SBUs.

GROWTH OPPORTUNITIES

Long-term survival requires that the organization be able to redirect its efforts in response to environmental change and to increase the organization's resources by identifying and pursuing profitable growth opportunities. The marketplace and its environments have the potential of presenting each SBU with one of three types of growth opportunities—intensive, integrated, or diversified.

INTENSIVE GROWTH OPPORTUNITIES Opportunities found within the organization's current portfolio of businesses are referred to as **intensive growth opportunities**—occasions when current products and current markets have potential for generating increased sales volumes. The organization may be able to realize considerable growth potential by more aggressively marketing current products to existing markets (market penetration), by introducing current products to new markets (market development), or by developing new products for existing markets (product development).

Market Penetration One possible growth opportunity available to organizations is the option of increasing SBU market share within existing markets. **Market penetration** is the strategy of trying to increase the sales productivity of current SBUs by more effectively meeting the needs of consumers within existing markets. In pursuit of this strategy, SBU managers can

- Increase purchase frequencies and order sizes of current customers.
- Attract trial business from nonpatrons who reside in the market.
- Lure business from competitors.

Market penetration opportunities are realized through more aggressive and effective promotions, enhanced product variety and quality, improved service offerings and levels, intensive and convenient distribution networks, and fair and competitive pricing structures. To gain greater market penetration, Tropicana increased production of single-serve containers of fruit-based juices and introduced vending machines to expand its distribution points and its coverage of the marketplace.[10]

Market Development Market development opportunities allow an SBU to increase sales of existing businesses by expanding into new markets. It is an attempt to find growth opportunities by identifying and developing markets that have not previously been served by the organization. In pursuing market development opportunities, strategic business planners can elect to

- Expand SBU operations into *new geographic markets*—as when an organization expands into international markets. Wal-Mart's expansion into Hong Kong [11] and the National Football League's expansion into Amsterdam, Barcelona, Dusseldorf, Frankfurt, London, and Edinburgh are current examples of this form of market development.[12]
- Serve new groups of customers (*new market segments*)—as does a fashion designer who develops a less expensive line of clothing for the mass market. Donna Karan's DKNY bridge line and Giorgio Armani's A/X line of pricey casual clothes are representative of what is commonly called "cheap chic."
- Extending into *new market levels* within the marketing distribution channel—as would a retailer or manufacturer who elects to sell to a nontraditional channel customer. Gateway and Dell now target both the corporate and home computer markets.[13] Wal-Mart's chain of warehouse clubs, Sam's Club, targets both businesses and final consumers.[14]

Product Development The final form of intensive growth opportunity is product development—the creation of new goods and services that are capable of increasing SBU sales within existing markets. Both Pizza Hut and Domino's have added Buffalo wings to their limited menus in hopes of gaining additional sales from existing customers.[15] It is an attempt to identify unmet consumer needs and to develop new product offerings to meet those needs. Product development can involve both **pruning decisions,** replacing old products with new product lines, and **extending decisions,** adding new product offerings to the existing product mix. Haggar Apparel, one of the nation's largest producers of ready-made custom-fit suits, has responded to the dress-down trend at work by adding jeans and a "relaxed, yet tailored" line of suits called City Casuals.[16]

INTEGRATED GROWTH OPPORTUNITIES Integrated growth opportunities are those that occur within the organization's current industry. Integration involves those occasions in which an organization establishes a strong position or a leadership role within a given industry by gaining greater control over its channels of distribution or competitive business enterprises. The organization's strategic business planners can pursue either a vertical or horizontal integration approach to growth.

Vertical Integration By vertically incorporating one or more levels of the marketing distribution channels into current SBU operations, corporate managers seek to generate increased sales revenues. A vertically integrated distribution channel is one in which one of the channel members (a manufacturer or retailer) controls and manages all or most of the functions performed by all of its members. **Forward integration** involves the control of channel operations or the outright acquisition of channel members that occupy positions closer to the intended consumer (such as a producer who acquires a wholesaler or retailer). Alberto-Culver, the personal goods manufacturer, pursued a forward integration policy with the acquisition and expansion of Sally Beauty Supply, a chain of beauty products stores.[17] **Backward integration** is to gain ownership and control of an SBU's supply system. It involves developing or acquiring businesses that are closer to sources of supply (such as a retailer acquiring a manufacturer or raw-resource producer). Whether integration is accomplished through outright ownership, contractual arrangements, or operational and marketing leverage, the ultimate goal is to develop strategic alliances and partnerships that create greater business growth.

Horizontal Integration Growth opportunities exist in cases where the organization can gain ownership or control of competing SBUs at the same level within the marketing channel. Quaker Oats Co. established itself as the third-largest soft-drink company when it acquired the Snapple line of fruit drinks to complement its Gatorade line of sport drinks.[18] In its bid to become a dominant player in the food distribution business, Supervalu, the nation's largest food wholesaler, recently acquired Wetterau, a St. Louis-based wholesaler.[19] By obtaining control of competitors, the business planner gains both an extensive distribution network and a less competitive marketplace. The rise of "megadealers" that own many car dealerships and sell competing brands of automobiles provides an excellent example of gaining distribution economies while limiting the number of competitors, if not the intensity of competition.[20] Horizontal integration, because it diminishes competition, is subject to closer scrutiny by government regulators than is vertical integration.

DIVERSIFIED GROWTH OPPORTUNITIES When an organization adds attractive SBUs whose business nature and format are dissimilar to current SBUs, the company is pursuing **diversified growth opportunities,** an attempt to enter new markets with new businesses. Diversification is directed at spreading an organization's risk by operating different businesses in different industries in different markets. Seagrams, the Canadian-based producer of spirits and wine, has pursued a diversified growth strategy by acquiring Tropicana beverages and taking a significant equity share in Time Warner, the media company.[21] Diversification opportunities can be classified on the basis of the degree of dissimilarity to existing SBU operations. The three types of diversified growth opportunities are concentric, horizontal, and conglomerate.

Concentric Diversification Opportunities that allow an SBU to attract new customers and serve new markets by adding businesses that have technological, operational, or marketing similarities to existing business formats are classified as concentric diversification. Brinker International, one of the largest restaurant operators in the United States, has developed several retail food chains that have considerable synergies. The six chains that make up the Brinker organization include Grady's American Grill, purveyor of steak and seafood; Cozumel's, a chain of Mexican restaurants featuring food from the Yucatan peninsula; Chili's Grill & Bar; Romano's Macaroni Grill; Spageddies; and On The Border.[22] Because of the close similarities in business policies and practices, concentric diversification provides growth opportunities that are less risky and more successful than other ventures might be. The operational and marketing synergies generated by these ventures make it the most preferred form of diversifying the organization's business portfolio.

Horizontal Diversification In pursuing a horizontal diversification, the corporate planner intends to increase sales revenues by annexing SBUs whose product mix will appeal to the organization's current customer base even though the acquired businesses are not technologically and functionally related to its current businesses. Horizontal diversification is an attempt to gain additional sales from current markets by offering those markets the different product offerings of newly acquired businesses. Labatt, the Toronto-based brewer, has combined its brewery businesses (Canadian brands Labatts and Wildcat; Mexican brands Dos Equis, Carta Blanca, and Femsa; and American brand Rolling Rock) with sporting (Toronto Blue Jays, Toronto Argonauts, and Toronto Skydome) and broadcasting (four cable channels) enterprises in hopes of gaining complementary sales opportunities.[23] Grand Metropolitan PLC recently acquired Pet, Inc. This horizontal diversification scheme has created a brand name juggernaut that includes Pillsbury, Green Giant, Häagen-Dazs, Burger King, and Smirnoff from Grand Metropolitan and Old El Paso, Progresso, Van de Kamp's, Downyflake, and Pet Milk from Pet Inc.[24]

3. *Conglomerate Diversification*   Conglomerate diversification is directed at taking advantage of new markets by developing or acquiring new businesses that are totally unrelated to current businesses. While the difficulties of operating unrelated businesses are great, and the risks of successfully managing unrelated business are high, the opportunity to serve multiple consumer segments within different industry markets can be attractive to corporate managers seeking new growth opportunities. The General Electric conglomerate includes financial services, electricity generation, appliances, lighting, medical systems, plastics, locomotives, and jet engines.[25]

RESTRUCTURING OPPORTUNITIES

Changing organizational structures are inevitable if the firm is to make the necessary adjustments to its dynamic operating environment. Corporate management is faced with a number of restructuring decisions ranging from supporting productive SBUs and repositioning underperforming SBUs to eliminating unproductive SBUs. Reasons for restructuring are numerous; some of the more common causes include the following:

❏ Response to changing business cycles

❏ Concentrating on organizational efforts

❏ Altering target market structures and their associated marketing programs

❏ Using managerial strengths better

❏ Using organizational resources more efficiently and effectively

A list of the most common opportunities for restructuring would include building, maintaining, harvesting, niching, and divesting.

BUILDING   In cases where an organization has a strong SBU in an attractive growth industry, a viable strategic business option is to increase the SBU's market share through an infusion of cash and other organizational resources. This **building** option is used to expand smaller stars into bigger stars or to transform question marks into stars. Building is also the most appropriate option for those SBUs that occupy the green zone as identified by the GE screen. By making aggressive investments in those SBUs that show the greatest promise, the strategic business planner is restructuring the organization's business portfolio to take advantage of the growth opportunities.

MAINTAINING Maintaining is a defensive approach to restructuring the organizational portfolio. It involves expending resources in amounts sufficient only to hold the existing portfolio as is. Maintenance is used by corporate management with SBUs that have relatively good market shares and positive cash flows (cash cows) but experience uncertain market conditions, face lower industry growth rates, and have limited business strengths with which to compete effectively (those businesses that occupy the yellow zone within the GE screen). This holding option requires actions that protect and reinforce the SBU's market share support through selective investment of resources. SBU maintenance dictates that an adequate level of financial investment and operational support must be provided in order to ensure acceptable customer service levels, ample advertising and sales promotion efforts, suitable target market coverage, correct price level structures, and appropriate product quality development. Maintaining SBU market share necessitates gaining repeat purchases from current customers and retaining customer loyalty by developing meaningful relationships with those patrons. As part of a maintenance strategy, companies such as Procter & Gamble, Miller Brewing, and Kodak created "fighting brands" by lowering prices on Joy dishwashing detergent, Miller High Life beer, and Funtime film, respectively, in order to battle the aggressive pricing of store brands.[26]

HARVESTING The third restructuring opportunity is **harvesting**—the practice of milking an SBU of its cash in order to finance other SBU alternatives that provide greater growth potential. Harvesting is a cash-extraction process designed to generate cash quickly by maximizing short-term profitability. It typically consists of making no additional investments in the SBU being milked, reducing the SBU's operating expenses to a minimum, and perhaps, increasing prices in order to create greater profit margins. The pace at which an SBU is harvested ranges from a rapid milking for quick cash to slow milking for a longer, positive cash flow contribution. The need for cash in managing the organizational portfolio is the determining factor in choosing between a quick or slow milking approach. The degree and speed by which investments and expenses are curtailed and prices are increased will govern whether corporate management will select a quick or slow milking of an SBU. Weak cash cows, together with some dogs (BCG portfolio approach), and occupants of the red zone (GE portfolio approach) whose future prospects are dim with little chance of survival, are the chief candidates for harvesting.

NICHING For an SBU with restricted market shares and confined business strengths in an industry whose growth rate and attractiveness is limited, niching might be the appropriate restructuring opportunity. Niching is the strategy of repositioning an SBU into a market niche or a narrowly defined market segment that is best suited to the SBU's business strengths and in which the business is protected somewhat from the actions of competitors. Niching can also be viewed from the perspective of retrenchment in which the SBU retreats back to the core businesses and core markets in which it has greater competencies and competitive advantages. By focusing on one or a few market segments and by carefully controlling investments and expenses, the niched SBU can achieve an acceptable level of profitability and a reasonable chance of long-term survival. Within the BCG portfolio, question marks and dogs are candidates for niching.

DIVESTING For SBUs with unfavorable industry environments and market positions, little to no business strengths, and little hope of improvement, divestiture may be the only realistic option open to the portfolio manager. Red zone SBUs, as identified by the GE screen, and SBUs classified as question marks and dogs by a BCG analysis are all potential candidates for divestiture. Divesting is an exit decision that is executed by either selling the SBU and its products or liquidating the assets of the SBU. Government restrictions, customer expectations, managerial pride, corporate image, contractual obligations, vender commitments, and capital investments all strongly influence the decision whether to exercise the divestment option. B.F. Goodrich has divested itself out of automobile tires, industrial rubber products, and polyvinyl chloride (PVC) plastics. Today, Goodrich focuses on producing specialty chemicals and aircraft components.[27] Having failed to protect its cash cow (its core discount store business), Kmart is being forced to sell some of its specialty operations (such as Payless Drugs) in order to secure the cash needed to update its core business of discount stores and expand its chain of supercenters (discount stores combined with supermarkets).[28]

CONCLUDING REMARKS

The strategic business plan is the first of three plans that must be completed in order to develop, execute, and control a successful marketing program. This corporate-level plan is created by top management to give direction to the organization's efforts and to provide guidance to middle and lower management as to how the organization intends to proceed. Planning at this level tends to be strategic in character and is directed at the entire business organization. Business planning is a three-stage process consisting of stage one—identifying desired outcomes in the form of an organizational mission; stage two—assessing current situations by conducting a portfolio analysis; and stage three—evaluating possible options by considering different business opportunities.

Endnotes

1. Alex Taylor, III, "GM's $11,000,000,000 Turnaround," *Fortune* (October 17, 1994), 66.

2. Geoffrey Smith and Ron Stodghill II, "Are Good Causes Good Marketing?" *Business Week* (March 21, 1994), 64.

3. Russell Mitchell, "Managing By Values, Is Levi Strauss' Approach Visionary—or Flaky?" *Business Week* (August 1, 1994), 46.

4. James B. Treece, "Hardball Is Still GM's Game," *Business Week* (August 8, 1994), 26.

5. "Just Business", *Financial World*, (August 16, 1994), 66.

6. The discussion is based on an article by Michael Treacy and Fred Wiersema, "How Market Leaders Keep Their Edge," *Fortune* (February 6, 1995), 88–98. Also see Michael Treacy and Fred Wiersema, *The Discipline of Market Leaders* (Reading, MA: Addison-Wesley, 1995).

7. See Laura Zinn, "Will the Pepsi Brass Be Drinking Hemlock?" *Business Week* (July 25, 1994), 31.

8. Stephanie Anderson, "Radio Shack Goes Back to the Gizmos," *Business Week* (February 28, 1994), 102.

9. John Kimelman, "Defensive Maneuver," *Financial World* (June 21, 1994), 32–34. Also see Alexandra Ourusoff, "When the Smoke Clears," *Financial World* (June 21, 1994), 38–42.

10. Matt Walsh, "Juice Wars," *Forbes* (April 11, 1994), 58.

11. Neil Herndon, "Wal-Mart Goes to Hong Kong, Looks at China," *Marketing News* (November 21, 1994), 2.

12. Paula Dwyer, "The Long, Muddy Field Ahead of Marc Lory," *Business Week* (March 6, 1995), 97.

13. Peter Burrows, "The Computer Is in the Mail (Really)," *Business Week* (January 23, 1995), 76.

14. Wendy Zellner, "Why Sam's Wants Businesses to Join the Club," *Business Week* (June 27, 1994), 48.

15. Chad Rubel, "Pizza Chains Winging It," *Marketing News* (March 27, 1995), 1, 15.

16. Cyndee Miller, "A Casual Affair," *Marketing News* (March 13, 1995), 2.

17. Amy Feldman, "When Lenny Met Sally," *Forbes* (February 13, 1995), 62.

18. Greg Burns, "Tea and Synergy," *Business Week* (November 12, 1994), 44.

19. Matthew Schifrin, "Middleman's Dilemma," *Forbes* (May 23, 1994), 67.

20. Gabriella Stern, "Car Dealerships Seem About to Be Combined Into Big Retail Chains," *Wall Street Journal* (February 10, 1995), A1.

21. Laura Zinn, "Edgar Jr.'s Not So Excellent Ventures," *Business Week* (January 16, 1995), 79.

22. Christopher Palmeri, "The King of Yuck! and Other Casual Foods," *Forbes* (August 15, 1994), 63.

23. Gregory E. David, "Strange Brew," *Financial World* (September 13, 1994), 26–30.

24. Tara Parker-Pope and Susan Carey, "Grand Metropolitan to Buy Pet Inc. in $2.6 Billion Pact," *Wall Street Journal* (January 10, 1995), A3.

25. James R. Norman, "A Very Nimble Elephant," *Forbes* (October 10, 1994), 89–90.

26. Jonathan Berry and Zachary Schiller, "Attack of the Fighting Brands," *Business Week* (May 2, 1994), 125.

27. John Kimelman, "Ohio Nocturne," *Financial World* (June 7, 1994), 40–41.

28. Debra Sparks, "Attention Bottom Fishers," *Financial World* (March 28, 1995), 30–32.

The Strategic Marketing Plan

Chapter Outline

- Introduction
- The Strategic Marketing Plan
- Marketing Goals
- SWOT Analysis
    - Internal Organizational Scan
    - External Environmental Scan
    - SWOT Matrix
- Marketing Strategies
    - Differentiating Strategies
    - Positioning Strategies
- Concluding Remarks

INTRODUCTION

The nature, scope, and tone of the business as established by corporate management is transmitted to each strategic business unit (SBU) in the strategic business plan. The general, long-term intentions and directions of this plan must be translated into more specific goals and strategies by SBU management. The focus of this chapter is the divisional-level planning process by which strategic marketing plans are developed for each SBU within the organization. Strategic marketing plans represent the second, or middle tier of plans each organization must develop in order to ensure a smooth transition from high-level strategic plans to low-level operational actions.

THE STRATEGIC MARKETING PLAN

The **strategic marketing plan** outlines a set of goals and strategies that defines the individual marketing efforts of each SBU. The divisional-level plan developed by SBU marketing managers must

1. Designate a marketing course of action consistent with the directions outlined in the organization-wide strategic business plan

2. Profile the methods and procedures needed to achieve the marketing components of the organizational mission

3. Assess the strengths and weaknesses and recognize the opportunities and threats associated with each business operation

4. Identify specific marketing strategies required to operationalize the annual marketing plan

An additional aim of the strategic marketing plan is to effectively coordinate and control the allocation and use of SBU resources relative to the marketing function.

The three stages of the strategic planning process are the same for the strategic marketing plan as for the strategic business plan. Figure 3-1 describes the issues to be addressed during each of the three planning stages. Stage I is directed at identifying desired outcomes in the form of clearly articulated goals. In Stage II, the procedures for conducting a SWOT analysis (strengths, weaknesses, opportunities, and threats) is presented as the principle vehicle for assessing current situations. Finally, in Stage III key marketing strategies are distinguished and investigated in an attempt to evaluate possible options that might be pursued by SBU marketing managers in the quest for customer satisfaction and organizational profitability.

FIGURE 3-1

THE STRATEGIC MARKETING PLAN

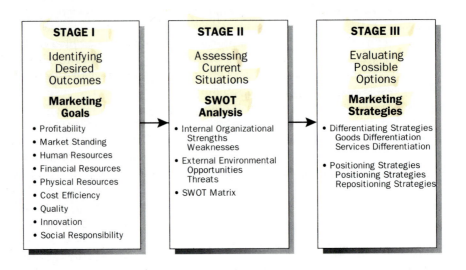

MARKETING GOALS

The general business purpose espoused in the organization's mission statement must be translated into more specific guidelines as to how these universal intentions will operate. Organizations and the people who manage them tend to be more productive when they have established standards to motivate them, specific directions to guide them, and stated achievement levels against which to compare their performance. The terms *goals* and *objectives* are defined and used in a variety of ways and many times are treated as interchangeable concepts. For our purposes, the terms *goals* and *objectives* have different meanings and uses.

A **goal** is a general and qualitative expression of a desired outcome that provides general guidelines by which management can direct its actions. Goals help identify, clarify, and prioritize intended accomplishments and help bridge the gap between the organization's mission and its objectives by focusing the efforts of the SBU management team. By refining and illuminating the mission statement, goals provide more specific direction as to which business opportunities the organization intends to pursue. In contrast, an **objective** is a specific and quantitative expression of a desired outcome. It indicates a measurable benchmark against which performance can be judged. Objectives provide management with clearly defined reference points against which to measure the organization's progress in reaching its goals and achieving its mission. Marketing goals are the benchmarks that establish direction for a strategic marketing plan. Marketing objectives direct the actions outlined in the annual marketing plan and are discussed in Chapter 4.

Marketing goals are the general results the organization hopes to achieve through its marketing efforts. These goals also identify the general focus through which marketing resources will be directed and allocated. Peter Drucker's classic list of key organizational goals can be applied to any functional business area. From Drucker's list, some general marketing goals might include:

- *Profitability*—marketing goods and services at a net profit (for-profit organizations) or providing goods and services within budget allowances (nonprofit organizations)
- *Market standing*—gaining an acceptable market share or establishing a competitive position for the organization's goods and services
- *Human resources*—recruiting, training, and maintaining a high-quality workforce that is capable of meeting productivity standards and dealing effectively with the organization's customers
- *Financial resources*—acquiring and retaining a sufficient level of financial capital to support the marketing effort
- *Physical resources*—developing, acquiring, and maintaining the physical assets (plant, equipment, and technology) needed to support the marketing program
- *Cost efficiency*—using and controlling the application of human, financial, and physical resources in a low-cost, productive fashion
- *Quality*—monitoring and regulating the quality of the goods and services offered by the organization's marketing program
- *Innovation*—developing and introducing new goods and services using unique marketing programs to retain a competitive edge over time
- *Social responsibility*—serving and enhancing the public welfare by making positive contributions to the community and the general public

Once marketing managers have a better indication of the direction in which the organization is heading, they can then proceed with a more directed effort at analyzing their current situation relative to marketing issues.

SWOT Analysis

In the second stage of developing a strategic marketing plan, a SWOT analysis is performed to assess an SBU's current situation. **SWOT analysis** is an analytical tool that allows strategic planners to compare the internal strengths and weaknesses of the organization to its external environmental opportunities and threats. SWOT, by providing a systematic framework for organizing and evaluating information, has proven to be extremely useful in developing viable marketing strategies. This flexible tool permits the planner to integrate and synthesize diverse information from a wide variety of sources.

In assessing current situations, SWOT analysis attempts to identify one or more strategic relationships or matchups between an SBU's current strengths or weaknesses and its present or future opportunities and threats. Organizations face *strategic windows* in which key requirements of a market and the particular competencies of the organization best fit together.[1] Identifying these limited time periods is a purpose for employing a SWOT analysis. A SWOT analysis involves an extensive scan and analysis of

1. Current and projected external environmental trends

2. Current and future internal organizational capabilities

3. How, if, and when it will be feasible to reconcile the two by implementing one or more marketing strategies[2]

Figure 3-2 provides an illustration of the major components of a SWOT analysis.

INTERNAL ORGANIZATIONAL SCAN

An **internal organizational scan** attempts to ascertain the type and degree of each SBU's strengths and weaknesses. By recognizing their special capabilities and serious limitations, firms are better able to adjust to the external environmental conditions of the marketplace. "Know thyself" is the basic tenet that guides this assessment of the abilities and deficiencies of the organization's internal operations.

Strengths are the bases for building competitive advantages and distinctive competencies. **Strength** is the quality or state of being strong; it suggests an ability to resist force (such as the unfriendly actions of competitors) and a capacity for enduring hardships (such as unfavorable changes in government regulations). An ability or capability becomes a strength when it benefits the organization in some fashion. Undeveloped or untapped abilities and capabilities are not counted as strengths until they have been transformed into useful strategies and tactics that allow the organization to take advantage of an external opportunity or to overcome an environmental threat.

Internal strengths can emanate from any of the organization's functional business areas or gain potency in various operational circumstances. Examples of functional business strengths include marketing (extensive product line), human resources (productive workforce), physical resources (modern facilities), financial resources (large capital base), and management (experienced and adaptive managers). A loyal customer base, effective distribution system, strong dealer network, favorable company image, and efficient management information system are potential operational

FIGURE 3-2

SWOT Analysis

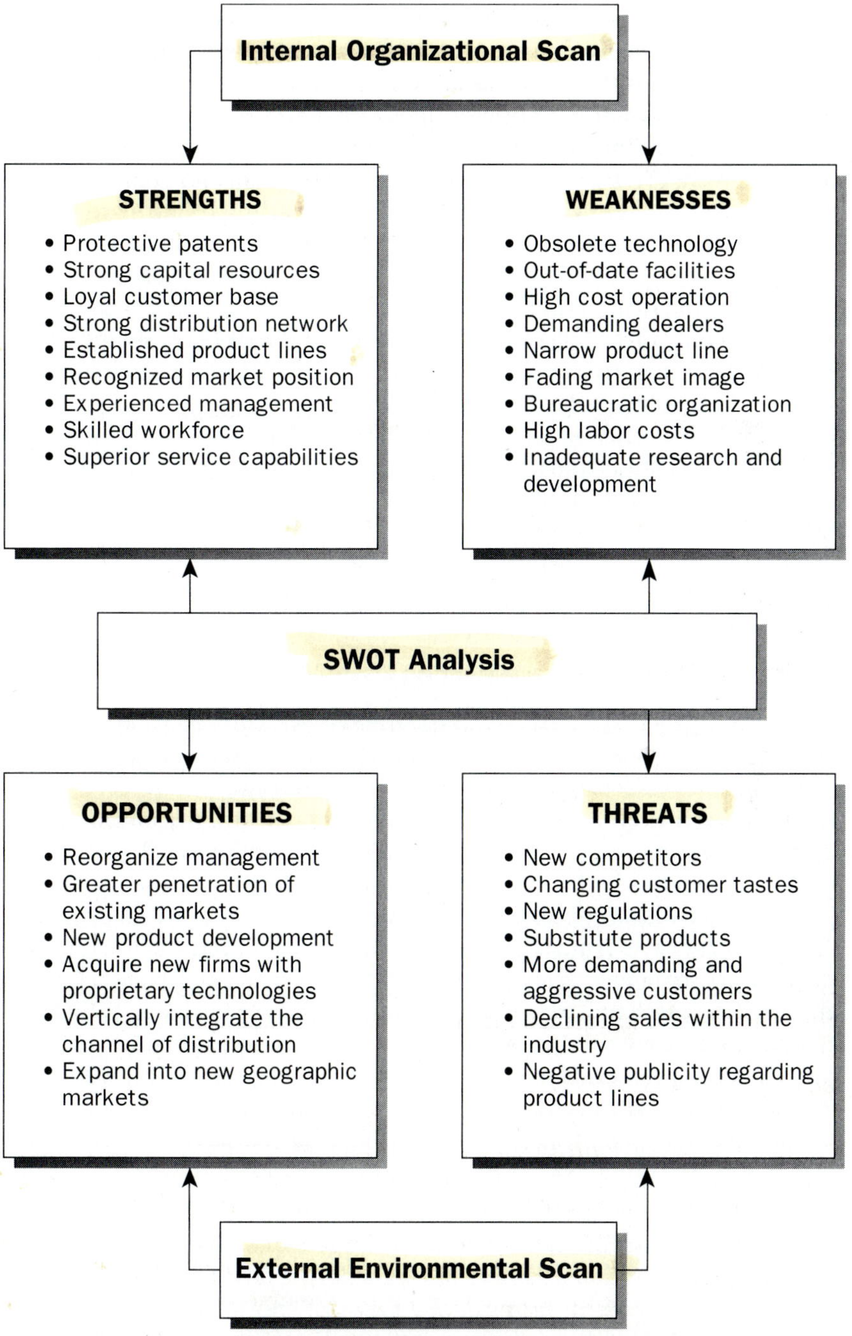

Internal Organizational Scan

STRENGTHS
- Protective patents
- Strong capital resources
- Loyal customer base
- Strong distribution network
- Established product lines
- Recognized market position
- Experienced management
- Skilled workforce
- Superior service capabilities

WEAKNESSES
- Obsolete technology
- Out-of-date facilities
- High cost operation
- Demanding dealers
- Narrow product line
- Fading market image
- Bureaucratic organization
- High labor costs
- Inadequate research and development

SWOT Analysis

OPPORTUNITIES
- Reorganize management
- Greater penetration of existing markets
- New product development
- Acquire new firms with proprietary technologies
- Vertically integrate the channel of distribution
- Expand into new geographic markets

THREATS
- New competitors
- Changing customer tastes
- New regulations
- Substitute products
- More demanding and aggressive customers
- Declining sales within the industry
- Negative publicity regarding product lines

External Environmental Scan

strengths (see Figure 3-2). In recent years, companies such as W.R. Grace & Co. have been able to leverage their considerable buying power by centralizing their purchasing functions, by concentrating their purchases with key vendors, and by cooperating with vendors to reduce total costs.[3]

All businesses have weaknesses. Successful businesses try to minimize or conquer their shortcomings. A **weakness** can be any business function or operation that is not able to resist external forces or withstand attack. A weak business function or operation is one that is deficient or inferior in its ability to reap the benefits presented by an external opportunity or to avoid the penalties of failing to adjust to a threatening environmental condition. Whirlpool Corporation has pulled its leading brand-name appliances from Best Buy, the consumer electronics retail chain, in order to avoid overdependence on a single customer. From Whirlpool's close association with Sears, the firm had learned a hard lesson: it is a major weakness to rely too heavily on one channel of distribution.[4] Weaknesses are most often viewed in comparative terms; a company has a weakness when it is unable to perform a business function or conduct a business operation as effectively and efficiently as its competitors. Frito-Lay dominates the sale of snack foods in supermarket outlets. It gained superior distribution efficiencies using new 40-foot tractor-trailers. These oversize delivery trucks have become somewhat of a weakness when it comes to servicing smaller convenience stores, drugstores, and gas stations.[5] Figure 3-2 provides some specific examples of weaknesses that might plague an organization.

EXTERNAL ENVIRONMENTAL SCAN

The second part of a SWOT analysis involves the organization's external environments. This environmental scanning process represents the opportunities and threats that are part of a SWOT analysis.

Opportunities are unsatisfied customer needs that the organization has a good chance of meeting successfully. The 1994 elections placed Republicans in control of Congress with a political agenda of reducing the size of the national government by limiting, among other things, spending for social programs. These changes have created considerable opportunity for cause marketing campaigns by other nongovernment organizations.[6] For an environmental occurrence to be considered an opportunity by a particular business, a favorable juncture of circumstances must exist. A unique business strength must fit an attractive environmental need in order to create a high probability of a successful match, as when a low-cost producer identifies an unserved market of low-income consumers. Good opportunities are needs that the firm can satisfy in a more complete fashion than can existing competitors. A sustainable competitive advantage is a key determinant in establishing what is and what is not a good need opportunity for a particular business.

Threats are hostile aspects of the external environment that could potentially injure the organization. For example, the new government-ordered nutrition labels represent a considerable threat to Ben & Jerry's once robust sales by calling attention to the high amount of total fat in the firm's super-premium ice cream.[7] The seriousness of a threat can range from a mere annoyance to outright hostility. Threats represent challenges that must be either avoided or conquered. For soft-drink companies, the growing popularity of flavored teas, sports drinks, and juice waters represents a threat to the conventional soft-drink market. Both Coca-Cola and PepsiCo are responding by acquiring or establishing brand-name product lines to serve this new expanding market.[8] From a marketing perspective, threats are most commonly defined in terms of any negative impact that an environmental trend or development might have on the firm's sales revenues, market shares, or profits.

The external environmental scan usually involves a systematic process by which environmental trends and developments are closely scrutinized and carefully analyzed in order to assess their potential positive impacts (opportunities) or negative impacts (threats) on the organization's businesses.

> The shift to a digital, networked office environment presents both a threat and an opportunity for Canon. The threat is that as copying, faxing, and printing functions converge, Canon will lose control of its copier markets to computer peripheral makers (like HP) that aren't now making copiers. ... The opportunity is that with the different office equipment markets increasingly converging in this fashion, just about everything is up for grabs.[9]

Astute strategic planners study the influences of the following external environments.

- ❏ Population/Demographic
- ❏ Competitive/Economic
- ❏ Social/Cultural
- ❏ Political/Legal
- ❏ Physical/Natural
- ❏ Technological/Informational

The specific issues associated with each of these environments is the focus of discussion in Part III.

SWOT MATRIX

To gain an overall perspective of the relationships among the four components of a SWOT analysis, a **SWOT matrix** can be constructed that not only classifies each relationship but suggests the most appropriate action, as shown in Figure 3-3. The following four relationships are illustrated:

- ❏ *Leverage*—matching an internal business strength with an external environmental opportunity. Leveraging represents the "ideal" business

FIGURE 3-3

THE SWOT MATRIX

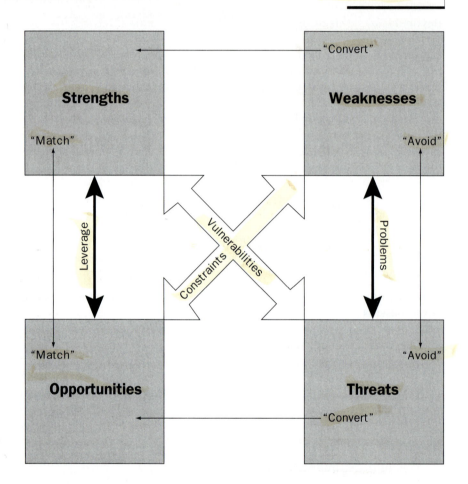

SOURCE: Adapted from Ramon J. Alday and Timothy M. Stearns, *Management* (Southwestern Publishing Co., 1991), 199–201, and Nigel Piercy, *Market-Led Strategic Change* (Oxford, U.K.: Butterworth-Heineman Ltd., 1992), 260.

relationship because it affords the organization a chance to develop a sustainable competitive advantage.

❑ *Vulnerability*—matching an internal business strength with an external environmental threat. This type of matchup leaves a business open to attack and may neutralize a competitive advantage.

❑ *Constraint*—matching an internal business weakness with an external environmental opportunity. An SBU might be restrained from taking advantage of a good business opportunity due to internal marketing or operating limitations.

❑ *Problem*—matching an internal business weakness with an external environmental threat. A problem is the most difficult business situation, wherein the firm is not equipped to compete effectively in an unfriendly environment due to limited resources and abilities.

The following actions suggested by the SWOT matrix are those that might be expected and provide the strategic marketing manager with some options:

❑ Match strengths and opportunities

❑ Convert weaknesses to strengths

❑ Convert threats to opportunities

❑ Minimize, if not avoid, weaknesses and threats

MARKETING STRATEGIES

The third stage in developing a strategic marketing plan is the evaluation of the various options that the marketing manager might pursue. Having completed a SWOT analysis, strategic marketing planners have identified possible courses of action that are best fitted to the organization's strengths and weaknesses. It is in this stage of the planning process where specific strategic marketing options are explored and evaluated in order to determine which marketing strategy is best suited to an identified opportunity. A **marketing strategy** is a functional strategy that guides and directs the marketing activities of an SBU. The strategic issues to be addressed by each marketing strategy are "How can we best apply our marketing strengths to satisfy the specific needs of targeted consumer groups and to meet the performance expectations of corporate management?" and "Is this the best match between our marketing competencies and marketplace opportunities?"

Practically an unlimited number of ways exist to classify the myriad of strategies employed by the marketing manager. Throughout this text we will be examining various marketing strategies from several different perspectives with respect to a host of marketing issues and decisions. In this initial preview of marketing strategies, two broad categories of marketing reference strategies will be discussed—differentiating strategies and positioning strategies.

Like most things, business organizations and marketing programs are understood and evaluated in relative terms. Customers, competitors, and the general public mentally organize information and make value judgments by comparing people, places, and things. **Reference strategies** are marketing activities that help to differentiate one organization and its marketing programs from competitive organizations and their marketing efforts and to position an organization and its marketing activities within the marketplace. Differentiating and positioning are the two key reference strategies employed by the marketing manager.

DIFFERENTIATING STRATEGIES

"Being different" is the core concept underlying the use of differentiating strategies. **Differentiation** is the marketing strategy of developing a set of unique and meaningful differences that will distinguish the organization's marketing programs from themselves and from the offerings of competitors. To correct previous problems of internal divisions competing against each other (such as Pontiac and Chevrolet competing for younger buyers), General Motors (GM) now controls model-line cannibalism by requiring every car and truck to hit one of twenty-six precisely defined market segments (such as small sporty cars or full-size pickup trucks). No two vehicles are allowed to overlap. Even in large market segments, such as midsize sedans, GM entries have to be clearly differentiated (sporty or conservative styling).[10] By being different, the marketing manager hopes to establish particular impressions that will serve as a basis for competing in the marketplace. This basis is often referred to as a **differential advantage**—any feature of the organization or any of the organization's activities perceived by customers to be highly desirable and notably different from those offered by competing organizations. The degree to which an organization enjoys a differential advantage over the competition will depend on how valuable the customer believes the difference to be.

Strategic planners pursue differentiating strategies by seeking to be different in one or more ways that are highly regarded by customers. By offering different goods and services in unique places at various prices, the marketing manager aims to gain a competitive advantage that is meaningful and sustainable.

GOODS DIFFERENTIATION The distinctiveness of goods can range from fairly standardized (salt and steel) to highly unstandardized offerings (personalized services and art). Due to the multidimensional character of goods, the strategic marketing planner has an expansive range of choices by which to differentiate the organization's offerings of goods. Tangible goods can be differentiated by functional features, aesthetic features, or psychological benefits.

A good's **functional features** include the tangible elements of size, shape, and weight, together with the chemical and biological makeup. The importance of functional features is that they determine to what extent a good can perform the functions that it was designed to perform. That is, they determine the performance quality of the good; e.g., how well does the lawnmower cut grass? Functional features also govern each good's

❑ Durability or life expectancy—how long will the lawnmower last?

❑ Reliability or performance dependability—will the lawnmower start each time with the same level of effort?

❏ Serviceability or repair convenience—how easy is it to fix the lawn-mower?

A good's **aesthetic features** are those elements that appeal to the consumer's five senses. Consumers have preconceived and different ideas about how a good should look, smell, sound, feel, and taste. The aesthetic features of Crystal Pepsi did not meet customer expectations. Crystal Pepsi will be reincarnated as a citrus cola in an effort to compete with Sprite and 7-Up. "Gone will be the hints of cinnamon, ginger, and pepper that gave Crystal Pepsi its peculiar noncola flavor."[11] Style and design are the two elements most often cited as aesthetic determinants. *Style* incorporates those special characteristics that distinguish one good from another of a similar type. For example, in fashion apparel, the specific style features that distinguish one skirt from another include length (floor, ankle, knee, mini), cut (wraparound, accordion-pleated, bias) and fabric (denim, gabardine, chiffon). *Design* is an individual interpretation or version of a style as created by different forms, lines, colors, and textures. Ethan Allen, the bastion of colonial credenzas and chintz couches, has refashioned itself by creating five new styles to appeal to younger consumers. The new styles include American Impressions, a mix of sturdy wooden pieces inspired by Shaker designs; Country Crossings, a rustic line of maple furniture; American Dimensions, a modern look that accents geometric shapes; Legacy, styles that borrow from Italian architecture; and Radius, sleek designs reminiscent of the 1960s.[12]

With the purchase of a good comes the expectation that the purchaser will benefit in some fashion beyond just the tangible rewards of using the good. The consumer expects **psychological benefits**, as well, from buying, using, or possessing the good. Marketers who have recognized that a good's psychological endowments are as important as its physical characteristics have greatly expanded the dimensions by which a good can be differentiated. Love and belongingness, safety and security, esteem and recognition, and freedom and individualism are all psychological needs that can serve as an effective means for creating a unique and distinctive perception of a good. "TAG Heuer's chunky, brushed steel watches with big numerals are becoming an emblem of the down-to-earth 1990s—even though the average price is $1,200."[13] According to the firm's senior management, TAG Heuer doesn't sell products to tell time; it sells image.

SERVICE DIFFERENTIATION Customer service incorporates all of the features, acts, and information that augment the customer's ability to realize the potential value of a core product or service.[14] As suggested by the definition and illustrated in Figure 3-4, total customer service is a multidimensional concept centered on two components: customer service features and actions. Total customer service is the degree to which services meet customer satisfaction and enhance the customer's perceived value from the exchange process. Marketing managers can differentiate their

FIGURE 3-4

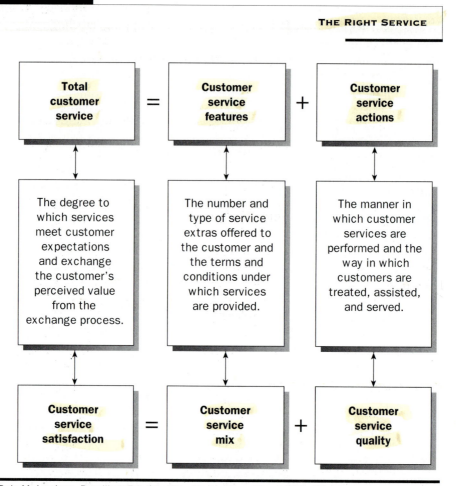

SOURCE: Dale M. Lewison, Retailing, 5th Ed., (New York: Macmillan, 1994), 29.

service offering by the number and type of services offered and the manner in which those services are executed. More posh hotels are now paying almost as much attention to their canine guests as to their human ones, gladly accepting four-legged clients and lavishing them with all sorts of four-star services. The Chicago Ritz's Pet Recognition Program provides a linen-covered pillow, a squeaky rubber toy, or personal dog biscuits on each visit. An on-site kennel provides grooming at a moment's notice.[15]

The distinction created by **customer service features** depends on the number and type of service extras offered to the customer and the terms and conditions under which the services are provided (see Figure 3-4). The number of services offered can fluctuate along a continuum from full service to limited service to self-service to no service. Some of the more common types of services offered by marketing organizations include delivery and installation, packaging and wrapping, labeling and coding, alteration and repair, credit and transactional assistance, and customer information and training, as well as returns and adjustments. American Express's new Optima True Grace credit card lets the customer avoid paying interest on new purchases for twenty-five days, even if there's a balance on the account. Other credit cards allow a grace period only when accounts have no outstanding balance.[16] The nature and structure of the customer service mix provides abundant opportunities for marketers to differentiate themselves from their competitors.

Customer service actions are the manner in which customer services are performed and the way in which customers are treated, assisted, and served (see Figure 3-4). In the package wars between FedEx and UPS, both companies are using technology to become more timely, convenient, faster, friendlier, and more adaptable and reliable in their struggle to gain more market share.[17] The competence, courtesy, credibility, willingness, responsiveness, reliability, and communication skills of the service provider are all characteristics that describe customer service actions and determine customer service quality. How services are provided can have equal value to customers as the services themselves. This delivery of services can be a key consideration when implementing a differentiation strategy.

POSITIONING STRATEGIES

Establishing a "place in the consumer's mind" is the underlying concept in the use of a positioning strategy. Positioning strategies are closely associated with the process of **target marketing** whereby the entire marketing effort of an organization is directed at a select group of customers in an attempt to meet "all" or "most" of their individual needs. By tailoring their entire marketing program to satisfying the needs of a chosen few, the target marketer is creating a consumer mind-set by engaging in market positioning and market repositioning strategies.

MARKET POSITIONING A **market positioning strategy** is one in which a distinctive and interesting position for the organization and its marketing program is created in the minds of consumers. This is accomplished by relating the organization or program to other marketing organizations and programs or by establishing a perception of being the most appropriate marketing organization and program for a preferred group of customers. Market positioning is one means by which strategic marketing managers hope to focus their company's efforts with regard to both the markets to be served and the marketing programs to be developed. Market positioning strategies are implemented by employing the three-stage process known as the **ABCs of positioning**—attributes, benefits, and claims.[18]

1. *Identify attributes*—Identify the intrinsic qualities of the company's marketing effort and the characteristics that distinguish one marketing program from another. Specific and distinctive attributes associated with product features, service levels, pricing points, promotional themes, and distributor networks are all elements of the marketing program that could provide a basis for creating a distinctive position within the market.

2. *Delineate benefits*—Delineate the comparative advantages that one marketing organization and program has over another company's marketing and operational attributes. To qualify as a comparative advantage, delineated benefits should be important, deliver high value; distinctive, deliver something different; superior, deliver higher quality; communicable, promote ease of understanding; preemptive, difficult to copy; affordable, consistent with consumer's ability to buy; and profitable, provided within reasonable cost structures.[19]

3. *Communicate claims*—Communicate the company's attributes and benefits to existing and potential customers by making specific claims or promises. Establish market positions by promoting the company and its marketing program as bigger, better, cheaper, faster, or some other description of the relative advantages offered to the consumer. Successful, long-term market positioning campaigns are based on real claims that can be substantiated; otherwise it becomes more illusion than reality, more hype than honesty.

MARKET REPOSITIONING The dynamic character of external environments and markets and the fickle nature of consumer buying behavior necessitate an adaptive approach to positioning strategies. When the Oldsmobile division of General Motors introduced its new luxury sedan, Aurora, company policy required the division to develop a product strategy that would make the automobile different from Buick. Management decided to "reposition Olds toward an 'international flavored' sedan aimed at the import buyer." All Olds models would be five-passenger cars with an overhead cam and a good suspension system. The Buick, meanwhile, would stick with its current success formula as a six-passenger, upscale car aimed at traditional American buyers.[20] **Market repositioning** is the process of altering the customer's existing mind-set relative to the market position occupied by a particular business operation. This alteration is accomplished by changing how the customer perceives the company relative to other businesses and their marketing programs. Or stated differently, it is accomplished by scrambling the previous ABC positioning mix. By identifying different attributes, delineating new benefits, and making fresh claims, the strategic marketer can alter the relative position the company occupies within the consumer's mind and develop a new image of where the company stands in relationship to its competitors. Laura Ashley, the British-based chain of women's apparel and accessories, thrived on a product line featuring florals and prints. Unfortunately, yesterday's frilly has become today's fussy. Plain, neutral colors are far more popular than busy patterns. These changing tastes have required the firm to reposition itself away from its English country tradition toward a more modern and contemporary image.[21] Something all marketing managers should remember is the fact that it is a very difficult task to change established mind-sets. Sears provides an excellent example of the difficulty that an organization can encounter in its attempts to remake itself. Prior to the current makeover, Sears' repositioning strategies in recent times "have all bombed badly, including their efforts to remake Sears into a mass merchandiser, a discounter, a specialty store, and a collection of specialty stores."[22]

CONCLUDING REMARKS

The second plan in our three-tier hierarchy of plans is the strategic marketing plan. These divisional-level plans are developed by the marketing management team within each of the SBUs. The strategic marketing plan establishes a set of goals and identifies a series of strategies that defines the marketing programs of each SBU. Acting as a bridging document, the strategic marketing plan links the broad aims of corporate management as outlined in the mission statement (Chapter 2) with the action plans of the annual marketing plan (Chapter 4).

ENDNOTES

1. See Derek F. Abell, "Strategic Windows," *Journal of Marketing* (July 1978), 2–26.

2. See Louis E. Boone and David L. Kurtz, *Contemporary Marketing*, 7th edition (Fort Worth, TX: The Dryden Press, 1992), 26.

3. See Shawn Tully, "Purchasing's New Muscle," *Fortune* (February 20, 1995), 75–83.

4. Marcia Berss, "We Will Not Be in a National Chain," *Forbes* (March 27, 1995), 50.

5. See Peter Samuel, "Chipping Away at the Champ," *Forbes* (April 25, 1994), 107.

6. Cyndee Miller, "Gaze into the Crystal Ball for '95 and Beyond," *Marketing News* (January 30, 1995), 1, 10.

7. William M. Bulkeley and JoAnn S. Lublin, "Ben & Jerry's New CEO Will Face Shrinking Sales and Growing Fears of Fat," *Wall Street Journal* (January 1, 1995), B1.

8. Howard Rudnitsky, "Lots of Fizz," *Forbes* (August 1, 1994), 44.

9. Gale Eisenstodt, "Crazy Is Praise for Us," *Forbes* (November 7, 1994), 182, 184.

10. Alex Taylor III, "GM's $11,000,000,000 Turnaround," *Fortune* (October 17, 1994), 70.

11. Laura Zinn, "Does Pepsi Have Too Many Products?" *Business Week* (February 14, 1994), 64.

12. Chris Roush, "Rearranging the Furniture at Ethan Allen," *Business Week* (July 11, 1994), 102.

13. Stewart Toy, "Trendy? Heaven Forbid!" *Business Week* (November 21, 1994), 106

14. William H. Davidow and Bro Uttal, *Total Customer Satisfaction: The Ultimate Weapon* (New York, NY: Harper & Row, 1989), 22.

15. Lisa Gubernick, "Dogs Very Welcome," *Forbes* (March 13, 1995), 138.

16. Leah Nathans Spiro, "Is This Amex' Trump Card?" *Business Week* (October 24, 1994), 32.

17. David Greising, "Watch Out for Flying Packages," *Business Week* (November 14, 1994), 40.

18. Martin R. Lautman, "The ABCs of Positioning," *Marketing Research* (Winter 1993), 2–8.

19. See Philip Kotler, *Marketing Management* (Englewood Cliffs, NJ: Prentice Hall, 1994), 306.

20. Robert Stowe England, "Piece of Cake," *Financial World* (March 28, 1995), 35.

21. Joshua Levine, "Wilted Flowers," *Forbes* (April 10, 1995), 94.

22. Robert Stowe England, "Penney-Wise," *Financial World* (April 26, 1994), 37.

The Annual Marketing Plan

Chapter Outline

- **Introduction**
- **The Annual Marketing Plan**
  - Title Page
  - Table of Contents
  - Executive Summary
  - Marketing Objectives
  - Situation Analysis
  - Marketing Programs
  - Marketing Actions
  - Marketing Issues
  - Reference Sources
- **Marketing Objectives**
  - Market Objectives
  - Financial Objectives
  - Societal Objectives
- **Situation Analysis**
  - Corporate Review
  - Environmental Analysis
  - Consumer Analysis
  - Competitor Analysis
  - Market Analysis
- **Marketing Programs**
  - Product Decisions
  - Distribution Decisions
  - Promotion Decisions
  - Price Decisions
- **Concluding Remarks**

Introduction

Functional plans are the focus of the third and final level of planning. These operational plans are designed to transform the strategic plans of the corporate and divisional levels into tactical actions that govern the day-to-day operations of the various functional departments within each business unit. It is at this functional level of planning that each organization finds out the degree to which the desired outcomes expressed in the mission statement and marketing goals can be realized in applied and practical terms. This tactical planning process takes the form of the annual marketing plan.

The Annual Marketing Plan

The **annual marketing plan** is a written document that governs all of the firm's marketing activities in terms of planning, executing, and controlling. As a tactical plan, this blueprint of marketing activities tends to be short term (annual), focused (marketing-related decisions), and functional (steps needed to implement a strategy). The emphasis in the annual marketing plan is more on *how* to accomplish a goal and less on *what* goal to accomplish. It is an action plan that gives specific directions to the firm's cadre of middle and lower management.

Before we focus on the three key components of the plan (marketing objectives, situation analysis, and marketing programs), a short overview of the reporting format for the entire annual marketing plan will prove instructive. Figure 4-1 identifies the nine sections that would normally be included within a professionally prepared annual marketing plan. Each of these sections will be briefly described.

Title Page

The **title page** is an identification document that provides the reader with the following essential information:

1. The business unit for which the plan was prepared

2. The individual or group of individuals for whom the plan was developed

3. The names and addresses of the individuals or agencies who authored the plan

4. The time period covered by the plan

5. The date on which the plan was submitted

FIGURE 4-1

REPORTING FORMAT FOR THE ANNUAL MARKETING PLAN

I.	Title Page
II.	Table of Contents
III.	Executive Summary
IV.	Marketing Objectives
V.	Situation Analysis
VI.	Marketing Programs
VII.	Marketing Actions
VIII.	Marketing Issues
IX.	Reference Sources

TABLE OF CONTENTS

The **table of contents** lists the subject matter of the plan, identifies where various topics are to be found within the report, and shows how the plan is organized and presented. The table of contents is often a listing of titles and subtitles used within the text of the report together with an enumeration of various types of exhibits—tables, graphs, and photos.

EXECUTIVE SUMMARY

The **executive summary** is a short and concise summary of the key points of the marketing plan. It is designed to give busy executives a quick overview of the report and to inform them of key provisions of the organization's marketing effort with regard to a particular product or business unit. The executive summary centers around a brief description of the objectives to be achieved, the situations to be considered, and the programs to be launched. Special issues that impact the marketing plan might also be reviewed.

Marketing Objectives

The **marketing objectives** section of the marketing plan should answer the question "Where does the organization want to go?" By identifying desired outcomes, objectives give direction to the firm's marketing efforts. Marketing objectives are stated in specific and measurable terms, thereby establishing clear standards against which performances can be judged.

Situation Analysis

The **situation analysis** attempts to address the question "Where is the organization now?" An assessment of internal organizational strengths and weaknesses together with a scan of environmental opportunities and threats provide the necessary background for developing effective marketing programs and for directing the marketing actions of the firm.

Marketing Programs

The **marketing programs** part outlines the specific tactics to be used by the organization's managers in their efforts to get where they want to be from where they are now. Marketing programs are traditionally structured around the four major components of the marketing mix—product offerings, distribution systems, promotional programs, and pricing practices.

Marketing Actions

The **marketing actions** segment of the marketing plan concerns itself with the implementation and control of the plan. By measuring actual outcomes against stated objectives, management is able to assess the effectiveness of its marketing programs and to determine what adjustments are needed.

Marketing Issues

The **marketing issues** section of the plan discusses those special or unusual concerns that might have either a positive or negative impact on the marketing plan now or in the future. These special issues are addressed separately because of both their unique character and the lack of clarity surrounding their potential impact.

Reference Sources

The **reference sources** concludes the marketing plan and is a list of information sources used in generating the marketing plan or that might be useful in implementing the plan. Sources include individuals, organizations, published materials, internal documents, and any other reference from which relevant information might be obtained.

As was the case for the previous strategic business and marketing plans, the three planning stages of the annual marketing plan are focused on identifying desired outcomes (marketing objectives), assessing current

■ FIGURE 4-2

THE ANNUAL MARKETING PLAN

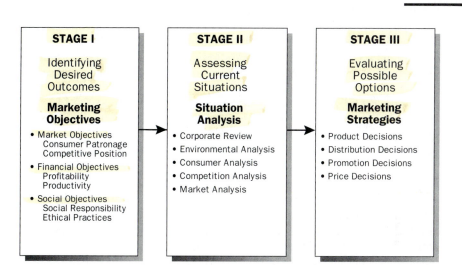

situations (situation analysis), and evaluating possible options (marketing programs). Figure 4-2 outlines the specific issues to be addressed within each stage of this planning process.

MARKETING OBJECTIVES

Marketing objectives are specific and quantitative expressions of desired outcomes that provide a clear blueprint or "road map" of what is expected from the organization's marketing efforts. They provide measurable benchmarks against which the firm's actual marketing activities will be judged and furnish marketing managers with a clear reference point against which to measure their contributions to the organization's stated mission and supporting goals. As suggested by Figure 4-2, marketing objectives can be classified into one of three groups—market, financial, or societal objectives.

MARKET OBJECTIVES

Market objectives are concerned with two issues: (1) securing the patronage of one or more customer segments, and (2) gaining a more favorable competitive position with the marketplace. Both of these market objectives require that the marketing manager carefully develop and implement marketing programs that enhance the organization's ability to meet the selective needs of targeted consumers.

CONSUMER PATRONAGE OBJECTIVES

Sales Objectives   Increase in sales revenues is perhaps the most common form of sales objective. A sales growth objective is commonly stated as a certain percentage increase for a particular product/brand/model (such as tennis shoes, Avia, or cross-trainers) or business/operating unit (such as the sporting goods stores or shoe department) over a definite period of time. Such an expansive objective is an ambitious one that will require additional investment of resources and encourage retaliatory action by competitors.

Customer Traffic   Consumer patronage can also be measured in terms of customer traffic, the number of customers attracted to the marketer's program. The entertainment (concerts and theaters) and recreation (amusement parks and golf courses) services industries are keenly interested in increasing the level of attendance at their events and facilities.[1] Retailers strive to increase customer traffic within their stores where visual displays, merchandising programs, and sales associates can turn shoppers into buyers. Unplanned purchases and complementary sales are two additional ways in which total revenues are enhanced through increased traffic counts. A customer traffic objective might be expressed as a 20-percent increase in concert attendance or a 30-percent expansion in the number of store visits by qualified customers during the weekend-advertised close-out sales period.

Customer Loyalty   Encouraging customers to buy the firm's products or patronize the firm's outlets on a frequent and regular basis is the focus of a customer loyalty objective. Repeat business through customer retention is an essential ingredient in any organization's successful marketing strategy. Chrysler has traditionally held the dominant market share in the minivan market. When Ford introduced its new aerodynamic Windstar version of the minivan, Chrysler sought to retain the loyalty of its customers by "carefully wooing millions of its own satisfied minivan owners with direct-mail advertising and special deals so they wouldn't defect. And it offered discounts of up to $1,600 on the vans, making it tough for Windstar to gain momentum."[2] High customer satisfaction levels are clearly reflected in the repeat trade of loyal customers. Higher profit levels, associated with the lower costs of doing business, are an additional benefit of dealing with an established customer base. For a dental clinic, a customer loyalty objective might be expressed as: to increase the average number of office appointments for dental hygiene services from one to two visits annually. A consumer goods company might express its loyalty objective in terms of increasing customer usage rate for one or more of its products.

COMPETITIVE POSITION OBJECTIVES

Market Share   Competitive position is generally expressed in terms of market share—an organization's or product's sales position relative to all other competing firms or products within a particular market area. Market share is calculated by dividing the organization's or product's sales by the total sales for the defined market. Market share growth (expanding an organization's share of the market, usually at the expense of competitors within the market) and market share maintenance (protecting current market share against the aggressive competitive actions of other organizations) are the two most commonly expressed market share objectives. The former is most appropriate when operating in growth markets while the latter is best suited to mature and stable market conditions. Generic drug producers have gained control of approximately 50 percent of the total drug market. Big drug companies are fighting to retain market share by cutting prices on brand products and by introducing generic versions of their own branded drugs, sometimes even before their brands go off patent.[3] Apple's share of the world computer market varies from 10 to 14 percent. A major marketing goal of the beleaguered Apple Computer Inc. is "to get enough market share to ensure that it does not become a marginal—and therefore endangered—player in the PC game."[4]

Consumer Image   How an organization and its products are perceived by the consuming public is an issue that concerns every organization. An **image** is the mental picture of the organization and its products as held by a group of consumers or the general public. **Consumer image** is the symbolic representation of the basic attributes of the organization or product. Often expressed in relative terms (cheaper, larger, better, faster, easier), images can be used by organizations to position themselves and their products in the minds of consumers. Gymboree, the mall-based chain of togs for tots, has successfully created a distinctive trademark look by featuring vibrant colors and bold patterns. "It's a childlike image, compared with rival GAPKids' tiny-grown-ups approach."[5] A consumer image objective might be expressed as: to be recognized and named by 22 percent of the respondents in a consumer survey as the product offering the best quality at the lowest price. Low prices and good quality are two images that would be associated with McDonald's. A lean and healthy menu is not an image that would immediately come to mind when talking about the world's largest purveyor of hamburgers. Hence, McDonald's has a goal to correct its image as an unhealthy (high calories and high fat content) place to eat. Other fast-food chains are pursuing a similar objective.[6]

Vendor Relations   Supply-side relationships are also important in determining an organization's competitive position. Being well positioned with respect to established vendors and emerging sources of supply can be the determining factor in creating a competitive organization or product line. Strategic alliances and partnerships with suppliers have become key elements in most strategic marketing plans and an essential component in any successful marketing program. In developing relationships, with its vendors, McDonald's does not shop for the lowest price; rather, its goal is to have close relationships with vendors in order to obtain a quality product at a low price, supported by excellent service. This "McDonaldizing" of suppliers involves an open-book relationship in which McDonald's actually sets vendor profits in return for assurances of long-term business relations and other production and distribution assistance.[7] Quick-response replenishing systems and the need for nonadversarial relationships have increased the importance of developing marketing objectives that deal with vendor relations. A stated goal to conduct 90 percent of all vendor transactions using electronic data processing and quick response systems by the year 2000 exemplifies this type of specific marketing objective.

FINANCIAL OBJECTIVES

The operational issues of profitability and productivity are the two key groupings of financial objectives. By establishing quantifiable measures of profit and production levels, the marketing manager creates standards by which the organization's performance can be judged. Targeted returns, earnings per share, and stockholders' dividends are among the profitability objectives that will be discussed. Productivity objectives usually center on three of the organization's most important resource on categories—labor, space, and inventory.

PROFITABILITY

Targeted Returns   For its investments in time and money, the organization has the right to expect something in return. Targeted return objectives reflect what management expects from its efforts. Some of the more commonly cited targeted return objectives include

1. Return on net sales—net profit divided by net sales
2. Return on net assets—net profit divided by total assets
3. Return on net worth—net profit divided by net worth

Each of these ratios permits the marketing manager to make an overall assessment of the performance of the business unit or product in terms of profit. A targeted return objective might be expressed as earning an 18-percent return on net sales for the fourth quarter during the current operating year.

Earnings Per Share   Stockholders' interests need to be protected if the organization expects to attract investment capital. Many organizations establish projected earnings-per-share-of-common-stock objectives in order to ensure that a certain dividend payment will be available to the owners of common stock. An earnings goal could be designated as $3.50 per share of common stock.

Stockholder Dividends Dividends and the increase or decrease in the market value of the stock represent the return on stockholder investment. The investment community and potential investors are keenly interested in what proportion of the organization's total earnings is allocated to stockholder dividends. As part of the management team, the marketing manager is partially responsible for ensuring a fair return for investors. A stockholder dividend objective is expressed as an annual dollar dividend yield per share of common stock.

PRODUCTIVITY

Labor Productivity Given the rather labor-intensive nature of many marketing activities, labor productivity is a high priority issue within many organizations. The productivity of the firm's labor force can be measured by dividing net sales by total number of employees, total number of worker hours, or total dollars of labor expense. To increase net sales per worker hour or per wage dollar by 2 percent during the fall selling season are two possible examples of labor productivity objectives. Reduction in labor turnover might also be considered as an objective in enhancing labor productivity.

Space Productivity Productive and effective use of facilities are common marketing objectives. Retailers, for example, establish productivity objectives by dividing either net sales or gross margin by some measure of the selling, storage, or service space for a store, department, or display area, such as net sales per square foot, cubic foot, or linear foot. Recognizing the importance of space productivity goals, Renaissance Cosmetics sends its sales representative to individual retailers and offers to analyze fragrance operations of each of the firm's stores. The representative then returns with plans showing how the store can turn inventories faster, not just by using Renaissance discount coupons, stand-alone displays, and aisle displays but also by employing a space management technique known as category management—reorganizing store shelves to maximize retail profits on each category of products.[8]

Inventory Productivity Inventory turnover is one of the most widely used measures of merchandise productivity. The inventory turnover rate is defined as the number of times during a specific time period that the average stock on hand is sold. Within certain constraints, the higher the inventory turnover rate the better the financial productivity of the merchandise. Profit per unit times product turnover rate determines the total revenues generated by a business unit or product line. Colgate-Palmolive assisted retailers to achieve their inventory productivity goals by switching to an everyday low-price policy. This change allowed retailers to buy just enough for their immediate needs rather than stock up several times a year when promotional prices were offered. The net result was a lower average stock on hand and a higher inventory turnover rate.[9]

SOCIETAL OBJECTIVES

Societal objectives support the organization's philosophy that its marketing efforts should satisfy not only the market and financial objectives but also serve the best interests of society. Societal objectives can be classified as those relating to social responsibility or ethical business practices.

SOCIAL RESPONSIBILITY Social responsibility objectives are concerned with the well-being of society. Levi Strauss takes pride in its reputation for being on the cutting edge of social responsibility. The jeans maker requires contractors to meet specific standards regarding minimum age of employees, overtime pay, plant safety, and healthful working conditions.[10] Social responsibilities are often statements in support of charitable causes, educational institutions, social organizations, or community projects. Being socially responsible means being a good corporate citizen. Personal involvement, financial contributions, technical support, marketing efforts, and managerial expertise are the more common vehicles by which marketing managers can demonstrate their commitment to the welfare of society.

ETHICAL BUSINESS PRACTICES Ethics statements are marketing objectives that guide marketing managers and employees in determining right from wrong, fair from unfair, and trustworthy from untrustworthy. Organizations that operate under a clearly stated and communicated ethical code are less likely to have moral or ethical lapses during the execution of the organization's marketing program. Ethics codes and related objectives seek to eliminate problems associated with job discrimination, unfair labor practices, operating violations, misleading warranties, false advertising claims, counterfeit products, price discrimination, price fixing, deceptive sales promotions or practices, and illegal distribution arrangements. To be successful in their mission as moral guidelines, ethics objectives must be more than just a public relations ploy.

SITUATION ANALYSIS

As was the case with both the strategic business and marketing plans, the second planning stage in the development of the annual marketing plan is the assessment of the current situation faced by the business unit or product line. At this lower level of the planning process, the annual marketing planner has the advantage of the availability of the vast amount of information generated by previous strategic business and marketing plans. For marketing managers the issue becomes one of determining which previously generated information is relevant and applicable to the particular business unit or product line and what new information is needed. Like the portfolio and SWOT analysis conducted for strategic business and marketing plans, the situation analysis is organized around internal and external components. Figure 4-2 identifies the important factors to be considered in completing this stage of the planning process.

CORPORATE REVIEW

To ensure conformity and compliance with higher level plans and expectations, marketing planners need to conduct careful reviews of all plans and documents that impact their operations. Reviewing mission statements and marketing goals, examining portfolio and SWOT analysis results, and scrutinizing corporate business opportunities and SBU marketing strategies are some of the prerequisites to the successful development of an annual marketing plan. The previous two chapters addressed each of these issues.

Additional corporate review activities might include a historical appraisal of the business unit or product line in terms of profit history as reflected by past sales and cost structures, product features and technologies, pricing strategies and tactics, distribution networks and relationships, sales policies and practices, and sales promotions and advertising campaigns. Historical market trends and competitive patterns might also be reviewed. Past accomplishments often provide beneficial information in planning for future performances. Chapters 10 through 13 will provide specific details regarding each of these marketing activities.

Finally, a corporate review makes a comprehensive assessment of the company's resources. An audit of the company's human, financial, and physical resources is necessary in order to know what resources will be available to implement the annual marketing plan.

ENVIRONMENTAL ANALYSIS

Environmental forces can either hamper or enhance the marketing manager's ability to accomplish stated goals. Having an understanding of the current state of the environment and making projections as to its future impact on the development and implementation of marketing programs are core concerns of the environmental analysis. Actually "the environment" includes several different environments. Most annual marketing plans include an extensive review and analysis of a number of external environments: population/demographic, competitive/economic, social/cultural, political/legal, physical/natural, and technological/informational. The specifics of each of these environments are considered in Chapter 6. It is sufficient here to mention that the nature of multienvironmental situations is highly volatile. Therefore, the annual marketing plan must remain fluid and capable of being adapted to new environmental opportunities and threats.

CONSUMER ANALYSIS

Consumer analysis attempts to delineate and describe the firm's buying population by answering the following questions:

1. How many are they? (total population)
2. Who are they? (demographic makeup)
3. Where are they? (geographic location)

In addition, a consumer analysis addresses the following buyer behavior issues:

1. What do buyers buy? (goods, services, and ideas)
2. How much do consumers buy? (ability, willingness, and authority to buy)
3. Which consumers do the buying? (individual or group buying centers)
4. Why do consumers buy? (psychological, personal, and social influences)
5. How do consumers buy? (stages of the buying process)

While such questions are appropriate for consumer markets, a similar list of questions can be developed for organizational markets. The information and insight developed and discovered during this phase of the situation analysis provides essential inputs for the final phase of the situation analysis—the market analysis. Chapter 7 explores the buying behavior of both final consumers and organizational buyers.

COMPETITOR ANALYSIS

While the consumer analysis phase dealt with the issue of "how much" business is available in terms of total market potential, the competitor analysis phase directs its attention to "what share" of the total market a given business or product can expect to capture. In other words, what marketing opportunities exist for the firm and its products? The annual marketing plan catalogs the type (direct or indirect), size (large or small), number (chain or single unit), scope (national or local), and relationship (affiliated or unaffiliated) of competing businesses in order to gain an idea of the level of competition existing within various markets. The competitor assessment is frequently accomplished through the use of a **competitor audit**, which lists and evaluates the marketing effort (strategies and tactics, programs and activities, and plans and actions) of competitive businesses. Competitor analysis forms the focus of the discussion in Chapter 8.

MARKET ANALYSIS

Market analysis is centered around delineating, segmenting, and targeting markets and submarkets. Market delineation involves the recognition and separation of consumption units into two types of markets. **Consumer markets** are made up of ultimate consumers of goods and services who purchase products for personal or family use. **Organizational markets** are made up of intermediate industrial, retail, institutional, or organizational buyers of goods or services who purchase products in order to resell them or to use them in the operation of their businesses. **Market segmentation** is the process of dividing a heterogeneous total market into several more homogeneous market segments based on geographic, demographic, psychographic, product-benefit, or brand-loyalty factors for consumer markets; and geographic, customer type, or product end-use characteristics for organizational markets. Target marketing entails the selection of market segments to be served and the development of marketing programs that are tailored to the special needs of targeted markets. Chapter 9 focuses on market analysis.

Marketing Programs

The last stage in the planning process is the evaluation of marketing programs to determine which are best suited to assist the business in meeting stated marketing objectives. **Marketing programs** are sets of activities organized around the four general marketing functions of creating, distributing, pricing, and promoting products (see Figure 4-2). This *mix* of functional marketing activities is often referred to as the *marketing mix* because it represents an appropriate blend of marketing activities designed to satisfy the needs and tastes of a particular group of ultimate consumers or organizational buyers. It is at this point in the planning process that specific tactical actions are identified in sufficient detail to implement the annual marketing plan as well as plans that preceded it.

Marketing programs are the actionable *means* of achieving desired *ends*. They outline *what* needs to be done, *how* it will be done, *when* it will be done, and *who* will do it. The actionable nature of the marketing program suggests its decision-making character. That is, the development of the marketing program is a series of decisions directed at the achievement of specific performance standards outlined by the measurable objectives in the annual marketing plan. We will briefly describe each of the four marketing subprograms, but a detailed discussion of each subprogram and the decisions that comprise them is the focus of Part IV.

Product Decisions

Product decisions involve the actions directed at developing and delivering a "bundle of benefits" to a select group of consumers. Customers expect to benefit in some way from buying a product; the extent to which the product meets those expectations determines the level of customer satisfaction and the degree of success enjoyed by the product. Products can be either tangible goods or intangible services and ideas; hence, the range of potential products and combination of products is enormous. The product or brand manager faces an interesting and challenging array of decisions relative to development and maintenance of a product program. A limited sample would include the following:

- Which product line or items will be included or excluded from the firm's total product mix?
- What process will be used to add or delete lines and items from the product mix?
- How will the product mix be structured relative to its makeup of products in different stages of the product life cycle and in different phases of the product adoption process?
- What, when, where, and how will new products be developed and introduced into the marketplace?
- What branding strategies will be employed to build recognition and maintain loyalty?
- What are the product's packaging and labeling requirements, and how can they be best used to support the product?
- How will products be differentiated from and positioned against competitive products?

DISTRIBUTION DECISIONS

Distribution decisions deal with the problems of moving products from points of origin to points of consumption. Often referred to as the *place* variable, distribution decisions are directed at ensuring that the right product is in the right place at the right time and in the right quantities. The creation of place, time, and possession utility for a select group of customers located in a specific geographic location provides the focus of the logistics manager's efforts. The distribution network is referred to as a **marketing channel**—a team of marketing institutions that directs a flow of goods and services from the original producer to the final consumer. The distribution team is made up of two or more of the following marketing institutions:

- raw resource producers
- distributors
- final manufacturers
- wholesalers
- retailers

A limited sample of the distribution issues faced by the marketing managers would include the following:

- Which marketing institutions should be included within the distribution network as full-fledged channel members, and which institutions should perform a facilitating and supportive role?
- How many different levels of middlepersons or intermediaries should be used in structuring the marketing channel of distribution?
- What degree of market coverage is desirable? Should the marketing channel be arranged to provide an intensive, selective, or exclusive coverage of the market?
- Is vertical integration of the marketing channel advisable? What level of integration is appropriate? How will the integrative process be accomplished?
- How will channel conflict be resolved? What means of control will be used to ensure cooperation and create close relationships among channel members?
- What form of order processing, inventory control, and materials handling systems will be used to manage the physical flow of goods and services?

Promotion Decisions

Effective communications is the core aim of most promotion decisions. The marketing manager's job is to combine various forms of promotional activities to effectively communicate specific messages concerning the firm and its market offering to targeted consumers, channel partners, company shareholders, and the general public. This promotion mix consists of such communications activities as advertising, sales promotion, personal selling, public relations, and direct marketing. Promotional messages tend to be informative and/or persuasive in nature. Informative messages provide the receiver with specific factual information concerning the product, its price, and where it can be purchased. In a persuasive message, the marketer presents arguments in an attempt to convince the audience that its marketing program offers the best value, the largest quantity, the finest quality, the longest life, the easiest terms, the closest outlet, or some other comparative advantages. Persuasive messages are cast in terms of either rational or emotional appeal. A selective listing of promotional issues could include the following:

- Which components of the promotion mix are best suited to helping the company reach its marketing objectives?
- How many different promotion mix components will be included in the company's promotional efforts?
- What will be the role and relative emphasis of each of the promotion mix components?

- What are the key messages that the firm wants to communicate about its products, prices, and the places where it sell its products?
- What form of appeal is most appropriate given the intended audience?
- How large a promotional budget is needed in order to ensure that the firm's messages are being effectively communicated to its intended audience?
- Who will be responsible for planning and implementing the promotion program?

PRICE DECISIONS

Price decisions deal with what the customer must pay to obtain a product. Prices are usually expressed in monetary terms. Price is a key input variable into the value equation—price plus quality plus service plus intangibles. A product's price is an expression of its worth to both the buyer and seller. As a powerful element of the marketing mix, price is expected to act as a revenue generator, a competitive tool, and an image builder. In making the price decision, marketing managers consider demand conditions, competitive positions, cost structures, and vendor recommendations. The following are some of the more interesting pricing questions:

- What objectives are to be achieved by the firm's price strategy?
- What type of price-level structure is appropriate for the type of customer targeted by the firm?
- Which and how many price determinants will be used in setting prices?
- What policies and practices will be used in making price adjustments?
- Is price a primary competitive strategy for the firm?

CONCLUDING REMARKS

The annual marketing plan is the third and final plan of the business planning process. This functional plan is created to provide specific directions as to how the firm's marketing program is to be implemented. As a short-term tactical blueprint, the annual marketing plan transforms the business and marketing strategic plans into a set of actions that guide low and middle managers in the daily operation of their business unit. A typical reporting format for an annual marketing plan includes a title page, table of contents, and executive summary together with a description of the plan's marketing objectives, situation analysis, marketing programs, marketing actions, marketing issues, and reference sources.

ENDNOTES

1. See Michael J. Mandel, Mark Landler, and Ronald Grover, "The Entertainment Economy," *Business Week* (March 14, 1994), 58–64.

2. David Woodruff, "Chrysler Is Burning up the Minivan Lane," *Business Week* (September 5, 1994).

3. John R. Hayes, "Drug Wars," *Forbes* (August 29, 1994), 81.

4. Kathy Rebello, "Spindler's Apple," *Business Week* (October 3, 1995), 89.

5. Russell Mitchell, "A Children's Retailing That's Growing up Fast," *Business Week* (May 23, 1994), 95.

6. See R. Lee Sullivan, "Leaner Menus," *Forbes* (March 13, 1995), 154. Also see Howard Rudnitsky, "Leaner Cuisine," *Forbes* (March 27, 1995), 43.

7. Andrew E. Serwer, "McDonald's Conquers the World," *Fortune* (October 17, 1994), 114.

8. Phyllis Berman, "The Spray Lingerie," *Forbes* (November 7, 1994), 108.

9. Howard Rudnitsky, "Making His Mark," *Forbes* (September 26, 1994), 47.

10. D. Kirk Davidson, "Marketers Can't Ignore New Ethics Issue," *Marketing News* (February 27, 1995), 34.

The Marketing Information System

Chapter Outline

- **Introduction**
- **The Marketing Information System**
    - Stage 1: Locating Information
    - Stage 2: Gathering Information
    - Stage 3: Processing Information
    - Stage 4: Utilizing Information
- **Marketing Intelligence**
    - Library Sources
    - Government Sources
    - Association Sources
    - Commercial Sources
- **Marketing Research**
    - Step 1: Problem Definition
    - Step 2: Hypothesis Formulation
    - Step 3: Research Design
    - Step 4: Data Collection
- **Records Search**
- **Analytical Models**
- **Concluding Remarks**

Introduction

Marketing managers need useful information concerning a wide range of external happenings and internal activities. Some of the more common external information needed include environmental opportunities and threats, the buying behavior of individuals and organizations, and the actions of competitors. Internally, data on the performances of various operations are needed to provide marketing managers with information about manufacturing, financial, and service activities that affect marketing decisions.

A massive amount of data is available from a wide variety of sources. The trick is to transform that data, ranging from statistics and facts to opinions and predictions, into information that is useful to the organization's marketing decision makers. The importance of a timely and comprehensive information system is becoming more evident with the increased need to develop closer customer relationships, the spiraling costs of making wrong marketing decisions, the greater complexity of the marketplace, and the elevated level of competitor aggressiveness.

The Marketing Information System

Effective problem solving and decision making depend on sufficient amounts of reliable and useful information. The need for current and relevant knowledge has resulted in the development and implementation of information systems that incorporate data management procedures involving generating new data or gathering existing data, storing and retrieving data, processing data into useful information, and disseminating information to those individuals who need it. The **marketing information system (MIS)** is an interacting organization of people, machines, and processes devised to create a regular, continuous, and orderly flow of information essential to the marketer's problem-solving and decision-making activities. As a planned, sequential flow of information tailored to the needs of a particular marketing manager, the MIS can be conceptualized as a four-stage process consisting of locating, gathering, processing, and utilizing information. Figure 5-1 illustrates the central issues to be addressed in each of the four MIS stages.

Stage 1: Locating Information

Finding relevant and useful information is predicated on having an understanding of the types and sources of information. Information can be classified as either secondary or primary. **Secondary information** is existing information that has already been collected and published by the organization or by some other organization for another purpose. Trade associations, government agencies, public institutions, and private businesses are a few of the organizations that collect and disseminate secondary information.

FIGURE 5-1

FOUR STAGES OF THE MARKETING INFORMATION SYSTEM

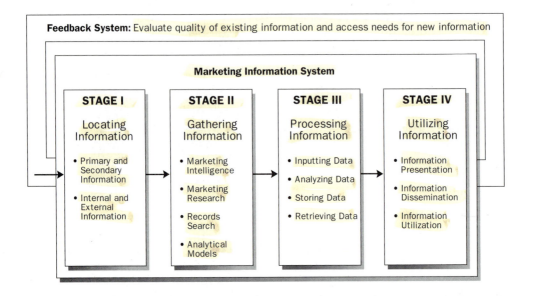

Often, secondary information is in an unsuitable form and has to be adapted to be useful and appropriate for the needs of the researcher. The usefulness of secondary data can be limited due to obsolescence. Dated information is simply not very helpful in solving contemporary problems. The accuracy of secondary data can also be questionable. Sources of secondary information need to be checked in order to eliminate the possibility of biased reporting. The advantages of secondary data are its lower acquisition costs and its immediate availability.

Primary information is new information in which the data collection process is tailored to the needs of the user. Surveys, focus groups, research panels, laboratory experiments, and quantitative methodologies are some of the means for collecting original data. The researchers select primary information sources for the greater accuracy, currency, and suitability of that information. When the advantages of primary information are great enough to justify the higher costs (time, money, and effort), marketing managers generally prefer this type of information.

Sources of information can be classified as either internal or external. **Internal information** is existing data or new data that can be generated from operations and activities found within the organization. Financial statements (income and net worth), operation reports (production and inventory), and marketing records (sales and margins) are but a few of the many internal sources of information. **External information** is knowledge obtained from sources outside of the organization. Formal sources of external information include public libraries, government and trade publications, and commercial studies and reports. Informally, external information can be gathered from customers, suppliers, competitors, and the general public.

STAGE 2: GATHERING INFORMATION

Figure 5-2 presents a taxonomy of information-gathering methodologies based on the types and sources of information. As illustrated in Figure 5-2, the four methods of gathering information are marketing intelligence, marketing research, records search, and analytical models. We will limit our discussion here to a brief definition of each method. A complete review of each method will follow later in the chapter. **Marketing intelligence** is the gathering of external secondary information. Marketing intelligence involves search procedures for probing public and private sources

• FIGURE 5-2

TAXONOMY OF INFORMATION-GATHERING METHODOLOGIES

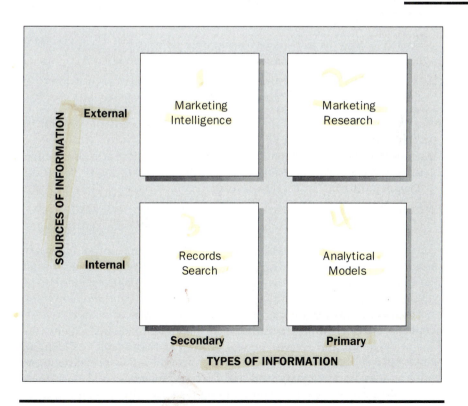

of published information. **Marketing research** involves the process of collecting external primary information from consumers, vendors, competitors, and the general public in order to solve a particular marketing problem. Research also entails the use of a set of scientific procedures to conduct experiments and surveys.

A **records search** is directed at scrutinizing internal, secondary sources of data for useful information on past, current, and planned performances and activities of the organization. Understanding existing internal operations is often a prerequisite for planning future organizational programs and activities. **Analytical models** are various statistical and quantitative methods used internally by marketing researchers to generate new information applicable to a particular problem or decision. These analytical techniques are used to explore new relationships and test new ideas by generating primary information from secondary information using a complex set of quantitative procedures.

Stage 3: Processing Information

The third stage of the marketing information system is the processing of information gathered in the second stage. As suggested by Figure 5-1, information processing consists of the four activities of inputting, analyzing, storing, and retrieving data. The goal of the processing stage is to produce marketing information that is as follows:

- ❏ *Reliable*—Does the information accurately reflect what it is intended to portray? Important decisions will be made based on what is reported.
- ❏ *Usable*—Can the information be used to make practical decisions and solve actual problems? Data that are not useful are irrelevant.
- ❏ *Understandable*—Can the significant findings be grasped, interpreted, and used in the decision-making process?
- ❏ *Meaningful*—Is the information relevant to the decision or problem under consideration? Useful information addresses the issues under consideration.
- ❏ *Current*—Does the information reflect what is presently happening? New information is often the lifeblood of successful marketing efforts.

Manual processing systems with their reliance on human labor and mechanical devices are a thing of the past for most organizations. Today, the data management system of choice is electronic data processing—analysis by computer-based systems that manipulate data and develop information. With computer configurations of all types and sizes readily available, electronic data processing systems can be developed for any type or size organization. Advancing computer hardware (such as compact disks, optical disks, and electronic imaging) and software technologies (such as standardized programs and databases) have greatly facilitated the capability of electronic data processing systems to input, analyze, store, and retrieve data. Perhaps the most significant advances in the processing of information in recent times have been the development and implementation of bar codes and the use of optical scanners for inputting data into the marketing information system quickly and inexpensively. Electronic scanning also increases the accuracy of the data being stored.

STAGE 4: UTILIZING INFORMATION

Information differs from raw data in that information is *useful* to the marketing manager. In order for information to be useful it must be

1. Presented in an appropriate format
2. Disseminated to the appropriate user
3. Utilized in an appropriate fashion

Information presentation is concerned with how information is reported to its users. The reporting format for the output generated by the information processing stage of the MIS can take several different forms. The primary output from the processing stage is a series of marketing research and marketing intelligence **reports** and a collection of current and accessible **databases** that marketing managers use in making decisions and solving problems. These marketing data banks are typically large and complex computer storage and retrieval systems, which provide the user with quick and easy access to electronic files. The MIS's processing stage can also yield information used to construct conceptual (why consumers prefer a certain brand) and applied (how to select a successful store location) **models**. Furthermore, processed information can be reported in the form of strategic and tactical **plans** that frame the decisions and actions of marketing managers.

Information dissemination deals with the issues of who gets what information and in what form. It is costly to locate, gather, and process information. To justify such costs, organizations strive to gain maximum internal exposure and usage by all appropriate decision makers within the firm. Because processed information is often viewed as proprietary, organizations usually restrict its external distribution to a few trusted business partners. While information has traditionally been disseminated in hard-copy form, on-line electronic access to information is fast becoming the preferred method for distributing information in a quicker and cheaper fashion. In sum, a highly effective and efficient marketing information system is a major competitive advantage that can be exploited.

Information utilization takes the form of making marketing decisions and initiating actions that implement those decisions. It is up to the decision maker to determine how the information is to be used relative to a particular problem or situation. Translating facts, opinions, relationships, associations, common tendencies, unusual occurrences, and other findings into actionable marketing decisions is the central purpose of the marketing information system. If marketing managers ignore these findings, then the gathered information has no meaning or value. Information-based decisions have proven to be better decisions, both in the short and long run, than decisions based on hunches and hearsay.

Marketing Intelligence

Marketing intelligence is that part of the marketing information system designed to monitor and collect information on existing and emerging developments and events within the organization's operating and marketing environments. It is a form of surveillance in which external scans are conducted to identify and evaluate environmental threats and opportunities. These uncontrollable and dynamic surroundings can have a huge impact on the firm's strategic plans and tactical operations. Current knowledge of what's happening in the marketing environment can prove to be essential to the avoidance of marketing mistakes and to take advantage of marketing opportunities. Using external secondary sources, the firm's marketing intelligence officer gathers information on population and demographic trends, competitive and economic shifts, social and cultural changes, political and legal developments, physical and natural fluctuations, and technological and informational advancements. Also, the gathering of marketing intelligence can address issues relating to the industry in which the organization operates and to member institutions that make up that industry. Marketing intelligence can be gathered from a variety of sources including public libraries, government agencies, trade associations, and commercial outsources.[1]

Library Sources

The library serves a dual information-gathering role. First, it is a source of intelligence on many different issues relating to business and marketing. Second, the library is a place where the researcher can identify and locate other sources of marketing intelligence. To access the tremendous amount of information on the library's reference shelves, the research librarian's information retrieval skills must include traditional card catalogs and index systems, although these systems are being replaced with new computer search technologies. In addition to the library's listings catalog, such source guides as *Business Periodicals Index* and *Marketing Information Guide* can be used to locate specific books and articles. The value of a good library is that it represents a centralized location for many sources of marketing intelligence. It also represents an economical source of general marketing intelligence.

Government Sources

Federal, state, and local government agencies are the most prolific compilers of marketing intelligence. At the federal level, various agencies and

FIGURE 5-3

SELECTED U.S. GOVERNMENT SOURCES OF MARKETING INTELLIGENCE

- Census of Population
- Census of Housing
- Census of Governments
- Census of Agriculture
- Census of Construction
- Census of Business
- Census of Manufacturing
- Census of Mineral Industries

- Census of Transportation
- County and City Data Book
- American Statistics Index
- Business Statistics
- Federal Reserve Bulletin
- Monthly Labor Review
- Monthly Vital Statistics Report
- Survey of Current Business

bureaus publish a wide variety of descriptive studies and statistical reports. Figure 5-3 identifies some of the more pertinent sources of environmental intelligence gathered and published by the federal government. Additional sources of information produced and distributed by federal agencies can be discovered by consulting the *Monthly Catalog of U.S. Government Publications*. The *Statistical Abstracts of the United States* is an inexpensive annual that provides information and serves as a guide to other, more complete sources of information.

Many government agencies require individuals and organizations to register or report their activities. Births, deaths, marriages, school enrollments, income tax statements, vehicle registrations, business licenses, building permits, crime statistics, and public utility payments are but a few of the databases created by state and local governments that could prove useful in judging the marketing climate of a geographic area.

ASSOCIATION SOURCES

Professional, business, and trade associations can be excellent sources of environmental intelligence. These associations often publish newsletters, journals, magazines, and special reports on issues related to the interests of the association's membership. In addition to their publications, associations also sponsor research, conduct training sessions, offer professional development courses, hold trade shows, and sponsor conventions. Association sources provide highly accessible industry and trade data for affordable fees. A selective sample of associations that a marketing manager might consult include the American Advertising Association, the American Management Association, the American Marketing Association, the U.S. Chamber of Commerce, the Conference Board, the International Franchise Association, the National Retail Federation, and Sales & Marketing Executives. The *Encyclopedia of Associations* is an index of associations that identifies additional association sources for specific industries and provides information on how to contact them. Figure 5-4 provides a list of selected association publications for marketing intelligence.

COMMERCIAL SOURCES

The high demand for marketing intelligence has spawned a vast array of organizations that collect and distribute information on environmental developments as a commercial venture. These organizations locate, gather, and process information and then sell it to their clients. A list of

FIGURE 5-4

SELECTED ASSOCIATION SOURCES OF MARKETING INTELLIGENCE

- American Demographic
- Chain Store Age Executive
- Direct Marketing
- Industrial Marketing Management
- Journal of Academy of Marketing Science
- Journal of Advertising
- Journal of Advertising Research
- Journal of Business Research
- Journal of Consumer Research

- Journal of Health Care Marketing
- Journal of Marketing
- Journal of Marketing Research
- Journal of Personal Selling and Sales Management
- Journal of Retailing
- Journal of Services Marketing
- Progressive Grocer
- Sales & Marketing Management
- Stores

such organizations can be found in *Bradford's Directory*. These commercial sources differ greatly in terms of the variety of services offered and the types of industries served. They range from standardized to specifically tailored marketing-intelligence services.

Syndicated marketing-intelligence services compile specific types of information on a regular basis and make it available to clients for an established fee. Services offered by selected syndicated marketing-intelligence services are shown in Figure 5-5. In addition to syndicated services, standardized information services include **on-line database vendors.** These serve as intermediaries between their clients and database creators by arranging on-line (electronic) delivery of information. The availability of on-line databases has increased dramatically in recent years from a few hundred to several thousand. The *Directory of On-line Databases* provides a description of available databases. Figure 5-6 identifies and describes the services offered by four of the most popular on-line database vendors.

Tailored services are **custom marketing-intelligence services** that provide information located, gathered, and processed according to specific client needs. The type of intelligence collected, the means by which the data are analyzed, and the format by which the information is reported are all carried out to the client's specifications. These customized services are typically offered on a project-by-project basis and are directed at solving particular marketing problems.

Additional sources of marketing intelligence include asking customers, vendors, competitors, and resellers what they think is happening or going to happen within the various marketing environments. Different perspectives and opinions often prove to be enlightening when the discussion is about the complex dimensions of the many different environments that impact the organization's marketing efforts.

MARKETING RESEARCH

Marketing research is the process by which marketers gather primary information concerning the external world of customers, competitors, suppliers, and the public. The American Marketing Association has developed the following widely accepted definition of marketing research:

> Marketing research is the function which links the consumer, customer, and public to the marketer through information—information used to identify and define marketing opportunities and problems; generate, refine, and evaluate marketing actions; monitor marketing performance; and improve understanding of marketing as a process.
>
> Marketing research specifies the information required to address these issues; designs the method for collecting the information; manages and implements the data collection process; analyzes the results; and communicates the findings and their implications.[2]

FIGURE 5-5

SELECTED EXAMPLES OF SYNDICATED MARKETING INTELLIGENCE SERVICES

1. *A.C. Nielsen Co., Northbrook, Ill.*
This, the world's largest marketing/advertising research company, specializes in monitoring television program viewing. Its "audimeter" device is attached to 1,700 household television sets through the nation. The company also provides syndicated and custom audits of retail product sales.

2. *IMS International, New York*
IMS's research activities consist mainly of syndicated audits in the pharmaceutical, medical, and health care industries throughout the world. The company tracks the movement of products through panels of doctors, drugstores, hospitals, medical laboratories, nursing homes, and the like.

3. *Selling Areas Marketing Inc., New York*
The major activity of SAMI is to monitor product movement through warehouses. In this way it is able to provide information on the wholesale movement of thousands of packaged goods sold through food stores.

4. *Arbitron Ratings Co., New York*
The focus of this company is measurement of radio and television audiences in local markets. The company also offers a computerized program that provides audience data merged with information on viewer life styles.

5. *Burke Marketing Services, Cincinnati*
This multidivisional company offers pre- and post-television copy testing and custom survey research, educational seminars, special market modeling, television campaign testing in controlled laboratory settings, and physiological measurement of reactions to advertising.

6. *NFO Research, Toledo*
The main business of NFO is a fixed mail panel of 240,000 households to track purchases of beverages, home furnishings, women's tailored apparel, and home computers and video games.

7. *Information Resources Inc., Chicago*
The main business of IRI is its BehaviorScan system, which collects product sales data via in-store optical scanner equipment; monitors buying behavior through a panel of households that use an identification card tied to the optical scanner; controls television advertising to selected homes via cable to test the relationship of advertising to purchase behavior; and measures in-store promotions.

8. *Yankelovich, Skelly & White, New York*
This marketing and social research company offers two widely used services—Monitor, a survey of opinions and trends in special segments of society, and Laboratory Test Market, a market simulation that evaluates new products in the planning stage.

9. *Simmons Market Research Bureau, New York*
Simmons conducts an annual survey of 19,000 adults regarding their media usage, purchase behavior, and demographic characteristics. These data are combined with the Dun & Bradstreet data bank to produce measures of advertising effectiveness by geographic area.

10. *The Gallup Organization, Princeton, N.J.*
Gallup specializes in quantitative attitude and public-opinion research and provides syndicated surveys in the areas of packaged goods, video, and financial services.

SOURCE: Reprinted by permission from Charles D. Schewe, *Marketing: Principles and Strategies* (New York: Random House, 1987), 107.

FIGURE 5-6

SELECTING MARKETING INTELLIGENCE OFFERINGS OF THE MOST POPULAR ON-LINE VENDORS

DOW JONES
- *Disclosure II*
- *Dow Jones News*
- *Current Notes*
- *Wall Street Journal*
- *Academic American Encyclopedia*
- *Cineman Movie Reviews*
- *AP News*
- *Comp *U* Store*

DIALOG
- *Disclosure II* (business database)
- *Management Contents*
- *Standard and Poor's Corporate Description*
- *Books in Print*
- *Electronic Yellow Pages*
- *Magazine Index*
- *AP News*

COMPUSERVE
- *Standard and Poor's General Information File*
- *Washington Post*
- *World Book Encyclopedia*
- *MicroQuote* (stock information)
- *Business Information Wire*
- *AP News*
- *Comp *U* Store*

THE SOURCE
- *Management Contents*
- *Commodity News Service*
- *Cineman Movie Reviews*
- *U. S. News Washington Letter Travel Services*
- *Travel Services*
- *Employment Services*
- *AP News*
- *Comp *U* Store*

SOURCE: Reprinted by permission from Charles W. Lamb, Jr., Joseph F. Heiser, Jr., and Carl McDaniel, *Principles of Marketing* (Cincinnati, OH: Southwestern Publishing Co., 1992), 185.

The goals of marketing research are to reduce the uncertainty involved in making marketing decisions and to lessen the risks associated with taking marketing actions. These goals are achieved by identifying and evaluating the firm's marketing opportunities and threats.

Marketing research is one of the four methods employed by the marketing information system to gather data (see Figure 5-7). As suggested by the definition of market research, it is the method directed at collecting primary data from external sources. Marketing research is carried out in a scientific fashion as a multistep process that includes

FIGURE 5-7

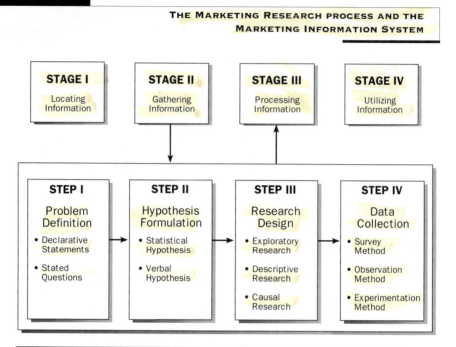

THE MARKETING RESEARCH PROCESS AND THE MARKETING INFORMATION SYSTEM

Step 1: Problem Definition

Step 2: Hypothesis Formulation

Step 3: Research Design

Step 4: Data Collection

STEP 1: PROBLEM DEFINITION

Problem definition is the process of clearly identifying and describing the problem that is to be the focus of the marketing research effort. A sharp research focus directs the marketing researcher to gather only information that is applicable to finding a solution to a well-specified problem. Research that is well focused is faster, cheaper, and usually more accurate. A well-defined problem provides the road map to guide the researcher through the remaining steps of the marketing research process.

Problem definition is typically accomplished through the use of one of two methods. The **declarative sentence** expresses the problem as a statement. For example, the problem is to determine the relationship between advertising expenditures and additional sales revenue. The **stated question** defines the problem in the form of a question, such as What value perception is being created by our pricing policies? The importance of this first step is best expressed by the old adage "A problem well defined is a problem half solved." In addition to basic knowledge and skills, defining problems requires that the researcher have a creative perception and insight into the issues being studied and the ability to look beyond problem symptoms to find underlying causes.

Step 2: Hypothesis Formulation

The **research hypothesis** is a tentative explanation of how the identified problem might be solved. It is the researcher's untested feelings and assumptions concerning the likely answer to the research question. In formulating a hypothesis, the researcher often takes a set of known facts or expressed opinions and proposes a relationship one step beyond existing knowledge. The hypothesis can be stated in either **statistical** or **verbal** form. With the creation of a hypothesis, the researcher then attempts to prove or disprove the basic premise of the hypothesis. Depending on the nature of the problem, the researcher might formulate several hypotheses to test.

Step 3: Research Design

The research design will be dictated by the study's research hypothesis. Marketing researchers have a choice of three types of research designs—exploratory, descriptive, and causal. **Exploratory research** studies are designed to collect additional information about the defined problem or the formulated hypothesis. The perceived problem, being limited in scope, is explored in more depth by the researcher. The goal of this type of study is to achieve greater clarification of the issues surrounding the identified problem prior to proceeding with a full-scale research effort. Exploratory research ranges from simply reviewing existing information in the organization's data bank to asking experts their opinions on the specific problem being explored. Examining customer feelings and behaviors through focus group studies or general customer surveys are additional methods used in conducting exploratory research.

Descriptive research consists of studies directed at gaining more extensive knowledge of the specific characteristics of a particular phenomenon associated with the stated research problem. The purpose of descriptive research is to describe what is happening within a particular consumer group (why customers choose national brands instead of private-label brands), market segment (the number of individuals within each income category), or marketing activity (the response rate to a sales promotion event). Descriptive studies are most often presented using descriptive statistics supported by quantitative analysis.

Causal research examines cause-and-effect relationships among the various phenomena being studied. This method starts with the general hypothesis that a particular *independent variable (X)* causes a *dependent variable (Y)*. For example, the research might examine the causal relationship between increased advertising expenditures (X) and the increased number of customer store visits (Y). This is a complex method of research that requires careful control of other independent variables in order to accurately assess the cause-and-effect relationship being studied. Because many independent variables are beyond the control of the researcher, causal research results must be viewed with a reasonable amount of caution. Experimental methodologies are the vehicle by which most causal studies are conducted.

STEP 4: DATA COLLECTION

The fourth step in the marketing research process is the collection of data that will allow the researcher to accept or reject the research hypothesis. As we identified in Figure 5-7, the researcher has three choices of data collection: the survey, observation, or experimentation methods. Each method has advantages and disadvantages. The method selected depends on the type and accuracy of information needed and the amount of time, money, and effort the researcher can justify in pursuing a particular research project.

THE SURVEY METHOD Survey research is a contact method of gathering primary information directly from the appropriate respondent. The contact is made using a questionnaire, which is administered in person, over the telephone, or by mail. Surveys are most commonly used when the researcher wants to discover how customers feel or what customers believe about a product, an advertisement, a retail outlet, a pricing practice, or some other element of the marketing mix. Surveying is the most widely used method of collecting primary data. Each of the survey research approaches must follow correct research practices and sampling procedures.

Personal Interviews Researchers select the personal interview approach to gathering primary data when they want to explore certain issues in great depth. The **personal interview** approach constitutes a face-to-face, question-and-answer session between the interviewer and one or more individuals. Because of the personal nature of this interviewing approach, researchers have greater flexibility in exploring complex issues and examining emotional concerns. In a face-to-face encounter, interviewers can observe the respondent's reaction to questions, thereby gaining some sense of their attitudes and opinions. They can also record information based on their observation of race, sex, apparent age, and other visible characteristics. Personal interviewers can also adjust the questioning process depending on the type of responses being received. Recently, computer-assisted interviews have been used in administering questionnaires. By having the respondent read questions on a screen and record answers by keying them into the computer, the possibility of interviewer bias is substantially reduced. Personal interviews can be conducted in one of the following ways:

- ❏ *Mall intercept interviews*—the practice of intercepting customers within a shopping mall and securing their participation in the survey

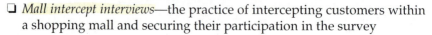

- *Home or office interviews*—the practice of securing permission to interview the individual at the home or office
- *Focus group interviews*—the practice of conducting an in-depth interview with a small group of individuals who freely discuss issues related to the problem being studied

Telephone Interviews As the fastest method of collecting primary information, **telephone interviews** involve calling potential respondents and asking them a series of predetermined questions. The immediacy of response and a fairly good response rate make this type of survey highly suited to a political candidate who needs timely feedback on where he or she stands in the polls or a business executive who is seeking immediate answers concerning the impact of a new advertising campaign or a competitive price adjustment. Due to respondent impatience and the interruptive nature of many telephone interviews, only a limited amount of information can be obtained.

Mail Surveys A **mail survey** is a written questionnaire that potential respondents receive and return by mail. Variations of the mail survey include attaching questionnaires to a product package, passing out written surveys on the street or in a shopping mall, and placing questionnaires in a newspaper or magazine. In each of the cases, respondents fill out the survey and return it by mail. Because no interviewer is present, the frankness and honesty of responses is increased due to respondent anonymity. Additionally, mail surveys offer the ability to cover a geographically dispersed population. These are good reasons for using mail surveys. The difficulty in compiling an appropriate mailing list, the uncertainty as to who actually filled out the questionnaire, and the problems associated with low response rates are limitations that have to be accepted and accounted for when using mail surveys.

In selecting one survey method over another, the researcher compares and contrasts the various survey methods with respect to their relative advantages and disadvantages. Figure 5-8 provides a comparison of those methods and a convenient means of determining which one to use. Conducting effective surveys also requires that the researcher carefully construct the questionnaire and plan the sampling procedures to be used in administering the questionnaire.

Survey Research Practices A good questionnaire is one key to gathering reliable information using the survey research method. A **questionnaire** consists of a series of carefully structured, worded, and sequenced questions in order to solicit complete and unbiased answers concerning topics that are germane to the research problem. Questionnaires are the most common research instrument for gathering primary information. In deciding which questions to ask, the survey researcher is guided by the problem definition and the stated hypothesis. Successful questionnaires ask only those questions that are essential and easy to understand and answer.

FIGURE 5-8

COMPARISON OF MAIL, TELEPHONE, AND PERSONAL INTERVIEW SURVEYS

Criteria	Mail Survey	Telephone Survey	Personal Interview Survey
Cost (assuming a good response rate)	Often lowest	Usually in-between	Usually highest
Ability to probe	No personal contact or observation	Some chances for gathering additional data through elaboration on questions, but no personal observation	Greatest opportunity for observation, building rapport, and additional probing
Respondent ability to complete at own convenience	Yes	No	Perhaps, if interview time is prearranged with respondent
Interviewer bias	No chance	Some, perhaps because of voice inflection, etc.	Greatest chance
Ability to decide who actually responds to the questionnaire within a household	Least	Some	Greatest
Sampling problems	Up-to-date, accurate mailing list and low response rates	Up-to-date, accurate phone subscriber list, unlisted numbers, no phones, refusals	Not-at-homes and refusals
Impersonality	Greatest	Some because of lack of face-to-face contact	Least
Complex questions	Least suitable	Somewhat suitable	Most suitable
Visual aids in survey	Little opportunity	No opportunity	Greatest opportunity
Opportunity for building rapport	Least	Some	Greatest
Potential negative respondent reaction	"Junk mail"	"Junk calls"	Invasion of privacy
Interviewer control over interview environment	Least	Some in selection of time to call	Greatest
Time lag between soliciting and receiving response	Greatest	Least	May be considerable if a large area is involved
Suitable types of questions	Simple, mostly dichotomous (yes-no) and multiple-choice questions	Some opportunity for open ended questions, especially if interview is recorded	Greatest opportunity for open-ended questions
Requirement for technical skills in conducting interview	Least	Medium	Greatest

SOURCE: Reprinted by permission from William F. Schoell and Joseph P. Guiltinan, *Marketing: Contemporary Concepts and Practices* (Boston: Allyn and Bacon, 1990), 132.

Questions can be structured as either open-ended or closed-ended. **Open-ended questions** are unstructured questions that allow respondents to answer in their own words. By permitting interviewees greater freedom of expression in communicating their answers, the researcher hopes to solicit answers that truly reflect individual feelings, beliefs, and attitudes.[3] The unstructured nature of open-ended questions is especially useful in conducting exploratory research. The major limitation of open-ended questions is that they are difficult to tabulate and interpret. A number of open-ended projective techniques have been devised by marketing researchers, including the following:

- *Completely open questions*—a string of questions is presented to respondents, who are totally free to answer any way they wish

- *Word association tests*—a set of words or phrases is presented to respondents, who in turn are asked to react immediately by relating what they associate with each word or phrase

- *Sentence completion tests*—a series of incomplete sentences is presented to respondents, who are then asked to complete each sentence in their own words

- *Story completion tests*—an incomplete narrative or story is presented to respondents, who are then asked to write a paragraph that would complete the story

- *Thematic apperception tests*—a cartoon, drawing, painting, or photo is shown to respondents, who are then asked to tell a story about or give an explanation of what is happening in the picture

The **closed-ended question** is a highly structured question format in which the respondent is given a set of answers from which to choose. Although closed-ended questions are easy to tabulate, analyze, and interpret, their restrictive nature has a tendency to limit the scope of possible answers and force respondents to choose an answer that may not truly or fully reflect their beliefs or opinions. In an attempt to gain the most accurate information, marketing researchers have developed a number of different forms for asking highly structured questions; some of the more common forms are

- *Dichotomous questions*—a set of questions that limits the respondent's answer to one of two choices: yes or no; true or false

- *Multiple-choice questions*—a series of questions in which respondents are provided several possible answers from which they must select an answer

- *Rank-ordered questions*—a list of factors are presented to respondents, who are then asked to rank each factor as to its importance relative to the other factors listed

❑ *Likert scale*—a list of statements is presented to respondents, who are then asked to indicate the extent of their agreement or disagreement by marking a five-point scale that ranges from "strongly agree" to "strongly disagree"

❑ *Semantic differential scale*—a set of seven-point, bipolar scales. At each end are descriptive terms (such as expensive and cheap) that are capable of measuring beliefs and attitudes that individuals have regarding a person, place, or thing. These scales are presented to respondents, who are asked to select the position on the scale that best describes their beliefs and attitudes toward the object.

The wording of questions is crucial to their success as information gathering tools. Poorly worded, ambiguous, or leading questions produce answers that are inaccurate, unreliable, and meaningless. To ensure accurate, reliable, and meaningful answers, the researcher should

1. Use simple and plain language and avoid technical and "buzz" words

2. Employ unbiased and uncolorful wording

3. Focus each question on a single idea by asking short and concise questions

4. Encourage accurate responses by asking for information that respondents can be expected to know and remember

5. Ask for only essential personal information in a general and non-threatening way

The sequence or ordering of questions within the questionnaire can impact the type, amount, and accuracy of the information provided. For best results, the researchers should

1. Develop a logical and consistent ordering of the questions

2. Use opening questions that are capable of gaining and holding respondents' attention

3. Place general questions at the beginning of the questionnaire and more specific questions toward the end

4. Locate all questions seeking personal information at the end of the questionnaire

Survey Sampling Procedures   The second key to gathering reliable and accurate information using the survey method is using an appropriate sampling procedure. Having determined what information is needed and how to gather it, the researcher then must decide from whom the information should be obtained. Identifying that portion of the population to be studied is the object of the researcher's sampling procedure. A **population**

is all people the researcher wishes to study; it represents the total group of people from which the researcher needs to gather information. Since this can be a very large group, the researcher needs to use a sample. A **sample** is a representative portion of the population to be studied. Samples are used because it is too costly to survey an entire population. By using proper sampling procedures, the researcher can obtain reliable and accurate information about the total population.[4] To ensure proper sampling procedures, researchers need to consider the following:

❏ *Sample frame*—a carefully identified list of the entire population from which a sample will be drawn

❏ *Sample size*—the number of individuals who will be part of the survey; larger samples result in greater accuracy and more reliable information but entail higher costs

❏ *Sample item*—the decision on which method (probability or nonprobability) will be used to determine who will be part of the survey. **Probability samples** give each individual in the population a known chance of being selected. **Nonprobability samples** result in a controlled selection of individuals from the population where chances of an individual being selected are neither known nor equal. Figure 5-9 describes the various types of probability and nonprobability samples.

THE OBSERVATION METHOD There can be a considerable difference between what people say they do and how they actually behave. That is why, for some research issues, researchers prefer to *see* what individuals do as opposed to *asking* them what they do. The **observation method** involves observing and recording the overt behavior of consumers. What consumers do and not what they say is the focus of this method of gathering primary data. The elimination of interviewer bias and the need to secure the cooperation of the individual are two key benefits in using this data collection method. On the other hand, this rather costly information-gathering method does not allow the researcher to explore the attitudes and beliefs of the individual being observed. The observation method is limited to examining *what* behavior occurred and not *why* particular actions were taken. The various considerations in designing and using the observation method are presented in Figure 5-10.

THE EXPERIMENTATION METHOD The **experimentation method** is a highly structured method of data collection in which the researcher attempts to measure the results that a change in one variable might create while holding all other variables constant. For example, what would be the impact on sales volume if a retailer lowered prices on a particular product item while keeping in-store displays, promotional activities, personal selling, and other relevant marketing activities constant? An experiment is used to determine cause-and-effect relationships among various marketing factors.

FIGURE 5-9

TYPES OF PROBABILITY AND NONPROBABILITY SAMPLES

Probability Samples

1. *Simple random:* A sampling procedure in which one sample is drawn from the entire population, with each individual or item having an equal probability of being selected.

2. *Stratified random:* A sampling procedure in which the population is first subdivided into groups based on some known and meaningful criteria (such as sex or age). Then a simple random sample is drawn for each subgroup.

3. *Cluster or area:* A sampling procedure in which geographical areas (such as census tracks or blocks) are randomly selected. Then a simple random sample is used to select a certain number of individuals or items (such as houses) from each of the selected geographical areas.

4. *Systematic:* A sampling procedure in which the first individual or item of a sampling frame is selected randomly. Then each subsequent individual or item is selected at every Nth interval (such as every fifth item on the list).

Nonprobability Samples

1. *Convenience:* A sampling procedure in which each sample individual or item is selected at the convenience of the researcher (such as whoever walks in the store).

2. *Judgment:* A sampling procedure in which each sample individual or item is selected by the researcher based on an idea of what constitutes a representative sample (such as every seventh person who walks past the display counter).

3. *Quota:* A sampling procedure in which the researcher divides the total population into several segments based on some factor believed to be important (such as sex and age). Then the researcher arbitrarily selects a certain number (quota) from each segment (for example, selects five females over age 40, five females under age 40, five males over age 40, and five males under age 40).

SOURCE: Reprinted by permission from Dale M. Lewison, *Retailing*, 5th Edition (New York: Macmillan Publishing Company, 1994), 680.

Experiments can be conducted in the laboratory or in the field. **Laboratory experiments** are research studies conducted within an environment in which all of the factors can be controlled and manipulated. The use of a simulated living room in which television viewing behavior is studied under controlled conditions is one example of a laboratory experiment. **Field experiments** are conducted in the marketplace where marketing activities actually occur (in the store, on the street, or at an event). Using these more realistic conditions is a good way to learn how consumers react to changes in the marketing effort. An example of a field experiment is the test-marketing of a new product within a retail store under reasonably controlled conditions.

FIGURE 5-10

USING THE OBSERVATION METHOD

Decision	Description	Example
Observation Methods		
1. Direct	Observing current behavior	Watching the number of consumers who stop to inspect a store display
2. Indirect	Observing past behavior	Counting the number of store branded products (Sears') found in the consumer's home
Recording Methods		
1. Personal	Recording observations by hand	Logging customer reactions to a sales presentation by visually observing and manually recording the process
2. Nonpersonal	Recording observations mechanically or electronically (counters, cameras, sensors)	Measuring television viewing habits using an "audiometer," measuring pupil dilation while viewing an advertisement as an indication of interest using a "perceptoscope," and using an "eye camera" to measure eye movement of a consumer as he or she views a display
Observation Setting		
1. Natural	Observing behavior in an unplanned and real setting	Observing the customer's natural and unobstructive trip behavior through the store
2. Artificial	Observing behavior in a planned and contrived setting	Observing sales personnel reaction to various customer "plants" who dress in a different fashion (well-dressed or shabbily dressed)
Observation Situation		
1. Disguised	Observing without the person being aware that he or she is being observed	Using a two-way mirror to observe how customers inspect a display
2. Nondisguised	Observing behavior in an open fashion, thereby allowing the person to be aware that he or she is being observed	Following the customer around the store to observe his or her shopping patterns

SOURCE: Reprinted by permission from Dale M. Lewison, *Retailing*, 5th Edition (New York: Macmillan Publishing Company, 1994), 675.

RECORDS SEARCH

A records search includes all sources of internal secondary information. Every organization routinely compiles and distributes internal reports based on financial, operating, and marketing records. Much of the information in these files can be organized and presented by customer groups, geographical areas, product categories, time periods, or a number of other useful formats for analytical purposes. Having knowledge of the who, what, where, when, and why of current organization operations is often a prerequisite to gathering information from external sources. "Customer database analysis can be a useful starting point when marketing questions arise. . . . the database can help define the problem and possibly alter the scope of required survey research."[5] Internal secondary information tends to be simple to locate, cheap to gather, quick to process, and easy to use. One common problem in securing and utilizing this form of information is the "turf issues" that can arise among various divisions of an organization. Some selected regular and special reports found through an internal records search are presented in Figure 5-11.

ANALYTICAL MODELS

A number of different statistical and quantitative methods are used to internally generate primary information. Essentially, analytical models generate primary information from other secondary and primary sources of data using various quantitative procedures. Analytical models are used to describe situations, to explain occurrences, to predict happenings, and to make decisions. Some of the more commonly used analytical models include the following.

❑ *Summarization procedures*—the use of percentages, measures of central tendencies, and trend analysis to simplify and organize information into new and meaningful measurements

❑ *Statistical inferences*—the use of hypothesis testing and analysis of associative data to make interpretations from a sample about the entire population that is the focus of study

❑ *Mathematical programming*—the use of linear and nonlinear programming and critical-path scheduling to find optimal solutions to problems

❑ *Simulation models*—the use of mathematical modeling to develop new models that imitate marketing situations wherein various factors can be manipulated in an attempt to identify problems, understand processes, or discover solutions

FIGURE 5-11

INTERNAL RECORDS

Report (frequency)	Information Provided (and Originating Department)
Regular Reports	
1. Sales call (after each call is made)	Customer location, date, whether sale was made, end use, news of company, competitors, industry development, and similar news (Marketing)
2. Sales invoice (when each sale is made)	Customer, location, date, item(s) sold, price, discount(s), industry, sales representative (Accounting)
3. Sales (weekly or biweekly)	Amount sold by item, time period, and sales territory (Accounting)
4. Sales forecast (depends on company—weekly, monthly, quarterly, or annually)	Item, amount forecast to be sold by time period and (in some cases) by geographic region (Marketing)
5. Inventories (daily, weekly, or monthly)	Amount of each item (by model number and size) by warehouse (Marketing, Production, or Traffic and Logistics, depending on how the company is organized)
6. Production schedules (weekly or biweekly)	Amount of each item to be produced by time period, and by plant if appropriate (Production)
7. Production costs (monthly)	Costs of production by item for a specified lot or time period (Accounting)
8. Research and development reports (monthly)	Schedule, progress, and (perhaps) expenditures by project (R&D or Engineering)
9. Marketing budget (monthly, quarterly, semiannually, or annually)	Amount budgeted by line item (advertising, sales, marketing research, and distribution, plus special line items such as market tests, new product introductions) by time period (Marketing)
10. Marketing expenditures versus budget (monthly)	Amount expended by line item for each time period versus amount budgeted (Accounting)
11. Income statement (monthly or quarterly)	Sales, expenses, and profit or loss by product line, or strategic business unit or market, depending on how the company is organized (Accounting)
12. Accounts receivable (monthly)	Accounts receivable by age of the account and by customer (Accounting)
13. Quality control	Quality levels of each product by time period (Quality Control or Engineering)
14. Field service	Number of items serviced by model, location, and time period (Field Service or Engineering)
Special Reports	
15. Long-range operating plan	Description of strategic directories and schedule of major events for implementing it/them (Chief Planning Office)
16. Annual operating plan	Description and schedule of major events in the planned operations of the various departments of the company (Chief Planning Office)

continued

FIGURE 5–11

CONTINUED

Report (frequency)	Information Provided (and Originating Department)
17. Marketing research	Depending on the study, may provide information on a market, a marketing program, or a development that may affect one or both of those (Marketing)
18. Legal	Reports on patent and trademark application, an assessment of the legality of competitor practices, legal risks associated with current or proposed company practices, and the like (Legal)
19. Production	Reports on potential new production processes, experience curve effects on costs, and the like (Production)
20. Research and development	Assessment of competitor products, the state of the art, and the like (Research and Development)
21. Consultants	Various

SOURCE: Reprinted by permission from Donald S. Tull and Lynn R. Kahle, *Marketing Management* (New York: Macmillan Publishing Co., 1990), 234.

CONCLUDING REMARKS

Information is the lifeblood of most business organizations and the basis of their marketing activities. The need for timely and accurate information must by addressed by the organization's entire management team. Effective problem solving depends on having a sufficient amount of reliable and useful information. Marketing managers develop and maintain marketing information systems to ensure that they have the necessary information for making correct decisions. The marketing information system is an interacting organization of people, machines, and processes devised to create a regular and continuous flow of essential information. The process of developing useful marketing information consists of four stages, which are designed to locate, gather, process, and utilize information. Marketing intelligence, marketing research, records search, and analytical models constitute the four primary methods used to gather the information so vital to the organization's success.

ENDNOTES

1. See Ruth Winett, "Guerrilla Marketing Research Outsmarts the Competition," *Marketing News* (January 2, 1995), 33.

2. *Marketing News*, "New Marketing Research Definition Approved," (January 2, 1987), 1, 14.

3. See Sidney J. Levy, "Interpreting Consumer Mythology," *Marketing Management,* Vol. 2, No. 4 (1994), 4–9.

4. See Ruth N. Bolton, "Covering the Market," *Marketing Research,* Vol. 6, No. 3 (1994), 30–35.

5. See Phyllis Ezop, "Database Marketing Research," *Marketing Research,* Vol. 6, No. 4 (1994), 35–41.

Marketing Situations

Chapter 6 **Environmental Analysis**

Chapter 7 **Consumer Analysis**

Chapter 8 **Competitor Analysis**

Chapter 9 **Market Analysis**

ENVIRONMENTAL ANALYSIS

Chapter Outline

- **Introduction**
- **Population and Demographic Trends**
  - Population Growth
  - Demographic Trends
- **Economic and Competitive Forces**
  - Economic Systems
  - Economic Conditions
  - Economic Issues
  - Competitive Market Structures
- **Social and Cultural Influences**
  - The Social Agenda
  - The Cultural Agenda
- **Political and Legal Issues**
  - The Political System
  - The Legal System
- **Scientific and Technological Advances**
- **Concluding Remarks**

INTRODUCTION

The **environment** is a set of external forces that directly or indirectly impact every organization. These environmental forces define the uncontrollable realm within which the firm must attempt to operate successfully. **Marketing environments** include those external forces that directly influence the decisions and actions of the marketing manager. These environmental forces affect how individual marketers define and satisfy the needs of selected target markets. As shown in Figure 6-1, effective marketing requires that the organization be able to successfully execute its marketing programs within various environmental settings.

Conceptually, the forces that comprise the marketing environment are viewed as existing at two levels. They are categorized as micro and macro influences (see Figure 6-1). The **microenvironment** consists of those forces

FIGURE 6-1

THE MARKETING ENVIRONMENT

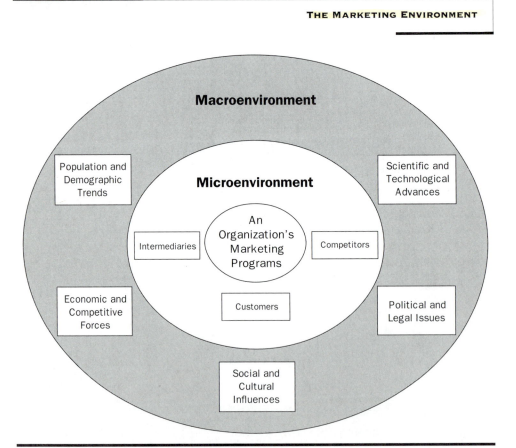

that directly affect the marketing programs of a particular firm. The activities of marketing intermediaries, customers, and competitors are all examples of external forces that influence the marketing actions of a specific organization. These activities are beyond the scope of our current discussion but are the subject of Chapters 7, 8, and 9. The **macroenvironment** encompasses the broad environmental system within which all organizations must conduct business. In one sense, it defines or creates the structure of the marketplace for all organizations. The particular elements that make up the macroenvironment are population and demographic trends; economic and competitive forces; social and cultural influences; political and legal issues; and scientific and technological advances. The macroenvironment serves as the focus of the discussion for the remainder of this chapter.

The dynamic nature of the macroenvironment requires that the organization constantly monitor all environmental elements and assess their impact on current and future marketing activities. As illustrated in Figure 6-2, **environmental monitoring** is the four-stage process of searching the macroenvironment for new and relevant trends and adapting the organization's marketing programs in response to those changes. In an **environmental scan** potentially relevant information is gathered in order to discover pertinent changes in any of the environmental elements. Both marketing research and marketing intelligence efforts are employed in scanning the environment for significant changes in any of the macroenvironmental patterns and trends. An **environmental analysis** is intended to identify the nature of each environmental change in terms of its direction, magnitude, and speed. With modern technologies, collecting data is not all that difficult. The greater challenge lies in making sense of what is gathered. The goal of environmental analysis is to determine whether identified environmental changes represent opportunities or threats (see Chapter 3).

The third monitoring stage is the process of making an **environmental forecast;** that is, predicting the degree of impact and type of consequences that an environmental change might have on the marketing efforts of the organization. As a logical extension of the environmental analysis process, the forecast attempts to project into the future the direction, magnitude, and speed of changing trends and patterns. Although the macroenvironment is made up of largely uncontrollable elements, **environmental management** is the final stage of the monitoring process. Here the organization attempts to gain some degree of management control by developing quick-response systems based on accurate and timely forecasts of changing environmental trends. Environmental management also encompasses the organization's attempts at influencing selective issues within one element of the macroenvironment (such as the cigarette industry's attempts to protect smokers' rights).

We have briefly outlined the four stages of the environmental monitoring process. Let us now focus our attention on identifying some of

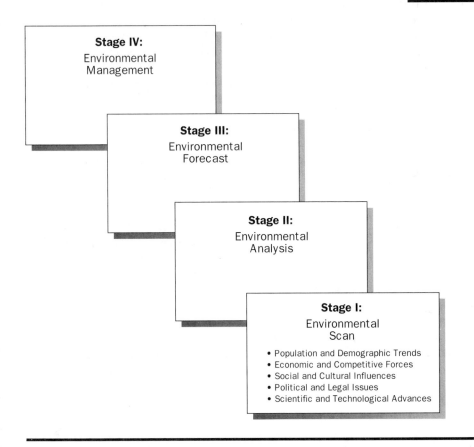

FIGURE 6-2

THE FOUR-STAGE ENVIRONMENTAL MONITORING PROCESS

the more important factors within each of the elements of the macroenvironment and on discussing some of the more dynamic changes in trends and patterns within the contemporary marketplace.

POPULATION AND DEMOGRAPHIC TRENDS

The first step in understanding the macroenvironment and its potential effects on the marketing effort of an organization is to examine the people who comprise the marketplace. The structure of buying populations should be examined in terms of *how many people are there?* (population growth) and *who are they?* (demographic trends).

POPULATION GROWTH

The actual and potential market for any organization is determined in part by **total population**—the total number of individuals living within a geographic area at a particular point in time. "By the projections the United Nations considers most likely, world population will leap from 5.6 billion in 1992 to 8.3 billion by 2025."[1] The current global population growth rate is approximately 1.6 percent per year. The growth rate varies from 1.9 percent in developing countries to 0.3 percent in industrial nations.[2] "The earth's population is almost certain to double in the next century, no matter what actions nations take to curb the population explosion."[3] While recent studies have confirmed that the earth might be able to feed this mass of humanity, the real threat is whether humans are capable of managing this type of growth.[4]

The total population of the United States was approximately 250 million in 1990. Experts project the annual growth rate to be less than 1 percent from 1990 to 2000. With a 7- to 8- percent growth rate during the final decade, the United States is expected to enter the new century with a total population of about 275 million people.[5] If total numbers were the only factor in determining marketplace potential, then future business prospects would indeed be bright. Unfortunately, total population is only part of the market potential equation.

DEMOGRAPHIC TRENDS

Demography is the study of human population characteristics and statistics used in profiling a particular population group. Demographic studies help organizations answer the population question *Who are they?* Demographic profiles are created using the descriptive elements described in Figure 6-3.

To illustrate the potential impact of demographics, we will examine three basic demographic trends—changing age profiles, evolving gender relationships, and emerging income inequalities.

CHANGING AGE PROFILES The population profile of the United States exhibits defined patterns that have and will continue to have a profound effect on the activities of marketers. Each age group that comprises the population profile not only represents a major market segment but can also be further segmented into additional market niches worthy of separate attention. Any serious consideration of consumer markets in the United States would include the following age categories:

- *Baby boomlets*—Kids under age twelve are a rapidly growing population group that is expected to continue expanding as baby boomers establish their families. Spending by dual-income parents and well-to-do grandparents has attracted the attention of many marketers, who have developed specific marketing programs for well-equipped

FIGURE 6-3

ELEMENTS OF A DEMOGRAPHIC PROFILE

- Age — the number of individuals within each age category, such as the zero to three baby market, four to twelve youth market, thirteen to nineteen market, twenty to twenty-nine young adult market

- Sex — the number of females and males within a defined geographic area

- Race — the number within each racial category, such as African-Americans, Hispanic Americans, Asian Americans, Pacific Island Americans, white Americans, and other racial groups

- Education — the number of individuals that have attained a certain level of education, such as elementary, secondary, junior college, college, graduate, and postgraduate

- Income — the number of individuals or families at various income levels, such as low income—under $25,000; middle income—$25,000 to $100,000; and high income—more than $100,000

- Occupation — the number of individuals employed within each occupation category, such as unemployed, professional, technical, clerical, supervisors, or retired

- Family — the number of individuals that are part of a particular family structure, such as single with no children, married with children, single with children, and so on

- Religion — the number of individuals that actively belong to a particular religious sect or follow certain religious beliefs, such as Jewish, Catholic, Muslim, or Protestant

---

baby boomlets who have become something of a status symbol in many social circles.[6] Kids 'R' Us, GAP Kids, and Discovery Zone are all examples of marketers who have achieved success targeting this age segment.[7]

❑ *Teens*—The teenage market (ages thirteen to nineteen) has started to grow again at a rate close to twice that of the overall population. The U.S. teen population hit 25 million last year, and over the next fifteen years it is expected to reach 30.8 million—about 900,000 more than during the peak baby boom years.[8] "They are the leading edge of a demographic wave that will wash over the United States during the next two decades, transforming our culture and economy. ... By the time this bulge peaks in 2010, it will top the baby-fueled teen explosion of the 1960s and 1970s in both size and duration."[9] Teens not only shop for themselves but have become the purchasing agents for families in which both parents work. Their multiple roles as buyers, influencers, and purchasing agents heighten the need to understand and appreciate this very different consumer. "Good as the teen business is in the United States, it ultimately may be even better abroad."[10]

❑ *Generation X*—The post–baby boom generation, those born between 1965 and 1978, are "the most ethnically diverse group of young folks in U.S. history. They are unshaped by grand defining events—like the Vietnam War—that forged a certain cultural unity in previous generations."[11] While Xers tend to be traditionalists in the sense that they aspire to the basics of career, home, and family, this "baby bust" group is also pessimistic about its future as a group sandwiched between the massive baby boomers and their offspring.[12] The great diversity of this 30-million-plus consumer group offers a considerable challenge for identifying meaningful market segments and tailoring successful marketing programs.

❑ *Baby boomers*—The baby boom generation consists of the 75 million consumers who were born between 1946 and 1964. This huge population bulge is heading toward a midlife crisis in the 1990s as all boomers enter, occupy, or exit middle age.[13] With the aging of the boomers, this moving target made up of many different marketing segments exhibits common traits that are useful to marketers. Middle-age boomers

1. Seek help in creating a balanced lifestyle that includes work, family, home, recreation, and personal time
2. Place greater emphasis on convenience and comfort
3. Want help in gaining greater control over all aspects of their lives[14]
4. Want to be involved and are becoming more interested in accumulating experiences rather than material things
5. Are experienced shoppers who have greater expectations relative to the organization's marketing program
6. Are keenly interested in their personal health and the maintenance of wellness

❑ *Mature Consumers*—The fifty-plus market is both large (60 million) and growing. The exaggerated importance of this market lies in the fact that mature consumers account for more than 50 percent of the nation's discretionary income. With the one-two punch of healthier habits and biomedical breakthroughs, the importance of this age group will continue to grow as life expectancies edge past ninety.[15] Corporate America is now in the process of making the adjustment to a less youthful population that refuses to act its age. This quality-oriented market requires appropriate adjustments in product offerings (baggier styles that fit and feel better), pricing (value pricing that offers good quality at reasonable prices), promotions (larger print on all forms of communication), and distribution (stores that offer better lighting and displays that are more accessible).[16] The needs of this multidimensional market are still being defined; "there now is a large gap between what marketers do and what social science recommends."[17]

EVOLVING GENDER RELATIONSHIPS The entrance of women into the workforce is one of the most important social changes that has occurred during the post–World War II period. With the advent of the twenty-first century, this trend is expected to continue.[18] More than one-half of the women in America are actively involved in the nation's workforce. Women are entering the workforce sooner and staying longer. The net result is a profound effect on relationships between men and women.[19] Stereotypical roles of women (the homemaker) and men (the breadwinner) are changing. These relational adjustments have carried over into their shopping behavior.

With both partners working, a team effort requires that each partner share in the responsibilities of securing needed goods and services. While the traditional divisions of shopping labors still predominate, men are now making significant purchases of foodstuffs, personal products, household products, home furnishings, family apparel, children's services, and other products that have long been the domain of women. In a similar vein, women have invaded the buying territories that had historically been assigned to men (such as automobiles, hardware, tools, lawn equipment, and financial and professional services). An important factor for marketers to realize is that men and women do not typically use the same shopping strategies. There is considerable variance in their attitudes toward brand choices, price comparisons, impulse purchases, and store preferences.[20] Discovering and respecting differences in gender shopping behavior is an essential part of the marketing manager's job.

With the rapid increase in the number of single-person households and single-parent households, many men and women have had to assume total responsibility for making all household purchases. Both men and women have had to learn to become supermarket whizzes, fashion critics, car-buying hagglers, and professional purchasing agents.

EMERGING INCOME INEQUALITIES One of the greatest challenges of the late 1990s is the growing income gap between America's rich and poor. Increasing inequality between the nation's "haves" and "have nots" looms as a central issue in the political, social, and economical environment of the United States. "From 1989 through mid-1993, earnings fell for most American workers, yet the drop was sharpest for those at the lower end of the income scale. New surveys show that the average corporate CEO earns

149 times the pay of the average factory worker, while nearly 18 percent of full-time workers do not make enough to keep a family of four out of poverty."[21] The most common delineating factor between richer and poorer Americans is education. "Today, you can all but forget about joining the middle class unless you go to college. . . . Top-fifth families now rake in 44.6 percent of U.S. income versus 4.4 percent for the bottom fifth."[22]

The market and marketing implications of the income gap are enormous. For example, the income polarization of the marketplace should further divide producers and retailers into two predominant retail formats: (1) upscale, focused businesses that target affluent consumers and (2) low-cost marketing channels that produce and distribute products to the less affluent, low-end buyers. This income split has implications with regard to product quality, product selection, brand strategies, pricing points, store choices, special promotions, and desired images. In addition, many experts believe that such inequalities are a major stumbling block to long-term economic growth. Perhaps the most serious consequence of the income gap was expressed by Labor Secretary Robert B. Reich: "A society divided between the haves and have nots or between the well-educated and the poorly educated . . . cannot be prosperous or stable."[23]

ECONOMIC AND COMPETITIVE FORCES

The **economic environment** consists of those factors that determine the way in which a nation's resources are allocated and used (economic systems), the health of the nation's economy (economic conditions), and the willingness and ability of consumers to buy (economic issues). The **competitive environment** can be described as the rivalry among various organizations in their attempt to satisfy the same target market consumers with similar marketing programs. These rivalries define the competitive market structure under which each marketer must compete. Both of these environmental forces create unique opportunities and present difficult threats to the organization's long-term growth and survival.

ECONOMIC SYSTEMS

Economic systems are allocation systems. They determine how resources are allocated among individuals, groups, and organizations within a defined political entity. Each economic system must resolve such issues as what and how many products to produce, and where and how to distribute those products. The continuum of economic systems ranges from a market economy at one end of the economic spectrum to a command economy at the other end. Economic systems that fall in the middle of the continuum are referred to as mixed economies.

Market economies are resource allocation systems in which supply-and-demand factors determine what resources are used for what purposes. In these "free-market" or "capitalist" systems the right of consumers to choose among different market offerings (consumer sovereignty) and the right of all marketers to have a fair and equal chance at serving all markets (competitive market structure) are the central economic premises of the resource allocation process. The United States, Japan, and some Western European nations are at this market end of the economic spectrum.

Command economies (also referred to as controlled or planned economies) rely on a central planning process in which the government establishes goals and creates plans to direct and control the allocation of resources, the purpose for which those resources are used, and who benefits from those resources. Government ownership and control are the hallmark of the command economy. The Chinese economy is the only remaining command economy of any significance, and it is becoming more market based.

Mixed economies are usually characterized by limited government ownership or support of basic industries, private ownership and control of most businesses, personal ownership of property, and a centrally planned and supported social welfare system. The economic systems of the Scandinavian nations and the United Kingdom typify mixed economies.

ECONOMIC CONDITIONS

The economic health of an economy directly influences all aspects of the marketing program. From expansion during times of prosperity to retrenchment during recessionary periods, the marketing manager must be prepared to adjust the entire marketing mix to meet changing economic prospects. The 1990–1991 recession had a devastating effect on many companies. American Express, for example, experienced declining market share "as companies cut travel and entertainment spending and cardholders and merchants rebelled against its high fees."[24] Economic growth is the most common benchmark for determining the health of an economy; it is most often described in terms of **gross domestic product (GDP)**—the value of all goods and services produced within the borders of the United States, and **gross national product (GNP)**—the value of all domestic and foreign goods and services produced by American companies operating in the United States and around the world. Strong economic growth creates higher employment which in turn increases consumer buying power. This results in greater spending and more marketing activity.

The ability and the willingness to buy are strongly influenced by the **business cycle**—the historic tendency of national economies to fluctuate between prosperous and less prosperous times. These boom-and-bust swings in the national economy take the form of the following four-phase cycle:

- *Prosperity*—a healthy economy characterized by strong demand, higher income levels, brisk consumer spending, low unemployment, high business output and investment, controlled inflation, and low interest rates

- *Recession*—a downturn in an economy that is troubled by rising unemployment, reduced wage growth rate, declining buying power, pessimistic consumer outlook, decreasing demand, and declining business output and investment

- *Depression*—a very unhealthy economy having the same negative characteristics of the recession phase but in the extreme. The last depression was in the 1930s. Most economists believe that a deep depression is unlikely to occur again due to strong economic policies used by the federal government to prevent such an occurrence.

- *Recovery*—a transitional phase in which both the economical and psychological outlooks are on the upswing. Pent-up demand, more consumer optimism, increased employment, and greater buying power lead to greater expansion in business investment, production, and marketing activities.

ECONOMIC ISSUES

Inflation, unemployment, and underemployment are all economic issues that have a negative impact on each consumer's willingness and ability to buy. **Inflation** is the economic condition wherein price levels of goods and services increase more rapidly than the personal incomes of consumers. A simple definition of inflation is "too much money chasing too few goods." **Unemployment** is defined as a state of affairs wherein an individual who is actively looking for employment cannot find it. **Underemployment** is the situation where individuals are working in jobs for which they are overqualified and undercompensated. Each of these threats reduces both what and how much consumers can buy. This reduction in the consumer's "willingness to buy" and "ability to buy" necessitates significant adjustments in each organization's product offerings, pricing strategies, distribution arrangements, and promotional campaigns. Greater price sensitivity, postponed purchase decisions, reduced brand and store loyalty, and changed buying behavior patterns are a few of the adjustments consumers make in response to these economic threats.

Shortages are a lack of available resources, which might include raw resources (coffee beans), component parts (engines), energy (gasoline), or labor (technical skills). Shortages can have a negative impact on the production or distribution of goods and services. For example, coffee bean shortages caused by severe frosts in Brazil in 1994 caused the price of a pound of coffee to increase by 45 percent.[25] When shortages are caused by excessive demand for a product, an organization might elect to pursue a strategy of **demarketing**—a marketing program designed to reduce the demand for a product by reducing consumption of the product or diverting demand to some other product or substitute. Demarketing strategies can be designed to achieve a temporary or permanent solution to a shortage problem.

COMPETITIVE MARKET STRUCTURES

The competitive structure of any market can be described in terms of the number of firms competing in the market and each competitor's share of the market. The four types of competitive market structures are pure competition, monopolistic competition, oligopoly, and monopoly.

Pure competition is a market structure in which there are many small buyers and sellers of fairly homogeneous products with few if any barriers to entering or exiting the market. The nature of a pure market structure prevents any organization from gaining much of a competitive advantage. This type of perfect market structure is not easily found in the real world. The exception might be the market for some agricultural products such as corn and rice.

Monopolistic competition exists when there are many competitors in the market who compete by differentiating themselves and their marketing programs. Organizations differentiate themselves by creating different images (such as value, convenience, or quality). Products are differentiated by offering different brands, designs, and styles. Price differentiation can be achieved by offering different quality products at different pricing points or by using different pricing policies (such as odd-even prices and multiple-unit pricing). The vast majority of businesses in the United States operate within this type of market structure. Because of "me-too marketers," organizations must continuously adjust their differentiation strategy in order to retain or gain market share.

Oligopoly market structures are those in which a few large organizations have large shares of the market and considerable influence on prices. Because of high entry barriers and few market competitors, firms that operate within an oligopoly enjoy considerable control of the market and its pricing structure. The automotive, telephone, and airline industries operate within an oligopoly market structure.

A **monopoly** exists when a single organization dominates the market by completely controlling the supply of a product for which there are no good substitutes. Because antitrust laws strictly limit monopoly market structures, public utilities (gas, electric, and sewage, so called "natural monopolies") are among the few monopolies allowed.

The complexity of the competitive environment needs to be recognized, appreciated, and accommodated. Focusing the organization's attention and actions only on direct competitors is a common and costly error. Adaptive competitive behavior is both specific and general in its response to environmental opportunities and threats.

Social and Cultural Influences

Social and cultural influences are some of the most powerful factors impelling human behavior. Human nature affects buying behavior, as do the responsive actions of marketers. Selected key issues that make up the social and cultural agendas of the consuming public must be examined in light of their potential impact on the marketing programs of organizations.

The Social Agenda

The **social agenda** is comprised of the social forces that determine "the structure and dynamics of individuals and groups and the issues that engage them."[26] Values, beliefs, and standards are some of the social elements that determine the type and extent of relationships and interactions among and within various social groups. They also influence how a particular marketing program is perceived and accepted. Because the social agenda reflects the concerns of contemporary society, it presents the marketer with business opportunities for alleviating those concerns.

Values and Beliefs **Values** are goals a society views as important and essential to the well-being of its members. Social values express a culture's shared ideas of how individuals and organizations should act and reflect in a general and somewhat abstract way what is good, fair, right, and desirable. "A **belief** is a conviction concerning the existence or the characteristic of physical or social phenomena. . . . Whether this belief is correct is not particularly important in terms of our actions. Even a totally foolish belief may affect how we behave."[27]

Values and beliefs provide consumers with a simple and preset way to respond to an organization's marketing program. Primary or core values and beliefs toward work and achievement, family and friends, or God and country are fairly stable, quite persistent, and very influential.[28] These behavioral guidelines have a strong and lasting effect on what, how, when, why, and where consumers buy. Secondary or surface values and beliefs are more likely to change on a more frequent basis and have a more modest influence on the individual's behavior. Being loyal to one's country is a core belief, while believing and supporting a particular national policy can often be a secondary belief.

Ethics and Standards **Ethics** is "a system or code of conduct based on universal moral duties and obligations which indicate how one should behave."[29] Ethical values guide individuals in their consideration of what is right and wrong, just and unjust, honest and dishonest, and acceptable and unacceptable. Both relative and absolute standards are used in judging the morality of an individual's or organization's behavior. Why would profit-driven organizations become unduly concerned with ethics? The bottom line on ethics is that "many companies are discovering that doing good and doing well go hand-in-hand."[30]

Relative standards or ethics are based on the set of circumstances that are involved with a particular decision or action. Judgments based on relative standards are made using criteria that are subjective, individual, situational, and socially determined. One such relative standard is "the end justifies the means." In this approach, the consequences of a decision or action are judged and not the decision or act itself.[31] Another relative ethical standard is based on the notion of intuitionism—if an individual's intuition or the collective conscience of an organization says a certain action is right, then it is okay. In recent years, "[c]orporations are increasingly trying to set ethical standards high enough so they do not break the law inadvertently. The gray area is no longer safe territory."[32]

Absolute standards are clearly expressed declarations of what constitutes ethical behavior. Right and wrong are based on rigid rules and standards that are outlined in basic religious teachings. The Rule of Reciprocity (the Golden Rule) of "do unto others as you would have them do unto you" is a good example of an absolute standard. Service Master, the $2.8-billion-in-sales company that operates Merry Maid (house care), Tru-Green/ChemLawn (lawn care), and Terminix (pest exterminators), has as its number-one operating principle "To honor God in all we do." According to its chairman, C. William Pollard, "making sure the company honors God in all it does is the best management principle ever derived ... it sets a clear direction, eliminates ethical dilemmas—when your first principle is to honor God, distinguishing between right and wrong is not that hard—and it makes it easier to manage."[33]

Developing a code of ethics is a demanding and complicated task. Codes of ethics must be more than legal or public-relations ploys; they must be useful, understandable, and practical. For codes to be accepted and followed by rank-and-file employees, visible signs of support for ethical behavior must be forthcoming from top management, where the moral tone of the organization is established and nurtured.[34] The American Marketing Association (AMA) has developed a Code of Ethics that governs all members of its association (see Figure 6-4). Even when an organization has an extensive ethics program, it does not assure it of complete protection from unethical behavior by some members of the organization. General Electric has one of the most extensive ethics programs in corporate America. "Unfortunately for GE, there are also few companies in the United States with as checkered an ethical record."[35] The adoption of the AMA code would provide an organization with an excellent set of guidelines for governing its marketing functions.

RELATIONSHIPS AND INTERACTIONS Social practices often suggest what makes up proper decorum or etiquette in the personal relationships between individuals within a society as well as between organizations and their customers and vendors. **Manners** can be thought of as the way individuals and organizations conduct themselves while engaging in personal interactions and negotiating business transactions. For example, in the area of verbal communications there are acceptable means of expressing oneself in terms of word choice, voice intonation, gestures, body position, eye contact, and symbolic aids.

Customs are patterned ways of maintaining relationships or conducting business in terms of rituals and ceremonies that create the setting for any interaction or transaction.[36] For example, in conducting business transactions, the customary way in which orders are handled (written versus verbal or credit versus cash), taken (personal versus nonpersonal selling), and processed (pickup or delivery) are a few of the issues that might arise. The impact of manners and customs becomes extremely important when dealing in international sales. More than one relationship has been permanently damaged by the failure to understand and appreciate cross-cultural differences in how personal and organizational relationships and interactions are conducted.

THE CULTURAL AGENDA

Culture establishes the general guidelines by which a society conducts its everyday life. A society's **cultural agenda** is the sum total of its basic knowledge, profound beliefs, fundamental values, and patterned behaviors, which are shared by a group of people and passed on from one generation to another. Culture includes everything that individuals learn and know as members of society. Some examples of important issues that comprise the cultural agenda and impact on most organizational marketing plans include cultural diversity, quality of life, and consumerism.

CULTURAL DIVERSITY With the advent of a new century, cultural diversity is replacing the "melting pot" premise of cultural assimilation as a core cultural value. **Cultural diversity** is the phenomenon of becoming a multicultural population group. This eclectic population structure of different ethnic and racial groups has made it necessary for many marketing managers to adopt a more cross-cultural approach to identifying target markets and tailoring marketing programs. A steady and significant flow of immigrants from many different cultural areas of the world and the relatively higher birthrates of minority groups have contributed to the diversification of the American culture. In the United States, the mosaic of key minority groups is made up of African Americans, Hispanic Americans, and Asian and Pacific Island Americans. By 2000, an estimated 28 percent of the U.S. population will be African American, Hispanic, or Asian American.[37]

The largest minority group in the United States are **African Americans.** They make up approximately 12 percent of the nation's total population.

FIGURE 6-4

AMERICAN MARKETING ASSOCIATION CODE OF ETHICS

Members of the American Marketing Association (AMA) are committed to ethical professional conduct. They have joined together in subscribing to this Code of Ethics embracing the following topics:

Responsibilities of the Marketer
Marketers must accept responsibility for the consequences of their activities and make every effort to ensure that their decisions, recommendations, and actions function to identify, serve, and satisfy all relevant publics: customers, organizations, and society.

Marketers' professional conduct must be guided by:
1. The basic rule of professional ethics: not knowingly to do harm
2. The adherence to all applicable laws and regulations
3. The accurate representation of their education, training, and experience
4. The active support, practice, and promotion of this Code of Ethics

Honesty and Fairness
Marketers shall uphold and advance clients, employees, suppliers, distributors, and the public:
1. Being honest in serving consumers, clients, employees, suppliers, distributors, and the public
2. Not knowingly participating in conflicts of interest without prior notice to all parties involved
3. Establishing equitable fee schedules including the payment or receipt of usual, customary and/or legal compensation for marketing exchange

Rights and Duties of Parties in the Marketing Exchange Process
Participants in the marketing exchange process should be able to expect that:
1. Products and services offered are safe and fit for their intended uses
2. Communications about offered products and services are not deceptive
3. All parties intend to discharge their obligations, financial and otherwise, in good faith
4. Appropriate internal methods exist for equitable adjustment and/or redress of grievances concerning purchases

It is understood that the above would include, but is not limited to, the following responsibilities of the marketers:

In the area of product development and management,
- Disclosure of all substantial risks associated with product or service usage
- Identification of any product component substitution that might materially change the product or impact on the buyer's purchase decision
- Identification of extra cost-added features

In the area of promotions,
- Avoidance of false and misleading advertising
- Rejection of high-pressure manipulations or misleading sales tactics
- Avoidance of sales promotions that use deception or manipulation

In the area of distribution,
- Not manipulating the availability of a product for purpose of exploitation
- Not using coercion in the marketing channel
- Not exerting undue influence over the reseller's choice to handle a product

In the area of pricing,
- Not engaging in price fixing
- Not practicing predatory pricing
- Disclosing the full price associated with any purchase

In the area of marketing research,
- Prohibiting selling or fundraising under the guise of conducting research
- Maintaining research integrity by avoiding misrepresentation and omission of pertinent research data
- Treating outside clients and suppliers fairly

continued

FIGURE 6-4

CONTINUED

Organizational Relationships
Marketers should be aware of how their behavior may influence or impact on the behavior of others in organizational relationships. They should not demand, encourage, or apply coercion to obtain unethical behavior in their relationships with others, such as employees, suppliers, or customers. Marketers should:
1. Apply confidentiality and anonymity in professional relationships with regard to privileged information
2. Meet their obligations and responsibilities in contracts and mutual agreements in a timely manner
3. Avoid taking the work of others, in whole, or in part, and representing this work as their own or directly benefiting from it without compensation or consent of the originator or owner
4. Avoid manipulation to take advantage of situations to maximize personal welfare in a way that unfairly deprives or damages their organization or others

Any AMA member found to be in violation of any provision of this Code of Ethics may have his or her Association membership suspended or revoked.

SOURCE: Courtesy of the American Marketing Association.

With a growth rate of 13 percent and increasing income levels, each segment of this multidimensional minority market requires a tailored marketing program to adequately meet its needs. The Spanish language, the Roman Catholic religion, family orientation, and sense of community are all common cultural traits that define the **Hispanic American** culture. At the same time, different Hispanic subcultures (Puerto Rican, Cuban, Mexican, Caribbean, and Central and South American) represent distinctive market opportunities. Accounting for about 9 percent of the total U.S. population, Hispanics have a growth rate (53 percent) that is four times that of African Americans and nine times that of the white population. Within thirty years, Hispanics are expected to become the second-largest cultural group in the United States. The **Asian and Pacific Island** cultures (Chinese, Japanese, Korean, Filipino, Vietnamese, and others) represent only 3 percent of the nation's total population but have the fastest growth rate (108 percent) of any group. While the level of diversity (different languages, customs, and needs) within the Asian and South Pacific market can be overwhelming, higher incomes and educational levels can make serving these subcultural groups very rewarding.

The most essential point is that each organization and its marketing program must learn to understand and appreciate the values, beliefs, attitudes, practices, and behaviors of people in all cultures.[38] Remember, new market opportunities are created by diverse needs and desires.

QUALITY OF LIFE Quality of life and standard of living are concepts that are often viewed as being synonymous, but they are not. **Standard of living** is concerned with the economic well-being of people in terms of quantity, quality, availability, and affordability of goods and services. Living standard incorporates the ideas of material wealth and determines what and how much typical members of a society can consume. On average, cultures with a higher standard of living offer greater marketing opportunities.

Quality of life is the cultural concept that embraces the notion of both economic and social well-being of all members of a society. Some quality-of-life factors include a clean natural environment, personal security, individual freedoms, and an adequate amount of leisure time. Each of these quality-of-life factors greatly extends the ways in which markets can be delineated and the basis upon which a successful marketing program can be built. **Green marketing** is a quality-of-life marketing tactic in which environmental causes and issues are used in the development, distribution, and promotion of the organization's products and programs.

CONSUMERISM The **consumerism** movement is a patchwork of individuals, groups, and organizations who seek to promote the rights of consumers. These consumer protection groups advocate consumer rights by pressuring businesses and government organizations and by publicizing consumer issues. Consumer rights were articulated by President Kennedy in 1962 as the following:

   1. The right to choose—each consumer should have a choice of goods and services

   2. The right to be safe—each consumer should be secure from defective goods and unsafe services

   3. The right to be informed—each consumer should be provided with information that is sufficient and reliable enough to make informed decisions

   4. The right to be heard—each consumer should be able to register their complaints and have them addressed by the responsible parties or proper authorities

Figure 6-5 identifies a small representative sample of some of the laws that have been passed in an attempt to ensure consumer rights and protect consumers from inappropriate marketing activities. With the advent of "retention marketing" and "relationship retailing," many marketing organizations are actively engaged in dealing with the issues championed by the consumer rights advocates.

POLITICAL AND LEGAL ISSUES

A nation's political and legal systems can either restrain or facilitate an organization's marketing activities. The **political environment** is concerned with the practices and procedures used by federal, state, and local governments to conduct business and make policy. The **legal environment** is the set of laws and regulations by which governments govern the conduct of individuals and organizations. Political and

▪ FIGURE 6–5

CONSUMER RIGHTS AND PROTECTIONISM LEGISLATION

1872 — **Mail Fraud Act.** Protects consumers against fraudulent use of the mail.

1906 — **Pure Food and Drug Act.** Forbids the manufacture and distribution of misbranded and adulterated foods and drugs in interstate commerce.

1939 — **Wool Products Labeling Act.** Requires that the label identify the type and percentage of wool used in products.

1951 — **Fur Products Labeling Act.** Requires that the label identify the type of animal used in the product.

1953 — **Flammable Fabrics Act.** Restricts the interstate distribution of flammable apparel and materials.

1958 — **Automotive Information Disclosure Act.** Requires that car dealers post suggested retail selling prices and prohibits the inflation of those prices.

1958 — **National Traffic and Safety Act.** Establishes safety standards for automobiles and tires.

1966 — **Fair Packaging and Labeling Act.** Requires disclosure of package contents, verification of manufacturer, and identification of the amount of product in package.

1967 — **Cigarette Labeling and Advertising Act.** Requires health warnings on all cigarette labels and advertisements.

1968 — **Consumer Credit Protection Act.** Requires full disclosure of interest rates and financial charges on credit purchases and loans.

1970 — **Fair Credit Reporting Act.** Requires accurate reporting on all consumer credit transactions, ensures consumer access to all credit reports, and provides procedures for correcting inaccuracies.

1972 — **Consumer Product Safety Act.** Created the Consumer Product Safety Commission and empowers the agency with the responsibility to set and enforce product safety standards.

1975 — **Equal Credit Opportunity Act.** Prohibits discrimination in lending practices.

1990 — **Nutrition Labeling and Education Act.** Requires food manufacturers to provide detailed information on the nutritional content of their product.

legal institutions most directly affect marketing activities by providing guidance. Laws, in effect, are codes of conduct that establish allowable limits within which marketing operations must be managed.

THE POLITICAL SYSTEM

In its basic form, the political system operates as a sequential process in which:

1. laws are enacted by legislative bodies,

2. legal issues are decided by the court system, and

3. legal decisions are enforced by regulatory agencies or court action.

This political process impacts every aspect of an organization's marketing program. It controls, among many other things, competitive tactics used in gaining additional market share, the wording of promotional messages, and the safety of product offerings. Congress, for example, is debating "legislation that would allow local and long-distance carriers, as well as cable-television companies into each others' markets."[39] Such legislation would have a profound effect on how each of these industries would respond to the market and each other. The typical organization interfaces with the political process on a regular and continuous basis. While the entire process is beyond the control of any organization or group (such as trade associations), influence can be exerted at each stage of the political process. Lobbyists influence what legislation is enacted and the form in which it is passed. Successful legal challenges can result in court ordered changes in enforcement of regulations. Public relations efforts aimed at appropriate political institutions develop the alliances necessary for the maintenance of good working relationships.

THE LEGAL SYSTEM

The legislative, executive, and judicial branches of federal, state, and local governments define the legal system under which every organization must operate. The legal system is comprised of a collection of legal measures and regulatory instruments that govern the behavior of the organization. Statutes, ordinances, licenses, contracts, and certificates constitute the building blocks of our legal system.

LEGAL ASPECTS OF MARKETING

Competitive Actions   Federal legislation has been enacted to ensure that virtually all markets are competitive business environments and that all competitors have a fair and equal chance to compete. To foster competitiveness within the marketplace, a series of laws known as **antitrust legislation** was passed in an attempt to prevent any "unreasonable restraint of trade" or "unfair trade practices." Antitrust laws have been both reactive (correcting present restraints on trade) and proactive (prohibiting probable restraints on trade or unfair trade practices). Figure 6-6 identifies the key legislative actions taken to promote a competitive market environment.

Company Operations All aspects of the organization's daily operations are regulated to some extent. Organizations are owned and operated as one of three types of legal entities—sole proprietorships, general and limited partnerships, or corporations. Each of these legal organizational formats creates unique advantages and limitations relative to personal liability, tax liability, licensing requirements, operational flexibility, and owner control. In addition, legal restrictions exist regarding gaining ownership and control of other competing organizations via mergers, acquisitions, and leveraged buyouts. If such activities lessen competition within a market, appropriate remedies would be required by law. Job discrimination, working conditions, worker compensation, and unemployment compensation are all human resource management issues that are covered under federal and state codes. Zoning ordinances, building codes, and business licenses are but a few of the physical facilities regulations that are covered by local ordinances.

Marketing Activities The organization's marketing mix is regulated by a series of laws commonly referred to as consumer protection legislation. This body of laws is designed to protect final consumers from unsafe products, inadequate product performance, unfair prices, misleading advertisements, improper selling techniques, deceptive packaging, unequal credit arrangements, and a host of other marketing activities that are considered unfair or inappropriate. Business-to-business marketing relationships are also regulated. Price discrimination, price fixing, price solicitation, exclusive dealing, refusal to deal, and exclusive territories are all transactions within the marketing channel that are controlled to ensure fair and equitable treatment for business partners.

REGULATORY FORCES IN MARKETING Both governmental and private regulatory agencies have been created to ensure compliance with applicable laws and standards. Federal, state, and local government regulators are assigned enforcement responsibilities and are empowered to take legal action against organizations in the event of noncompliance. Governmental regulatory agencies are most active in the supervision of transportation systems, public utilities, communication networks, environmental protection, commercial transactions, public education, and public safety.

Private regulatory agencies are attempts at self-regulation. Trade associations (National Retail Federation), accreditation agencies (American

FIGURE 6-6

ANTITRUST LEGISLATION

1890 — **Sherman Antitrust Act.** Prohibits monopolies or attempts at monopolizing commerce and outlaws any contract or combination in restraint of trade.

1914 — **Clayton Act.** Amends the Sherman Act by prohibiting such anticompetitive actions as price discrimination, tying contracts, exclusive dealings, and interlocking boards of directors when such actions substantially lessen competition or tend to create a monopoly.

1914 — **Federal Trade Commission Act.** Prohibits unfair trade practices that might injure either the competitive nature of the market or unduly harm another competitor. Established the Federal Trade Commission.

1936 — **Robinson–Patman Act.** Broadens and clarifies the meaning of unfair competition by declaring any competition that tends to injure, destroy, or prevent competition is unlawful.

1938 — **Wheeler–Lea Act.** Prohibits any unfair or deceptive business practices regardless of their impact on competition. Outlaws false and deceptive advertising.

1950 — **Kefauver Antimerger Act.** Prevents corporate mergers and acquisitions that reduce competition.

1980 — **FTC Improvement Act.** Limits the power of the Federal Trade Commission to decide unfairness issues.

Assembly of Collegiate Schools of Business), and business organizations (Better Business Bureau) are all voluntary membership groups that promote professional and ethical standards within a particular industry or profession. They rely on peer pressure, censorship, and loss of membership to persuade members to adhere to acceptable legal, traditional, and ethical practices.

SCIENTIFIC AND TECHNOLOGICAL ADVANCES

Science refers to the whole body of knowledge that is available to society. **Technology** is the application of scientific and engineering knowledge to practical problems. Technological changes can be evolutionary (slow and predictable) or revolutionary (fast and unpredictable). "Our society is in the midst of several technological revolutions, including an information revolution, an electronics revolution, a biotech revolution, a chemical revolution, a medical revolution, a transportation revolution, a computer-chip revolution, a superconducting revolution, and so on."[40] Future advances in technology are expected to occur at a more rapid pace and have a greater and more direct impact on the marketing activities of most organizations. For example, technology in the personal computer market is on a collision course with marketing. "The PC market demands faster chips, bigger screens, more memory, and fancier software. But these gadgets have far outstripped the technical competence of the typical user."[41] Strategic windows of opportunity created by new technologies come and go quite rapidly. The amount of reaction time afforded organizational management is severely restricted by the evolution of newer technologies. Future successes with new technologies will require rapid transition of these inventions and innovations through the technological phases of (1) conceptualization and experimentation, (2) adaptation and refinement, and (3) application and implementation.

From the perspective of the marketing manager, new and advancing technologies "can readily destroy or create markets, develop or make obsolete industries and products, and create economic surges or rapid declines. The likely impact of future technology is among the hardest of the external marketing factors to discern."[42] The following list contains just a few of the expected technological impacts that marketers will have to consider and manage:

- Quicker product obsolescence and replacement
- Faster new product development and introduction
- More rapid expansion of product lines and substitutes
- Better product quality capabilities
- More channels of distribution
- Different retailing formats
- More efficient cost reduction techniques
- New and innovative communications systems
- Novel modes of advertising
- Enhanced methods of sales presentations
- Greater use of visuals and other sensory technologies
- More advanced methods of handling customer transactions

The expansion of existing technologies and the development of new technologies will require that each organization carefully develop and foster the interface between technology and marketing. Ventritex, makers of a small but complex gadget known as an implantable heart defibrillator, which treats a dangerous heart condition called ventricular tachyarrhythmia, hopes to build a successful company by constantly obsoleting itself through the development of new product technologies.[43] Figure 6-7 outlines a set of guidelines for dealing effectively with the technology/marketing interface.

FIGURE 6-7

GUIDELINES FOR MANAGING THE TECHNOLOGY/ MARKETING INTERFACE

- Recognize technology as a major factor in the strategic marketing planning process.

- Track technology to help overcome the information and perception gaps between marketing and technological development.

- Understand and appreciate current and emerging technologies that relate directly to current markets, product/services, and customers.

- Put a formal technology scanning and technology assessment process in place.

- Generate a marketing climate and philosophy that supports and encourages technological advancements.

- Set up priority listing of likely future technological opportunities and explore the potential in each.

- Seek to close the gap between market wants and needs and technological know-how.

- Evaluate competitors' technological capabilities and approaches and explore their potential impact.

SOURCE: Reprinted by permission from Willlam Lazer, Priscilla LaBarbera, James M. MacLachlan, and Allen E. Smith, *Marketing 2000 and Beyond* (Chicago: American Marketing Association, 1990), 16.

CONCLUDING REMARKS

All organizations must operate within the macroenvironment. Population and demographic trends must be examined from the perspective of population growth, changing age profiles, evolving gender relationships, and emerging income inequalities. Economic systems, conditions, and issues are the economic and competitive forces that make up this sector of the macroenvironment. The social and cultural agendas that influence marketing activities include values and beliefs, ethics and standards, relationships and interactions, cultural diversity, quality of life, and consumerism. Political and legal issues and scientific and technological advances are also necessary in an analysis of the macroenvironment.

ENDNOTES

1. Emily T. Smith, "Too Many People," *Business Week* (August 29, 1994), 65.

2. Peter Waldman, "Population Conference Fallout Is Feared," *Wall Street Journal* (September 2, 1994), A6.

3. Emily MacFarquhar, "Population Wars," *U.S. News & World Report* (September 12, 1994), 52.

4. Stephen Budiansky, "10 Billion for Dinner, Please," *U.S. News & World Report* (September 12, 1994), 58.

5. Population Trends and Congressional Apportionment," *1990 Census Profile* (Washington DC: Bureau of the Census, U.S. Department of Commerce, March 1991), 1.

6. See Peter Newcomb, "Hey, Dude, Let's Consume," *Forbes* (June 15, 1990), 126. Also see Susan Caminiti, "Who's Minding America's Kids?" *Fortune* (August 10, 1992), 50–53. Also see Lisa Gubernick and Marla Matzer, "Babies as Dolls," *Forbes* (February 27, 1995), 78–82.

7. See Monica Roman, "Discovery Zone: Fitness for the Latchkey Set," *Business Week* (July 27, 1992), 76.

8. Cyndee Miller, "Teens Seen as the First Truly Global Consumers," *Marketing News* (March 27, 1995), 9.

9. Laura Zinn, "Teens, Here Comes the Biggest Wave Yet," *Business Week* (April 11, 1994), 76

10. Shawn Tully, "Teens: The Most Global Market of All," *Fortune* (May 16, 1994), 90.

11. Joshua Levine, "Generation X," *Forbes* (July 18, 1994), 294.

12. Larry Reibstein and Dante Chinni, "Extra! Extra! Will They, Like, Read It?" *Newsweek* (September 5, 1994), 65.

13. See Melinda Beck, "The New Middle Age," *Newsweek* (December 2, 1992), 50.

14. See Joan Warner, "The Baby Boomers' Triple Whammy," *Business Week* (May 4, 1992), 178–79.

15. Richard I. Kirkland, Jr., "Why We Will Live Longer ... And What It Will Mean," *Fortune* (February 21, 1994) 66. Also see Christopher Farrell, "The Economics of Aging," *Business Week* (September 12, 1994), 60

16. See David Young, "Aging Baby Boomers Have Consumer Clout," *The Akron Beacon Journal* (July 16, 1994), A1.

17. George P. Moschis and Anil Mathur, "How They're Acting Their Age," *Marketing Management,* Vol. 2, No. 2 (1993), 43. Also see Charles D. Schewe and Geoffrey E. Merredith, "Digging Deep to Delight the Mature Adult Consumer," *Marketing Management,* Vol. 3, No. 3 (1994), 20–35.

18. Robin Knight, "Gender, Jobs and Economic Survival," *U.S. News & World Report* (September 19, 1994), 63.

19. Amanda Bennett, "More and More Women Are Staying on the Job Later in Life Than Men," *Wall Street Journal* (September 1, 1994), B1.

20. See Suein L. Hwang, "From Choices to Checkout, the Genders Behave Very Differently in Supermarkets," *The Wall Street Journal* (April 22, 1994), B1.

21. Susan Dentzer, "Bridging the Bitter Income Divide," *U.S. News & World Report* (May 30, 1994), 53.

22. Aaron Bernstein, "Inequality, How the Gap Between Rich and Poor Hurts the Economy," *Business Week* (August 15, 1994), 78.

23. Ibid, 79.

24. Jon Berry, "Don't Leave Home Without It, Wherever You Live," *Business Week* (February 21, 1994), 76.

25. Dori Jones Yang, "Trouble Brewing at the Coffee Bar," *Business Week* (August 1, 1994), 62.

26. William M. Pride and O.C. Ferrell, *Marketing: Concepts and Strategies* (Boston, MA: Houghton Mifflin Company, 1993), 45.

27. Willian G. Zikmund and Michael d'Amico, *Marketing,* Fourth Edition (Minneapolis/St.Paul, MN: West Publishing Company, 1993), 74.

28. See Cyndee Miller, "People Want to Believe in Something," *Marketing News* (December 5, 1995), 1–2.

29. Michael Josephson, *Ethical Decision Making in the Trenches,* (Marina del Rey, CA: Joseph & Edna Josephson Institute for the Advancement of Ethics, 1989), 1.

30. Don L. Boroughs, "The Bottom Line on Ethics," *U.S. News & World Report* (March 20, 1995), 61.

31. Geoffrey P. Lantos, "An Ethical Base for Marketing Decision Making," *Journal of Business and Industrial Marketing,* 2 (Spring 1987), 14–16.

32. Nick Gilbert, "1-800-22 ETHIC," *Financial World* (Fall 1994), 22.

33. Jagannath Dubashi, "God Is My Reference Point," *Financial World* (Fall 1994), 36.

34. See Bruce Hager, "What's Behind Business's Sudden Fervor for Ethics?" *Business Week* (September 23, 1991), 65.

35. Nanette Byrnes, "The Smoke at General Electric," *Financial World* (Fall 1994), 32. Also see Jolie Solomon and Daniel McGinn, "Scratches in the Teflon," *Newsweek* (October 3, 1994), 50–52.

36. See Dale M. Lewison, *Retailing,* Fifth Edition (New York: Macmillan Publishing, 1994), 811.

37. Cyndee Miller, "Catalogers Learn to Take Blacks Seriously," *Marketing News* (March 13, 1995), 8.

38. See John Steere, "How Asian-Americans Make Purchase Decisions," *Marketing News* (March 13, 1995), 9.

39. Judy Ward, "Wires Crossed," *Financial World* (October 1, 1994), 37.

40. William Lazer, Priscilla LaBarbera, James M. MacLachlan, and Allen E. Smith, *Marketing 2000 and Beyond* (Chicago, IL: American Marketing Association, 1990), 14.

41. David C. Churbuck, "Help! My PC Won't Work," *Forbes* (March 13, 1995), 103.

42. Lazer, LaBarbera, MacLachlan, and Smith, *Marketing 2000 and Beyond*, 13.

43. Justin Doebele, "A Better Mousetrap," *Forbes* (October 24, 1994), 238, 240.

CONSUMER ANALYSIS

CHAPTER OUTLINE

- **INTRODUCTION**
- **CONSUMER BUYING BEHAVIOR**
    - CONSUMER BUYING BEHAVIOR MODEL
    - CONSUMER BUYING DECISION PROCESS
    - PSYCHOLOGICAL INFLUENCES
    - PERSONAL INFLUENCES
    - SOCIAL INFLUENCES
    - SITUATIONAL INFLUENCES
- **ORGANIZATIONAL BUYING BEHAVIOR**
    - ORGANIZATIONAL BUYING MODEL
    - ORGANIZATIONAL MARKETS
    - ORGANIZATIONAL BUYING
- **CONCLUDING REMARKS**

INTRODUCTION

Consumer analysis involves diagnosing past buying behavior and forecasting future buyer activities. Marketing managers, supported by their marketing information system, must continuously gather relevant information about what, where, when, why, and how consumers buy. **Buying behavior** involves the actions and activities in which people and organizations engage when making purchase decisions. Effective marketing management requires an appreciation of buyer behavior in terms of how buyers act and react to various situations involving the procurement of goods and services and the adoption of ideas and causes. A thorough understanding of buying behavior is essential to anticipating and responding to the buyers' needs.

Buyer behavior encompasses the buying actions and activities of both individual consumers and organizational buyers. **Consumer buying behavior** focuses on the buying conduct of individuals, families, or households who are the ultimate consumers of goods, services, and ideas. **Organizational buying behavior** deals with the procurement activities of industrial firms, resellers, and institutions. While there are common traits in the buying behavior of these two different markets, the numerous differences require that they be discussed independently.

CONSUMER BUYING BEHAVIOR

Consumers have become strategic shoppers with the knowledge and experience to go beyond simple searches for the cheapest or best-known products. Today, consumer buying activities have become multi-dimensional behaviors involving a complex set of interacting forces.

CONSUMER BUYING BEHAVIOR MODEL

Consumer buying decisions, and the resulting patronage behavior, involve a problem-solving process in which consumers are swayed by a wide variety of internal and external influences (see Figure 7-1). This consumer buying behavior model demonstrates the principal relationships between the five-stage consumer buying decision process and the four types of buyer influences. The **consumer buying decision process** is a sequential series of actions that progress from problem recognition to information search to alternative evaluation to purchase decision to postpurchase evaluation. This process is directed and influenced by a set of psychological, personal, social, and situational forces that have both a direct and indirect impact on the buying behavior of individuals. We will first examine the process by which consumers make buying decisions. Then we will review the factors that influence those buying decisions.

FIGURE 7-1

INFLUENCES ON THE CONSUMER BUYING PROCESS

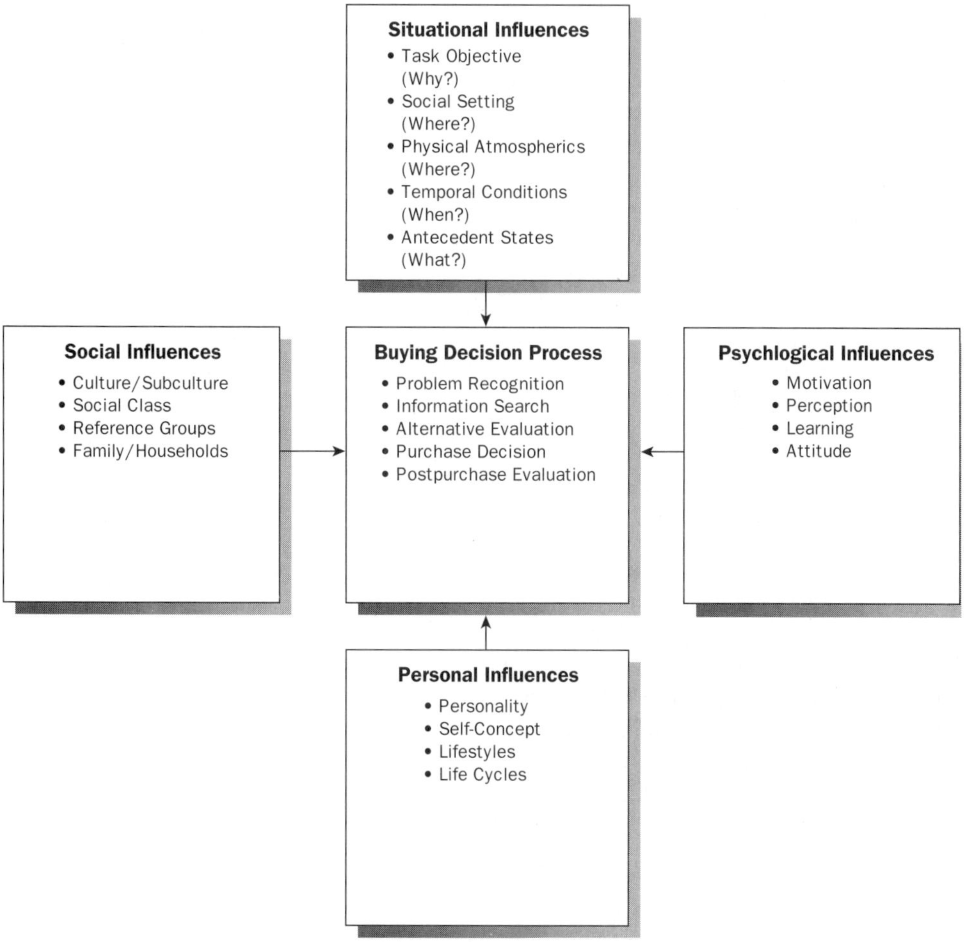

Situational Influences
- Task Objective (Why?)
- Social Setting (Where?)
- Physical Atmospherics (Where?)
- Temporal Conditions (When?)
- Antecedent States (What?)

Social Influences
- Culture/Subculture
- Social Class
- Reference Groups
- Family/Households

Buying Decision Process
- Problem Recognition
- Information Search
- Alternative Evaluation
- Purchase Decision
- Postpurchase Evaluation

Psychlogical Influences
- Motivation
- Perception
- Learning
- Attitude

Personal Influences
- Personality
- Self-Concept
- Lifestyles
- Life Cycles

CONSUMER BUYING DECISION PROCESS

Consumer buying decisions are purposeful judgments about whether a product is capable of satisfying the needs of the consumer well enough to justify its purchase and use. A buying decision can be viewed as the process by which consumers match product alternatives with expected capabilities for need satisfaction. Cosmetics marketers have come to recognize that their products for mature consumers need to be truly different from those sold to younger women. Extra moisturizers, sunscreens, and light diffusing ingredients to reduce the appearance of wrinkles are deemed essential in order to meet the needs of the more mature consumer.[1] By understanding the process by which consumers make purchase decisions, marketers stand a better chance of meeting the needs of a particular group of consumers by tailoring marketing programs to assist buyers at each stage of the buying process.

Buying decisions and the process by which consumers make them vary significantly depending on the buyer's need, the product, and the buying situation. Consumer buying decisions have been classified into one of three general categories—routinized response behavior, limited decision making, and extensive decision making. **Routinized response behavior** involves purchases of products without a great deal of thought or deliberation. When engaging in this type of behavior, consumers make decisions almost automatically because of their high level of familiarity with a purchase decision that has been made on a frequent and regular basis in the past. These repurchases are often made simply by selecting a preferred brand.

Limited decision making is practiced when the consumer has some knowledge and experience with a particular product purchase. For example, the consumer faces a limited decision-making situation when a new brand is introduced into a group of brand alternatives from which the consumer had previously chosen. Additional information and evaluation of the new brand becomes necessary prior to the final product decision and selection.

A buying situation in which the decision involves an expensive, unfamiliar, or important product purchased infrequently requires **extensive decision making.** Considerable time and effort is required to satisfactorily complete an extensive information search and to properly evaluate each viable alternative prior to making the purchase decision.

Although different circumstances call for different levels of involvement with the buying decision process, consumers do tend to follow an organized problem-solving process in most purchase situations.

PROBLEM RECOGNITION Consumers experience problem recognition when they become aware of an imbalance or discrepancy between a desired state of affairs and an actual condition. The consumer experiences a sense of dissatisfaction with the current state of affairs. For example, "Parents are increasingly disenchanted with the education kids are getting at school. Interactive computer games have become the 'Sesame Street' of a new generation. Probably the number-one reason computers are upgraded in the home is education."[2] A state of tension is often triggered by both internal physiological stimuli (for example, hunger pangs) and psychological stimuli (such as feelings of inadequacy) and such external sensory stimuli as seeing and hearing a television advertisement.

Some of the more common situations that cause problem recognition include the following:

- The routine depletion of a product used on a regular basis
- The inability to find a preferred product
- Dissatisfaction with a poorly performing product
- The interest created by promotional activities for a new or improved product
- An increase in the consumer's ability to buy such as brought about by a salary increase

When the consumer's sense of tension increases, the consumer is motivated to act in some fashion in order to reduce the tension. This motivated state leads the consumer into the next stage of the buying process.

INFORMATION SEARCH The consumer's information search is focused on gathering new and additional knowledge pertinent to the identified problem. The extent of an information search and the consumer's level of involvement in it will depend on the perceived importance of the problem. A quick review of readily available information is usually sufficient for minor problem-solving situations. An extensive search of many different information sources is common prior to making important buying decisions. Department stores such as Nordstrom, Neiman Marcus, and Dayton-Hudson are engaging in a practice known as "clienteling" in an attempt to reduce how much additional information their preferred customers seek. By showering their profitable consumers with special attention and special services, these high-end retailers hope to reduce the amount that regular customers shop the competition.[3]

Consumers tend have two general sources of information—internal and external. An **internal information search** involves recalling relevant information that might have a direct bearing on the buying problem. Past experiences with similar problems and former exposures to marketing programs that have been directed at the problem could yield enough information to proceed to the next step of the buying decision process. If not, the consumer engages in an **external information search,** involving gathering new information from one or several of the following sources:

1. Discussions with friends and family

2. Reviews of magazines, product labels, government publications, promotional literature, and other printed material

3. Store visits that include inspections of store displays or products and talks with sales personnel

4. Consultations with experts and other independent nonmarketing sources

To take advantage of the dress-down trend within the American workplace, Haggar Apparel created point-of-purchase (P-O-P) materials for men describing "how to dress down." Marshall Fields, the Chicago department store chain, featured articles in its newsletter on workday dressing down and followed up with a one-hour seminar on the subject.[4]

The desired outcome of the information search is the identification of what is termed the buyer's **evoked set**—a group of products and brands (or retail outlets) that the consumer views as potentially viable alternatives for overcoming the discrepancy between the consumer's desired state of affairs and the actual state of affairs. With the completion of a successful information search, the consumer is ready to consider the merits of alternative solutions to the problem.

ALTERNATIVE EVALUATION The alternative evaluation stage is the selection of the best alternative from the consumer's evoked set. Product or brand comparisons are used to discover which alternative has the greatest likelihood of achieving the best solution to the consumer's buying problem.[5] These comparisons are based on a set of criteria judged significant by the purchaser. Potential evaluation criteria might include the following:

1. The size, shape, and weight of the physical product

2. The material and workmanship used to produce the product

3. The aesthetic qualities created by the product's color, texture, odor, taste, sound, or style

4. The service "extras" that support the product

5. The prestige, image, and uniqueness associated with the product and the firm that produces and markets it

Make-up Art Cosmetics, Ltd., of Toronto has been able to successfully penetrate a tough market by projecting an authoritative image of its products as the brand used by professionals.[6]

Not all of these criteria are of equal importance to the consumer in making a particular purchase decision. Hence, in different buying situations, the consumer often assigns different weights (levels of importance) to the criteria used in the evaluation of a group of alternatives. A different buying situation with new alternatives produces a different set of criteria and a new assignment of weights.

PURCHASE DECISION In the fourth stage of the buying process, the consumer needs to make several decisions in order to successfully complete a purchase. These purchase decisions include the following:

❏ *Buy or No-Buy Decision*—the decision to select or reject the best product/brand alternative or one of the acceptable alternatives

❏ *Now or Later Decision*—the decision as to proceed with the purchase now or to postpone the purchase until a later time

❏ *Where and How Decision*—the decision as to which store to patronize and how (credit or cash) to pay for the purchase

It is hoped that the quality of the information search and the extensiveness of the alternative evaluation process have simplified each of these decisions. Clear-cut decisions generally prove to be more satisfying and successful.

POSTPURCHASE EVALUATION   Evaluation of the level of satisfaction with the purchase and the process that led to the decision is an essential task in order to determine whether the identified buying problem has been resolved. **Customer postpurchase satisfaction** has been previously defined as the case where actual performance of the product meets or exceeds expectations. When performance expectations are not met and aroused tensions stemming from the problem situation have not been relieved, the consumer then experiences **cognitive dissonance**—the unpleasant feelings or doubts that occur when consumers question whether or not they have made the right purchase decision.

To reduce these uncomfortable feelings or to overcome any doubts, the consumer might return or discard the product, choose to emphasize the positive aspects of the purchase experience and ignore the negative issues, or seek approval and positive feedback from friends and family. Whatever the outcome of a particular purchase situation, that experience becomes part of the consumer's field of purchase experiences that will be used as key inputs into the next buying decision process.

PSYCHOLOGICAL INFLUENCES

Psychological influences are forces within the individual that determine, in part, the buying behavior of that individual. As illustrated in Figure 7-1, motivation, perception, learning, and attitudes are the primary psychological influences that help to determine consumer responses to marketing programs.

MOTIVATION   A **motive** is an internal energizing force that directs a person toward a particular goal. It is a determination to meet one or more needs. Motives lead to drives that result in actions. **Motivation** is the mental process wherein **stimulated needs** (the lack of something that is necessary to the well-being of the consumer) lead to **aroused tensions** (the uncomfortable feeling that is activated by internal and/or external stimuli) which result in **goal-directed behavior** (the action taken by an individual to reduce aroused tensions and to satisfy stimulated needs). The need for comfort, rest, approval, affection, acceptance, pleasure, competition, sympathy, cooperation, or warmth are all motives that might influence buying behavior. Exploiting consumers' fears has allowed some marketers to sell a wide array of personal safety products ranging from remote entry systems on automobiles to security dummies designed to deter carjackers who prey on lone drivers.[7] As baby boomers age and sag, Playtex Apparel is rolling out more shapewear offerings (one-piece garments that go from bust to hip) that fulfill the need for more comfort and more control than previously provided by the Victorian instrument of torture—the corset.[8]

One popular theory concerning why and how humans are driven to satisfy particular needs is **Maslow's Hierarchy of Needs.** This well-regarded theory as applied to consumers suggests that they must first satisfy lower-order physiological needs before higher-order psychological needs can emerge as strong buying motivators. This hierarchical rank-ordering of the motivating power of human needs starts with satisfying physiological and safety needs and progresses to needs for socialization, esteem, and self-actualization. Figure 7-2 identifies each of these needs.

PERCEPTION Consumer behavior is strongly influenced by how individuals perceive their environment. Each individual's perceptions are unique, and they constitute a distinctive force in shaping consumer reactions to various environmental stimuli. **Perception** can be defined as the process by which consumers receive, organize, and interpret incoming stimuli. It is the impression created when humans consolidate sen-

FIGURE 7-2

MASLOW'S HIERARCHY OF NEEDS

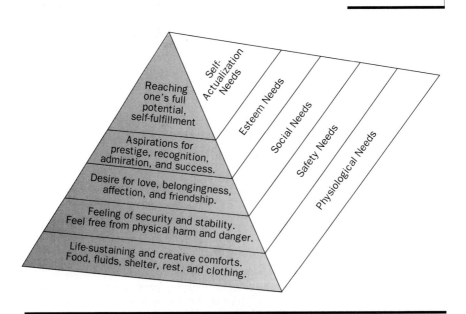

sory information. Consumers "constantly filter a barrage of clues, organizing them into a set of impressions—some of them rational, some emotional. These impressions can be very subtle—even subliminal—or extremely obvious. They may occur by happenstance or by purposeful design."[9] The consumer perception process is shown in Figure 7-3. The first stage in the perception process is **stimulus reception**—a highly individualized sensory function in which information inputs are received through sight, sound, taste, touch, and smell. In stage two, **stimulus organization,** consumers attempt to categorize and order the information they have received into meaningful and useful groupings that enhance understanding and communication. **Stimulus interpretation** is the final stage in the perception process; it entails the acts of assigning meaning to information inputs and using such information to make consumer behavior decisions.

Each stage of the consumer perception process can be unique to the individual person. Because of perceptual selectivity, notable differences in consumer behavior are common even under similar environmental conditions. By manipulating the perception process, each consumer creates a personal view of the world. These individualized views are important to the consumer and are keys to creating niche marketing programs. As illustrated in Figure 7-3, **selective perception** involves the following forms.

▪ FIGURE 7-3

CONSUMER PERCEPTION PROCESS

Selective Perception = Stimulus Reception + Stimulus Organization + Stimulus Interpretation

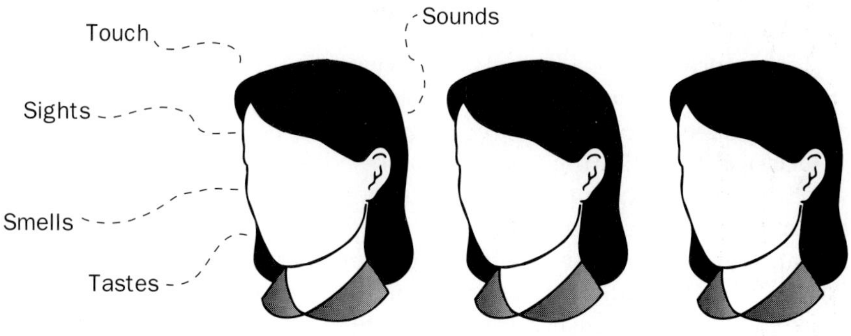

Touch, Sights, Smells, Tastes, Sounds

Selective Perception = Selective Exposure + Selective Retention + Selective Distortion

1. *Selective exposure*—the act of restricting both the type and amount of information input through the use of a screening process that limits our exposure to selective stimuli. For example, subscribing to and reading certain magazines.

2. *Selective retention*—the act of remembering information inputs that are consistent with and supportive of our feelings, beliefs, and attitudes. For example, remembering the safety message concerning a particular automobile but forgetting the high price tag associated with that level of security.

3. *Selective distortion*—the act of changing or misinterpreting information in order to make it more agreeable with current beliefs and attitudes. For example, criticizing a self-service, economy supermarket for not offering bagging service.

While each consumer's selective perception often does not agree with reality, it does serve as a basis for that consumer's decision-making process. It is essential that marketers appreciate and adapt to this rather distorted but operational view of the world as seen, remembered, and understood by a particular consumer.

LEARNING Learning is a behavioral change that results from personal experiences and the acquisition of knowledge. Consumer behavior is learned behavior that is the result of experiences with or knowledge of various marketing programs. Retailers like The GAP clothing stores taught the consuming public that cheap could be chic and coveted by focusing on apparel items that incorporate interesting fabric, texture, color, details, and other personal styling traits. To the dismay of some department stores and high-end specialty retailers, many consumers soon learned that it was acceptable to trade down to discount stores and other value-oriented outlets.[10] The fact that consumers learn to buy certain products or to patronize certain stores is good news to marketers because it means that they can directly or indirectly influence the consumer buying decision process. The bad news is that there is no common agreement on exactly how consumers learn. Three common theories of the learning process as applied to consumers are presented in Figure 7-4.

Classical conditioning is a stimulus-response conditioning process in which a strongly felt inner need is transformed into a drive that impels action. External cues (such as advertisements) direct consumers toward particular responses that can satisfy the need and reduce the drive to act (see Figure 7-4a). **Operant conditioning** is a slightly different stimulus-response process wherein consumers learn to associate specific behavioral actions with corresponding consequences (rewards or punishments). Correct responses, such as selecting a particular brand, beget appropriate rewards, such as dollar-off coupons to be used with the next purchase. **Cognitive learning** is goal-directed behavior that results from a reasoning process relative to new

FIGURE 7-4

CONSUMER LEARNING PROCESS

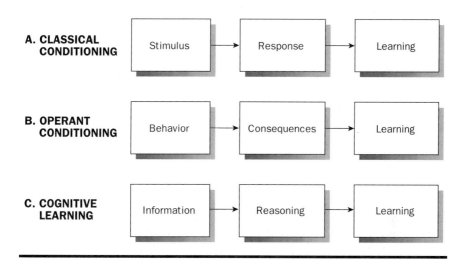

and additional information (see Figure 7-4c). This theory hypothesizes that new knowledge is acquired from problem-solving activities. For buying situations in which the consumer has no or few prior relevant experiences, cognitive learning becomes the focus of the marketer's attention.

Several of the following factors influence the extent and rate at which consumers learn:

- ❑ *Reinforcement*—the comparison of actual and expected results. Learning is greatly enhanced if actual results equal or exceed expected results. Reinforcement by positive buying experiences is a prerequisite to customer satisfaction and strong customer relationships.
- ❑ *Repetition*—the greater understanding that results from repeating a particular behavioral action. Familiarity reduces risks, enhances learning, and encourages repeat behavior.
- ❑ *Participation*—the active involvement with a particular process or task. Active engagement in hands-on experience promotes learning through a trial-and-error process.

The ultimate goal of the learning process, regardless of how it takes place, is to generate return trade and to promote customer loyalty. In developing each aspect of the marketing program, the marketer needs to consider how it can be translated into a positive learning experience for the consumer.

ATTITUDES An **attitude** is a consumer's knowledge and feelings about an object, either a good, firm, or person, or an activity, such as a service, commercial advertisement, or store event. Attitudes can be positive, negative, or neutral. These valuative mental orientations help direct the behavior of consumers by simplifying the consumer buying decision process. Favorable attitudes toward one set of goods and services result in patronage while unfavorable attitudes eliminate another set of products from further consideration. Attitudes are fairly stable feelings learned through personal experiences and social interactions.

Because attitudes are acquired through a learning process, attitudes can be changed by marketers, though considerable effort may be required. The likelihood of success in changing a consumer attitude depends on the strength of the attitude. Strongly held attitudes are difficult if not impossible to change while softer attitudes can be altered somewhat by a well-designed marketing program.

As suggested by the definition, an attitude is made up of three components: cognitive, affective, and behavioral elements. The **cognitive component** consists of the beliefs that the consumer has relative to an object or activity. As a strongly held opinion, a cognition is based on acquired knowledge and information. The **affective component** of an attitude incorporates feelings (fear, love, joy, anger) and emotional reactions that consumers experience with regard to an object or activity. Consumer beliefs and feelings are strong motivators. They lead to the final component of an attitude, the **behavioral component,** the predisposition to act or react in a particular fashion. Marketers impact consumer behavior by developing marketing programs that (1) provide consumers with useful information, (2) generate strong and positive feelings, and (3) solicit an appropriate emotional response.

Personal Influences

Personal influences on consumer buying behavior include several factors that affect how individuals see themselves and how they live their lives. As identified in Figure 7-1, the four personal influences include personality, self-concept, lifestyle, and the individual's stage in the life cycle.

Personality Personality is the composite of all the traits and behaviors that make up an individual's unique character. Personality traits include such characteristics as ambitiousness, competitiveness, aggressiveness, gregariousness, and degree of authoritarianism. An individual's personality is a function of both heredity and personal experiences. While marketers recognize the importance of consumer personalities, the problems associated with defining personality traits and classifying consumers based on those traits are considerable. Logic suggests that a consumer's personality has a significant impact on buying behavior. However, determining specific cause-and-effect relationships of consumer personalities on individual buying behavior is still in the exploratory research stage.

Self-Concept Consumers view themselves in certain ways. **Self-concept** is the set of perceptions, beliefs, and feelings that consumers have about themselves. Consumers have multiple self-concepts; that is, they perceive themselves in several different ways. **Self-image** is the private self; that is, how you see yourself. The **looking-glass self** is your conception of how you think others see you. How you would like to be constitutes your **ideal self.** The way you actually are is your **real self.**

Consumers buy products, choose brands, and patronize stores in a manner consistent and compatible with their self-concept. With the adoption of the self-concept of "thrifty" by a large segment of the market following the conspicuous consumption of the 1980s, many consumers found it acceptable to trade down to used cars and forgo the purchase of new automobiles. The result was that in 1993, middle-income Americans spent more than twice as much on used vehicles as on new.[11] Developing brand and store images that fit the prevailing self-concepts of a targeted group of consumers should be a key consideration in the creation of a successful marketing program. Advertising messages, store atmospheres, product packaging, brand names, and price points are but a few marketing decisions that need to accommodate the multidimensional character of the self-concept.

Lifestyles How consumers live has a profound effect on how they consume. **Lifestyles** are patterns of living. A lifestyle profile outlines the entire mode of living and how individuals interact with their environments. The overwhelming success of the practical minivan has come to symbolize the suburban lifestyle of a cargo-hauling "mommy" whose life revolves around the tasks of transporting kids to school, carting groceries home from the supermarket, and picking the players up after the ball game.[12] As illustrated in Figure 7-5, life-style patterns are the sum total of consumers' **activities** (how they spend their time), **interests** (what they enjoy doing), and **opinions** (what they think of people, places, and things). Lifestyle patterns are also strongly influenced by **demographics** (who they are). An understanding of how activities, interests, and opinions come together to create a lifestyle is an excellent basis for developing product, price, promotion, and distribution strategies. Harley-Davidson Motor Company developed a lifestyle to go along with the sale of its motorcycles. The company marketed its Harley Owners Groups (HOGs), magazines, clothing, and bike rallies in a highly successful effort to create a lifestyle for aging baby boomers trying to feel young.[13] As suggested by one group of researchers, the following is a list of some future lifestyle orientations:

❏ Living my life my way
❏ Enhancing psychological self
❏ Enhancing physical self
❏ Being cosmopolitan

FIGURE 7-5

LIFESTYLE DIMENSIONS

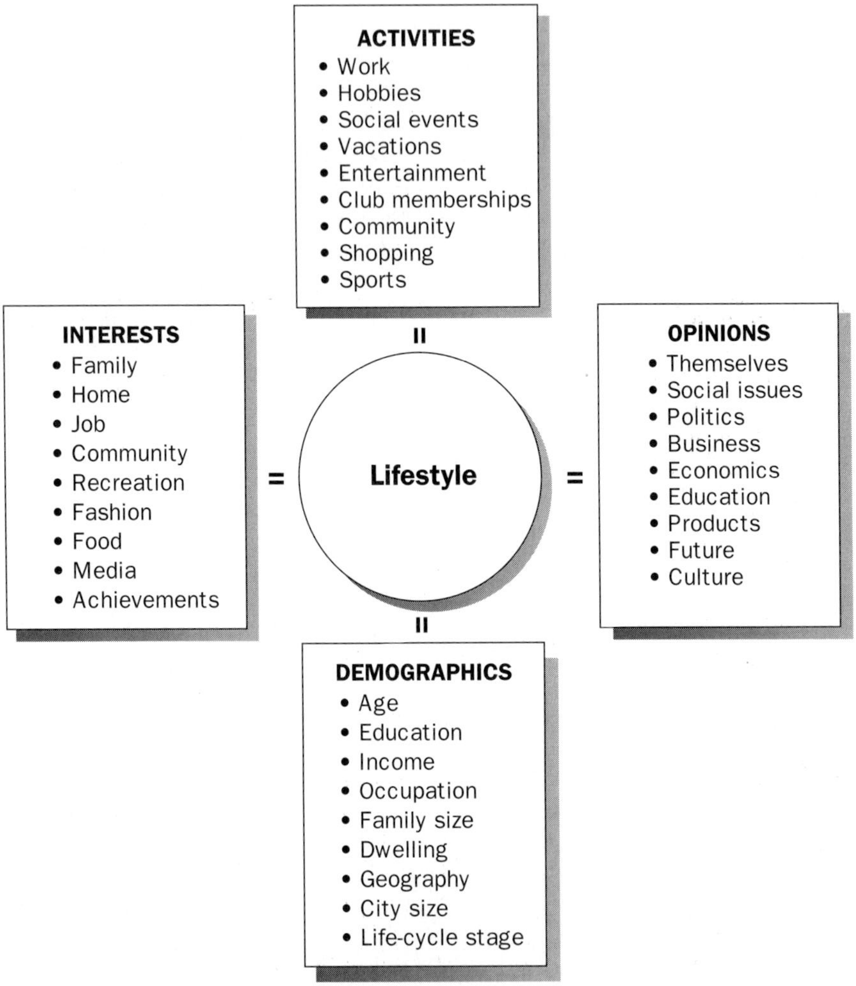

ACTIVITIES
- Work
- Hobbies
- Social events
- Vacations
- Entertainment
- Club memberships
- Community
- Shopping
- Sports

INTERESTS
- Family
- Home
- Job
- Community
- Recreation
- Fashion
- Food
- Media
- Achievements

= **Lifestyle** =

OPINIONS
- Themselves
- Social issues
- Politics
- Business
- Economics
- Education
- Products
- Future
- Culture

DEMOGRAPHICS
- Age
- Education
- Income
- Occupation
- Family size
- Dwelling
- Geography
- City size
- Life-cycle stage

❏ Seeking security and avoiding risk
❏ Valuing leisure and discretionary time
❏ Escaping from it all
❏ Wanting convenience and immediate gratification
❏ Expecting secure living spaces[14]

The analysis of consumer lifestyles, as outlined in Figure 7-5, is often referred to as **psychographics,** which will be discussed in Chapter 9.

LIFE CYCLES What products consumers buy and consume is strongly influenced by what stage in the family life cycle they currently occupy. The **family life cycle** is a series of stages through which a family goes during its lifetime. It profiles the family formation and dissolution process. The family life cycle begins with the singles stage and progresses through various family arrangements and ends with the solitary survivor stage. A description of the nine stages of the family life cycle is presented in Figure 7-6. As seen in Figure 7-6, consumers in each stage of the family life cycle have distinctive demographic, psychographic, and behavioral characteristics that affect what they buy (older married couples whose children are grown buy more expensive items for their homes), how much they buy (large families buy larger package sizes), how they buy (retired, older solitary survivors tend to use a buying process that has proven successful for them in the past), and where they buy (new couples with smaller children tend to patronize value-oriented retail outlets). Marketing managers recognize the practicalities associated with consumers who are in different stages of the family life cycle.

SOCIAL INFLUENCES

Group expectations and social interactions have a powerful influence on the buying behavior of individuals. Conformity to group norms, acceptance by peer groups, and recognition by contemporaries are all social factors that motivate consumers to buy certain products, select particular brands, and patronize certain retail outlets. As identified in Figure 7-1, socially influential groups include one's culture and subcultures, social class, reference groups, and family.

CULTURE AND SUBCULTURES The importance and role of culture and subcultures was reviewed in the Chapter 6 discussion of the social and cultural environment. Cultural influences on consumer buying behavior tend to be more generalized in character; they set the scene and provide the background for the more specific influences exerted by an individual's subculture. Mode of dress, forms of entertainment, use of credit, and types of foods are but a short list of behavioral activities that are determined in part by cultural and subcultural settings.

As cultural diversity becomes the norm instead of the exception during the next several decades, marketers will be faced with a situation wherein each of their marketing programs will be in a continuous state of flux. Changing cultural trends will create extremely difficult problems for the static and passive business organization. On the other hand, highly profitable opportunities will be created for the dynamic and adaptive business enterprise that develops fluid marketing programs capable of accommodating emerging cultural trends.

SOCIAL CLASS **Social class** is a society's relatively homogeneous and permanent division of individuals, families, or groups based on similar interests, activities, values, and behaviors. Social classes are rank-ordered

FIGURE 7-6

NINE STAGES OF THE FAMILY LIFE CYCLE

Singles
(Young people not living at home)

- Few financial burdens
- Fashion opinion leaders
- Recreation oriented
- Buy: Basic kitchen equipment
  Basic furniture
  Automobiles
  Equipment for the mating game such as clothing and accessories, vacations, and other entertainment and recreation activities

Newly married couples
(Young, no children)

- Better off financially than they will be in near future
- Highest purchase rate and highest average purchase
- Buy: Automobiles
  Refrigerators
  Sensible and durable furniture and household items
  Vacation and joint entertainment events

Full nest I
(Youngest child under six years old)

- Home purchasing at peak
- Liquid assets low
- Dissatisfied with financial position and amount of money saved
- Interested in new products
- Like advertised products
- Buy: Washers, dryers
  Televisions
  Baby food
  Chest rubs, cough medicine, vitamins
  Dolls, wagons, sleds, skates

Full nest II
(Youngest child six years old or over)

- Financial position still better
- Some wives work
- Less influenced by advertising
- Buy larger size packages multi-unit deals
- Buy: Wide variety of foods, cleaning materials
  Bicycles
  Music lessons, pianos
  Children's clothing, sporting equipment

Full nest III
(Older, married with dependent children)

- Financial position still better
- More wives work
- Some children get jobs
- Hard to influence with advertising
- High average purchase of durables
- Buy: New, more tasteful furniture
  Automobile travel
  Nonessential appliances
  Recreation and entertainment equipment
  Boats
  Dental services
  Magazines

Empty nest I
(Older, married couples, no children at home, head of household in labor force)

- Home ownership at peak
- Most satisfied with financial position and money saved
- Interested in travel, recreation, self-education
- Make gifts and contributions
- High average purchase of durables
- Buy: Vacations
  Luxuries
  Home improvements
  Club memberships
  Health improvement products and services

Empty nest II
(Older, married couples, no children at home, head of household is retired)

- Drastic cut in income
- Keep home
- Buy: Medical appliances
  medical care, products to aid health, sleep, and digestion
  Security products and services
  Inexpensive recreational products and services

Solitary survivor I
(Head of household in labor force or retired)

- Income still good, but likely to sell home
- Buy: Medical appliances, medical care, products to aid health, sleep, and digestion
  Products and services capable of reducing feelings of loneliness

Solitary survivor II
(Head of household retired, drastic cut in income)

- Some medical and product needs as other retired group
- Special need for attention, affection, security
- Buy: Medical products and services
  Inexpensive recreational and entertainment products and services

classifications based on several characteristics. The most common factors used in identifying social classes include occupation, education, place of residence, source of wealth, amount of income, and family ancestry. While social class standing does impact the buying and consumption behavior of the individual, it would be improper to make value judgments stating that one social level is happier or more fulfilled than another. The following list provides widely accepted classifications for the different social class groupings in existence.

- Upper-upper class (less than 1 percent)—the social elite who live on inherited wealth and come from well-known family backgrounds; tend to be conservative rather than conspicuous consumers; a major market for unique, personal, and expensive goods and services; serves as a reference group and an opinion leader for the consumption activities of other social class groups

- Lower-upper class (about 2 percent)—high-income professionals and business executives who have accumulated wealth from their investment portfolios; upwardly mobile individuals who started in the middle class; active in social and community affairs; buy expensive homes, fashion apparel, automobiles, and other personal items; some are conspicuous consumers in an attempt to impress lower social classes; seek peer class approval and acceptance by the upper-upper class

- Upper-middle class (12 percent)—career-oriented professionals, small-business owners, corporate managers with comfortable incomes; represent a substantial market for quality homes, apparel, furniture, appliances, and personal care products; are civic-minded individuals who seek and support quality education and community services for their friends and family; home serves as a focus for family activities and home entertainment

- Middle class (32 percent)—white- and blue-collar workers who have average incomes and want to live "on-the-right-side-of-town" in better school districts; buy name-brand merchandise and consume prestigious products that communicate their self-concept to other social classes; fashionable and trendy products find favor with this consumer; quality education and enriched personal experiences are seen as vehicles for upward class mobility

- Working class (38 percent)—blue-collar workers and skilled tradespeople with average incomes who prefer a blue-collar lifestyle; not particularly status conscious; tend to be concerned with buying goods and services that enhance personal enjoyment; modern and comfortable household furnishings tend to be more important purchases when home and family are central to social interactions; are traditionalists with respect to family roles and the importance of the extended family; a strong "buy America" tendency

- Upper-lower class (9 percent)—working poor whose standard of living is just above the poverty level; tend to be unskilled workers who are often educationally deficient; purchasing power is extremely limited; securing basic essentials consumes the entire income of this minimum-wage employee

- Lower-lower class (7 percent)—welfare recipients and other long-term unemployed individuals who rely on public and charitable organizations for their subsistence; commercial opportunities are extremely limited[15]

A quick scan of the brief social class descriptions outlined here demonstrates how our ranking within a particular social class affects our outlook on life and our aspirations. The products we buy, the brands we support, and the stores we patronize will be consistent with the social class we either belong to or aspire to.

REFERENCE GROUPS A **reference group** is a group of individuals who serve as a basis for self-appraisal and personal comparison. Reference groups are used as models or points of reference in the formation of attitudes and the development of behavioral patterns. Family, friends, neighbors, and coworkers represent close and personal groups that usually have a direct influence on an individual's behavior. Peer groups, public figures, professional relationships, and social acquaintances are all examples of secondary reference groups that might be influential in directing an individual's buying behavior.

A common practice is to classify reference groups into three different types of relationships. A **membership group** is any group or association to which an individual actually belongs and that has a direct impact on the attitudes and behavior of that person. For example, one's membership group usually includes nuclear and extended families, religious and cultural organizations, and immediate friends and peers, as well as professional organizations and social clubs. A group or association to which an individual aspires to membership is an **aspirational group.** A better neighborhood, a prestigious social club, an honorary fraternity, and a higher managerial position within an organization are some of the more common associative relationships that may be an individual's aspirational groups. Most individuals have associations and relationships with which they try to avoid being identified. Those groups whose values and behaviors are rejected by an individual are referred to as **dissociative groups.** Any group that is at odds with one's current belief structure or behavioral pattern is often considered an association to be rejected.

Marketers must assess the type and degree of influence that reference groups have on the buying behavior of their target markets. Reference group influence can take the following different forms:

- *Exposure*—introducing the individual to new goods, brands, services, and outlets

- *Conformity*—encouraging the individual to engage in specific buying behavior in order to "fit in" and be accepted by the group

❏ *Recognition*—requiring the individual to follow prescribed behavior patterns in order to achieve acknowledgment and appreciation

The role of reference group influence depends on the type of product and its branding characteristics. Reference group influence is quite significant in the purchase of highly conspicuous and visible products (clothing, beverages, and automobiles) and brands (Nike, Budweiser, and Honda). For teenage apparel purchases, "peer pressure is much stronger than any fashion message a store can sell. . . . It's a hormone-driven business."[16] The more distinctive and recognizable a product's brand, style, or model, the greater the likelihood that reference group influence will play an important role in shaping the buying behavior of the target market.

A key marketing strategy employed by many organizations is to identify opinion leaders within each target market and gain their acceptance and support for the marketing program. **Opinion leaders** are individuals within a reference group who exert strong influence on other members by assuming leadership roles based on their stronger personalities, greater knowledge, superior skills, or better abilities. Opinion leaders are often innovative trendsetters who try new products and brands and communicate their experiences to other members of the group. Thus word-of-mouth promotion is highly effective in getting other reference group members to try and adopt a particular product and brand.

FAMILY From childhood on, family influences play an important role in shaping the way we do things. Consciously and unconsciously, we adopt our parents' values and attitudes toward products, brands, retail outlets, and various types of shopping behavior, such as use of credit and reasons for buying. These behavior patterns are then imitated, adapted, or rejected when we establish our own families.

Family buying behavior is frequently described in terms of the various roles each family member might assume in the purchase decision. The family buying process involves several participants who assume one or more roles. Several classifications of how family members interact within the buying process have been proposed. One such classification of family buying roles includes the following five roles that might be assumed by any member of the household:

❏ *Initiator*—family member(s) who recognizes the problem and identifies the need

❏ *Influencer*—family member(s) who directly influences what to purchase and how, when, and where a purchase will be made

❏ *Decider*—family member(s) who actually makes the decision as to what to purchase and how, when, and where a purchase will be made

❏ *Buyer*—family member(s) who actually makes the purchase by visiting the store or placing the order

❏ *User*—family member(s) who actually uses and consumes the good or service

A second classification attempts to delineate the roles of spouses in purchase decisions. Among married couples, marketing research has identified which spouse has the dominant role in the purchase decision for various products. A study by Davis and Rigaux produced the following perceptions of marital roles in purchase decisions.

- *Wife dominant*—purchase decisions made predominantly by the wife with little or no input by the husband
- *Husband dominant*—purchase decisions made by the husband with little or no input by the wife
- *Syncratic*—purchase decisions made jointly through a process of negotiation and compromise
- *Autonomic*—purchase decisions made independently of each other

Wife-dominant decisions include those involving children's clothes, household goods, home furnishings, food, and cleaning products. Many financial and insurance service purchases are dominated by husbands. The purchase of children's toys, outside entertainment, vacations, schools, and housing tend to be joint decisions. Personal products and alcoholic beverages tend to be autonomic decisions. Having a better understanding of how families make buying decisions is one more means by which the marketing manager can gain that competitive edge in building strong and permanent customer relationships.

SITUATIONAL INFLUENCES

Situational influences are the circumstances surrounding a consumer purchase at a particular time and place that have a direct or indirect impact on the buying decision process. A consumer's buying behavior on a leisurely Saturday afternoon while browsing through a local bookstore will be quite different from that same consumer's behavior at an airport newsstand looking for something to read on the airplane. As identified and described in Figure 7-7, situational influences include task definition, social surroundings, physical surroundings, temporal perspective, and antecedent states.[17]

ORGANIZATIONAL BUYING BEHAVIOR

Like consumers, organizations require goods and services in order to accomplish their missions and meet the needs of their customers. Organizational buying behavior is the focus of **business-to-business marketing**—the marketing of goods and services to business users to produce other goods and services, to operate other businesses, or to resell the goods to other businesses or the final consumer.[18]

FIGURE 7-7

SITUATIONAL INFLUENCES

Physical Surroundings
The most readily apparent features of a situation. These features include geographical and institutional location, decor, sounds, aromas, lighting, weather, and visible configurations of merchandise or other material surrounding the stimulus object.

Social Surroundings
Provide additional depth to a description of a situation. Other persons present, their characteristics, their apparent roles, and interpersonal interactions occurring are potentially relevant examples.

Temporal Perspective
A dimension of situation, which may be specified in units ranging from time of day to season of the year. Time may also be measured relative to some past or future event for the situational participant. This allows conceptions such as time since last purchase, time since or until meals or payday, and time constraints imposed by prior or standing commitments.

Task Definition
The features of a situation include intent or requirement to select, shop for, or obtain information about a general or specific purchase. In addition, task may reflect different buyer and user roles anticipated by the individual. For instance, a person shopping for a small appliance as a wedding gift for a friend is in a different situation than he would be in shopping for a small appliance for personal use.

Antecedent States
Momentary moods (such as acute anxiety, pleasantness, hospitality, and excitation) or momentary conditions (such as cash on hand, fatigue, and illness) rather than chronic individual traits. These conditions are further stipulated to be immediately antecedent to the current situation in order to distinguish states that the current individual brings to the situation from states that result from the situation. For instance, a person may select a certain motion picture because he feels depressed (an antecedent state and a part of the choice situation), but the fact that the movie causes him to feel happier is a response to the consumption situation. This altered state may then become antecedent for behavior in the next choice situation encountered, such as passing a street vendor on the way out of the theater.

SOURCE: Adapted from Russell W. Belk, "Situational Variables and Consumer Behavior," *Journal of Consumer Research,* Vol. 2 (1975), 157–64.

Organizational Buying Model

Organizational buying behavior is different from consumer buying behavior. The types of products organizations buy and the methods used in procuring those products are significantly different from the consumer buying behavior process discussed earlier. Figure 7-8 conceptualizes the structure and nature of organizational markets and the buying process used by organizations within those markets.

Organizational Markets

The organizational market is a composite of several different markets. The **industrial market** is comprised of those firms that buy goods and services in order to produce other goods and services. American Airlines purchasing fuel from British Petroleum, Green Giant contracting with a local cannery to can its peas, Levi Strauss buying zippers for its jeans, and Republic Steel's acquisition of iron ore for the production of steel plate are all examples of industrial market transactions. **Reseller markets** involve the buying and selling activities of wholesalers and retailers. Resellers buy goods and services in order to resell them at a profit to end users. Merchant wholesalers, truck distributors, and rack jobbers are all examples of wholesalers who buy merchandise from producers and sell them to retail outlets. Department and specialty stores, discount and variety stores, direct marketers, and vending machines are but a few of the many types of different retailing formats that sell goods and services to the final consumer.

Government markets incorporate the vast array of local, state, and federal governmental units that need to purchase goods and services in order to provide those services for which they are responsible. Purchases range from sophisticated military equipment to basic office supplies. The U.S. government is the nation's largest buyer and accounts for approximately 20 percent of the gross national product. The **institutional market** is made up of a variety of public and private organizations (both profit and not-for-profit institutions) whose operations and buying behaviors tend to be quite diverse. Religious organizations, medical facilities, educational institutions, fraternal organizations, social clubs, foundations, and museums are a few of the organizations that comprise the institutional marketplace.

To facilitate the collection and presentation of information regarding organizational markets, the U.S. government developed the **standard industrial classification system (SIC),** which classifies businesses, resellers, governments, and other organizations according to their primary economic activity. Eleven major industrial divisions make up the SIC: agriculture, mining, construction, manufacturing, public administration, finance, retail trade, services, transportation, wholesale trade, and nonclassifiable establishments. These major divisions are further broken down into industry group, specific industry, product class, and specific product. Using SIC codes, organizational markets can be divided into many different submarkets that are more narrowly defined and more useful to the business-to-business marketer.

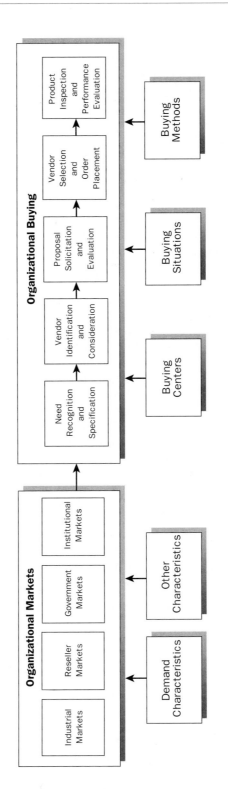

FIGURE 7-8 ORGANIZATIONAL BUYING MODEL

The Census Bureau conducts a census of each of these organizational markets and collects a wealth of knowledge that can be used in profiling the opportunities that each submarket represents. SIC numbers help the marketer to find specific and germane information.

DEMAND CHARACTERISTICS OF ORGANIZATIONAL MARKETS While many similarities exist between organizational markets and consumer markets, the differences between the two are significant enough to require that the business-to-business marketer develop marketing programs tailored to the demand characteristics of the organizational market. Organizational market demand differs from consumer demand in that it is derived, volatile, joint, and inelastic.

The demand for organizational products is **derived** from the demand for consumer products. Organizational products are purchased and used (directly or indirectly) to produce other products. The demand for lumber depends in part on the demand for housing, home furnishings, and other consumer goods made of wood. Close monitoring of current and projected consumer demand is essential in order to accurately forecast organizational demand. Many organizations participate in marketing activities that actively encourage the consumption of their customers' products, thereby building demand for their own products.

The derived nature of the demand for business products can create wide fluctuations. This **volatile demand** characteristic suggests that the demand for business products is more unstable than the demand for consumer products. A modest increase or decrease in consumer demand for a product can result in a much greater corresponding fluctuation in the demand for goods and services needed to produce the consumer product. This relationship is often referred to as the "accelerator principle" or the "multiplier effect." Being highly sensitive to the slightest change in the demand status of consumer goods is a prerequisite to effective organizational buying.

Joint demand means that the demand for one product is closely related to the demand for another business product. The demand for automobiles and original-equipment tires is closely connected. An increase or decrease in demand for automobiles will result in a corresponding change in demand for tires. For better or worse, the complementary nature of many business products results in a joint dependence for market success.

Finally, the demand of organizational products tends to be **inelastic**—an increase or decrease in the price of an organizational product does not significantly affect the demand for the product. This inelasticity of demand for business products stems from the fact that most of the products that go into the making of the final product represent an insignificant portion of the final product's total cost. An increase in the cost of ink to produce this book would have little or no effect on its total sales.

OTHER CHARACTERISTICS OF ORGANIZATIONAL MARKETS In addition to demand characteristics, there are a significant number of other characteristics that help to differentiate between organizational and consumer markets. These characteristics include important product, buyer, and marketing

FIGURE 7-9

CHARACTERISTICS OF ORGANIZATIONAL MARKETS

Characteristics	Business-to-Business Market	Consumer Market
Demand	Organizational	Individual
Purchase volume	Larger	Smaller
Number of customers	Fewer	Many
Location of buyers	Geographically concentrated	Diffuse
Distribution structure	More direct	More indirect
Nature of buying	More professional	More personal
Nature of buying influence	Multiple	Single
Type of negotiations	More complex	Simpler
Use of reciprocity	Yes	No
Use of leasing	Greater	Smaller
Primary promotional method	Personal selling	Advertising

SOURCE: Reprinted with permission from Charles W. Lamb Jr., Joseph F. Hair Jr., and Carl McDaniel, *Principles of Marketing* (Cincinnati, OH: Southwestern Publishing Co., 1992), 115.

differences that distinguish business-to-business marketing from consumer goods marketing. Figure 7-9 compares and contrasts organizational and consumer markets.

ORGANIZATIONAL BUYING

Organizational buying is centered on a five-stage process that takes the organizational buyer from the recognition and specification of needs to product inspection and the evaluation of its performance.

ORGANIZATIONAL BUYING CENTER The buying function within an organization tends to be a group process involving individuals from several different divisions or departments that might be directly or indirectly affected by the purchase. This group of individuals is organized into a **buying center.** This term encompasses all individuals who become active participants in the decision to purchase a good or service. The buying center is not a formal operation located in a specific building or office. Rather, it is more akin to a communications network of individuals who have a stake in a particular purchase. The participants within the buying center vary from one purchase to another and from one organization to another.

Regardless of its structure, all buying centers have individuals who tend to assume one or more of the following roles.

❑ *Initiator*—the individual who first identifies the problem and recognizes the need to make a purchase

- ❏ *Influencer*—an individual who helps to identify the specifications (what products and vendors) under which the product will be purchased
- ❏ *Gatekeeper*—an individual who controls all or part of the flow of information within a buying center relative to a given purchase
- ❏ *Decider*—the individual who actually makes the decision to purchase a particular product from a given vendor
- ❏ *User*—any individuals who actually use the product in the performance of their duties

The marketing manager is ultimately responsible for identifying the membership of each buying center and the roles that each member assumes in any buying decision concerning the manager's products. In prospecting for new business and in qualifying prospective customers, role identification becomes a critical step in the successful completion of the vendor's selling efforts.

Members who comprise the organizational buying center exhibit a wide range of personality types. Richard Lancioni and Terence A. Oliva have developed personality profiles of industrial customers that are useful as a market segmentation scheme and in customizing the seller's marketing and service strategies.[19] The nine personality types include the chiseler, intimidator, screamer, talker, airhead, loyal customer, rude and irate, abusive nitpicker, and stereotyper. Figure 7-10 profiles these nine industrial-customer personality types.

ORGANIZATIONAL BUYING SITUATIONS Organizational buying situations, or **buy classes** as they are commonly referred to, involve purchasing decisions that are made under various degrees of difficulty with various levels of effort. Straight rebuy, modified rebuy, and new task buy are the three buy classes faced by the organizational buyer. The **straight rebuy** is a buying situation in which the organization automatically places an order for a particular product item from an established vendor. Past experience with the product and vendor have been satisfactory; hence, the organization is not motivated to engage in a new information search-and-evaluation process that could be both costly and time consuming. Most organizations have purchasing departments that are responsible for making these routine purchase decisions.

Modified rebuy is the buying situation in which the organization is reconsidering part or all of its original purchase decision and is willing to consider additional proposals. Organizational purchases become modified rebuys when the organization becomes dissatisfied with either the products that are being secured through straight rebuys or the vendors who supply those products. Poor quality, higher cost structures, or inadequate service levels are some of the most common reasons why organizations consider modifying their purchase decisions.

When a new problem emerges or a new need is identified, the organization faces a **new task buy**—a first-time buying situation in which the organization lacks sufficient knowledge and experience to make the purchase without engaging in an extensive decision-making process. Product choice and vendor

FIGURE 7-10

INDUSTRIAL CUSTOMER PERSONALITY TYPES

Personality Type	%	Motivation	Marketing Strategy	Service Strategy
Chiseler	15	Low price	Discounts, volume, freebies	Demonstrate value of the deal
Intimidator	5	Control and power	Detailed specs and procedures	Be firm; follow procedures
Screamer	3	Quick problem resolution	Competitive comparisons	Fast response, empathy
Talker	4	Social interaction	Hand-holding, always available	Refocus on the issue, friendly
Airhead	2	Lazy	No effort, works out of box	Product problem diagnose
Loyal Customer	62	High degree of comfort	Provide extras	Special first-class treatment
Rude and Irate	3	Poor-quality product	Demonstrate product quality	Preemptive product fixes readily
Abusive Nitpicker	4	Distrust	Honest, clearly specified terms	Customer-developed solutions
Stereotyper	2	Low ambiguity	Factual competitive comparisons	Have information at fingertips

SOURCE: Richard Lancioni and Terence A. Oliva, "Penetrating Purchaser Personalities," *Marketing Management*, Vol. 3, No. 4, (1994), 24.

selection become high-involvement problem-solving situations in which the organizational buying center is expanded to handle the complex nature of the purchase. These high-risk purchases tend to involve extensive information searches and to require careful considerations of many alternative proposals.

ORGANIZATIONAL BUYING METHODS Organizations use different buying methods in the procurement of different goods or services. Based on the level of buyer involvement prior to making the purchase decision, buying methods can be classified as description, sampling, inspection, and specification buying. Leasing can also be an acceptable alternative to buying in some cases. **Description buying** involves making a purchase decision on the basis of a written narrative of the product or service. Catalog descriptions and price lists are usually all that are necessary for the purchase of highly standardized products such as cleaning supplies and office products. **Sampling** involves first examining representative samples of a product before making the decision to buy. Agricultural products and other raw resource materials are secured in this fashion.

Inspection buying requires that each item to be purchased first be inspected in order to ensure that it meets established standards. Products that can exhibit considerable variation in quality are often inspected before being purchased. **Specification buying** involves having goods made to the exact specifications of the buyer. Using this buying method, the buyer establishes the quality standards for workmanship and materials. The buyer also determines design specifications or styling elements for each product. The use of specification buying ranges from the procurement of machine tools to the buying of fashion apparel. **Leasing arrangements** are contractual agreements in which the organization agrees to rent a product for a specific time period. The lease contract identifies the terms and conditions of the agreement and identifies the rights and responsibilities of both the lessor and lessee. Leasing is common in the procurement of such high-priced items as facilities and capital equipment. Tax, cash flow, and operating advantages are often cited as the major reasons for leasing as opposed to buying.

ORGANIZATIONAL BUYING PROCESS Having examined the various buying situations faced by members of the organization's buying center and having identified the buying methods used in procuring goods and services, we can now look at how organizations make buying decisions. The organizational buying process is a sequence of five stages similar to the consumer buying process. The five stages are shown in Figure 7-8.

Need Recognition and Specification The first stage of the buying process involves the recognition that a problem exists that could be solved through the purchase of a good or service. Low inventory levels, malfunctioning equipment, rapidly expanding sales, customer complaints, employee concerns, and new production processes are but a few of the situations that could trigger need recognition. In essence, need recognition occurs when the actual state of affairs is not reasonably compatible with the desired state of affairs. Once the need has been identified and the buying center has been established, a detailed description of the need is developed. Need specifications describe the quantity and quality of the goods and services to be purchased and include a **value analysis**—a cost-benefits analysis that examines the cost of the potential purchase relative to the benefits it provides.

Vendor Identification and Consideration At this stage of the buying process, members of the buying center develop a list of alternative sources of supply and evaluate the capabilities of each supplier on the list to satisfactorily meet the specified need. Vendor identification might be accomplished by consulting catalogs or trade magazines, attending trade shows or conferences, visiting merchandise marts or producer markets, contacting sales representatives or sales offices, and listening to word-of-mouth comments of knowledgeable persons. Vendor evaluations are based on production capacities, quality control programs, marketing programs, and past performance records.

Proposal Solicitation and Evaluation In soliciting proposals the organizational buyer invites qualified vendors to submit a proposal. Depending on the nature of the buying situation, vendor response could range from sending a current catalog and price list, to having a sales representative call on the account, to developing highly sophisticated contract bids. Both the submitted proposal and the vendor's ability to perform in accordance with the contract are evaluated. Proposal evaluations are based on such criteria as the suitability and availability of the product, the adaptability of product features to buyer specifications, the order cycle time and the error rate in filling orders, the level of the vendor's delivery standards and special handling capabilities, and the terms and conditions of the sale.

Vendor Selection and Order Placement The fourth stage in the organizational buying process is the selection of a vendor from the list of acceptable alternatives and the placement of orders with chosen vendors. Buyers may elect to concentrate their purchases with one vendor. This **single sourcing** strategy is thought to lower total procurement costs and secure preferential treatment as a reward for quantity purchases and vendor loyalty. On the negative side, concentrated purchases lead to concentrated risks. **Multiple sourcing** is the strategy of spreading orders over several suppliers. This dispersion strategy is viewed as less risky because it offers greater choice of products, ensures backup supply sources, and promotes competition among suppliers.

Product Inspection and Performance Evaluation Product inspection is the process of determining whether vendors have shipped what was ordered (quantity and quality of product) and whether the shipment arrived in good condition. Any shortages, overages, or substitutions are carefully documented. Immediate resolution of any problems are sought from the vendor. Nonperformance records are kept and used in vendor evaluations in future purchase decisions. For the vendor, good performance records can be very rewarding. Because of the extensive costs associated with pursuing each stage of the entire organizational buying process, many organizations develop long-run strategic alliances with vendors who have established steady and reliable performance records. Superior performance by the vendor often leads to the routine placement of orders by the buyer organization.

CONCLUDING REMARKS

Individuals and organizations exhibit a wide variety of behaviors when buying goods and services. Effective marketing requires that the marketing manager not only understand but also appreciate the dynamic and interrelated forces that are at work in each purchase decision. Significant differences exist in what, where, when, why, and how individual and organizational consumers buy. The consumer buying decision process of problem recognition, information search, alternative evaluation, purchase decision, and postpurchase evaluation is greatly influenced by psychological, personal, social, and situational factors. The industrial, reseller, government, and institutional markets, which make up the organizational market, accomplish the buying function using a five-stage buying process that is similar to that of individual consumers.

Endnotes

1. Paulette Thomas, "Peddling Youth Gets Some New Wrinkles," *Wall Street Journal* (October 24, 1994), B1.

2. Kelly Shermach, "Teaching Tots Has Come a Long Way," *Marketing News* (February 13, 1995), 6.

3. Laura Bird, "Department Stores Target Top Customers," *Wall Street Journal* (March 8, 1995), B1.

4. Cyndee Miller, "A Casual Affair," *Marketing News* (March 13, 1995), 1–2.

5. See Milind M. Lele and Jagdish N. Sheth, "Chapter 4, The Four Fundamentals of Customer Satisfaction," *The Customer Is Key* (New York: John Wiley & Sons, Inc., 1991), 81–104.

6. Yumiko Ono, "Earth Tones and Attitude Make a Tiny Cosmetics Company Hot," *Wall Street Journal* (February 23, 1995), B1.

7. Kelly Shermach, "Scared Consumers Shop for Personal Safety," *Marketing* (January 16, 1995), 1.

8. Susan Chandler, "Remember When Bras Were for Burning?" *Business Week* (January 16, 1995), 37.

9. Lewis P. Carbone and Stephan H. Haeckel, "Engineering Customer Experiences," *Marketing Management*, Vol. 3, No. 3 (1994), 9.

10. Teri Agins, "Many Women Lose Interest in Clothes, to Retailers' Dismay," *Wall Street Journal* (February 28, 1995), A8.

11. Douglas Lavin, "Stiff Showroom Prices Drive More Americans to Purchase Used Cars," *Wall Street Journal* (November 1, 1994), A1.

12. Oscar Suris, "It's Useful, Practical, and No One Can Make Me Drive It," *Wall Street Journal* (February 27, 1995), B1.

13. Kevin Kelly and Karen Lowry Miller, "The Rumble Heard 'Round the World: Harleys," *Business Week* (May 24, 1994), 58.

14. William Lazer, Priscilla LaBarbera, James M. MacLachlan, and Allen E. Smith, *Marketing 2000 and Beyond* (Chicago: American Marketing Association, 1990), 39.

15. This discussion of social class groups is based on Richard P. Coleman, "The Continuing Significance of Social Class to Marketing," *Journal of Consumer Research* (December 1983), 265–80.

16. Nanette Byrnes, "Oh Mom, Those Jeans Are, Like, So Five Minutes Ago," *Business Week* (September 5, 1995), 36.

17. See Russell W. Belk, "Situational Variables and Consumer Behavior," *Journal of Consumer Research*, Vol. 2 (1975), 157–64.

18. See Michael P. Collins, *The Manufacturer's Guide to Business Marketing* (Burr Ridge, IL: Irwin, 1995).

19. Richard Lancioni and Terence A. Oliva, "Penetrating Purchaser Personalities," *Marketing Management*, Vol. 3, No. 4 (1994), 22–29.

COMPETITOR ANALYSIS

CHAPTER OUTLINE

- **INTRODUCTION**
- **COMPETITOR ANALYSIS MODEL**
- **COMPETITOR IDENTIFICATION**
  - LEVELS OF COMPETITION
  - FORMS OF COMPETITION
- **COMPETITOR INTELLIGENCE**
- **COMPETITOR RELATIONS**
- **COMPETITIVE ADVANTAGES**
  - COST LEADERSHIP
  - DIFFERENTIATION
  - FOCUS
- **COMPETITIVE STRATEGIES**
  - ATTACK STRATEGIES
  - DEFENSE STRATEGIES
- **CONCLUDING REMARKS**

Introduction

Implementing effective marketing strategies requires a realistic and complete analysis of competitors and their actions. For the vast majority of organizations, the competitive arena is the global marketplace in which competitive offerings fight for customer acceptance. Both domestic and international competitors present challenges that must be met and effectively countered. Competitiveness requires that each organization not only meet the needs of today's demanding consumers but also plan for tomorrow's market opportunities. As described by Hamel and Prahalad in their book *Competing for the Future:*

> Although many of tomorrow's mega-opportunities are still in their infancy, companies around the world are, at this moment, competing for the privilege of parenting them. Alliances are being formed, competencies are being assembled, and experiments are being conducted in nascent markets—all in the hopes of capturing a share of the world's opportunities. In the race to the future there are drivers, passengers, and roadkill.[1]

In the competitive global marketplace, drivers are organizations that orchestrate the terms and conditions under which all other organizations will compete and that strongly influence the nature of the reward system for each competitor. "Passengers will get to the future, but their fate will not be in their own hands. Their profits from the future will be modest at best."[2] Organizations that fail to adjust to current competitive conditions and to plan for new competitive opportunities end up as "roadkill"; they are simply run over by the oncoming traffic of more adaptive competitors.

Competitor Analysis Model

Successful competitive strategies are those actions undertaken by an organization to exploit the weaknesses of competitors in today's marketplace while positioning the enterprise for taking advantage of tomorrow's opportunities. Prior to the selection of the most appropriate competitive strategies, the organization needs to systematically analyze the nature, structure, and level of competition. As shown in Figure 8-1, the **competitor analysis model** involves the following five-stage, sequential process:

1. *Identify competitive situations*—classify competitors on the basis of the various levels and different forms of competition

2. *Conduct competitor audits*—gather intelligence on competitors and their actions from a variety of information sources

3. *Assess competitive relations*—examine the nature of potential relationships among competitors within a defined marketplace

FIGURE 8-1

COMPETITOR ANALYSIS MODEL

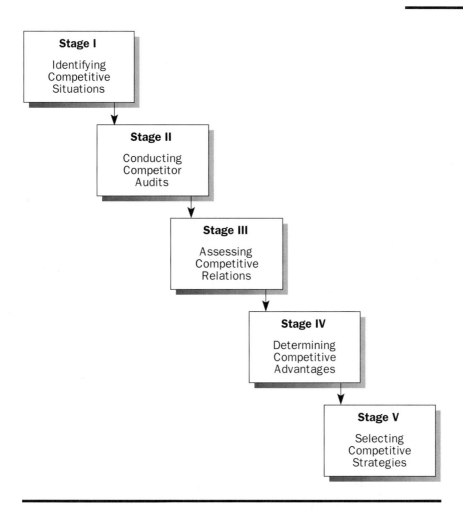

4. *Determine competitive advantages*—based on cost leadership and differentiation

5. *Select competitive strategies*—should be consistent with the needs of the organization and the realities of the marketplace

COMPETITOR IDENTIFICATION

Competitor identification is a precondition to competitor analysis. Identifying who the competitors are is the first stage in the competitor analysis process. At first glance, one might answer the question by making the simple observation that in a general sense everyone competes with everyone else. Lehmann and Winer suggest that the key question is not whether products and services compete; rather, it is the *extent* to which they compete.

> Defining competition therefore requires a balance between identifying too many competitors (and therefore complicating instead of simplifying decision making) and identifying too few (and overlooking a key set of competitors).[3]

In this section we examine the problem of competitor identification from the viewpoint of the various levels of competition and the different forms of competition. While these viewpoints are not always mutually exclusive, they will provide a multidimensional outlook on the nature of competition.

LEVELS OF COMPETITION

Competitive levels can be classified along a continuum ranging from direct to indirect or from specific to general. As illustrated in Figure 8-2, there are four levels of product competition—item, category, substitute, and generic.

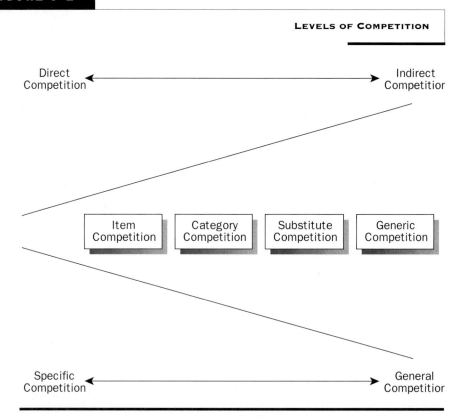

FIGURE 8–2 LEVELS OF COMPETITION

ITEM OR BRAND COMPETITION Figure 8-2 identifies the narrowest perspective of competition as **item competition**—the rivalry among organizations selling the same or similar products to the same target market at comparable price points. This form of contention is specific because it involves direct competition among product items in terms of brands, styles, sizes, models, and features. The competition between a twelve-ounce box of General Mills Total Corn Flakes and the same-size package of Kellogg's Corn Flakes is an example of item competition. This view of competition focuses on competing items that are currently being offered by rivals and typically does not concern itself with what competitors might offer in the future.

CATEGORY COMPETITION **Category competition** involves rivalry among marketers of closely related lines of products with similar features. Markets and the competitors that comprise them are identified on the bases of product categories, groups of products as distinguished by consumer need, and usage patterns. For example, toys, children's apparel, sporting goods, arts and crafts, home electronics, books, and office supplies are all product categories. These identify rather narrow and focused sectors of the competitive marketplace. The importance of this level of competition is made evident by the rapidly expanding retail format known as a **category killer**. Toys 'R' Us, Kids 'R' Us, Sports Authority, Michaels stores, Circuit City, Borders Books and Music, and OfficeMax are all examples of category killers that have the "killer instinct." Category killers use a power format and a sharp focus to competitively dominate their particular category of products and become the market leader within that product category.

SUBSTITUTE COMPETITION A more general perspective on product competition is to view it in terms of product substitutability (see Figure 8-2). **Substitute competition** exists when two different products satisfy the same basic need. The degree of substitution can vary from a perfect substitute, where consumers perceive a product to be essentially the same as another product, to general substitutes, where consumers perceive a product as different from another product but as serving the same general purpose. In both cases, product substitutes are viewed by consumers as viable alternatives to solving a problem or fulfilling a desire. Some examples of substitute competition include rice versus potatoes, popcorn versus corn chips, fruit juices versus soft drinks, movies versus videos, and visits to the Grand Canyon versus Disney World vacations. Currently, Sega Enterprises, Ltd., the video game powerhouse, is racing to build a high-tech entertainment empire that includes indoor virtual-reality theme parks, which will have rides featuring windowless capsules that inexpensively create the illusion of intergalactic warfare or the Wild West. With parks planned by 1997, Sega "will try to take a bite out of Disney. It will try to exploit the efficiency of electronics over iron and steel to create a new entertainment form."[4] In the analgesic market of painkillers crowded with me-too products, consumers have correctly perceived that there is little difference among products. As a result, they have been switching from brand merchandise (Bayer, Anacin, Ecotrin, Excedrin, and Nuprin) to private-label painkillers.[5] To create a perceived difference, Bayer has positioned its new Bayer Select lines as "the one brand to remember for pains from headaches to body aches, arthritis, cold and flu symptoms, sinus problems, and menstrual cramps."[6] By targeting different types of pain, Bayer hopes to make its products something more than just another substitute.

GENERIC COMPETITION The broadest and most indirect level of competition is termed **generic competition**—the general competition that exists among marketers of different goods and services for the limited income and patronage of the consuming public. Each consumer has only so much money to spend and a wealth of product choices on which to spend it. A consumer who elects to attend a concert might have to forgo the purchase of another sweater, contributing to a charitable cause, or taking the family out to dinner.

The preceding discussion of levels of marketing has allowed us to identify competitors from a market point of view, delineating competition based on those competitive efforts to satisfy the same or similar consumer needs and desires. Additional insight into the issue of competitor identification can be gained by examining different forms of competition.

FORMS OF COMPETITION

Competition extends beyond the various levels of product competition just described. Competition also involves interorganizational rivalry, firm versus firm, within a given industry, and rivalry within and among various marketing channels of distribution. In this discussion of competitive forms, we will examine competition from both industry and channel perspectives.

INDUSTRY PERSPECTIVE Viewing competition from the perspective of whole industries allows the analysis to be broad enough to identify the major forms of competition that directly or indirectly impact the organization's marketing effort. In this type of analysis, the competitive set might be defined as the automotive industry, the computer industry, the apparel industry, the pharmaceutical industry, or the consumer electronics industry. Within a given industry the similarity of products generates some degree of rivalry due to the substitutability of the goods and services within that industry. Hence, one of the first steps in identifying competition is to understand the nature of the industry within which a firm operates.

The typical industry analysis includes an examination of the structure of the industry and its attractiveness. Both of these issues have been covered previously. The four competitive market (or industry) structures of pure competition, monopolistic competition, oligopoly, and monopoly were examined in Chapter 6. The General Electric business screen discussed in Chapter 2 is a respected method for assessing the attractiveness of a particular industry. A review of those discussions should enhance appreciation of the complexities of industrywide competition and the type of information needed to conduct such an analysis.

CHANNEL PERSPECTIVE Market competition is more complex than just two organizations competing against each other for the patronage of a select group of consumers. The nature and structure of the relationships among various members of the marketing channel of distribution can greatly impact the form of competition that any particular organization might encounter. Figure 8-3 illustrates the four different types of competition based on the following adversarial relationships:

1. Between members of the same channel
2. Between members of different channels
3. Between one vertically integrated marketing channel and another
4. Between entire marketing channel systems

Intratype competition is the rivalry between two marketers from different marketing channels who occupy the same level within their respective channels of distribution. For example, a wholesaler from one channel of distribution may compete against a wholesaler in another marketing channel. In the case of intratype competition, both competitors use a similar business format to sell comparable products to the same target market. Hence, discount retailers such as Wal-Mart and Kmart are engaging in intratype competition by selling general merchandise to price-conscious consumers using similar retailing formats. The most recent form of intratype competition between Wal-Mart and Kmart involves their newer retailing format, the supercenter (a discount store combined with a supermarket).[7]

Intertype competition differs from intratype competition in that competing parties from different channels use unlike business formats to serve the same target markets with comparable product offerings. Department stores (Dillard's, Macy's, or Bloomingdale's) and specialty stores (The Limited, The GAP, or Eddie Bauer) both market casual clothing to the young adult market. To ensure better coverage of its market, the Goodyear Tire & Rubber Company elected to offer its tires through such mass-market outlets as Sears, Discount Tires, and Wal-Mart, as well as through its traditional outlets of franchise dealers and company-owned stores.[8] In essence, Goodyear created intertype competition by expanding its distribution network.

FIGURE 8-3

MARKETING CHANNELS PERSPECTIVE ON COMPETITION

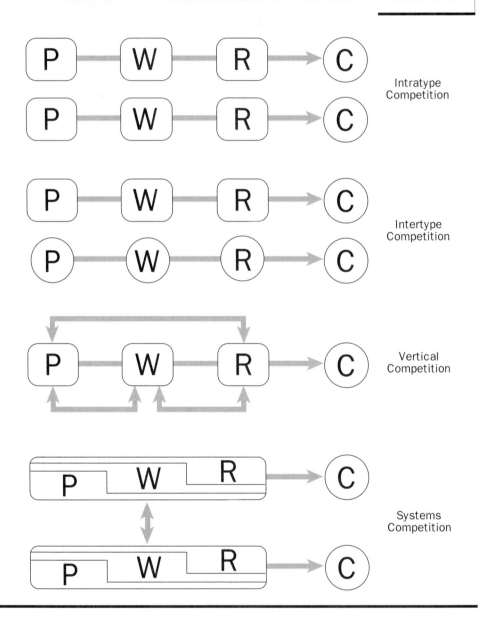

Vertical competition is the rivalry among members of the same channel of distribution. For example, when such apparel producers as Levi Strauss, Liz Claiborne, and Hanes market their clothing through independent retailers as well as company-owned factory outlet stores, the result is vertical competition. Another common example of vertical competition is the case of producers employing both direct marketing (catalogs) and retail outlets. Patagonia, the manufacturer of quality outdoor wear, uses an upscale catalog to complement its 1,200-dealer network.

Systems competition is the rivalry among entire marketing channel systems; it is the competitive relationship that exists among highly integrated vertical marketing systems. By the integration of all levels of the distribution system into a vertical marketing system, operating efficiencies and economies are created to provide the marketing channel with distinctive and sustainable competitive advantages. Many of the nation's largest fast-food chains (McDonald's, Taco Bell, and Wendy's) represent vertical marketing systems that successfully compete against each other.

COMPETITOR INTELLIGENCE

The goal of competitor analysis is to get to know the competition in order to understand their current actions and to predict probable future activities. In order to accomplish this goal, the organization has to gather timely and useful intelligence on what competitors are doing and can do. A competitor intelligence system should be able to answer the following questions:

❏ What are the competitor's core capabilities?

❏ What is the competitor's ability to grow?

❏ What is the competitor's ability to respond to change?

❏ What is the competitor's ability to tough it out? [9]

In answering these and other questions, marketing managers conduct competitor audits using a variety of information sources.

A **competitor audit** is a systematic gathering of information on a competitor's ability to conceive, design, produce, and market goods and services. It often takes the form of a comprehensive checklist of factors that affect an organization's ability to compete. A typical competitor audit includes both quantitative measures and qualitative evaluations of a competitor's capabilities. Figure 8-4 presents a fairly comprehensive list of factors to be considered in developing a competitor audit form. Using the factors in Figure 8-4, each organization designs a competitor audit form that is suitable to the uniquely competitive circumstances of the organization. A successful competitor audit form is able to serve as a diagnostic tool in identifying the strengths and weaknesses of competitive enterprises.

The information necessary for a competitor audit can come from a number of different sources. Our discussion of the marketing information system in Chapter 5 and the supporting material in Appendixes A and B provides a fairly comprehensive overview of the more relevant information sources. Figure 8-5 identifies and describes specific sources of competitor information.

FIGURE 8-4

A COMPETITOR ANALYSIS TEMPLATE

Competitor_____ Analyst_____ Date_____

Summary of Competitor's Position

Overall Management

• Goals	
• New product development strategy	
• Decision-making skills	
• Product and process R&D	
• Innovation/imitation skills	
• Implementation skills	
• Current success story	
• Current mistakes	
• Advantage with buyers	
• Disadvantage with buyers	
• Cost advantages	
• Cost disadvantages	

Comments and Rating of Competitor's Added-Value Chain

Financial Position

• Importance of this profit center to rival	
• Short-term liquidity	
• Access to working capital	
• Access to capital for major expansion	
• Contribution margin	
• Fixed cost/breakeven	
• Marginal cost structure	

Market Position

• Major geographical markets	
• Major target markets	
• Way they segment the market	
• Current expansion efforts	
• Current holding efforts	
• Overall strength	

continued

FIGURE 8-4

CONTINUED

Product Position

• Raw material quality	
• Workmanship quality	
• Design quality	
• Design efficiency	
• Durability	
• Ease of servicing	
• Feature innovations	
• Appearance	
• Brand strength	
• Product range	
• Fit to segments	
• Packaging effectiveness	
• Overall strength	

Pricing

• How much above/below average	
• Percent increase in last year	
• Increases in last two years	
• Margin to trade	
• Volume discounts	
• Payment terms	
• Promotional discounts	
• Leasing terms	
• Buyback allowances	
• Overall strength	

Inbound Logistics

• Sources of supply	
• Purchasing skills	
• Raw materials inventory control & efficiency	
• Overall strength	

Production

• Production capacity (long-term and seasonal)	
• Production efficiency	
• Labor relations	
• Labor turnover	
• Ability to retool/adapt	
• Quality control	
• Production costs	
• Overall strength	

continued

FIGURE 8-4

CONTINUED

Outbound Logistics

• Finished product stock control & efficiency	
• Warehouse/storage method	
• Transportation method	
• Order-delivery lag	
• Back order lost sales	
• Logistics service features	
• Overall strength	

Trade Relations

• Major channels used	
• Image of channels	
• Trade loyalty	
• Trade promotions	
• Trade advertising	
• Overall strength	

Advertising and Promotion

• Message theme	
• Past message themes	
• Media used	
• Schedule/seasonality	
• Effectiveness	
• Cost efficiency	
• Consumer promotions	
• Overall strength	

Sales Force

• Selling strategy	
• Sales force management	
• Sales force morale	
• Sales force turnover	
• Sales force selection	
• Sales force training	
• Sales force discipline	
• Territory allocation	
• Sales force calling cycle and patterns	
• Use of new technology (telemarketing, etc.)	
• Service reputation	
• Overall strength	

SOURCE: Reprinted by permission from Peter R. Dickson, *Marketing Management* (Fort Worth, TX: The Dryden Press, 1994), 140–41.

FIGURE 8-5

MAJOR EXTERNAL AND INTERNAL SOURCES OF PRIMARY COMPETITIVE INFORMATION

Source	Examples	Comment
Government	Freedom of Information Act	1974 amendments have led to accelerating use
	Government Control Administration	Examination of competitor's bids and documentation may reveal competitor's technology and indicate costs and bidding philosophy
	Patent filings	Belgium and Italy publish patent applications shortly after they are filed. Some companies (namely pharmaceutical) patent their mistakes in order to confuse their competitors.
Competitors	Annual reports and 10Ks	FTC and SEC line of business reporting requirements will render this source useful in the future
	Speeches and public announcements of competitor's officers	Reveal management philosophy, priorities, and self-evaluation systems
	Products	Systematic analysis of a competitor's products may reveal the competitor's technology and enable the company to monitor changes in the competitor's engineering and assembly operarations. Forecasts of a competitor's sales may often be made from observing serial numbers over time.
	Employment ads	May suggest the technical and marketing directions in which a competitor is headed
	Consultants	For example, if a competitor has retained Boston Consulting, then portfolio management strategies become more likely
Suppliers	Banks, advertising agencies, public relations firms, and direct mailers and catalogers, as well as hard-goods suppliers.	Have a tendency to be more talkative than competitors since the information transmitted may enhance supplier's business; can be effective sources of information on such items as competitor's business equipment installations and on which retail competitors are already carrying certain product lines; suppliers biases can usually be recognized
Customers	Purchasing agents	Generally regarded as self-serving; low reliability as a source
	Customer engineers and corporate officers	Valued sources of intelligence. One company taught its salespersons to perform elementary service for customers in order to get the salespersons past the purchasing agent and on to the more valued sources of intelligence.

continued

FIGURE 8-5

CONTINUED

Source	Examples	Comment
Professional Associates and Meetings	Scientific and technical society meetings, management association meetings.	Examine competitor's products, reseach and development, and management approach as revealed in displays, brochures, scientific papers, and speeches
Company Personnel	Executives, sales force, engineers and scientists, purchasing agents	Sensitize them to the need for intelligence and train them to recognize and transmit to the proper organizational location relevant intelligence that comes to their attention
Other Sources	Consultants, management service companies, and the media	Wide variety of special-purpose and syndicated reports available

SOURCE: David B. Montgomery and Charles B. Weinberg, "Toward Strategic Intelligence Systems," *Journal of Marketing*, Vol. 43, No. 3 (Fall 1979), 46.

COMPETITOR RELATIONS

Competitive relationships range from hostile conflict to illegal collusion. Dalrymple and Parsons identify and describe a continuum of competitor relations containing five forms of competitive relationships.[10] As seen in Figure 8-6, competitor relations might involve any of the following:

❑ *Conflict*—a serious confrontation between competing organizations that occurs when rivals have mutually incompatible goals, such as gaining market share, at the expense of each other. This type of threat creates considerable strain on marketplace relationships and leads to harsh reactions and retaliatory measures.

❑ *Competition*—a less extreme form of rivalry in which competing organizations attempt to meet and exceed customer expectations by developing a better market program that offers the consumer greater value. The focus of this form of rivalry is on meeting customer needs and less on beating competitor performances.

❑ *Coexistence*—a marketplace relationship that exists when organizations seek to serve different core market niches and compete indirectly in peripheral market segments. Direct competition is avoided via a live-and-let-live relationship with those competitors targeting different market segments.

❑ *Cooperation*—a mutually beneficial relationship in which competing organizations work together for a common goal. Joint ventures, for example,

FIGURE 8-6

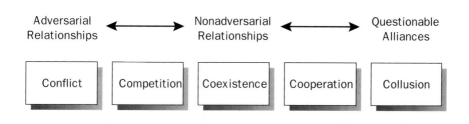

FORMS OF COMPETITIVE RELATIONSHIPS

represent cooperative efforts that are often undertaken to enter a foreign market or secure a scarce resource. Strategic alliances with one competitor are also formed to counter the threatening actions of a third party or to gain a competitive advantage within the marketplace. Delta Airlines has entered into a joint-marketing deal with Virgin Atlantic Airways in which Delta markets blocks of seats for Virgin and in return Delta gets access to London's Heathrow airport.[11]

❏ *Collusion*—a direct (face-to-face meetings, telephone calls, or written communications) or indirect (signaling via public announcements of intended actions) conspiracy to engage in cooperative behavior with the intent of injuring a third party. Collusive actions are often illegal and almost always questionable from an ethical viewpoint.

Given the complexities of the marketplace, most organizations are involved with a multitude of different relationships at any given time. Managing competitor relationships requires that the organization realize the benefits of gaining a competitive advantage without generating unnecessary and overly hostile reactions from competing firms.

COMPETITIVE ADVANTAGES

Competitive advantage is derived from providing customers a greater level of actual or perceived value. If customers believe that one competitor is providing greater value, that competitor has achieved a competitively superior position relative to its rivals within a defined marketplace. Value is defined by customers; that is, value is what customers think it is. Thus, value is a multidimensional concept that can be determined by a host of different factors.

Michael E. Porter argues that an organization can achieve a sustainable competitive advantage by pursuing (1) a differentiation strategy that avoids head-to-head competition by providing customers a new or unique set of benefits, or (2) a cost leadership strategy where the effects of competition are managed by controlling cost structures.[12] Porter also suggests that an equally important consideration is the scope of the competitive field. Is the competitive scope broadly defined (industry wide) or narrowly defined (limited to a particular market segment)? Porter's model of generic strategies for competitive advantage is presented in Figure 8-7; it identifies three basic business strategies for gaining competitive advantage—cost leadership, differentiation, and cost or differentiation focus.

COST LEADERSHIP

Cost leadership is the strategy of gaining a competitive advantage by being the low-cost producer and marketer in broadly defined markets. Southwest,

FIGURE 8-7

PORTER'S MODEL OF GENERIC STRATEGIES FOR COMPETITIVE ADVANTAGE

COMPETITIVE ADVANTAGE

	Lower Cost	Differentiation
Broad Target	Cost Leadership	Differentiation
Narrow Target	Cost Focus	Differentiation

COMPETITIVE SCOPE

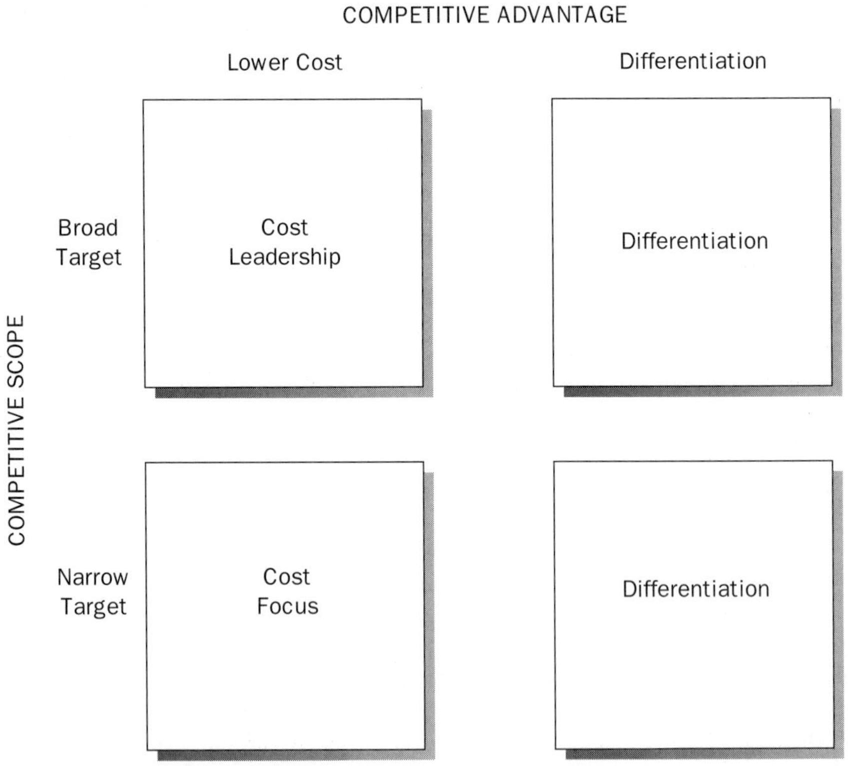

SOURCE: Adapted from Michael E. Porter, *Competitive Advantage: Creating and Sustaining Superior Performance* (New York: The Free Press, 1985).

the Dallas-based airline, has a significant cost advantage over its rivals. Southwest's cost per available-seat mile is 7.20 cents; only Continental Airlines is reasonably close at 7.91 cents. American (at 8.25 cents), Delta (at 9.26 cents), United (at 9.30 cents), and USAir (at 11.09 cents) must all compete at a considerable cost disadvantage.[13] According to Howard Banks,

> What's under way, in effect, is the Wal-Martization of the airline business. The high-cost carriers have no options but to shrink their unit costs to match those of their low-cost competitors.[14]

Chevy assumed a cost leadership role in producing the 1995 Lumina; it has "900 fewer parts than its predecessor and takes 30 percent less labor to assemble. Such efficiency was achieved partly by making many popular features standard equipment, so workers build fewer complicated variations."[15] By offering comparable products at the same price, cost leaders outperform other competitors within the industry because their lower cost structures make profit margins higher. McDonald's improved its cost leadership position by reducing the size of the average restaurant. Lower construction, installation, and operational costs have allowed McDonald's to sell products at prices low enough to draw value-conscious buyers yet high enough to make a profit.[16] By being a more efficient producer and marketer, the cost leader is better able to withstand the competitive threats that emanate from within or outside the industry. Mikasa, a leader in the tabletop industry, is able to market its lines of flatware, serving platters, and Christmas plates at slightly lower prices than either Noritake or Lenox and still achieve higher operating margins. Mikasa's cost leadership position is achieved by owning no factories and contracting production out to seventeen different countries where labor costs are lower and production runs more flexible in adjusting to varying demand for different china patterns.[17]

Cost leadership advantages are derived from a number of different strategies.[18] Cost management might include the following:

❏ Developing superior manufacturing and operating methods that lower capital investment and operating expenses

❏ Designing better products to optimize product performance and production costs

❏ Gaining economies of scale in production and marketing, thereby lowering overhead expenses

❏ Discovering an entirely new way of doing business that promotes operating efficiencies while enhancing product value

❏ Finding more conducive operating locations, which reduces procurement and distribution costs

❏ Improving operations in the sourcing of low-cost inputs

❏ Lowering overall costs by gaining experience in identifying and implementing cost reduction techniques

Cost leadership advantages are sustainable only if barriers (patents, exclusive arrangements, high initial-investment costs) exist that keep competitors from employing the same or similar strategies. The boom in direct-mail computer sales is over. "At one time, low overhead and toll-free order lines gave mail-order companies an immense advantage.... But PC makers got wise fast. Once you take away the price advantage, buying direct doesn't seem quite so good to customers."[19] A competitive advantage built on several cost management actions is usually more sustainable than an edge gained from employing a single action.

DIFFERENTIATION

Differentiation is the strategy of gaining a competitive advantage by offering the consumers products that provide unique benefits and distinctive features not typically associated with competing products. Bristol-Meyers Squibb's new shingles treatment drug, Sorivudine, requires only one daily dose as compared to competitive drugs, which require three doses daily.[20] By being different, the organization avoids direct competition. Competitive advantages can also be gained by developing a marketing program (such as a particular product, price, promotion, or place offering) that enhances the customer's perceived value of the organization's total market offering. Differentiation strategies are directed at broad, industry-wide markets.

Differentiation is more than just being different. As discussed in Chapter 3, it requires meaningful advantages that create superior value. Meaningful product differentiation can be achieved by the following:

1. Providing new functional capabilities that allow the product to satisfy customer needs not previously met

2. Providing a major improvement in product performance

3. Tailoring or fine tuning a product to the specific needs of the customer[21]

Americans want to be in constant touch with work and home. Pagers have some competitve advantages over cellular phones. "They're smaller, their batteries last longer, signals have better reach, their capabilities are expanding, and they are cheap."[22] Creative promotions that contribute to a unique image, new distribution networks that enhance convenience, and different pricing programs that produce better value packages are but a few of the actions that marketers employ to differentiate their marketing programs from the more common market offerings of their competitors.

FOCUS

Gaining a competitive advantage using a **focus** strategy is the result of both the selection of the target market and the choice of either a cost or differentiation strategy. By tightening and narrowing the scope of the target market, the marketer can gain a better understanding of the needs and desires of customers. This consumer focus allows the marketer to identify and develop differentiating factors that are more suitable to the unique expectations of a limited market segment. Organizations are also able to achieve a better cost structure advantage when production, operations, and marketing functions are more narrowly defined by a more focused approach to the market. Colgate-Palmolive has pruned its once unwieldy structure down to five core businesses: oral care, personal products, household cleaners, detergents, and pet foods. A sharper focus has lead to higher profit margins.[23]

COMPETITIVE STRATEGIES

Increased global competition, slow economic growth rates, new technological advances, shifts in population and demographic patterns, emerging sociocultural trends, introduction of new competitive business formats, and changing legal and regulatory constraints are but a few of the external environmental occurrences that have a direct impact on every organization's prospects for future prosperity and continued growth. These harsher environmental conditions have made it necessary for the marketing planner to develop competitive strategies that are capable of enhancing and supporting the reference strategies. **Competitive strategies** are maneuvers and tactics designed to take businesses away from the competition or prevent the loss of business to competitors. In their classic article "Marketing Warfare," Kotler and Singh describe how military strategy can be used to formulate marketing strategies that are effective in dealing with competitors within the context of the marketplace battlefield.[24] Competitive market warfare can be viewed from the perspective of "attack" and "defensive" strategies.

ATTACK STRATEGIES

Attack strategies are aggressive competitive actions in which one organization challenges another organization in an effort to realize some performance goal such as to gain market share or to increase total sales. Attack strategies are "market challenger" strategies wherein one organization becomes an "aggressor" and challenges a competitor who exhibits some weakness (such as limited resources) or who is vulnerable to a particular strength (advanced technology) of the aggressor. In pursuing an attack strategy, the challenger can choose one of the following:

1. Attack the market leader
2. Attack another market follower
3. Attack smaller local or regional firms
4. Attack any established competitor in an indirect fashion[25]

Figure 8-8 illustrates the five attack strategies identified by Kotler and Singh.

FRONTAL ATTACK A **frontal attack** is a competitive maneuver in which the challenger attacks the leader's strengths in head-to-head competition (see Figure 8-8). Publix Super Markets, the Florida-based supermarket chain, switched from a slow-growth approach toward entering the Georgia and South Carolina market to a direct frontal attack on the Winn-Dixie, Kroger, and Food Lion strongholds by opening 28 stores in just more than one year.[26] In this type of head-to-head engagement, the marketing manager attempts to match or top the opponent in all areas of the marketing mix—product offering, promotions program, distribution network, and price structures. In order to be victorious against an entrenched market leader, the attacker needs some differentiating strengths (lower costs, better technologies, or more managerial competencies) or greater endurance (a stronger financial, human, and physical resource base). Frontal attacks are most commonly associated with homogeneous markets that are reasonably covered and served by one or a few established competitors. United Airlines pursued a frontal assault on Southwest's lucrative intra-California air-travel market by developing a low-fare West Coast shuttle operating out of its San Francisco hub.[27]

FIGURE 8-8

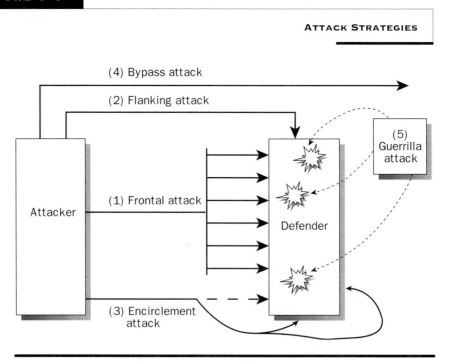

ATTACK STRATEGIES

SOURCE: Adapted from Philip Kotler and Ravi Singh, "Marketing Warfare in the 1980s," *Journal of Business Strategy* (Winter 1981), 31–40.

FLANK ATTACK **Flank attacks** are aggressive marketing maneuvers that greatly enhance the chances of success by matching the strengths of the challenger to the weaknesses of the opponent. Flank attacks are used in situations where the defender is well entrenched in at least one of several market segments and the attacker has limited resources with which to support aggressive competitive actions. When chances are slim that an attacker can directly dislodge a competitor from a heavily defended market segment, the attacker must rely more on outmaneuvering the defenders than on overpowering them (see Figure 8-8). The flanking maneuver involves identifying and pursuing markets (geographically, psychographically, or behaviorally defined and delineated market segments) that are undefended or poorly fortified. By creating a marketing program that is more suited to a market segment left exposed to competitive maneuvering, the attacker is able to meet the unsatisfied needs of a neglected market segment.

ENCIRCLEMENT An **encirclement** strategy involves simultaneously attacking all of a competitor's markets using the full array of the elements of an effective marketing program (goods, services, promotions, prices, and dealers). The objective of such an enveloping strategy is to dilute the opponent's defenses through a dispersion of the opponent's support resources (financial, human, and physical). When a defender has to protect several markets, it is extremely difficult to develop tailored marketing programs that are equally effective in meeting the individual needs of each market. The chances of finding a gap in an opponent's market coverage and capitalizing on a competitor's weakness is considerably enhanced with an all-encompassing strategic maneuver.

BYPASS ATTACK In an effort to build a larger resource base and to prepare for future competitive conflicts, a marketing manager might elect to engage in a **bypass attack** strategy. This maneuver calls for avoiding directly belligerent moves against well-entrenched market leaders. It involves skirting stronger competitors and attacking unserved markets or the underserved markets of weak competitors. U-Haul has targeted the owned-and-borrowed segment (people who own or borrow someone else's truck or van) of the moving market in order to achieve sales growth, thereby avoiding more direct competition with moving companies like Mayflower or other rental companies like Ryder Systems.[28] The bypass strategy can be accomplished by entering completely new product markets (product development) or by opening up new geographical markets (market development). One variation of this strategy is **leapfrogging**—developing and introducing new product technologies that allow an attacker to bypass a competitor by attracting customer patronage through the provision of new and enhanced product benefits. For example, the computer industry consistently introduced faster, more powerful hardware in order to appeal to new market segments. Rather than launch a direct marketing attack on a competitor, the attacker simply leaps over the opponent's defenses using superior product technology to successfully expand within a market segment.

GUERRILLA WARFARE   The objective of **guerrilla warfare** is to gain a limited victory in which the opponent becomes demoralized and grants some concessions (allows the attacker to enter the market on a limited basis). Typically, marketing guerrillas make surprise and sporadic raids on the competitor's smaller, less well-defended markets. These raids often take the form of a localized advertising campaign, a limited price war, an extra service offering, or a specialized sales promotion. To avoid serious retaliation, the challenger limits the frequency and degree with which these guerrilla tactics are used.

DEFENSE STRATEGIES

Defense strategies are competitive actions in which one organization (often a market leader) takes steps to protect and strengthen its current market positions. Most likely, the goal of the market defender is market share maintenance and the retention of acceptable growth rates. Successful defense strategies require the organization to carefully determine *what* markets will be defended and *how* those markets will be defended. Depending on the resource capabilities of the defender, the attack strategies of the challenger, and the sales or profit potential of each market, the defender may elect to defend all or only the most valuable markets.

Equally important are decisions determining what marketing elements will be used to defend each market. Innovative product developments, competitive pricing structures, aggressive advertising programs, comprehensive distribution systems, and creative sales promotions are but a few means for successfully defending markets. As outlined in Figure 8-9, defense strategies include positioning, flanking, mobile, preemptive, counteroffensive, and contraction defenses.

POSITION DEFENSE   The complete commitment of the organization's resources to the defense of existing markets provides the central focus of the **position defense** strategy. In hopes of building impregnable marketing fortifications around selected markets and their current product mixes, the position defender invests heavily in all aspects of the marketing program. Coca-Cola Co. is fortifying its defenses by "tweaking every aspect of its global marketing, adding cutting-edge advertising, new packaging, product sampling, and high profile sponsorships. It is also

FIGURE 8-9

DEFENSE STRATEGIES

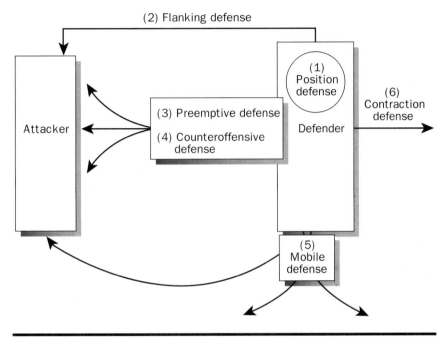

SOURCE: Adapted from Philip Kotler and Ravi Singh, "Marketing Warfare in the 1980s," *Journal of Business Strategy* (Winter 1981), 31–40.

pushing new products out the door faster than ever before."[29] Being a stationary target is the chief limitation of this competitive strategy.

MOBILE DEFENSE Creating more depth to its defense system by broadening its operating base into new and different markets is the core strategic consideration in employing a **mobile defense.** It also involves redefining the organization's business interests away from a product-specific focus to that of satisfying a more generic need (moving from being a simple steakhouse restaurant to becoming a recreation and entertainment facility). Xerox used to call itself an information company because it created products for the office of the future (computers and computer peripherals). Today, Xerox has redefined itself as the "document company" with a focus on products that serve as on- and off-ramps to the digital highway (copying and printing).[30] The strength of this strategic move is that it creates a more fluid situation that is much more difficult for competitors to attack. Moving targets are much more difficult to hit. This market diversification and broadening maneuver also provides the organization with multiple market positions from which to launch counterattacks and strikes against aggressive competitors.

PREEMPTIVE DEFENSE The **preemptive defense** strategy is built around the concept that "the best defense is a good offense." In order to keep potential aggressors off balance and cut off competitive threats, the preemptive defense involves attacking competitors first before they can effectively position themselves to attack you. Both Coca-Cola Co. and PepsiCo have launched fierce counterattacks to halt the spread of private-label colas into new markets. Aggressive pricing, new products, creative advertising, and extensive merchandising are some of the tactics used to limit the spread of private-label soft drinks.[31] By taking the initiative, preemptive defenders put their competitors in a defensive posture, thereby reducing their ability to engage in offensive maneuvers. With a 90-percent share of the microprocessor market, Intel has startled rivals by launching an unprecedented price war. By slashing prices, Intel hopes to establish its Pentium chip as the mainstay of the IBM-compatible, PC microprocessor business before rivals can make much of a showing.[32] Any of the attack strategies discussed earlier could be employed in a preemptive strike.

FLANKING DEFENSE In this hedge-betting strategy, the defender attempts to guard against possible competitor attacks by entering into new and underdeveloped market segments before anyone else. Recognizing that its warehouse concept was easily copied, Office Depot, a chain of no-frills, warehouse-type stores selling brand-name office products at 30 percent to 60 percent off manufacturer's list price, has pursued a superfast expansion strategy in order to forestall competition. Office Depot's strategy calls for moving into ten new markets a year and adding 50 stores a year.[33] While these peripheral marketing segments may not have the same potential as more mainstream markets, they can be denied to the enemy if they are entered first and effectively served. Lowe's Construction, the second-largest player in the home-improvement retailing industry, has limited its expansion to small cities and towns in the Southeast. This selective expansion strategy has so far avoided going head-to-head with Atlanta-based Home Depot, the nation's largest chain of home-improvement centers.[34]

COUNTEROFFENSIVE To nullify the offensive moves of a competing organization, the defender can elect to counterattack in order to force the aggressor to defend its own markets. A **counteroffensive** strategy might involve slugging it out by meeting the attacker head-on (engaging in a price war) or by outmaneuvering the aggressor with a flanking move (developing a special sales promotion program targeted to a specific market segment). What distinguishes this strategy is that it is not a "hold the line" maneuver. Rather, it requires offensive moves that are designed not only to reverse the attacker's intended outcome but also to retaliate for any losses. The Good Guys, Inc., a San Francisco-based retailer of high-quality stereos, VCRs, televisions, and other consumer electronics equipment, responded to an invasion by Circuit City, the largest chain of consumer electronics stores, into northern California by moving into Circuit City's southern California territory.[35]

CONTRACTION DEFENSE Strategic withdrawal from an indefensible market or when facing a superior competitive force might be the only realistic option open to the organization. Overextension into marginal market segments and product categories are common cases in which an organization becomes strategically vulnerable to the aggressive actions of competitors. Eliminating vulnerable markets and products and consolidating defendable markets and products are essential moves in a **contraction defense.** Herman's Sporting Goods had made a clumsy effort to take its Northeast Corridor retail firm national. The organization was saddled with too many stores in too many locations and was losing ground even on its home turf. To save the firm, management conducted a strategic withdrawal from all markets west of Pennsylvania and south of Virginia.[36]

CONCLUDING REMARKS

Every organization must analyze its competitive position in order to gain a clear understanding of its capabilities and the strengths and weaknesses of the competition. To accomplish this goal, marketing managers systematically identify competitive situations, conduct competitor audits, assess competitive relations, determine competitive advantages, and select competitive strategies. From market selection to product development, the impact of competitor actions must be dealt with and planned for if the organization is to be more effective in meeting the needs of consumers.

ENDNOTES

1. Gary Hamel and C.K. Prahalad, *Competing for the Future* (Boston: Harvard Business School Press, 1994), 28.

2. Ibid.

3. Donald R. Lehmann and Russell S. Winer, *Analysis for Marketing Planning,* Second Edition (Homewood, IL: Richard D. Irwin, Inc., 1991), 19.

4. Richard Brandt and Neil Gross, "Sega," *Business Week* (February 21, 1994), 68.

5. Joseph Weber, "Painkillers Are About to O.D.," *Business Week* (April 11, 1994), 54.

6. Ibid.

7. Chad Rubel, "Discount Stores Battle Each Other with Supercenters," *Marketing News* (January 16, 1995), 1, 10.

8. Seth Lubove, "The Last Bastion," *Forbes* (February 14, 1994), 58.

9. John A. Czepiel, *Competitive Marketing Strategy* (Englewood Cliffs, NJ: Prentice Hall, 1992), 346–48.

10. See Douglas J. Dalrymple and Leonard J. Parsons, *Marketing Management—Text and Cases*, Sixth Edition (New York: John Wiley & Sons, Inc., 1995), 224–27.

11. Peter Fuhrman, "Brand-name Brandson," *Forbes* (January 2, 1995), 41–42.

12. This discussion is based on material adapted from Michael E. Porter, *Competitive Strategy: Techniques for Analyzing Industries and Competitors* (New York: The Free Press, 1980), and Michael E. Porter, *Competitive Advantages: Creating and Sustaining Superior Performance* (New York: The Free Press, 1985).

13. Ronald Henkoff, "Smartest & Dumbest Managerial Moves of 1994," *Fortune* (January 16, 1995), 94.

14. Howard Banks, "A Sixties Industry in a Nineties Economy," *Forbes* (May 9, 1994), 109.

15. David Woodruff, "Can a Tune-Up Make Chevy a Contender?" *Business Week* (July 25, 1994), 71.

16. Richard L Papiernik, "Mac Attack?" *Financial World* (April 12, 1994), 28.

17. Damon Darlin, "Accessorizing the Dinner Table," *Forbes* (December 19, 1994), 289.

18. See Czepiel, *Competitve Marketing Strategy*, 47–49.

19. Paul M. Eng, "The PC Is Not in the Mail," *Business Week* (July 11, 1994), 42.

20. Suzanne Oliver, "We're Making Good Business," *Forbes* (December 19, 1994), 191.

21. Czepiel, *Competitve Marketing Strategy*, 52.

22. Matt Walsh, "Beep! Beep!" *Forbes* (August 15, 1994), 66.

23. Jane A. Sasseen, "For Colgate-Palmolive, It's Time for Trench Warfare," *Business Week* (September 19, 1994), 56.

24. This discussion is adapted from Philip Kotler and Ravi Singh, "Marketing Warfare," *Journal of Business Strategy* (Winter 1981), 30–41. Also see Philip Kotler, Liam Fahey, and Somkid Jatusripitak, *The New Competition* (Englewood Cliffs, NJ: Prentice-Hall, Inc., 1985).

25. See Orville C. Walker, Jr., Harper W. Boyd, Jr., and Jean-Claude Lerreche, *Marketing Strategy: Planning and Implementation* (Homewood, IL: Irwin, 1992), 283.

26. Matt Walsh, "The Schwarzkopf Gambit," *Forbes* (November 21, 1994), 170, 174.

27. Wendy Zellner, "Dogfight Over California," *Business Week* (August 15, 1995), 32.

28. Seth Lubove, "American Gothic," *Forbes* (November 21, 1994), 120–21.

29. Maria Mallory, "Behemoth on a Tear," *Business Week* (October 3, 1994), 54.

30. Subrata N. Chakravarty, "Back in Focus," *Forbes* (June 6, 1994), 72.

31. William C. Symonds, "A Third Front in the Cola Wars," *Business Week* (December 12, 1994), 66.

32. Robert Hof, "Fortress Intel," *Business Week* (August 22, 1994), 28.

33. Zina Moukheiber, "A Lousy Day for Golf," *Forbes* (May 9, 1994), 60.

34. Maria Mallory, "This Do-It-Yourself Store Is Really Doing It," *Business Week* (May 2, 1994), 108.

35. Marc Ballon, "We're the Good Guys," *Forbes* (January 16, 1995), 48.

36. David S. Fondiller, "A Turnaround Is a Turnaround," *Forbes* (November 21, 1994), 60.

MARKET ANALYSIS

CHAPTER OUTLINE

- **INTRODUCTION**
- **MARKET ANALYSIS**
    - DEFINING A MARKET
    - ANALYZING A MARKET
- **MARKET SEGMENTATION**
    - STEP 1: IDENTIFYING MARKET SEGMENTS
    - STEP 2: PROFILING MARKET SEGMENTS
    - STEP 3: EVALUATING MARKET SEGMENTS
- **MARKET TARGETING**
    - STEP 4: SELECTING MARKET SEGMENTS
    - STEP 5: TARGETING MARKET SEGMENTS
- **MARKET POSITIONING**
    - STEP 6: DEVELOPING POSITIONING STRATEGIES
    - STEP 7: TAILORING MARKETING MIXES
- **CONCLUDING REMARKS**

INTRODUCTION

The important tasks of identifying and selecting markets are essential prerequisites to developing a viable marketing program and a successful organization. Poorly defined markets lead to poorly designed marketing programs. An incorrect delineation of the marketplace puts the organization at a competitive disadvantage that even the best conceived marketing mix of products, places, prices, and promotions might not be able to overcome. The ability to conduct a well-conceived market analysis is a key component of any marketing manager's list of competencies.

MARKET ANALYSIS

DEFINING A MARKET

What is a market? The term *market* has a number of different connotations. The term *market* can refer to a specific location, a geographic area, the demand for a particular product, or the act of selling something. Our usage of the term *market* is very specific. As illustrated in Figure 9-1, a **market** is a group of individuals or organizations (**consumer population**) who have needs and desires they want satisfied (**consuming purpose**) and who have the willingness, ability, and authority to patronize those marketing programs capable of meeting their needs (**consumption potential**).

A consumer population can be either final consumers who buy products for their own use (consumer markets) or such organizational buyers as producers, wholesalers, retailers, and institutions who purchase products for use in their businesses (organizational markets). Individuals and organizations create demand for goods and services only when they have

FIGURE 9-1

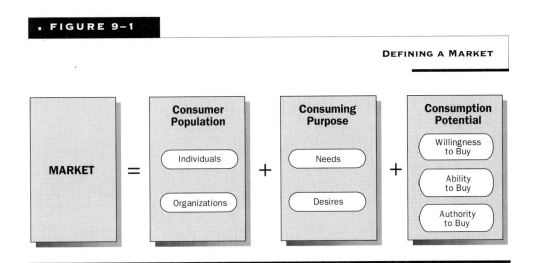

DEFINING A MARKET

needs (essential physiological or psychological requirements) and desires (nonessential wants or wishes) that are unfulfilled or otherwise unsatisfied (see Chapter 1). Markets are made up of qualified consumers who have the willingness to buy (the belief that the marketer is offering something of value), the ability to buy (the availability of sufficient financial resources in terms of income, credit, and assets), and the authority to buy (the individual or the person within the organization buying center who makes the purchase decision).

Figure 9-2 presents a hierarchy of markets based on consumer needs, similar consumer characteristics, and the size of the market. This hierarchical structure of the marketplace is described by one writer in the following manner:

> First came the mass market, that vast, undifferentiated body of consumers who received identical, mass-produced products and messages—any color of car so long as it was black. Then came market segmentation, which divided still-anonymous consumers into smaller groups with common demographic and psychographic characteristics. Now, new generations of faster, more powerful computers are enabling marketers to zero in on ever-smaller niches of the population, ultimately aiming for the smallest consumer segment of all: the individual.[1]

FIGURE 9-2

SEGMENTING A MARKET

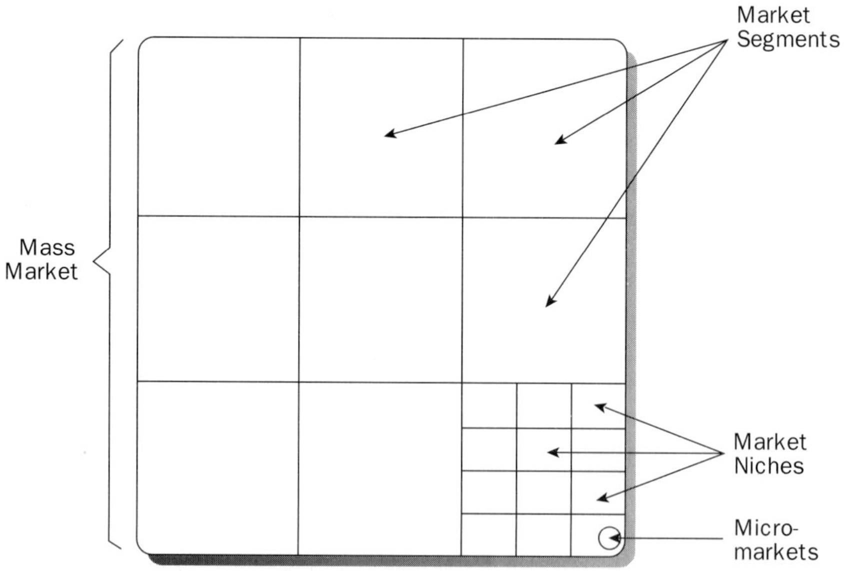

Mass Market

Market Segments

Market Niches

Micro-markets

Market structures range from large, heterogeneous mass markets to small, homogeneous submarket segments, niches, and micromarkets.

A **mass market** is a heterogeneous grouping of actual or potential consumers for a general category of products. For example, the mass market for shoes would include everyone who is in the market for a pair of shoes regardless of their specific needs. Household goods, apparel, building supplies, toys, automotive, legal services, recreation, and entertainment are all broad product descriptions that identify mass markets. In mass market structures, consumers are not differentiated on the basis of their needs or characteristics.

Market segments are more narrowly defined homogeneous subdivisions of the mass market. They consist of individuals or organizations who have one or more similar characteristics that influence their buying behavior with respect to a specific category of goods or services. In the car-rental business, Hertz, Avis, and Alamo specialize in airport rental cars for business and leisure travelers while Enterprise has made its mark in the low-budget insurance-replacement market.[2] Within these broader market segments, car-rental companies further segment their markets based on such needs as comfort, economy, and safety; these product markets include subcompact, compact, midsize, full size, and luxury segments.

Market niches are small and narrowly defined submarkets that are comprised of consumers who have distinctive needs and several unique characteristics that strongly impact their buying behavior. As such, niches represent homogeneous markets. Reebok and Nike have convinced consumers that owning a single pair of sneakers is not enough. A serious athlete has tennis shoes, basketball shoes, running shoes, walking shoes, aerobic shoes, cross-training shoes, boating shoes, and so on. "Today, 24 percent of all Americans aged eighteen to seventy-five own four or more pairs of sneakers."[3] Callaway Golf offers its oversized Big Bertha drivers with a larger "sweet spot," which enables most duffers to drive the ball farther and straighter. Cobra Golf targeted the same market niche by specializing in irons with oversized heads and graphite shafts.[4] Small specialty breweries like New Belgium Brewing Co. in Fort Collins, Colorado, are carving out a market niche by offering such fruit-flavored brews as Raspberry Beer and Old Cherry Ale.[5] Oldsmobile's new model, the Aurora, is a niche car designed to attract the affluent, quality-conscious baby boomer who never considered buying an Oldsmobile before.[6]

A **micromarket** is defined as a single individual or organization with a unique set of needs or desires. Levi Strauss has been able to sell made-to-order Levi's jeans for women. Store clerks "use a personal computer and the customer's vital statistics to create what amounts to a digital blue jeans blueprint. When transmitted electronically to Levi's factory in Tennessee, this computer file instructs a robotic tailor to cut a bolt of denim precisely to the women's measurements."[7] The term is also used to describe other small markets consisting of a limited number of customers in a restricted geographical area. For example, many companies are now developing store-specific marketing programs to meet the needs of a localized customer base.

ANALYZING A MARKET

Market analysis attempts to simplify and organize the rather complex marketplace by identifying clusters of consumers who have similar needs and exhibit similar buying behavior patterns. By grouping consumers into more meaningful submarkets, marketers can then target those market segments that are most consistent with the organization's mission. Having a greater understanding of the marketplace also allows the organization to gain a competitive advantage by uniquely positioning its marketing programs to the specific needs of a more homogeneous market segment. The rationale behind market segmenting, targeting, and positioning is that marketing managers are better able to develop marketing programs that meet the needs of a limited number of consumers than they are to satisfy the highly diverse needs of the total market.

Figure 9-3 conceptualizes market analysis as a three-stage process with several steps within each stage. Our discussion of market analysis is organized around this three-stage model.

FIGURE 9-3

A MARKET ANALYSIS MODEL

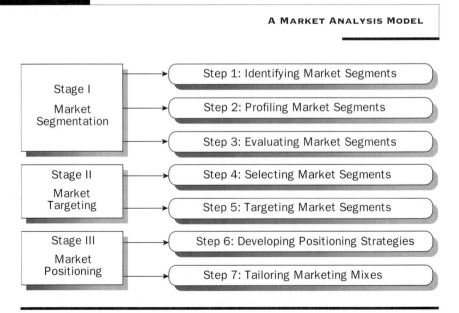

Market Segmentation

Market segmentation is the act of dividing the mass market into smaller, homogeneous submarkets. Groupings of similar consumers have similar needs. The market segmentation process identifies individual market segments that are more meaningful to the individual marketing manager than is the totality of the market. The ultimate goal of market segmentation is to identify target market segments for which the marketer creates and tailors the marketing mix and focuses company operations. In this first stage of the market analysis process, market segmentation is accomplished by identifying, profiling, and evaluating individual market segments (see Figure 9-3).

Step 1: Identifying Market Segments

Markets can be subdivided on the basis of any variable or combination of variables that clearly distinguishes consumers from one another. Among these variables are customer needs, desires, preferences, and characteristics. By segmenting markets into more similar and therefore more meaningful consumer groupings, marketing managers can better predict how those consumers will respond to different marketing programs. The trick is to select variables that are important to the marketing of a particular product classification. Figures 9-4 and 9-5 provide an overview of the basic means by which marketers identify markets. As seen in Figure 9-4, consumer markets are segmented using geographic, demographic, geodemographic, psychographic, and behavioristic variables. Segmentation variables used in segmenting organizational markets are highlighted in Figure 9-5.

Geographic Segmentation Geographic segmentation is accomplished by identifying and describing markets in terms of their physical location and the extent of the area they encompass. This spatial approach to market segmentation divides markets into international, national, regional, and local markets. Geographic segments are also identified in terms of trading areas, neighborhoods, sites, and physical or environmental areas. Figure 9-4 identifies and describes the key variables used in geographic segmentation.

Some of the most useful and readily available sources for delineating geographic market segments are the various census areas that have been established by the U.S. Census Bureau. Each of the bureau's nine different censuses (Censuses of Population, Housing, Governments, Agriculture, Construction, Business, Manufacturing, Mineral Industries, and Transportation) reports data by national, regional, state, county, and city areas. Local city and neighborhood market areas can be identified by using census tract and census block designation.

Demographic Segmentation Demographic variables are personal characteristics by which every individual can be described. Marketers use age, sex, race, education, income, occupation, family structure, and reli-

FIGURE 9-4

MARKETING SEGMENTATION VARIABLES USED IN IDENTIFYING CONSUMER MARKET SEGMENTS

Geographic Segmentation	
International	Western Europe, Pacific Rim, Latin America, Africa, Islamic nations
Regional	U.S. Census regions (New England, Mid-Atlantic, South-Atlantic, East South-Central, East North-Central, West North-Central, Southwest-Central, Mountain, and Pacific states); and media regions (*Newsweek's* regional markets—Western, West Central, East Central, Eastern, and Southern)
Local	U.S. Census Areas (Metropolitan Statistical Areas, Primary Metropolitan Statistical Areas and Consolidated Metropolitan Statistical Areas); local political areas (counties, cities, and townships); media areas (Arbitron Company's Areas of Dominant Influence); and population density areas (urban, suburban, and rural areas)
Trading Areas	Central business districts (Seattle, Kansas City, Milwaukee, and Orlando); shopping centers (megamalls, mixed-use centers, superregional centers, regional malls, power strips, and community and neighborhood convenience centers.
Neighborhoods	U.S. Census Units (Census Tracts and Census Blocks); and ZIP Code Area
Sites	Mailing addresses, telephone numbers, and fax numbers
Physical	Land use (residential, commercial, industrial, and recreational); soil groups (red, podzol, prairie, and steppe); natural vegetation (broadleaf-coniferous forest, grasslands, desert, and chaparral); and weather zones (temperature, precipitation, sunshine, and humidity)
Demographic Segmentation	
Age	Age categories (0 to 3 baby market, 4 to 12 youth market, 13 to 19 teen market, 20 to 29 young adult market, 30 to 49 middle-age market, 50 to 69 mature market, and 70 and above senior citizens market)
Sex	Gender categories (females and males)
Race	Racial categories (African-Americans, Hispanic-Americans, Asian-Americans, Pacific Island Americans, white Americans, and other racial groups)
Education	Educational levels (elementary, secondary, junior college, college, graduate, and postgraduate)

continued

gious affiliation, among other variables, to identify and profile market segments. Figure 9-4 presents several ways markets might be divided using demographic segmentation. Demographic characteristics describe

FIGURE 9–4

CONTINUED

Income	Income levels (low income—under $25,000, middle income—$25,000 to $100,000, and high income—over $100,000
Occupation	Occupational categories (unemployed, professional, technical, clerical, supervisors, retired)
Family	Family structures (single with no children, married with children, single with children)
Religion	Religious sect or beliefs (Jewish, Catholic, Muslim, Protestant, Hindu)
Geodemographic Segmentation	
Geodemographic Markets	Gannett Company's Nine Geodemographic Nations; Claritas Corporation's Potential Rating Index for ZIP Markets (PRIZM); National Data Systems' VISION program; and European database A Classification of Residential Neighborhoods (ACORN)
Psychographic Segmentation	
Social Class	Upper-Upper, Lower-Upper, Upper-Middle, Middle, Working, Upper-Lower, Lower-Lower
Lifestyles	SRI International's Values and Lifestyles (VALS) segments (Actualizers, Fulfilled, Achievers, Experiencers, Believers, Strivers, Makers, and Strugglers)
Personality	Authoritarian, Ambitious, Aggressive, Compulsive, Competitive, Extroverted, Gregarious, Innovative, and Persuasible
Behavioristic Segmentation	
User Status	User, Nonuser, Former User, and Potential User
Usage Rate	Heavy Users, Moderate Users, and Light Users
Usage Occasion	Common Use and Special Use
Usage Regularity	Sporadic User and Continuous User
Benefits Sought	Acceptance, Convenience, Dependability, Economy, Image, Quality, Security, Selection, Service, Status, Recognition, and Value
Patronage Reason	Product Variety and Assortment, Store Location and Atmospherics, Service Offering and Levels, Pricing Programs and Levels, and Promotional Programs and Activities
Loyalty Status	Unreliable, Minimally Loyal, Moderately Loyal, and Totally Loyal
Readiness Stage	Unaware, Aware, Informed, Interested, Disposed, and Intending to Buy

who we are; hence, they are important factors in determining how we behave as consumers. Having discussed demographics in Chapters 6 and 7, we will limit this discussion to the following examples of demographic segmentation: Mail-order companies such as Lands' End, Spiegel,

FIGURE 9–5

MARKET SEGMENTATION VARIABLES USED IN IDENTIFYING ORGANIZATIONAL MARKETS

Geographic Location	The geographic location and extent of the market—international, national, regional, and local market segments
Customer Type	Standard Industrial Classification (SIC) system of organizational types—agriculture, forestry, and fishing; mining; construction; manufacturing; transportation and utilities; wholesale and retail trade; finance, insurance, and real estate; services; government; and other
Customer Size	Organizational size in terms of sales volume, number of employees, number of facilities, and volume of purchase; account size in terms of small, medium, and large order quantities
Product Usage	End-use application of products in terms of how consumers use a product; performance, design, quality, and cost specifications; usage rate in terms of heavy or light use of the product
Purchase Criteria	Purchase decision criteria in terms of what factors are used in making the buying decision and how important is each of the factors; product quality, delivery standards, terms and conditions of sale, service support, and pricing program
Purchase Situation	Level of experience with the purchase situation: straight rebuy, modified rebuy, or new buy

and Fingerhut experienced rapid growth by targeting two-earner families who do not have time to make lots of trips to the mall. For this demographic market segment, "shopping at home is more comfortable and a time-saver."[8] Tower Records, Musicland, Wherehouse Entertainment, Music Plus, and most of the other big record store chains target urban adolescents and postadolescents—the MTV crowd. In contrast, Borders Book and Music aims for a demographic segment that can be described as college educated, more than age thirty-five, with higher income levels.[9] Educational toy marketers aim for a different market segment by practicing "stealth marketing" in which they peddle pedagogically correct diversions by targeting parental anxiety—buying toys that are supposed to be good for children.[10] Colgate-Palmolive (Fabuloso household cleaners), Nestlè (Nestum instant cereals), PepsiCo Food International (Gamesa cookies and pasta), CPC International (Fruquo spicy ketchup), and Goya Foods (nopalitos—sliced cactus) are all food giants who have discovered the U.S. Hispanic market and have developed immigrant brands to serve that market.[11] Walt Disney is expanding its demographic appeal beyond the traditional family by advertising to couples without kids and to retirees.[12]

GEODEMOGRAPHIC SEGMENTATION   **Geodemography** is the practice of linking demographic characteristics with various geographic locations in order to identify more meaningful market segments based on both the "who" and "where" of consumer behavior. This approach to market segmentation epitomizes the old saying "birds of a feather flock together."[13] Several commercial marketing research firms have developed their version of a geodemographic segmentation process, but we will discuss only two of them.

Nine Geodemographic Nations   A unique regional perspective of the United States divides it into nine geodemographic nations based on demographic and lifestyle characteristics. This broad yet useful view of regional differences and preferences is presented in Figure 9-6.

Potential Rating Index for ZIP Markets (PRIZM)   This geodemographic segmentation procedure was developed by the Claritas Corporation, combining lifestyle dimensions and ZIP Code areas into neighborhood markets. This segmentation system defines every neighborhood in the United States down to the ZIP + four level. PRIZMs represent geodemographic clusters of shoppers that are delineated by combining ZIP Code locations with census data, consumer surveys, and other primary and secondary information. Figure 9-7 presents a sample of PRIZM clusters.

PSYCHOGRAPHIC SEGMENTATION   Social classes, lifestyles, and personality traits form the bases for psychographic segmentation. Each of these psychographic variables was defined and described in Chapter 7. Our discussion here will be limited to one of the most widely used psychographic segmentation schemes, the **VALS 2 System,** based on individual values (VA) and lifestyles (LS). VALS 2 divides consumers into eight groups as defined by their psychological makeup or self-orientation (that is, patterns of attitudes and activities that help people reinforce, sustain, or even modify their social image) and their available resources (their education, income, self-confidence, health, eagerness to buy, intelligence, and energy level).[14]

Based on self-orientation, consumers are grouped into (1) principle-oriented individuals who are guided by their beliefs and opinions, (2) status-oriented individuals who are influenced by others, or (3) action-oriented individuals who seek activity and take risks. Resource availability ranges from individuals with minimal resources to those with abundant assets. The eight VALS 2 segments are profiled in Figure 9-8. As seen in Figure 9-8, the goal of the VALS 2 system is to explain why and how individual consumers make purchase decisions.

BEHAVIORISTIC SEGMENTATION   Descriptive segmentation schemes identify market segments in terms of who consumers are (demographic) and where they are (geographic). A more useful segmentation can be achieved using variables that describe how consumers behave relative to brands, products, firms, and stores. **Behavioristic segmentation** is the

FIGURE 9-6

THE NINE GEODEMOGRAPHIC NATIONS

New England	Contains Maine, Vermont, New Hampshire, Massachusetts, Connecticut, and Rhode Island. Residents are typically older than in other regions and boast the highest proportion of executives and professionals; they reflect a high incidence of two-earner couples, and they are open to alternative shopping methods, such as shopping by mail.
Atlantic Expanse	Comprised of New York, New Jersey, Pennsylvania, West Virginia, Maryland, and Delaware. The most populous region with the highest proportion of white-collar workers, it has one of the highest proportions of single, young adults but is last in terms of households with children. As consumers, they are individualistic in their buying styles and, with a fast-paced lifestyle, prefer the centralized convenience and variety of stores found in malls.
New South	Lining the southernmost point in the U.S. coastline from Virginia to Key West, Florida, New Southerners are characterized as "belongers" and tend to be conservative in outlook. They are also cosmopolitan and like to keep pace with the trends. They have, for example, the distinction of having one of the highest ownerships of compact disc players.
Traditional South	States located in the center of the Cotton Belt. Residents are still struggling with economic and social problems, and retail sales per household are lower by far than in any other region of the country. However, these customers are very brand loyal.
Gulf Coast	Described as the bridge between the South and the West. Populated by many more "self-made" men and women, the region's consumers tend to be value-oriented and conformist in their shopping—and shopping is a popular sport for them.
Heartland	Made up of seven "breadbasket" states and including urban centers such as Kansas City, Des Moines, and Minneapolis. Consumer buying styles reflect conservative values, and shoppers lead the nation in purchases of kitchen conveniences like dishwashers and microwaves. These consumers are also "world-class browsers."
"Made in the U.S.A."	This "nation" is located east of the Heartland and encompasses the U.S. motor capital, Detroit. Living here are the greatest number of economic nationalists; Sears catalogs are probably the most-thumbed reading material in their homes.
Western Horizons	Geographically the largest of the regions and includes Wyoming, Montana, Oregon, and the Pacific Northwest. The region boasts a highly educated populace and more children under age eighteen than any other. Its consumers tend to be impulsive shoppers, doing more than average buying by mail or telephone.
Multicultures Region	Dominated by California, plus New Mexico, Arizona, and southern Texas. Residents are young, affluent, highly educated, dynamic, and informed, with active lifestyles. As consumers, they reflect their upscale situations in buying patterns and boast above-average per-household retail sales.

SOURCE: "Geodemography: Tracking Where Customers Live," *Stores* (November 1989), 42–43. Reprinted by permission of *Stores*. Copyright by National Retail Merchants Association.

FIGURE 9-7

PRIZM CLUSTERS

Furs and Station Wagons	3.2% of U.S. households—Median household income, $50,086. Age group, 35–54. New money in metro suburbs; white, college-educated families. Belong to country clubs; have second mortgages; drive BMW 5-series; read *Gourmet* and *Forbes;* eat cold cereals. Sample ZIPs: Plano, TX 75075; Reston, VA 22091; Glastonbury, CT 06033; Needham, MA 02192; Pomona, CA 91765; Dunwoody, GA 30338.
Young Suburbia	5.3% of U.S. households—Median household income, $38,582. Age group 25–44. White, college educated; upper middle class; child-rearing families. Buy swimming pools, mutual funds; drive Mitsubishi Galants, Toyota vans; read *World Tennis;* eat frozen waffles. Sample ZIPs: Eagon, MN 55124; Dale City, VA 22193; Pleasanton, CA 94566; Smithtown, NY 11787; Ypsilanti, MI 48197.
Blue-Chip Blues	6.0% of U.S. households—Median household income, $32,218. Age group 25–44. White families, high-school educated; wealthiest blue-collar suburbs. Use CB radios, belong to unions, drive Chevy Springs, Buick Rivieras; read *Gold, 4 Wheel & Off Road;* eat natural cold cereal, frozen pizzas. Sample ZIPs: Coon Rapids, MN 55433; S. Whittier, CA 90605; Mesquite, TX 75149; Ronkonkoma, NY 11779; St. Charles, St. Louis, MO 63301; Taylor, Detroit, MI 38180.
Levittown, U.S.A.	3.1% of U.S. households—Median household income, $28,742. Age group 55-plus. High-school educated, white couples; postwar track subdivisions. Watch ice hockey; go bowling; read *Stereo Review, Barron's;* drink instant iced tea, eat English muffins. Sample ZIPs: Norwood, MA 02062; Cuyahoga Falls, OH 44221; Donelson, Nashville, TN 37214; Stratford, CT 06497.
New Beginnings	4.3% of U.S. households—Median household income, $24,847. Age group 18–34. Middle-class, urban apartment dwellers; some college education. Use slide projectors, jazz records; drive Mitsubishi Mirages, Hyundais; read *Scientific American, Rolling Stone;* drink bottled water, eat whole-wheat bread. Sample ZIPs: Bloomington, MN 55420; Northeast Phoenix, AZ 85016; Reseda, Los Angeles, CA 91335; Englewood, Denver, CO 80110; Parkmoor, San Francisco, CA 95126; Park Place, Houston, TX 77061.
Middle America	3.2% of U.S. households—Median household income, $24,431. Age group 45–64. High-school educated, white families; middle-class suburbs. Use domestic air charters, Christmas Clubs; drive Plymouth Sundances, Chevy Chevettes; read *Saturday Evening Post;* eat pizza mixes, TV dinners. Sample ZIPs: Marshall, MI 49068; Sandusky, OH 44870; Hagerstown, MD 21740; Oshkosh, WI 54901; Stroudsburg, PA 18360; Elkhart, IN 46514.

SOURCE: "Using ZIP Codes to Segment Customers," *Stores* (November 1989), 42–43. Reprinted by permission of *Stores*. Copyright by National Retail Merchants Association.

FIGURE 9-8

PSYCHOGRAPHIC SEGMENTATION USING THE VALS-2 SYSTEM

Actualizers	Successful, sophisticated, active, "take charge" people with high self-esteem and abundant resources. They are interested in growth and seek to develop, explore, and express themselves in a variety of ways—sometimes guided by principle and sometimes by a desire to have an effect, make a change. Their possessions and recreation reflect a cultivated taste for the finer things in life.
Fulfilleds	Mature, satisfied, comfortable, reflective people who value order, knowledge, and responsibility. Most are well educated and in, or recently retired from, professional occupations. Content with their careers, families, and station in life, their leisure activities tend to revolve around their homes. Although their incomes allow them many choices, they are conservative, practical consumers, concerned about functionality, value, and durability in the products they buy.
Believers	Conservative, conventional people with concrete beliefs and strong attachments to traditional institutions: family, church, community, and the nation. They follow established routines, organized in large part around their homes, families, and social or religious organizations. As consumers, they are conservative and predictable, favoring American products and established brands.
Achievers	Successful career- and work-oriented people who like to, and generally do, feel in control of their lives. They value structure, predictability, and stability over risk, intimacy, and self-discovery. They are deeply committed to their work and families. As consumers, they favor established products that demonstrate their success to their peers.
Strivers	Seek motivation, self-definition, and approval from the world around them. They are striving to find a secure place in life. Unsure of themselves and low on economic, social, and psychological resources, they are deeply concerned about the opinions and approval of others. They emulate those who own more impressive possessions, but what they wish to obtain is generally beyond their reach.
Experiencers	Young, vital, enthusiastic, impulsive, and rebellious. They seek variety and excitement, savoring the new, the offbeat, and the risky. Still in the process of formulating life values and patterns of behavior, they quickly become enthusiastic about new possibilities but are equally quick to cool. They are avid consumers and spend much of their income on clothing, fast food, music, movies, and videos.
Makers	Practical people who have constructive skills and value self-sufficiency. They live within a traditional context of family, practical work, and physical recreation, and have little interest in what lies outside that context. They experience the world by working in it (building a house, canning vegetables) and have sufficient skill, income, and energy to carry out their projects successfully. They are unimpressed by material possessions other than those with a practical or functional purpose.
Strugglers	Strugglers' lives are constricted. Chronically poor, ill educated, low skilled, without strong social bonds, aging and concerned about their health, they are often despairing and passive. Their chief concerns are for security and safety. They are cautious consumers; while they represent a very modest market for most products and services, they are loyal to favorite brands.

SOURCE: Adapted from Penny Gill, "New VALS 2 Values and Lifestyles Segmentation," *Stores* (November 1989), 35.

practice of segmenting markets on the bases of product usage characteristics and consumer buying behavior. Figure 9-4 identifies four product-usage variables employed by marketers in identifying market segments. Benefits sought, patronage reason, loyalty status, and readiness stage are four of the more popular means for segmenting markets based on buyer behavior characteristics.

User status groups consumers into one of four groups depending on their involvement with the product at any given time. Consumers can be identified as current users, nonusers, former users, or potential users. Weight Watchers International is marketing its new health-oriented programs (as opposed to diet programs) and refresher courses by using its "prodigious database of 11 million former and current customers."[15] This database of users gives the firm a distinctive advantage over Jenny Craig International and Nutri/Systems Inc., which lack comparable lists.

Usage rate is the rate at which consumers use or consume a product. One common usage-rate segmentation divides product users into heavy, moderate, and light user segments. Others simply describe usage-rate segments as the "heavy half" and the "light half." Many marketers are especially interested in the heavy half since this segment often accounts for the vast majority of sales for a given product category. This heavy-half phenomenon is so prevalent in numerous situations that marketers have coined a term to describe it. The **80/20 rule** suggests that about 20 percent of all users will account for 80 percent of all product category sales.

Usage occasion is a product-related segmentation process that groups consumers by the purpose or nature of their purchases. Product segments are viewed as being common or special-use situations. For example, you might buy a cheaper store-brand shirt for yourself but not as a Father's Day present. Generic beer might be suitable for personal consumption but not considered appropriate to serve during a Super Bowl party.

Usage regularity is concerned with how consistent the consumer's usage pattern for a particular product or brand might be. Is it constant or erratic? Usage regularity classifies consumers as sporadic users or continuous users. Some people will buy no toothpaste other than Crest, while others switch brands constantly.

Benefit segmentation subdivides markets on the basis of the primary benefit or benefits sought when buying a good or service. Market segments are identified using such benefit characteristics as convenience of product use, dependability of product design, image of brand name, selection of product features, status of product category, and perceived value of the entire product package. Hence, some people will purchase only those face soaps that include moisturizers. Wrinkle-free, no-iron slacks represent one of the fastest-growing segments in men's apparel.[16]

Retailers often segment their markets on the basis of **patronage reasons**—the motivating force behind selecting one store over others as the supplier of a particular good or service. Consumers are grouped according to the most compelling reason(s) for choosing a retailer. Those reasons range from the variety and assortment of goods offered by different retailers to the convenience of the store's location and the store's atmospherics. The typical American family does the greatest part of their weekly grocery shopping at a favorite, conveniently located supermarket that offers a wide selection of products within a clean and well-organized store. The Birmingham-based Parisian department store chain does not attempt to compete on price. It targets customer segments that want service and ambience. "Zero-interest credit cards, play areas for toddlers, hand-signed thank-you notes from salespeople" are some of the reasons for patronizing Parisian.[17]

Consumers exhibit different degrees of loyalty to brands and products. **Loyalty status** is the degree to which a consumer is predisposed to purchase a particular firm's goods and services. For example, a consumer is minimally to moderately loyal to the Ford Motor Company if the desired Ford truck (the right color, features, accessories, and services) is conveniently available from the local Ford dealer at the lowest price when the consumer is ready to buy. Consumers are defined as totally loyal when they consider only Ford products.

Readiness stage refers to the consumer's mental state during the consumer buying decision process (see Chapter 7). The first distinction to be identified is whether consumers are aware or unaware of the firm and its offering. Consumers who are aware can be grouped according to their readiness to make a purchase decision. Initial readiness stages include consumers who are becoming informed and interested in the firm's goods and services. Market segments containing consumers who are in more advanced stages of readiness are populated by consumers who either are disposed to the firm's offerings or intend to buy the firm's products. The marketer's task with respect to unaware market segments is to build awareness if the segment justifies the effort and if the segment is selected as a viable target market.

STEP 2: PROFILING MARKET SEGMENTS

Having selected the variable or variables by which the organization plans to segment the mass market, the marketing manager proceeds to profile market segments by developing cross-classification matrices—single- or multiple-dimensional grids in which one or more of the axes are defined by different categories of the selected segmentation variable. **Single variable segmentation** uses only one variable to define individual market segments (see Figure 9-9). This simple approach to market segmentation is easy to perform but provides the marketer with limited information about how the market might react to various marketing programs.

Multiple variable segmentation requires the use of two or more variables in identifying and profiling individual market segments. As seen in Figure 9-9, this multidimensional cross-classification approach to market segmentation provides a more in-depth profile of the consumers who

FIGURE 9-9

PROFILING MARKET SEGMENTS

Single Variable Segmentation

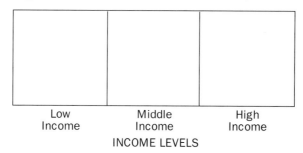

Multiple Variable Segmentation

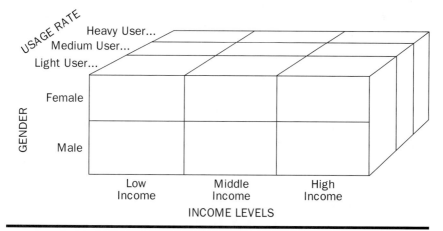

make up each market segment. This greater understanding of consumers and their buying behavior allows the marketer to create a marketing program that is uniquely suited to the needs of the targeted segments. One cautionary note on the use of multiple variable segmentation is necessary. The marketing manager should avoid identifying too many market segments by using too many variables. This could lead to the identification of micro-markets that are too small to be profitable.

STEP 3: EVALUATING MARKET SEGMENTS

Having identified and profiled various market segments, the marketing manager must then evaluate each group of consumers in terms of its ability to generate sufficient sales to support the organization's marketing programs. Evaluating market segments requires that the marketing manager make several forecasts of each segment's support capabilities using one or more forecasting methods.

SALES FORECASTING Sales forecasting requires that the following three questions be answered with respect to each market segment:

1. What is the total amount of business for a particular product that each market segment can generate now and in the future?

2. What is the maximum share of a market segment's total business that can be captured by the product offering of a particular firm?

3. How much of a particular product can a company expect to sell given an assumed marketing environment and a specified level of marketing effort?

The answers to these questions entail making demand estimates in terms of market potential, sales potential, and sales forecasts.

The **market potential** for a certain product or product line is an estimate of the maximum total sales possible for all competing organizations within a market segment within a given time frame. Snowboarding (half surfing, half skiing) is expected to double by the end of the decade. What factors might account for this rapidly expanding market potential? More and more ski resorts are beginning to permit snowboarding, and it is extremely popular with young Americans who have both the time and money to pursue such a sport.[18] Market potential forecasts establish the upper limit on total demand for a product within each market segment. Both dollar and unit sales estimates are created in order to provide the marketing manager with insight into the full potential of each identified consumer group. In establishing the market potential for each segment, the forecaster assumes both a given marketing environment and a composite level of marketing effort involving all competing organizations. Hence, the first decision in the evaluation of various segmented consumer groupings is to determine which, if any, market segments have a level of total business sufficient to warrant the organization's attention and investment.

The second decision is centered on the issue of **sales potential**—the maximum percentage of each market segment's total market potential that an organization can reasonably expect to seize given various levels of marketing effort over a stated period of time. The results of this evaluation are estimates of the probable market shares that one company can expect to realize relative to the marketing efforts of all competing organizations.

Sales forecasts are projections of the amount of product that a particular organization actually expects to sell to a select group of consumers with a specific level of marketing effort during a given time period. These company- and product-specific forecasts differ from sales potential in that they are specific sales estimates for a particular product at a given level of marketing effort. Sales forecasts are often translated into marketing objectives that are used in evaluating and measuring the performance of the marketing team.

FORECASTING METHODS Marketing managers use a number of different methodologies for forecasting market potential, sales potential, actual sales, and a range of forecasting methods follow.

❏ Projecting past experiences into the future

❏ Asking various knowledgeable persons what they think will happen in the future

❏ Using commercially generated projections of future happenings

❏ Conducting market tests of how consumers might respond to certain situations and marketing programs

Figure 9-10 identifies and describes some of the more commonly used forecasting methods.

MARKET TARGETING

Once a market has been segmented, profiled, and evaluated, the second stage of the market analysis model (see Figure 9-1) requires that the marketing manager select and target those market segments that are most consistent with the organization's mission. Market targeting concerns determining which market segments should be the focus of the organization's marketing effort and how many market segments should be targeted. **Target marketing** is the process of selecting the market segment or segments to be served by the organization and identifying the strategic option or options the organization will employ to implement its target marketing program. A **target market** is a group of individuals or organizations for which the firm develops a marketing program tailored to that target's needs and expectations.

STEP 4: SELECTING MARKET SEGMENTS

The purpose of market segmentation is to identify submarkets on the basis of meaningful differences that directly impact consumer behavior

FIGURE 9-10

FORECASTING METHODS

Executive Opinion	A survey of the opinions and judgments of executives from different functional areas (marketing, finance, and production) within the organization. Forecasts are based on the intuition and experience of company executives.
Customer Forecasts	A survey of the existing and potential consumers in order to ascertain purchase intentions, purchase motives, buyer reactions, future expectations, rates of consumption, and any other buyer behavior actions that might influence sales now and in the future.
Expert Opinion	A jury of outside experts is polled as to their opinions and estimates of future sales with respect to particular products in identified market areas during specified time frames. Forecasts are based on their expertise and special knowledge of a product or market segment. Delphi techniques are often used to arrive at a consensus opinion.
Sales-Force Opinion	A survey of the organization's sales representatives as to their opinions of customer actions and future intentions, competitor strengths and weaknesses, and market trends and patterns. A composite of sales force opinions is used to make territorial sales forecasts.
Test Markets	The practice of conducting a market test in which a product is placed in one or more market areas (cities) to study consumer reactions to the product and its marketing program. National or regional sales forecasts are made based on test market results.
Trend Analysis	A quantitative technique involving the analysis of past sales information in order to discover sales patterns or trends that can be projected into the future. Trend analysis assumes that future market conditions are an extension of past market circumstances.
Correlation Method	A quantitative method that assumes that an identifiable relationship exists between sales for a particular product category and one or more market area characteristics (total number of consumers who are over the age of fifty and have disposable income of $50,000 or more). This special knowledge of these relationships is used by the forecaster to make future sales projections.

and are therefore useful to the marketer when developing a marketing program. A number of guidelines exist for choosing meaningful market segments.

❏ *Accessibility*—Is the market segment reachable using the firm's current distribution channels and communication methods? What marketing program changes will be required to access any given market segment? What costs are associated with such changes?

❏ *Profitability*—Is the market segment large enough to be profitable? What is the current and future sales potential, relative to cost structures, in serving the proposed target market? Are the financial rewards sufficient to warrant the development of a special marketing program?

❏ *Compatibility*—How consistent are the needs and expectations of the market segment with the organization's business mission and marketing objectives? Are the operational and marketing requirements for serving this market segment compatible with the resources and capabilities of the organization?

❏ *Responsiveness*—Will the market segment respond favorably to a marketing program that is specifically designed to meet its individual needs? Does the market segment require a unique and individualistic marketing mix?

❏ *Competencies*—What relative advantages does the organization have in serving a particular market segment relative to competing organizations? Can a sustainable competitive position be developed and implemented?

Market segments that offer greater accessibility, higher profitability, and better compatibility, and are likely to be more responsive and conducive to the organization's operations, are the preferred choices for market targeting.

STEP 5: TARGETING MARKET SEGMENTS

A mass market that has been segmented affords the marketing manager four strategic options in selecting target markets. Those strategic options include undifferentiated, differentiated, concentrated, and custom marketing. Figure 9-11 illustrates each of these strategic options.

UNDIFFERENTIATED MARKETING When there are insufficient differences among various market segments to justify developing individualized marketing programs, the marketing manager might elect to practice **undifferentiated marketing**—the strategy of treating all market segments as a single segment and developing one marketing program to meet the needs of the entire market. Using this market aggregation or mass market strategy, the marketer develops the same product mix, pricing program, and distribution system to service all potential customers. Promotions are directed at the mass audience.

From a marketing viewpoint, undifferentiated marketing represents an absence of market segmentation and lacks the degree of customer focus that promotes long-term relationships and customer loyalty. As such, undifferentiated marketers are highly vulnerable to the marketing actions of target marketers. From an operations point of view, the mass market approach offers considerably more opportunities to gain production, distribution, and marketing efficiencies due to economies of scale and more

FIGURE 9-11

TARGET MARKET STRATEGIES

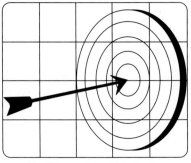
Undifferentiated Marketing

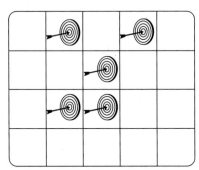
Differentiated Marketing

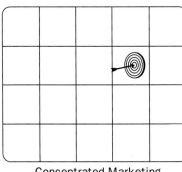
Concentrated Marketing

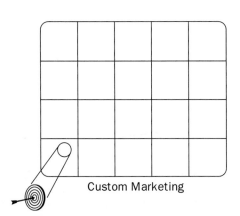
Custom Marketing

standardized operations. In previous times, when demand exceeded supply for many products, mass marketing was a viable option. Today, in most product categories, the level and intensity of competition for a limited number of customers has relegated the undifferentiated marketer to a minor role. Such staples as salt, flour, and sugar are marketed to some extent using an undifferentiated strategy.

DIFFERENTIATED MARKETING Differentiated marketing is a multiple-segment strategy in which the marketer selects several market segments to target and develops a separate marketing program for each chosen segment (see Figure 9-11). For example, gambling is a fragmented market. In Las Vegas, "Hilton aims at two distinct but related segments. The

Flamingo caters to the tour-and-travel crowd, the middle-market folks enticed by a $5.95 all-you-can-eat dinner buffet and plenty of twenty-five-cent slots. The Las Vegas Hilton, by contrast, serves the premium market, or high rollers, as well as the convention trade from its own meeting space and the Las Vegas Convention Center next door."[19] The number of selected targets can range from two to all of the identified market segments. The total number of segments selected by a particular organization will depend on the relative market potential of each segment, the resources available to develop tailored marketing programs, the cost structures associated with serving any particular market target, and the type and degree of competition connected with various multiple-segment options. Holiday Inns Worldwide developed a multibrand strategy so that customers can choose from the upscale Crowne Plaza, the traditional Holiday Inn, the budget Holiday Express, and the business-oriented Holiday Inn Select or Holiday Inn Suites and Rooms.[20]

Employing a differentiated approach to the marketplace allows the marketer to exploit the meaningful differences among consumer groups by tailoring product offerings to the specific product needs of each target market. With strong supporting programs in pricing, promotion, and distribution, this highly individualized marketing effort should ensure greater customer satisfaction and loyalty. An additional advantage of this multiple-segment approach is that market risks are spread out over several consumer groups. If marketers carefully select market targets that are clearly different, lower returns from poorly performing market segments can be offset by high-performance markets. On the negative side, differentiated marketing can be quite expensive to implement due to the number of individualized marketing programs that have to be developed.

Concentrated Marketing As Figure 9-11 illustrates, **concentrated marketing** involves targeting a single market segment and developing a marketing program tailored to the specific needs of those consumers who comprise the target market. This highly focused strategy is most often used by smaller organizations, which lack the resources to target more than one market segment. Concentrated marketing is also a viable option for the organization that finds only one segment worth targeting or compatible with the company's mission.

By zeroing in on a single target market, the organization gains the marketing advantages of a focused effort in which the organization's entire marketing program is totally centered on a highly homogeneous group of consumers. A sharply focused marketing strategy increases the likelihood of successfully fulfilling the needs of targeted consumers. By aiming at a single market niche, the organization is better able to achieve greater market penetration. This success comes from being recognized as that segment's market leader and being acknowledged as "the expert" in knowing and meeting its selective needs. The downside hazards are that a concentrated market results in a concentrated risk in which the organization does not have any backup position if, for unforeseen reasons, the market should prove to be unproductive or the market segment experiences unexpected negative environmental changes.

CUSTOM MARKETING The ultimate in market segmentation and target marketing is **custom marketing**—the strategy of totally disaggregating the mass market by treating each individual or organization as a market segment and developing a unique marketing program designed to satisfy the totally individualized needs of the individual or organization. In many industrial markets, machine tools are custom-designed to meet specific production needs. In the world of high fashion, designers create collections of original designs that are later modified for individual customers on a made-to-order basis.[21] Doctors, lawyers, and consultants tend to practice custom marketing in the provision of their highly personal services. While treating customers on an individual basis almost always ensures a high level of customer satisfaction, it represents an expensive approach to meeting consumers' needs.

One variation of custom marketing employed by retailers is the practice of **mass customization** through modularization—a point-of-sale customization in which standardized parts and components are used to customize a product in the retail store. This new mass customization paradigm "is based on the goal of developing, producing, and delivering affordable goods and services with enough variety and customization that nearly everyone finds exactly what he or she wants."[22] For example, an electronics store might encourage a customer to buy one manufacturer's disc player, another's amplifier, and speakers from a third vendor; the final stereo system is tailored to one individual's specific needs, but the parts are standard mass-produced components. Dell Computer practices mass-customizing when it bundles each PC with software and peripherals that the customer wants.[23] On a larger scale, D.R. Horton, Inc., of Fort Worth, Texas, is a large, regional builder of standardized houses that customizes each house by offering such options as higher-priced kitchens, fancier bathroom fixtures, sitting areas in the master bedroom, additional windows, and raised ceilings. These major options are on top of the customary options of choosing different carpets, wall coverings, and light fixtures.[24]

MARKET POSITIONING

The third stage of the market analysis process is market positioning. With the selection of the target market segment or segments accomplished, the marketing manager proceeds to position the organization's marketing program within those targeted segments. As described in Chapter 3, **market positioning** is the process of creating in the minds of the targeted buyers a distinctive *position* for the organization and its marketing program. A **market position** is the target consumer's perception of an organization's products and marketing program relative to those of competing organizations.

Step 6: Developing Positioning Strategies

The processes by which marketers position their product mixes, prices, promotional messages, and distribution systems were discussed earlier in the text. For a review of the *ABCs* of positioning, see Chapter 3. Because market positioning strategies involve consumer mind-sets, marketers often visually portray market positions by constructing **perceptual maps**—a multidimensional graphic image of consumer perceptions. Perceptual maps typically display one competitor's marketing program in terms of attributes, benefits, or claims relative to the market positions of all other relevant competitors. These visual representations of marketing positions greatly aid in the development of marketing mixes focused on the core needs of the targeted consumer group and assist the marketing manager in judging the organization's marketing program's relative advantages over competitors' market offerings.[25] Figure 9-12 is a perceptual map showing how different department store retailers position themselves in terms of merchandise selection, price levels, and service levels. As seen in Figure 9-12, department store merchandise-selection strategies range from full-line stores offering both soft and hard goods (such as Sears) to specialty department stores offering only soft goods (Nordstrom). Popular-priced department store chains (JCPenney and Montgomery Ward) are positioned to compete with the midmarket prices offered by Dillard's and The May Company, which in turn compete with the high-end prices of Bloomingdale's and Nordstrom.

Step 7: Tailoring Marketing Mixes

The last step in the market analysis process is to create a new marketing mix, or to adapt an existing marketing mix, for the individual needs of consumers comprising each of the market segments targeted by the organization. Product, distribution, price, and promotion decisions and tailoring marketing mixes will be covered in Chapters 10, 11, 12, and 13.

Concluding Remarks

Markets are comprised of individuals or organizations who have needs and desires to be satisfied and who are willing, able, and have the authority to make purchase decisions for themselves, their families, or the organizations they work for. Market structures can be described in terms of a hierarchy ranging from the broadly defined mass markets, which are sub-

FIGURE 9-12

A PERCEPTUAL MAP OF THE DEPARTMENT STORE INDUSTRY

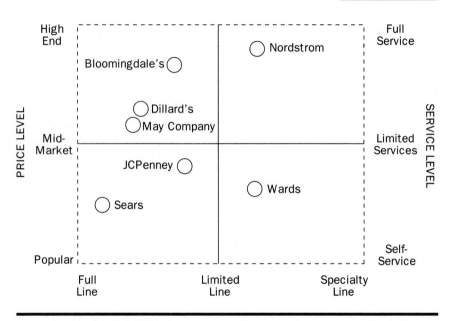

SOURCE: Adapted from Dale M. Lewison, *Retailing*, Fifth Edition (New York: Macmillan Publishing Company, 1994), 52.

divided into more narrowly defined market segments, to market niches, and micromarkets. The market analysis process consist of three major stages (market segmentation, market targeting, and market positioning), which, in turn, are broken down into seven steps: identifying, profiling, evaluating, selecting, targeting market segments, developing positioning strategies, and tailoring marketing mixes.

ENDNOTES

1. Jonathan Berry, "A Potential New Tool for Selling—Database Marketing," *Business Week* (September 5, 1994), 56–57.

2. Greg Burns, "It Only Hertz When Enterprise Laughs," *Business Week* (December 12, 1994), 44.

3. Suzanne L. Jennings, "Niches within a Niche," *Forbes* (April 25, 1994), 122.

4. Damon Darlin, "Borrow from Thy Neighbor," *Forbes* (November 7, 1994), 214.

5. Annetta Miller and Seema Nayyar, "Make It a Lemon Light Ice, Please," *Newsweek* (October 3, 1994), 53.

6. "GM's Aurora," *Business Week* (March 21, 1994), 89.

7. Glenn Rifkin, "Made-to-Order Levi's Create a Fit Like a Glove," *Akron Beacon Journal* (November 11, 1994), A1.

8. Howard Rudnitsky, "Growing Pains," *Forbes* (February 27, 1995), 59.

9. Nina Munk, "Shopping in Peace," *Forbes* (March 14, 1994), 94–96.

10. Robert La Franco, "Barbies with Brains," *Forbes*, (December 19, 1994), 294, 298.

11. Laura Zinn, "Run to the Supermarket and Pick Me Up Some Cactus," *Business Week* (June 20, 1994), 56.

12. Lisa Gubernick, "We Will Not Dilute," *Forbes* (February 27, 1995), 50–51.

13. See Peter Brimelow, "Al Gore's Lousy Latin," *Forbes* (August 15, 1994), 72–73.

14. See Penny Gill, "New VALS 2 Values and Lifestyle Segmentation," *Stores* (November 1989), 35.

15. Keith L. Alexander, "A Health Kick at Weight Watchers," *Business Week* (January 16,1995), 36.

16. Stephanie Anderson Forest, "Pumping No-Iron Slacks," *Business Week* (February 7, 1994), 30.

17. Amy Feldman, "But It Wasn't Broken," *Forbes* (March 14, 1994), 66.

18. Randall Lane, "The Culture That Jake Built," *Forbes* (March 27, 1995), 45.

19. Seth Lubove, "Barron's Big Bet," *Forbes* (October 24, 1994), 118.

20. David Greising, "Major Reservations," *Business Week* (September 26, 1994), 66.

21. Frederick E. Webster, Jr., "Defining the New Marketing Concept," *Marketing Management*, Vol. 2, No. 4 (1993), 27.

22. See Blanca Riemer and Laura Zinn, "Haute Couture That's Not So Haute," *Business Week* (April 22, 1991), 108; Phyllis Berman, "Closer to the Consumer," *Forbes* (January 20, 1992), 57; and Susan Caminiti, "The Petty Payoff in Cheap Chic," *Fortune* (February 24, 1992), 71.

23. Neil Gross and Peter Coy, "The Technology Paradox," *Business Week* (March 6, 1995).

24. R. Lee Sullivan, "Just Say Yes," *Forbes* (February 28, 1994), 84.

25. See Richard M. Johnson, "Market Segmentation: A Strategic Management Tool, *Marketing Management*, Vol. 3, No. 4 (1995), 49–53.

Marketing Decisions

- Chapter 10 **Product Decisions**
- Chapter 11 **Distribution Decisions**
- Chapter 12 **Promotion Decisions**
- Chapter 13 **Price Decisions**

Product Decisions

Chapter Outline

- **Introduction**
- **Product Concepts**
    - Total-Product Concept
    - Product-Mix Concept
    - Product Life Cycles
- **Product Classification**
    - Consumer Products
    - Organizational Products
- **Product Management**
    - Product-Item Management
- Product-Line Management
- Product-Mix Management
- New Product Management
- Product Development Process
- Product Adoption Process
- Product Diffusion Process
- **Concluding Remarks**

Introduction

In the broadest sense, *product* is a generic term used to identify what is being marketed. Products represent anything and everything that consumers might receive as part of the exchange process. In specific terms, a **product** can be a tangible *good* (a physical entity that has precise specifications in terms of its composition and description), an intangible *service* (an activity involving the application of human skill or mechanical effort in order to solve a consumer problem), or an *idea* (a concept or way of thinking about a particular issue, event, person, or situation). This textbook is a good. Your professor's lecture is a service. And the product concepts that we are about to discuss are all ideas on how we should view the nature of products. Jimmy Buffett, the singer/songwriter, has become a textbook lesson in how to cross-market goods, services, and ideas. Buffett's core business is the sale of records, which he markets through his own Margaritaville Records label. His Margaritaville Store in Key West, Florida, merchandises a wide range of personalized trinkets, tapes, CDs, T-shirts, sweatshirts, Hawaiian shirts, and the "lost shaker of salt." Buffett has added a mail-order catalog, newsletter, nightclub, and cafe. The latest additions to his collection of goods, services, and ideas are two novels—*Tales from Margaritaville* and *Where is Joe Merchant?* Buffett's collection of products has made him one of the highest-earning entertainers in the world.[1]

Product Concepts

Prior to a discussion of the many issues associated with the management of an organization's product offering, it is necessary to understand several basic product concepts. Product offerings should be understood from the perspective of the total-product concept, the product-mix concept, and the concept of the product life cycle.

Total-Product Concept

Most organizations offer consumer products that represent a combination of tangible goods and intangible services and ideas. From a marketing perspective, it is essential to recognize that a product is more than just a tangible object having specific functional attributes. A more comprehensive and useful approach to the issue of what constitutes a product is to view products in their totality. The total-product concept recognizes that a product is a great deal more than just the physical and functional attributes of a tangible good. It is the all-encompassing perception that a product is the sum total of all the benefits that consumers might expect in buying, using, and possessing the product. Figure 10-1 illustrates the **total-product concept** as the sum of the tangible, augmented, and generic products.

FIGURE 10-1

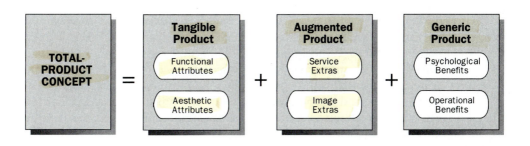

THE TOTAL-PRODUCT CONCEPT

TANGIBLE PRODUCT The **tangible product** encompasses both the product's functional attributes and aesthetic features that define and describe an actual physical good. The tangible product represents the physical bundle of characteristics that describe what a product is and what a product does.

Functional attributes are the product's biological or chemical structure together with its physical design specifications in terms of its size, shape, weight, and other operating features. A product's functional attributes are important because they determine, to a large extent, whether a product is capable of providing the functions it was designed to perform. A computer's design specifications determine what functions it can perform and how fast it can perform them. Product quality is defined, to a considerable extent, by its functional attributes and ability to meet the functional needs of the consumer. Functional attributes are the first consideration in evaluating the potential success of a product. Without adequate functional performance, most other considerations associated with the total-product concept become irrelevant.

The second component of the tangible product is its **aesthetic features**—those physical elements of a good that appeal to the consumer's five senses. How does the product look, feel, smell, taste, and sound? Aesthetic features are important because they are a key element in generating customer awareness and product trial. Most consumers have strong preconceived notions of what a product should be in an aesthetic sense. If the aesthetic features of the product do not match up to preconceived notions or create new and exciting reactions, it is unlikely that the product will enjoy wide market acceptance and success. In the apparel industry, for example, if the color is wrong, the entire garment is wrong regardless of its other redeeming qualities. There are some notable exceptions, however. "A pair of Joe Boxer's shorts typically features brightly colored images of chili peppers, trout, or motorcycles. One popular pair says 'no, no, no'; turn off the lights and the words 'yes, yes, yes' glow in the dark. Another model has 3-D images visible only when accompanying glasses are worn."[2]

AUGMENTED PRODUCT The **augmented product** is an enhancement of the tangible product through the addition of service and image extras. These product enhancements greatly magnify the actual and perceived value of the organization's product offering.

Service extras are any activities offered as a conditional part of the sale. They enhance and extend the actual value and utility of the tangible product. An organization's list of service extras might include any or all of the following extras:

- Delivery and installation
- Repair and alteration
- Credit and layaway
- Returns and adjustments
- Warranties and guarantees
- Telephone and mail ordering
- Toll-free customer service number
- Lessons and instructions
- Maintenance contracts

Manufacturers and retailers can enhance the product offering by providing services individually or in combination with one another.

Image extras are features that enhance the perceived value of the tangible product. Brand names, logos, exclusive distribution, prestige pricing, distinctive design, and unusual packaging are some means by which marketers generate a favorable image for the product. Images are overall composite impressions of how consumers see and what consumers feel about a particular product. These mental pictures are important because consumers use them to make value judgments concerning competitive product offerings. Sperry Top-Siders reinforced its image as a professional boat shoe by becoming the official supplier to the U.S. Sailing Team and the Team Dennis Conner.[3]

GENERIC PRODUCT The **generic product** encompasses all of the product dimensions (functional attributes, aesthetic features, service extras, and image extras) plus underlying personal benefits that the individual or organization expects to realize in the exchange process. In any purchase decision, the buyer expects to benefit in some fashion. Benefits might be psychological or operational in nature.

Psychological benefits include a wide range of advantages that customers feel that they gain in *buying* and *possessing* the product. An attorney might buy a Mont Blanc pen because he or she thinks that the mere possession of such a fine writing instrument suggests success and a greater sense of professionalism. An organizational buyer might enter an exchange arrangement in the expectation that a successful deal will enhance his or her chances for promotion.

Operational benefits are the advantages realized by the customer in *using* the product. Operational benefits focus on what the product does for the consumer. It is the basic benefit that a product provides. For example, cleaning, entertaining, transporting, processing, cooling, and problem solving are all core benefits that a consumer might expect from a product. From a product operations viewpoint, people do not buy snowblowers; they buy cleared driveways. Organizational buyers do not buy lubricants; they buy maintenance-free operations, longer machine life, and better returns on the company's capital investments.

Marketers who recognize the multifaceted character of products by viewing them in their totality have considerably more to market than the marketer who assumes the more narrow viewpoint of products as simply physical entities. Satisfying the comprehensive needs of customers requires assuming the broader perspective of the total-product concept.

PRODUCT-MIX CONCEPT

Rarely does an organization market just one product. Most organizations offer a collection of different products to different market segments. The **product mix** is comprised of the full range of products that an organization offers the marketplace. It represents "appropriate combinations" of products that are grouped together because they have the capability to satisfy the needs of one or more market targets. As seen in Figure 10-2, the composition of a product mix is described in terms of the relationship among product lines, items, and units.

Product lines are groupings of closely related products. Products might be grouped together because they are used together (lawn and garden), are purchased by similar groups of customers (designer fashion apparel), have comparable price points (generic brands), meet a particular need (recreation and entertainment), or are sold through similar retail outlets (discount stores and warehouse clubs). There is no single agreed-upon product-line classification scheme. Organizations create product-line groupings that work for them. For example, Early Learning Centers, an educational toy store chain, groups its products into different categories or departments based on children's play behavior: first year—rattles and pull-alongs; activity play—swings and climbing and sand toys; sound and music—instruments and tapes; pretend play—cooking, driving, and shopping; manipulative play—building, stitching, and blocks; numbers—games and flash cards; and finding out—dinosaur models, microscopes, and shell and rock collections.[4]

A specific version of a particular product is described as a **product item**—a particular good or service within a product line that is unique and

FIGURE 10-2

THE PRODUCT-MIX CONCEPT

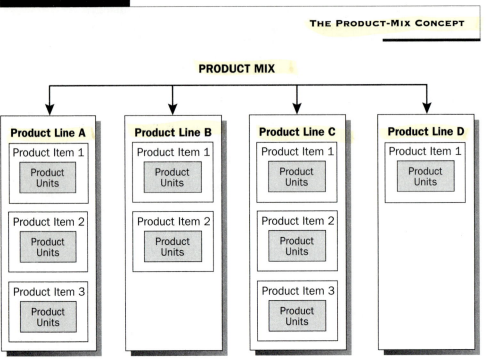

clearly distinguishable from other goods or services within and outside the product line. The distinctive identity of a product item is based on a combination of such product features as brand, style, model, color, material, size, price, or any other unique feature that can be used to distinguish the item. Individual product items are commonly referred to by retailers as **stock-keeping units (SKUs)** and form the basis for keeping track of inventory levels. Product items are important to the marketing manager because it is at this level within a product line where goods and services are directly comparable and substitutable. Consumer comparison shopping is conducted with respect to product items.

Marketers use the expression **product units** to describe the total number of a particular product item that the organization has in stock at any given time. The number of units that an organization has on hand describes the inventory support level that the organization is willing to assume in order to meet expected sales. For example, the number of units your local bookstore stocked of this particular textbook was based on expected enrollment for this class.

Issues and decisions concerning the product mix and the lines, items, and units that comprise it will be covered later in the chapter in our discussion of product management. First, we must examine the product life cycle and some means by which marketers delineate and classify products.

PRODUCT LIFE CYCLES

The product life cycle is a highly regarded model that conceptualizes the nature and evolution of products. It is widely accepted as one of the marketer's most valuable tools. The product life cycle provides useful inputs into making product decisions and formulating product strategies. Like human beings, products have life cycles characterized by distinctive stages. The **product life cycle** is the conceptualization of the life of a product as a series of stages through which products progress. Each stage in the cycle is identified by its sales performance record and characterized by different levels of profitability, various degrees of competition, and distinctive marketing programs. The four stages of the product life cycle are introduction, growth, maturity, and decline. Figure 10-3 describes the product life cycle and each of its four stages. It should be noted that this concept was originally developed for application to products and product categories within a particular industry. Its use in planning individual brand strategies may be inappropriate, though the basic "lifetime" idea does apply to brands.

▪ FIGURE 10-3

THE PRODUCT LIFE CYCLE

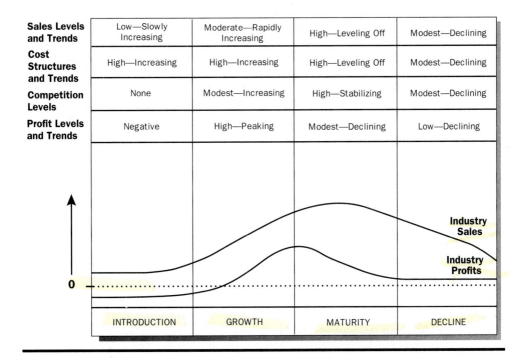

	INTRODUCTION	GROWTH	MATURITY	DECLINE
Sales Levels and Trends	Low—Slowly Increasing	Moderate—Rapidly Increasing	High—Leveling Off	Modest—Declining
Cost Structures and Trends	High—Increasing	High—Increasing	High—Leveling Off	Modest—Declining
Competition Levels	None	Modest—Increasing	High—Stabilizing	Modest—Declining
Profit Levels and Trends	Negative	High—Peaking	Modest—Declining	Low—Declining

INTRODUCTION STAGE The first stage of the product life cycle is the introduction of a newly developed product into the marketplace. As shown in Figure 10-3, the introduction stage is characterized by negative profits resulting from low sales and the high costs of developing and launching a new product. Perfume designer Christian Dior on average spends $40 million to launch a new fragrance.[5] New product introductions do not typically face direct competition; however, the likelihood of competitors having similar product development projects is quite high. In any case, the introduction of a new product will attract "me-too marketers" who will soon be offering their substitute versions of the product. The exceptions might be product introductions that are protected to some extent by patents or trademarks.

The organization's marketing program during the introduction stage is to build primary demand for the product by:

1. Gaining the support of marketing channel participants through effective trade promotions

2. Creating awareness among consumers who might be early adopters of the product by informing them of its unique attributes and relative advantages

3. Offering potential adopters various sales incentives in the form of samples, coupons, and rebates

Initially, product distribution tends to be rather limited as the organization builds its channel relationships. Pricing practices at the introductory stage tend to follow one of two strategies. First, the organization may elect to pursue a "skimming policy" wherein prices are set high in order to rapidly recapture initial investment costs and to quickly generate profitable sales. The danger associated with this practice is that competitors are attracted to the market by higher profit margins. The second pricing practice involves a "penetrating policy" in which prices on new introductory products are set low in order to penetrate the market faster and to gain a higher and more sustainable share of the market. The downside to this policy is that it takes longer to recapture development costs and to become profitable.

GROWTH STAGE The growth stage is characterized by rapidly increasing sales and profits. It is during this stage of the life cycle that the marketer attempts to build specific demand for the organization's brands and labels. The primary marketing objective during this stage is to increase both sales and market share by building brand preference and customer loyalty. While the level of competition may be limited during the early parts of this stage, it slowly increases as competing organizations recognize and respond to the newly identified market opportunities. One of the greatest benefits in developing and introducing new products is realized during this stage: product profitability reaches peak levels (see Figure 10-3).

Growth-stage marketing initiatives include making continuous product quality improvements, extending product-support services, expanding product-distribution networks, promoting greater awareness, providing more sales incentives, and communicating brand benefits. Pricing is usually an extension of the price skimming or penetration strategy begun in the introduction stage. With increased competition, however, price levels tend to fall as the product begins to age.

MATURITY STAGE The maturity stage is composed of two substages. The product profile during early maturity is one of moderately increasing sales but continually declining profits. With the peaking of sales, the latter part of maturity is marked by falling sales and profits (see Figure 10-3). During this highly competitive maturity stage, organizations concentrate on defending market share and building brand loyalty. To accomplish these goals, the marketing manager attempts to gain distribution and marketing efficiencies in an effort to control costs and improve customer service. Remaining competitive within the product category is the key component for long-term survival during this "mid-life crisis."

Mature product strategies include product differentiation (adding product features to distinguish the item from competing brands), market penetration (attempting to get current customers to increase their usage rate or to find entirely new uses for the product), and product development (engaging in line-extension strategies by adding new but related product items). Promotion programs focus on reminder advertising to maintain product image and encourage brand loyalty. Sales incentives are also used to retain current customer patronage and induce brand switching from competitive products. Building strategic alliances within channel networks and introducing quick-response inventory programs are two highly regarded distribution strategies employed by organizations that intend to survive until the end of the product's profitable life. While maintaining adequate profit margins is the desired pricing goal during this stage, the organization must be willing and able to defend market share should rivals attempt to use aggressive pricing tactics to increase their share of the market.

DECLINE STAGE In the final stage of the life cycle, products experience steadily declining sales and profits. Old technology, limited uses, changing markets, legal constraints, environmental problems, and better or new product alternatives are but a few of the reasons why products decline. In the hotly contested video-game market, software purchases for 16-bit game computers have declined dramatically as the industry shifts to 32-bit and 64-bit machines.[6] With decreasing demand comes fewer competitors. Products that have entered the decline stage are subject to one of several possible fates. If a particular product item (brand) remains profitable, the organization may elect to maintain it by continuing to provide an appropriate level of support or to niche it by finding a protected market niche where it can continue to survive. For products that still have marginally adequate sales and profit levels but do not fit into the organization's strategic plans, the alternative is often one of divestiture through sale of the product to a firm where its strategic fit is more appropriate. Finally, the organization may elect to harvest the product by reducing its support and continuing to milk it for sales until it is no longer profitable. When the product is no longer productive, it is liquidated or sold. There are cases where products are given new life or revived by dramatic market conditions or new product applications. Baking soda as a key ingredient in a wide variety of deodorant products is a commonly cited example.

PRODUCT CLASSIFICATION

Marketers develop product classification schemes in order to gain a better understanding of the differences among various product lines and items and to bring order to their product mix. These differences are often the focal point around which marketing programs are developed and distinguished from the marketing efforts of competitors. Product classifications are also essential to the successful management of such operational tasks as sales planning, order processing, and inventory control. Previously, we distinguished between consumer and organizational markets. We will continue that differentiation by approaching product classification from the viewpoint of consumer products and organizational products.

CONSUMER PRODUCTS

Marketers have developed a number of different consumer product classifications. One of the more commonly used classifications is based on the specific product characteristic of durability. Another focuses on the buying behavior of consumers.

PRODUCT DURABILITY **Durability** is the quality of surviving many uses. **Durable goods** are products that last through numerous uses and endure over an extended period of time. Sporting goods, automotive parts, appliances, and furniture are all examples of durable hard goods. Apparel items and many home furnishings are illustrative of durable soft goods. The highly successful marketing strategy and ad campaign "The Softer Side of Sears," in which the retailer emphasized women's apparel and other soft goods, was a major contributor to Sears' turnaround in the mid-'90s after years of weak performance results.[7] How long consumers make durable goods last depends on the general state of the economy and the specific situation of the individual consumer. During bad economic times consumers tend to extend the life of durable products; good times usually result in faster replacement rates. **Nondurable goods** are perishable products that are consumed in one or a few uses. Food products, beverages, and personal care products are typically classified as nondurables. Additional products lacking durability include faddish products, personal services, and unusual ideas. Regular and frequent shopping patterns tend to be associated with nondurables.

BUYING BEHAVIOR The amount of shopping effort exerted by consumers in finding and buying a particular product serves as the criterion in this second consumer-product classification scheme. This product classification system is based on consumers' reasons to buy, need for product information, and actual shopping behaviors. In this consumer-oriented classification system, four major categories of consumer products are identified. They are convenience, shopping, specialty, and unsought goods and services.

Convenience Products Convenience products are goods and services to which consumers give little forethought prior to making a purchase. They represent purchases to which the consumer is unwilling to devote time, money, and effort. Candy bars are examples of such products. Due to their previous buying experience with convenience items, consumers require little or no additional information to make a purchase decision. Quick and easy availability of the product is the most important purchase motive for most convenience goods and services. If a particular convenience item is not readily available, the lack of customer loyalty is made quite evident by the customer's willingness to switch to another available item. Convenience products are commonly broken down into the following three categories: staples, impulse items, and emergency products.

Staples are convenience goods that consumers buy and consume on a regular and continuous basis. Typically, staples are inexpensive items that consumers have purchased many times. Staples include such items as coffee, milk, produce, bread, and paper products. **Impulse items** are convenience goods that consumers buy on the spur of the moment without any planning or forethought. They are goods that consumers buy as a result of strong and often irresistible urges. Impulse purchases range from inexpensive items such as candy or magazines at the supermarket checkout counter to more costly apparel items (a shirt and tie that complement a new suit). **Emergency products** are convenience goods that consumers buy under duress when the need is urgent. Emergency items are totally unplanned purchases in response to unexpected situations. Snow chains, umbrellas, medical supplies, auto parts, and flashlights are all examples of goods that may be purchased as a result of unexpected situational circumstances.

Shopping Products Shopping products are items for which consumers are willing to shop. That is, they are prepared to spend time, money, and effort in order to compare various product alternatives. Quality, features, durability, suitability, brand, style, and price are some of the characteristics used by consumers in their comparison shopping activities. The need for additional information prior to making the purchase decision is the trigger for this shopping behavior. Shopping goods tend to be more expensive than convenience goods but may not command brand loyalty. For example, an alternative VCR may be purchased with no regard to brand name.

Comparison shopping varies depending on how consumers view certain products. These goods are commonly subclassified into homogeneous and heterogeneous shopping goods. **Homogeneous shopping goods** are product items that consumers view as essentially the same in terms of product features. Hence price is often the sole basis on which consumers make comparisons among the product offerings of different firms. Household appliances such as washers, dryers, refrigerators, and dehumidifiers are viewed as homogeneous shopping goods by most consumers. **Heterogeneous shopping goods** are items that consumers view as having important differences in terms of product features, aesthetic attributes, and service extras. Consumers make multiple comparisons in terms of brands, styles, models, colors, sizes, workmanship, materials, and prices. Clothing, personal care products, jewelry, automobiles, recreation equipment, and home furnishings are some of the product categories that tend to be classified as heterogeneous shopping goods.

Specialty Products Specialty products are items for which there is no acceptable substitute from the perspective of the consumer. Hence, consumer acquisition of specialty products is accomplished with little regard to expense and effort. Unique product features, original brand identification, distinctive product image, and personal product benefits are some of the characteristics that make a product item "special" in the eyes of the consumer. For example, Dr. Scholl's Toe Squish Preventer is a shoe cushion for spike heels. This specialty good "acts like a speed bump for your foot, keeping your toes from getting jammed into the pointed toe."[8] Just about any product can be a specialty item for any particular customer. A special mustard, a preferred brand of scotch, an apparel item carrying a certain designer label, a particular model of automobile, or an item secured from a prestigious retail outlet can translate into a specialty product item. Specialty blends of coffee have been the foundation of the rapid chain expansion of such coffee bars and houses as Gloria Jean's Coffee Bean and Starbucks Coffee.[9] The uncommon nature of specialty products leads the customer to engage in shopping activities that result in extra effort and extensive search behavior.

Unsought Products An unsought product item is one that the consumer does not normally seek out. Unsought products are purchased when a sudden need arises (funeral services), when customers become aware of the product (new products), or when aggressive selling tactics generate a sale that might have not otherwise been made (a financial services program). Creating consumer awareness, understanding, and conviction through promotional activities is essential to the sale of unsought goods and services. One cemetery in Cleveland, Ohio, has "updated its marketing, no longer promoting the cemetery as a place to visit but as a place to reside."[10]

ORGANIZATIONAL PRODUCTS

Organizational products can be classified according to durability and cost of the product item or the product's usage and its form.

DURABILITY AND COST   Organizational goods can be grouped according to how long they last and how much they cost. **Expense goods** are low-cost items that the organization rapidly consumes on a regular basis. Office supplies are treated as expense goods. **Capital goods** are expensive goods used to make other goods. These long-lasting items include installations and accessory equipment.

USAGE AND FORM   Organizational products are most commonly categorized on the basis of their intended uses and functional characteristics and can be grouped into seven classes. The first three product categories, which include raw materials, component parts, and manufactured materials, are referred to as production-oriented products because they are integrated into the final product. Installations, accessory equipment, operating supplies, and business services are all operations-oriented organizational products because they are used to support the production of the product. Figure 10-4 describes each of the seven classes of organizational products.

PRODUCT MANAGEMENT

Marketing managers are concerned with the whole spectrum of product decisions. That spectrum begins with the management of individual product items, continues through the management of existing product lines and mixes, and ends with the new product management. Figure 10–5 outlines this bottom-up process that profiles the key decisions facing every product manager.

PRODUCT-ITEM MANAGEMENT

In this section, we will examine the decisions that deal with the development and management of individual product items. As suggested in Figure 10-5, our discussion will focus on those decisions relating to the quality, designing, branding, and packaging of individual product items.

PRODUCT QUALITY   What is product quality? As defined by one quality expert, "Quality is what your customer says it is—not what you say it is. To

FIGURE 10-4

ORGANIZATONAL PRODUCTS

Raw Materials	A basic commodity that becomes part of the finished product. Raw materials are either farm products (wheat, eggs, livestock, cotton, milk, or soybeans) or natural products (lumber, coal, iron ore, granite, or fish).
Component Parts	A manufactured product of one producer that is used as part of the finished product of another producer. Tires, computer chips, switches, and chains are all component parts that go into the making of automobiles, computers, lamps, and bicycles.
Component Materials	A semiprocessed good that undergoes further processing before it becomes part of the finished product. Component materials include textiles for the home furnishings industry, chemicals for the plastics industry, wood pulp for the paper industry, and iron ore for the steel industry.
Installations	A building (a factory used to house the production process or an office complex that provides business support services) or a major piece of fixed equipment (crane, generator, large machine tool) used in the production of the finished product. Installations represent long-term investments that are usually very costly.
Accessory Equipment	A portable piece of equipment that is used in the production process hand tools, motors, and forklifts) or in office activities (word processors, calculators, and office furniture). Accessory equipment includes less costly items whose life spans are considerably shorter than installations.
Supplies	A product item that expedites the production of a finished product or the completion of an office task. Supplies are subclassified into MRO items: (1) maintenance items such as cleaners, brooms, and lubricants; (2) repair items such as tapes, screws, nuts, and bolts; and (3) operating supplies such as stationery, pens, and paper clips.
Services	A business service that facilitates the production of a finished product (engineering, designing, and manufacturing services) or the operation of the business (legal, financial, and security services).

find out about your quality, ask your customer."[11] From this marketing viewpoint, **quality** is the ability of the product to match or exceed the customer's performance expectations and to satisfy the customer's needs and desires.

In defining quality from a consumer perspective, the marketer faces the problem that consumers often disagree on what constitutes product quality. Perceived quality can be based on some combination of the following product characteristics that consumers value highly—durable construction, distinctive styling, low cost, prestigious image, convenient packaging, support services, reliable performance, and a host of other value-creating attributes.[12] Each customer has his or her own viewpoint as to what constitutes quality. Regardless of how they define quality:

FIGURE 10-5

PRODUCT-MANAGEMENT DECISIONS

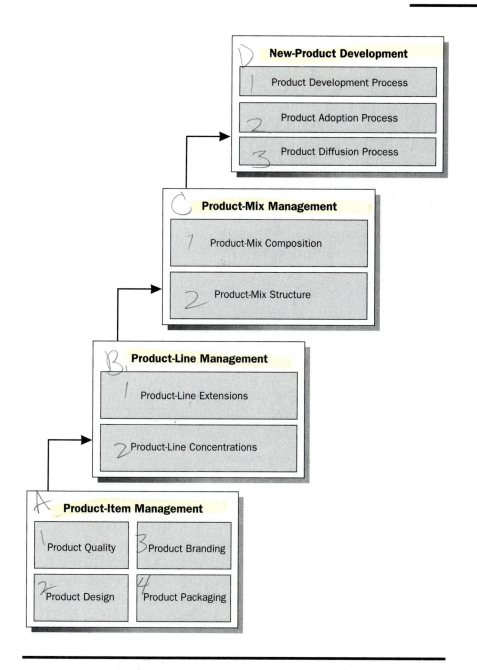

[c]ustomers today want more of those things they value. If they value low cost, they want it lower. If they value convenience or speed when they buy, they want it easier and faster. If they look for state-of-the-art design, they want to see the art pushed forward. If they need expert advice, they want companies to give them more depth, more time, and more of a feeling that they're the only customer.[13]

Developing a quality image is a task assigned to the marketing manager.

Apparently, there are a number of very different ways of achieving a high quality image. Evident are the draw of sentimentality and caring of brands like Disney and Hallmark, ... the hard-working practicality of brands like UPS and Levi's, the technical superiority of brands like Mercedes-Benz and AT&T, and the purity and wholesomeness of Chiquita and Fisher-Price.[14]

From the more utilitarian viewpoint of the production manager, quality is more likely to be defined in terms of tangible product attributes created by better raw materials, superior craftsmanship, more efficient production processes, and cutting-edge product design. Quality production goals are centered on improving both the level and consistency of product performance. A certain **quality level** is achieved by reducing the number of defects that hinder a product from performing the functions it was designed to perform. While zero defects is usually not economically feasible, quality assurance control reduces or eliminates defects through a process of continuous improvement. **Quality consistency** is the goal of producing and marketing a product with dependable quality. Product performance should always meet or exceed customer expectations.

The marketing and production perspectives on product quality come together in what has become known as **total quality management (TQM)**, a management philosophy that encourages all organization employees from all functional areas to continually work together to improve products and processes. The goal is to achieve superior customer satisfaction and world-class performance. Meeting and exceeding customer expectations by implementing a TQM program requires an organization-wide commitment to the following precepts:

1. Create a customer focus by establishing quality standards that direct the organization's attention toward customer satisfaction

2. Make product quality the organization's top priority

3. Ensure that all of the organization's partners (employees, suppliers, managers, stockholders) are supportive and committed to each quality initiative

4. Establish a goal of defect prevention, not defect correction, through an attitude of "doing it right the first time"

5. Use cooperative, cross-functional teams to solve customer problems and improve organizational processes

6. Empower employees by providing them with information and the responsibility for making decisions[15]

Two tangible expressions by which organizations state their confidence in the quality of their products are the product warranty and guarantee. A **product warranty** is an expression of the product's quality. It is a statement that communicates what the producer will do to correct any product defects. **Product guarantees** are statements by producers and resellers that inform customers of the marketer's general responsibility for the product and its performance capabilities. They represent a performance pledge that the product is what it was represented to be and that it will perform the functions that it was designed to perform. Both product warranties and guarantees help reduce the customer's perceived risk of making a purchase or patronizing a store.

PRODUCT DESIGN Products must be both functionally and aesthetically correct. While the relative importance of functional and aesthetic features varies from one product to another, both have a key role to play in creating customer satisfaction. **Product design** is how a product is engineered and styled. It is a determining factor in the operational capabilities and the aesthetic acceptance of the product. The highly successful Joan & David line of women's shoes is designed for women who move—heels are low and the shoes are chic, simple, soft, and easy. As explained by Joan, "Our designs relate to people of style, rather than people who get involved with momentary fashion."[16] The practical side of design determines the product's usability, reliability, and functional capabilities. For a family with young children, the built-in child safely seats available in several Chrysler models provide those products with a distinctive and important relative advantage. Other automotive safety design features might include child-protection door locks, driver- and passenger-side air bags, rear window defroster, and an antilock braking system. The aesthetic side of design plays a significant role in helping producers differentiate their products. Automotive styling has always played a significant role in creating a distinctive difference among the many models offered by both foreign and domestic automobile producers. Good product design is essential to good product quality.

PRODUCT BRANDING Product branding is essentially a product identification process whereby an organization distinguishes its products from those of its competitors. Customers recognize the output of a particular organization by its brand and attach both positive and negative associations to it. "Knowing who stands behind a product is the fundamental purpose of a brand."[17] Given the number of organizations that offer the same or similar products, effective branding has become a necessary prerequisite for success in most product categories. Our discussion of branding will center on product identification, brand development, and brand strategies.

Product Identification A **brand** is a name, term, phrase, symbol, design, or any other feature used to identify and represent an organization's goods or services. It helps the organization differentiate its goods and services from the competition's. A **brand name** is that part of the brand that can be verbalized; it consists of numbers, letters, and words. Taco Bell, Dodge Stratus, G.E. Soft White Light Bulbs, Gateway 2000, and Surf Liquid Laundry Detergent are all examples of brand names. Michelin's brand names can be confusing to consumers. The firm "dubs most of its tires with numbers and letters, instead of easy-to-remember names. Michelin has the XH, the XA4, the XH4, and the MX4."[18] Figure 10-6 summarizes several characteristics that make for a good brand name.

Brand mark is that part of the brand expressed as a symbol or design; it is that part of the brand that cannot be vocalized. The insurance industry makes effective use of brand marks to communicate the feeling of security. For example, the "good hands" of Allstate, the Travelers' umbrella, and Prudential's Rock of Gibraltar are all brand marks that promote a comfortable image of safety.

A **trademark** is a brand, or part of a brand, that is registered with the U.S. Patent and Trademark Office. A trademark is intellectual property owned by an organization. Trademark registration affords the organization considerable protection by granting exclusive use of its property—the brand.[19] In some cases, an organization may preclude other organizations from using a similar brand name or brand mark if it represents too great an infringement on the registered brand.[20] Trademark protection can include characters—Barney, Betty Crocker, and the Pillsbury Doughboy; shapes—Coca-Cola bottle or McDonald's golden arches; and phrases—"You're in goods hands with Allstate."

FIGURE 10-6

CHARACTERISTICS OF A GOOD BRAND NAME

A good brand name

- suggests product uses
- implies product benefits
- is easy to recognize
- is easy to remember
- is easy to spell
- is easy to pronounce
- is distinctive
- is translatable
- is positive

Brand Development Successful branding is the result of a carefully orchestrated development process wherein the brand progresses through several stages, and brand recognition, image, loyalty, and equity are created. Figure 10-7 illustrates this brand development and marketing process.

The first step in the brand development process is to gain **brand recognition**—a state of **brand awareness** in which consumers recognize the brand. The brand is familiar to consumers who have seen the brand advertised or observed it in the marketplace (such as on store shelves or being used by other consumers). In addition to brand recognition, at this stage of the development process brand marketing seeks to build some specific consumer knowledge of the product and its benefits. Greater awareness and knowledge lead to greater probability of product trial.

Having achieved brand recognition, the brand manager then proceeds to establish a **brand image**—how the brand is viewed by consumers. These convictions are important in developing **brand acceptance**—a favorable impression for the brand in the eyes of potential customers. Positive brand image is basic to a product's acceptance as a viable choice within the consumer's set of acceptable alternatives. Brand image represents the symbolic value of the product in terms of what consumers think and how consumers feel about the product.

The third stage of brand development involves enhancing the product level of acceptance. **Brand loyalty** suggests customer satisfaction with the brand as evidenced by repeat purchases. Loyalty is a matter of degree. **Brand preference** is a somewhat limited degree of brand loyalty; the customer will choose a preferred brand if it is readily available (if they can find it conveniently displayed at the local retail outlet). The lack of availability of a preferred brand results in brand switching—the purchase of an available competitive brand. The ultimate degree in brand loyalty is **brand insistence**—the customer will accept no substitute; there is no acceptable alternative. Consumers treat such brands as specialty goods and services

■ **FIGURE 10-7**

THE BRAND DEVELOPMENT PROCESS

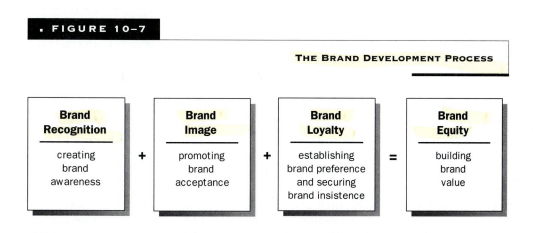

and will search extensively in order to find and secure them. The level of loyalty attained by a particular brand is the result of how comprehensive and effective the marketing program is that supports the brand development process.

The total worth or strength of the brand in the marketplace is referred to as **brand equity**. It represents the *value* of the brand to the company that owns it. The rise or fall in a company's brand equity is one measure of its changing fortunes and competitive position. For example, during the early 1990s, Nintendo plummeted from number 27 to number 103 in Total Research Corp.'s survey of brand equity. "Sega, meanwhile, showed steady growth, moving from number 131 to number 67 during the same period."[21] The top-ten most valued brands in 1994 were Coca-Cola, Marlboro, Néscafe, Kodak, Microsoft, Budweiser, Kellogg's, Motorola, Gillette, and Bacardi.[22] As illustrated in Figure 10-7, brand equity is the composite of the proprietary assets created by brand recognition, image, and loyalty. The value inherent in brand equity is often expressed in financial terms. Mergers and acquisitions are frequently predicated on the value of a company's brands in terms of their ability to generate additional sales, attract new customers, and enhance existing images. As more and more products are viewed by consumers as basic commodities, the few remaining distinguishing product features include their brand names and the equity they represent.

Brand Strategies Organizations can pursue one of four different brand mix strategies. Commonly employed brand strategies include individual branding, family branding, combination branding, and brand licensing.

The practice of using different brand names for each product line or item within the product mix is referred to as **individual branding**. Individual brand names are typically used when substantially different products make up the organization's product mix. Other circumstances when individual brand names might be used include significant variations in product quality, diverse requirements for effective marketing, and different usage behavior among various target markets. An important benefit of individual branding is that a negative image or the performance failure of one product is not transferred to another item with the same brand name. On the other hand, building brand equity for many different products is an expensive proposition.

When an organization uses the same brand name for all of the goods and services that comprise its product mix, or all of the items within a particular product line, that organization is practicing **family branding**. Family brands include such names as Campbell's, Heinz, Jell-O, and Kenmore. Movies such as the four *Rocky* films represent a family branding strategy. Mattel Inc. has created a whole family of products from its highly successful Barbie doll: ninety different dolls; a Barbie dollhouse; Barbie's sports car; Barbie on a cruise ship; kid-size Barbie; Barbies that come in wearable wedding dresses that retail for $140; and adult collector Barbies that wear clothes designed by Nicole Miller.[23]

Combination branding occurs when the organization combines individual brands with the company name. Walt Disney Studio's animated films *Dumbo, Aladdin,* and *101 Dalmatians;* Post's cereals Banana Nut Crunch, Raisin Bran, and Fruit & Fiber; and Dodge Automobiles' Intrepid, Stratus, and Dynasty are all examples of a combination branding strategy. Operating economies and marketing effectiveness are two of the more common benefits that accrue to those organizations that utilize family and combination branding strategies.

Brand licensing is an agreement by which one organization (the licenser) grants another organization (the licensee) the right to use a brand name, a brand mark, or a trademark. In essence, one company rents its name and image to another company. Licensed brands include cartoon characters (Mickey Mouse), TV characters (Big Bird), sports organizations (National Football League), corporations (Harley-Davidson), fashion designers (Gucci), and celebrities (Jack Nicklaus). Walt Disney's *The Lion King* licensed more than 5,000 different products in eighty different countries.[24] A well-conceived brand licensing program allows an organization to gain extra mileage from its name and image with a limited amount of effort or risk. To reduce risks in the very risky fashion apparel business, Perry Ellis International licenses its designs and lets others bear the manufacturing and distribution risks.[25] Overexposure, poor quality, negative associations, and inappropriate marketing activities are some of the possible pitfalls connected with brand licensing. Lacoste's classic polo shirt with its crocodile logo was once an American icon. By being plastered on a wide variety of apparel items, including infant and toddler outfits, the crocodile logo lost its snob appeal and its crisp image.[26]

Types of Brands   The branding process can be viewed from the perspective of no-name generic products, manufacturer brands, and private brands. **Generics** are unbranded and no-frill products that typically are unadvertised and offered as low-cost alternatives to brand-name products. These plain-packaged, starkly labeled products identify only the product category (cornflakes) and not the company that produced it (Kellogg's). **Manufacturer brands** are produced and distributed by the manufacturer. Also referred to as national or vendor labels, these brands are owned and controlled by manufacturers. National brands include those produced and marketed by Procter & Gamble, Ford Motor Company, IBM, Kodak, Goodyear, Century 21, Avis, and Federal Express. **Private brands,** also referred to as distributor brands or store labels, are branded product items that are produced by a manufacturer to the specifications of retailers or distributors and sold under their labels. Store brands have successfully competed against national labels because they provide retailers better profit margins.[27] Specialty stores (such as The Limited and The GAP), department stores (JCPenney and Macy's), and supermarket chains (Kroger and Winn-Dixie) are but a few of the retailers who have pursued a private label strategy for all or part of their merchandise mix. There has been a significant increase in the market share for private labels in recent years.[28] In what is commonly referred to as "the battle of the brands," national labels are fighting back by focusing on new product development, using resources to strengthen "power brands" and weed out marginal labels, closing the price gap between national and private labels, finding ways to offer greater perceived value, building closer relationships with resellers and final consumers, and improving real and perceived product quality.[29]

PRODUCT PACKAGING Product packaging is still another means to influence the buying behavior of consumers. The importance of product packaging becomes evident when one realizes that 70 to 80 percent of customer purchase decisions are finalized while consumers are in the store inspecting the merchandise.[30] A **package** is a box, carton, wrapper, or container that houses the product. Good package design is essential in order for the product to provide the many functions expected of it. Packaging functions include the following:

❑ *Promoting the product* by attracting the consumer's attention, maximizing the product's exposure, enhancing the product's appearance, stimulating the customer's interest, and supporting the product's image.[31]

❑ *Informing the customer* by identifying the product and its producer, providing information on product composition, and imparting instructions on how, when, and where to use the product.

❑ *Facilitating distribution* by safeguarding the product during distribution, assisting in the handling of the product, and providing product storage.[32]

❑ *Protecting the product* by offering tamper-resistant containers and providing aseptic containers to remove oxygen and moisture for product preservation.

Product packaging is also important in assisting customers in using the product (such as spill-proof containers) and disposing of the product (recyclable packaging materials).

PRODUCT-LINE MANAGEMENT

The next level of product decisions faced by the product manager are those associated with managing the organization's product lines. Figure 10-5 identifies product-line extensions and contractions as the key decisions to be made relative to product-line management.

PRODUCT-LINE EXTENSIONS In **product-line extensions** the product manager elects to add new products to existing product lines. For example, red beers have become a growth market for brewers. Miller has added Leinendugel Red and Red Dog to its product line. Red Wolf represents a line extension for Anheuser-Busch.[33] This expansion strategy extends the product line beyond its current mix of products in an effort to appeal to new market segments and to provide greater selection for existing customers. Extension strategies can take the form of stretching or filling a particular line of products.

Product-Line Stretching Product-line stretching can be accomplished by extending the product line downward, upward, or both ways. A **downward stretch** is achieved by adding products to the lower end of the product line in order to attract the price-sensitive consumer. It typically involves adding less expensive products that may or may not entail lower quality, fewer features, and less service. Downward stretching has characterized the computer industry (IBM and Compaq offer inexpensive personal computers), the automotive industry (Mercedes and BMW offer downsized models of their automobiles), and the fashion apparel industry (Yves-Saint Laurent and Christian Dior offer luxury ready-to-wear versions of their original designs).

An **upward stretch** strategy is one in which the product manager adds products at the high end of the product line. Higher profit margins and enhanced product image are often two of the more important reasons for pursuing upscale markets. Ford Motor Company's acquisition of Jaguar and Chrysler's purchase of Lamborghini are two examples of this high-end extension strategy. Japanese automakers (Honda and Nissan) have also successfully stretched their product lines upward.

Finally, a **two-way stretch** is accomplished when the organization adds products at both the upper and lower ends of the product line. The Marriott Hotel chain successfully stretched both ways by adding a high-end hotel (Marriott Marquis) and lower-end hotels (Residence Inn, Fairfield Inn, and Courtyard) to their established chain of Marriott Hotels.[34]

Product-Line Filling The product-line strategy of adding new product items within an established product line is called product-line filling. **Item addition** increases the depth of the product line by filling in those lines with an increased selection of brands, styles, models, sizes, colors, materials, and price points. Retailers are particularly interested in having an appropriate combination of products to offer their customers. To accomplish this goal they expect their vendors to provide them with an adequate selection of product items within each product line in order for them to develop the type of product assortments demanded by their customers.

PRODUCT-LINE CONTRACTIONS When product lines become overextended, the product manager faces the decision of whether or not to eliminate certain product lines and items. **Product-line contraction** is the process of decreasing the product offering by deleting unsuccessful products from the firm's total product offering. In order to deliver better value to its customers, Procter & Gamble has moved aggressively to cut costs, keep prices down, and improve customer service. To accomplish its goal, Procter & Gamble eliminated many unproductive product lines or combined them with other lines. Since 1991, Procter & Gamble has eliminated almost a quarter of the different sizes, flavors, and other variety brands that have not met their performance targets.[35] Products that have become overexposed, outdated, unprofitable, unmanageable, or incompatible with current product lines are all candidates for elimination. Products are terminated by discontinuing them or selling them to other organizations. Given the tendency of most organizations to achieve growth objectives through product-line expansion, these product abandonment decisions can be difficult but necessary if the firm is to reach its profit goals. Marginal products restrict the company's ability to realize profitable growth from existing as well as new product offerings.

PRODUCT-MIX MANAGEMENT

An organization's product mix represents its total selection of products offered to the marketplace. As such, the product managers must manage, plan, and control both the composition and structure of the product mix (see Figure 10-5).

Product-mix composition is concerned with the nature of the relationships among various product lines; that is, what level of consistency exists among the various product lines that make up the product mix. **Product-line consistency** refers to the extent that product lines are similar or related in terms of production methods, product quality, distribution requirements, end use, target markets, price ranges, or any other factor that strongly impacts the marketing of the product. Highly consistent product lines allow for greater economies of scale in producing and marketing the product. High product-line consistency also accrues a sharp market focus and greater market expertise. By adhering too closely to a high consistency strategy, the firm might expose itself to concentrated risk and forgo the opportunity of capitalizing on new and different product lines.

The two-dimensional structure of an organization's product mix is described in Figure 10-8. **Product-mix width,** also referred to as product variety, is the number of different product lines the organization produces, distributes, or sells. Product-width strategies can range from a narrow and highly focused product mix consisting of a limited number of product lines to a broader product-mix strategy comprised of many different product lines. As shown in Figure 10-9, Vanguard, the mutual fund company, offers investment opportunities in a wide array of stock and bond funds. Equity funds are broken down into the following product lines: balanced, growth, growth and income, international, and specialized. Income funds include taxable income, tax-free municipal, and tax-free state funds. **Product-mix depth,** referred to as product assortment by retailers, is the number of different product items within each product line.

FIGURE 10-8

THE DIMENSIONS OF PRODUCT-MIX STRUCTURE

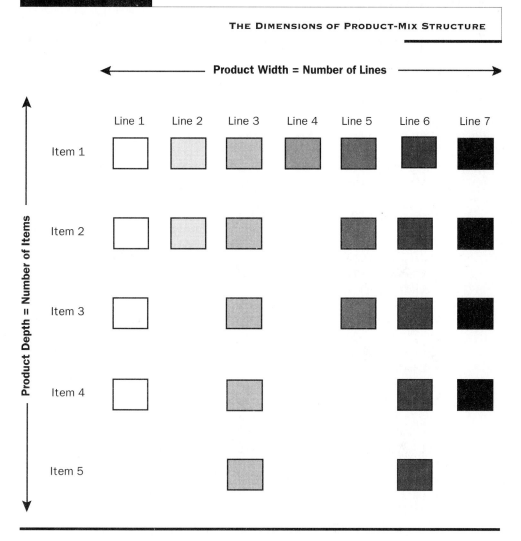

The strategic choices associated with product depth range from offering a limited selection of product items to an extensive choice of items within each product line. Vanguard, for example, offers a choice of four international funds while providing the investor a greater selection of growth funds. Category killers are retailing formats that specialize in offering the customer an extensive selection of merchandise within a particular product category. For example, Barnes & Noble, Borders Books and Music, Crown Books, and Books-A-Million are all category killers that operate superstores that offer an extensive selection of books and related reading materials.[36]

FIGURE 10-9

The Structure of Vanguard's Mix of Mutual Funds

Equity Funds

Balanced/Hybrid
- Asset Allocation
- Convertible
- Index: Balanced
- Star
- Wellesley
- Wellington

Growth
- Explorer
- Index: Extended
- Index: Small Cap
- Morgan Growth
- PRIMECAP
- U.S. Growth

Growth and Income
- Equity Income
- Index: S&P 500
- Index: Total Stock Market
- Index: Value
- Quantitative
- Trustees U.S.
- Windsor
- Windsor II

International
- Index: Europe
- Index: Pacific
- International Growth
- Trustees International

Specialized
- Energy
- Gold and Precious Metals
- Health Care
- Service Economy
- Technology
- Utilities Income

Income Funds

Taxable Income
- GNMA
- High-Yield Corporate
- Index: Total Bond Market
- Intermediate-Term Bond Market
- Long-Term Corporate
- Long-Term Treasury
- Money Market: Federal
- Money Market: Prime
- Money Market: U.S. Treasury
- Preferred Stock
- Short-Term Corporate
- Short-Term Federal
- Short-Term Treasury
- Admiral Intermediate-Term Treasury
- Admiral Long-Term Treasury
- Admiral Money Market Treasury
- Admiral Short-Term Treasury

Tax-Free Municipal
- High-Yield
- Insured Long-Term
- Intermediate-Term
- Limited-Term
- Long-Term
- Money Market: Municipal Bond
- Short-Term

Tax-Free State
- CA Money Market
- CA Insured Tax-Free
- FL Insured Tax-Free
- NJ Money Market
- NJ Insured Tax-Free
- NY Insured Tax-Free
- OH Money Market
- OH Insured Tax-Free
- PA Money Market
- PA Insured Tax-Free

NEW PRODUCT MANAGEMENT

The final set of product-related issues faced by the marketing manager is the successful introduction and acceptance of new products. As outlined in Figure 10-5, new product management is concerned with three processes—product development, product adoption, and product diffusion.

What is a new product? The answer to this question depends on one's perspective. A new product can be one that is new to a particular producer or reseller, new to a specific market, or entirely new to the world. One classification of new products identifies the following five commonly accepted categories:

1. *New-to-the-world products*—new and innovative products that represent new inventions

2. *New category entries*—new product-line additions to an organization's product mix

3. *Additions to product line*—additions to the organization's existing product lines

4. *Product improvements*—refinement and betterment of existing products

5. *Repositioning*—products that are redirected for a new use or application.[37]

PRODUCT DEVELOPMENT PROCESS

Achieving significant sales-revenue increases from existing mature products is extremely difficult. To remain competitive the organization must usually develop new product offerings. The Gillette Co. introduced twenty-two new products in 1994 and expects to top that figure in subsequent years.[38] Hewlett-Packard counts on products that are less than two years old to generate more than 60 percent of its current equipment orders.[39] Even products that are functionally sound still need updating in order to meet customer expectations.

Product development consists of several stages, which provide a systematic approach to reducing the considerable risk associated with introducing a new product into the marketplace. As outlined in Figure 10-10, the seven stages of the new product development process consist of idea generation, idea screening, concept development, business analysis, prototype development, test marketing, and commercialization.

Stage 1: Idea Generation The initial stage of the new product development process involves a systematic search for new product ideas that are consistent with the organization's mission and strategic goals. During this brainstorming stage of product development, the purpose is to identify any product ideas that could meet an unsatisfied consumer need or an underserved consumer market. Good product ideas can come from any number of different internal or external sources and can be generated by

FIGURE 10-10

THE NEW PRODUCT DEVELOPMENT PROCESS

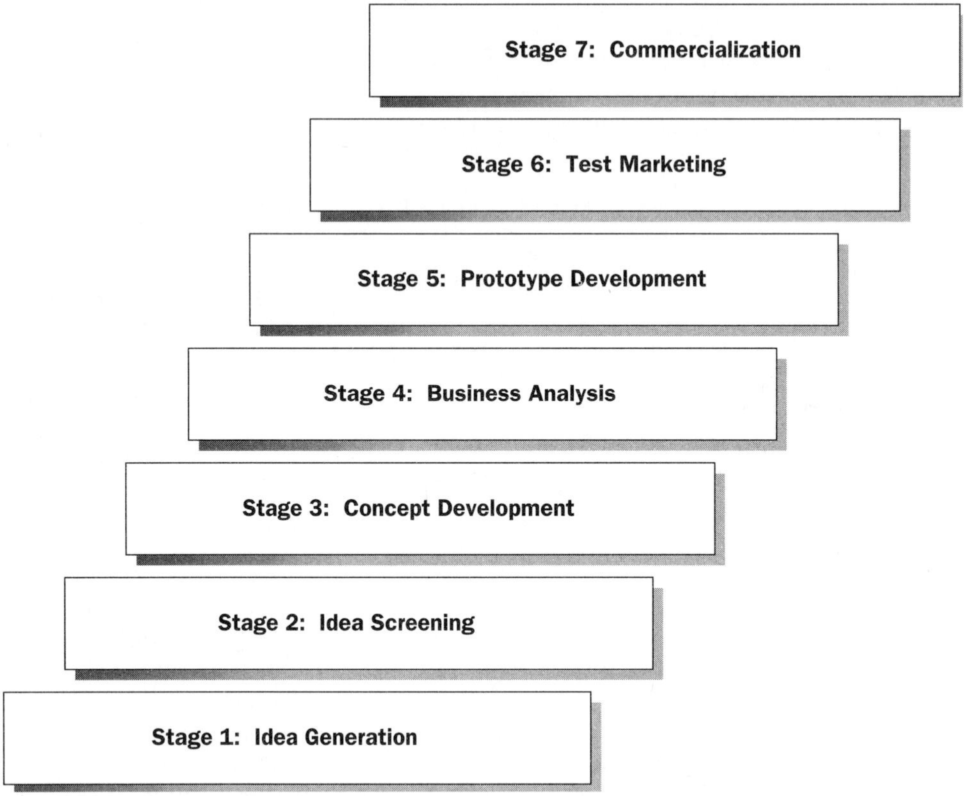

Stage 7: Commercialization

Stage 6: Test Marketing

Stage 5: Prototype Development

Stage 4: Business Analysis

Stage 3: Concept Development

Stage 2: Idea Screening

Stage 1: Idea Generation

---

using a variety of different techniques. Figure 10-11 identifies several sources of innovative and imitation product ideas.

Some of the more commonly used idea-generating techniques include the following:

- *Benefit analysis*—identify any product benefit that existing products are currently not providing
- *Use analysis*—identify any new and different applications for an existing product
- *Relative brand profile*—identify different types of products that an existing brand name might be stretched to cover
- *Systems analysis*—study systems of activities in order to identify products that might improve the performance capabilities of the system

FIGURE 10-11

SOURCES OF INNOVATION AND IMITATION IDEAS

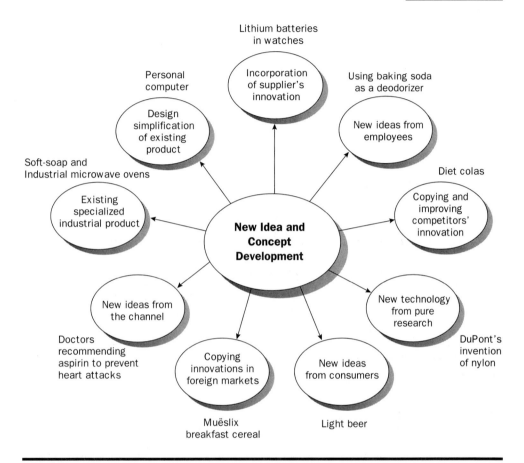

SOURCE: Reprinted by permission from Peter R. Dickson, *Marketing Management* (Fort Worth, TX: The Dryden Press, 1994), 299.

- ❑ *Unique properties*—identify any special characteristics of an existing product and determine if distinctive traits have value in the form of new applications of the existing products or possible modification for new uses
- ❑ *Achilles' heel*—identify weakness in both the organization's and competitor's existing products and distinguish the key weaknesses that might be translated into new product ideas
- ❑ *Free association*—record any and all potential product ideas associated with a particular product attribute, product use, or market need

❑ *Failures*—examine why a particular product failed in order to identify a problem that might justify a product modification

❑ *Big winners*—study products, people, and organizations that have enjoyed considerable market success in an attempt to discover their secrets to success[40]

Stage 2: Idea Screening   Product ideas generated in the first stage are screened, or evaluated, in terms of their potential as new products. Deciding which product ideas are worth pursuing requires a careful assessment of each product idea relative to the organization's strategic goals and distinctive competencies. Additional screening criteria include the size of the market, level of competition, type of environmental barriers, nature of consumer response, level of profitability, and nature of cost structures. The purpose of the screening process is to identify a limited number of new product ideas that might be described as innovative and distinctive. New products that represent a technological edge, a patentable idea, or a unique style will not only increase the likelihood of success, they will also improve the organization's chances of gaining a sustainable competitive advantage. Given the rather subjective nature of this initial screening effort, a checklist approach is quite common. Figure 10-12 identifies a checklist used by Johnson Wax to screen new product ideas.

Stage 3: Concept Development   During the third stage of the product development process, general product ideas are transformed into more precise product concepts. As described by C. Merle Crawford, a **product concept** is a verbal or pictorial version of a proposed product. This conceptualization of a product includes a description of the following:

1. One or more of the benefits that it will provide the customer

2. Its general form

3. The technology used to achieve the form[41]

The goal of concept development is to obtain a complete description of the proposed product and its intended uses so that the organization's marketing team can properly evaluate it.

Once a product idea has been transformed into a product concept, the next step usually involves conducting a **concept test**—an evaluation of the product concept by potential customers. A common practice is to develop several versions of the product concept and ask consumers to rate each version relative to several different criteria. Personal interviews are used to administer most concept tests. This testing process has proven to be fairly reliable with respect to new product proposals that do not require major changes in the buying behavior of consumers. Radically new product concepts that dictate significant behavioral changes require considerably more testing than a basic concept test. Most new product ideas do not make it past the concept test and are rejected during this filtering process.

FIGURE 10-12

JOHNSON WAX'S CHECKLIST FOR SCREENING NEW PRODUCT IDEAS

No.	Element	Yes	No
1.	The idea represents high value-added products, not commodity-type products.		
2.	It requires consumer-oriented development and presentation of products using existing marketing capabilities.		
3.	The idea has high advertising or promotional content that allows for intensive communications.		
4.	It's not a major capital investment for the consumer (such as an appliance or motor home).		
5.	There is opportunity for developing logical extensions.		
6.	The product offers a significant "plus" that is discernible by a large majority of consumers.		
7.	There is an opportunity to expand into many overseas markets.		
8.	The idea ties in with existing key Johnson's functions—technology, marketing, sales force.		
9.	Labor will be of average or lower intensity relative to national norms.		
10.	Capital will be of average or lower intensity relative to national norms.		
11.	The product is compatible with Johnson's physical packaging capabilities.		
12.	The product is preferably nonperishable.		
13.	The idea is related to entomology, microbiology, polymer chemistry, emulsion or film formation, or substrate technology.		
14.	The product uses existing distribution channels.		
15.	There is an extended product life cycle (that is, years versus months).		
16.	The product can be a building block for a multiproduct line or business.		

SOURCE: Adapted from Rodger L. DeRose, "New Products—Sifting through the Haystack," *Journal of Consumer Marketing* (Summer 1986), 83. Reprinted by permission of Marketing Journals Publishing Company.

Stage 4: Business Analysis Does the new product concept make good business sense? This question must be answered during the fourth stage of the new-product development process. A **business analysis** is an examination and evaluation of the business parameters surrounding the production and marketing of the proposed new product. Developing an explicit business proposal necessitates consideration of the following issues:

❑ *Demand analysis*

  1. Make projections of short- and long-term sales potential
  2. Identify price/sales relationship

3. Delineate sales cycles
4. Discover consumer behavioral patterns

❑ *Profit analysis*
1. Project fixed and variable cost structures
2. Conduct break-even analysis
3. Estimate short- and long-term profit margins

❑ *Competitor analysis*
1. Recognize competing products and organizations
2. Identify competitive strengths and weaknesses
3. Devise competitive strategies and tactics
4. Estimate probable market shares

❑ *Production analysis*
1. Estimate materials requirements
2. Identify sources of supply
3. Outline production processes in terms of facilities, equipment, and human resources.

❑ *Marketing analysis*
1. Configure a distribution network
2. Explore potential pricing strategies
3. Design possible product-mix strategies
4. Determine service support requirements
5. Ascertain promotional requisites

The above considerations are only a sampling of the issues that would normally be addressed at this product development stage. Few new product concepts have the overall potential to survive the business analysis stage.

Stage 5: Prototype Development   A favorable business analysis report results in the decision to develop a product prototype. The **prototype development** stage involves transforming the product concept into an actual product. It is during this design stage that product specifications (materials, workmanship, style, and features) and product performance standards are identified and evaluated. During this stage of the product development process, the organization faces key decisions concerning such issues as the type and number of product features and the nature of the value package to be offered the consumer in terms of the relationship between product quality and product price. Technical feasibility tests, production engineering checks, customer acceptance studies, and marketing program analysis are part of the prototype development process.

Stage 6: Test Marketing How will targeted consumers react to the new product? To get a preliminary answer to that question, marketing managers may conduct limited market tests of the product. **Test marketing** is a limited introduction of the product prototype and its proposed marketing program. By restricting the new product introduction to a particular geographical area (such as carefully selected cities representative of the targeted consumer markets and the marketing conditions under which the product will compete), the marketing management team can study consumer reactions to different product versions and different marketing programs. Product modifications and the fine-tuning of marketing strategies are inherent parts of this developmental stage. The Limited's merchandising calendar is a sophisticated computer analysis program that pinpoints the days of the year and the stores for testing a given item so that the test yields a better reading of how well that item will do nationally.[42]

Stage 7: Commercialization Successful test market results lead to the full-scale introduction of the product. **Commercialization** is the rollout of a new product. This requires the complete support of the organization's senior management and a major commitment of the firm's resources. Acclaim Entertainment supported its introduction of Mortal Kombat, a video game featuring blood, gore, and human dismemberment, with a $10-million market blitz that helped it to finish the year as the top-selling video game.[43] New product rollout can be gradually phased in over time by introducing the product on a market-by-market basis. Alternatively, the firm can elect to introduce the product to the entire marketplace in one major campaign. Even with a carefully conceived and implemented product development process, the chance of failure still looms above each new product introduction. A number of reasons have been identified for new product failures. Figure 10-13 outlines several of these reasons and identifies suggested safeguards for avoiding the same mistakes in the future.

PRODUCT ADOPTION PROCESS

An understanding of how new products are accepted by the consuming public is essential to the new-product development process. The **adoption process** is a mental and behavioral procedure consisting of a series of stages that a prospective buyer goes through in trying, using, and adopting a new product. The marketing manager's goal is to get the buyer to make regular use of the product and to eventually become a loyal customer.

New-product adoption is a five-stage process consisting of creating awareness, generating interest, encouraging evaluation, promoting trial, and gaining adoption. During the **awareness** stage, the prospective consumer is

FIGURE 10–13

New Product Failures: Reasons and Safeguards

Failure Reason	Elaboration	Suggested Safeguard
1. Market too small	Insufficient demand for this type of product	Market is defined and rough potential estimated in the opportunity identification and concept test phase
2. Poor match for company	Company capabilities do not match product requirements	Opportunities are matched to company's capabilities and strategic plans before development is begun
3. Not new/not different	A poor idea that really offers nothing new	Creative and systematic idea generation. Also, early communication check to see how idea is perceived.
4. No real benefits	Product does not offer better performance	In the design stage, perceived benefits of concepts as well as benefits from actual product use are tested
5. Poor positioning/ misunderstanding of consumer needs	Perceived attributes of the product are not unique or superior	Use of perceptual mapping and preference analysis to create well-positioned products
6. Inadequate support from channel	Product fails to generate expected channel support	Assessment of trade response to pretest market phase
7. Forecasting error	Overestimation of sales	Use of systematic methods in design, pretest, and test phase to forecast consumer acceptance
8. Competitive response	Quick and effective copying by competitors	Good design and strong positioning to preempt competition. Quick diagnosis of, and response to, competitive moves.
9. Changes in consumers' taste	Substantial shift in consumer preference before product is successful	Frequent monitoring of consumers' perceptions and preferences during development and after introduction
10. Changes in environmental constraints	Drastic change in key environmental factor	Incorporation of environmental factors in opportunity analysis and design phases. Adaptive control.
11. Insufficient return on investment	Poor profit margins and high costs	Careful selection of markets, forecasting of sales and costs, and market-response analysis to maximize profits
12. Organizational problems	Intraorganizational conflicts and poor management practices	Multifunctional approach to new product development to facilitate intraorganizational communication. Recommendations for a sound formal and informal organizational design.

SOURCE: Reprinted by permission from Glen L. Urban, Jorn R. Hauser, and Nikhilesh Dholakia, *Essentials of New Product Development* (Englewood Cliffs, NJ: Prentice-Hall, 1987), 37–38.

exposed to the new product but lacks information regarding its use, features, and benefits. Awareness generates **interest.** In this second stage, the potential adopter actively seeks out additional information about the new product and its uses. Having accumulated sufficient information for **evaluation,** the prospective buyer judges the relative strengths and weaknesses of the new product and forms a favorable or unfavorable opinion concerning its merits. If the opinion is favorable, the potential consumer becomes an actual buyer by proceeding to the trial stage of the adoption process. During this fourth stage, the individual becomes a customer by adopting the product on a limited basis by sampling the product. If the trial also proves favorable, and the customer experiences consistent satisfaction, the individual may become a regular customer by adopting the product as a preferred alternative. When customers elect to use the product on a regular basis, the fifth and final stage of **adoption** is completed.

The rate or speed at which prospective consumers adopt a new product innovation depends on a variety of factors. The type of marketing effort, the nature of prospective buyers, the conditions of the marketplace, and the degree of competition are some of the factors that impact how fast a new product might be adopted. The characteristics of the new product innovation are also extremely important in determining adoption rates. Figure 10-14 describes how relative advantage, compatibility, complexity, observability, and trialability impact the rate of adoption for new products.

PRODUCT DIFFUSION PROCESS

The **diffusion process** describes the spread of a new product over time. It depicts how a new product penetrates the marketplace and the manner by

FIGURE 10–14

PRODUCT CHARACTERISTICS THAT INFLUENCE THE RATE OF NEW PRODUCT ADOPTIONS

Relative Advantage	The extent to which a new product is perceived to be better than existing products
Compatibility	The extent to which a new product is consistent with existing patterns of consumer buying and usage behavior
Complexity	The extent to which a new product can be easily understood and used by potential adopters
Observability	The extent to which potential adopters can observe the product's favorable attributes and benefits
Trialability	The extent to which a new product can be tested on a trial basis and the degree to which its benefit can be experienced through demonstrations, samples, and trials

which consumers accept and adopt a new product innovation. Some people are quick to try a new product; others prefer to delay adoption until more information is available. Still others wait until the product becomes widely accepted. Some consumers rarely adopt anything new. These varying behavioral traits with respect to the dispersion of new products have led to the classification of adopters into the following five categories:

- *Innovators*—venturesome consumers who tend to be quick to adopt new products. They tend to be younger, better educated consumers who are relatively financially secure. Innovators have broad social relationships and use multiple sources of information in their consideration of product innovations. They represent a limited segment of the total market (2.5 percent).

- *Early Adopters*—community leaders who adopt new products after innovators but long before most other consumers. Early adopters have above-average education and frequently serve as opinion leaders within certain social groups. As such, early adopters play an important role in influencing the larger market to accept the new product innovation. Early adopters comprise 13.5 percent of the total market.

- *Early Majority*—consumers who make up a significant proportion of the mass market (34 percent) and who carefully deliberate their decision to adopt a new product. Early majority consumers have above-average incomes and educations; therefore, their social status allows them to serve as a reference group to the rest of the market.

- *Late Majority*—skeptical consumers who tend to adopt a new product only after it has been accepted by a significant majority of the total market. Peer pressure, economic advantage, and an absence of risk tend to trigger acceptance by this consumer group. On average, the late majority is made up of individuals who have lower incomes, have lesser social status, and are less responsive to change. Nevertheless, they represent a significant share of the total market (34 percent).

- *Laggards*—tradition-bound consumers who are the last to adopt almost any new product or idea. Often laggards get around to adopting a product after innovators and early adopters have discarded it. These conservative consumers tend to have lower incomes and social status. Laggards (16 percent of the market) are often ignored by some organizations due to the limited size and potential of the market segment.

The nature of the consumer adoption process helps explain why products go through life cycles. Because of the time it takes to gain product acceptance by different consumer groups, competitive product offerings can be developed and marketed as alternatives for those consumers who make up the early and late majority. The interplay of the adoption process and competitive response contributes to product evolution in the form of life cycles.

Concluding Remarks

A product can be a tangible good or an intangible service or idea. It is essential that marketers view products from the perspective of the total-product concept—the sum of the functional attributes, aesthetic features, service extras, image extras, psychological benefits, and operational benefits associated with the product. Marketers develop product mixes (product lines, items, and units) in order to meet the diverse needs of various target markets. To better understand products and their development, product managers use a product concept known as the product life cycle, a management tool that explains how products develop over time.

Consumer products can be classified on the basis of their durability (durables and nondurables) or on the basis of the buying behavior employed by consumers (convenience, shopping, specialty, and unsought products). Organizational products are also classified on the basis of their durability and cost (expense and capital goods) and on their usage and form (raw materials, component parts, manufactured materials, installations, accessory equipment, operating supplies, and business services).

Product-line management is a bottom-up process in which the product manager is responsible for product-item management (quality, design, branding, and packaging), product-line management (extensions and contractions), product-mix management (composition and structure), and new product management (development, adoption, and diffusion processes).

Endnotes

1. Robert La Franco, "Margarita Marketing," *Forbes* (January 16, 1995), 84.

2. Randall Lane, "The Boxer Rebellion," *Forbes* (September 12, 1994), 74. Also see Cyndee Miller, "Men Drop Their Dull Drawers for Something More Colorful," *Marketing News* (October 24, 1994), 1–2.

3. Zina Moukheiber, "They Want Mules, We'll Sell Mules," *Forbes* (September 12, 1994), 44.

4. Nancy Cohen, "Toys: Selling Education," *Stores* (February 1991), 29. Also see Andrea Rutherford, "Educational Toys Spell H-O-T as Parents Seek to Give Kids an Edge," *Wall Street Journal* (July 9, 1992), B1, B8; and Dana Wechsler Linden, "Mr. Smith Builds His Dream Store," *Forbes* (June 20, 1994), 94, 98.

5. Alexandra Ourusoff, "Brands, What's Hot. What's Not." *Financial World* (August 2, 1994), 44.

6. Jim Carlton, "Nintendo, Video-Game Retailers Discover Treasure Trove in Donkey Kong Country," *Wall Street Journal* (January 11, 1995), B1.

7. Susan Chandler, "Sears' Turnaround Is for Real—For Now," *Business Week* (August 15, 1994), 102.

8. Teri Agins, "Fashion Slaves Get Kicks from Spike Heels," *Wall Street Journal* (January 20, 1995), B1.

9. Kelly Shermach, "Coffee Drinking Rebounds; Specialty Blends Lead Way," *Marketing News* (September 12, 1994), 2.

10. Kelly Shermach, "Pay Now, Die Later," *Marketing News* (October 24, 1994), 1, 6.

11. Douglas MacDonald, "A Conversation with Dr. Val Feigenbaum," *Tenneco Symposium* (Summer 1992), 20.

12. See David A. Garvin, "Competing on the Eight Dimensions of Quality," *Keeping Customers* (Boston, MA: Harvard Business School Press, 1993), 119–36. Also see Hirotaka Takeuchi and John A. Quelch, "Quality Is More Than Making a Good Product," in *Keeping Customers*, ed. John J. Sviokla and Benson P. Shapiro (Boston, MA: Harvard Business School Press, 1993), 137–50.

13. Michael Treacy and Fred Wiersema, "How Market Leaders Keep Their Edge," *Fortune* (February 6, 1995), 88.

14. John Morton, "Predicting Brand Preferences," *Marketing Management*, Vol.2, No.4 (1994), 35.

15. See Philip B. Crosby, *Quality Is Free: The Art of Making Quality Certain* (New York: McGraw-Hill, 1979); Tom Peters, *Thriving on Chaos* (New York: Knopf, 1987); and Allan J. Magrath, "Marching to a Different Drummer," *Across the Board* (June 1992).

16. Richard C. Morais, "If You Stand Still, You Die," *Forbes* (January 30, 1995), 45.

17. Peter H. Farquhar, "Strategic Challenges for Branding," *Marketing Management*, Vol. 3, No. 2 (1994), 10.

18. Roula Khalaf, "Le Tire, C'est Moi," *Forbes* (August 1, 1994), 49.

19. See Steven A. Meyerowitz, "Surviving Assaults on Trademarks," *Marketing Management*, Vol. 3, No. 1 (1994), 44–46.

20. See "Combating Counterfeiting," *Marketing Management*, Vol. 2, No. 3 (1993), 49–51.

21. Cyndee Miller, "Sega vs. Nintendo," *Marketing News* (August 29, 1994), 1.

22. Alexandra Ourusoff, "Brand, What's Hot."44.

23. Seth Lubove, "Barbie Does Silicon Valley," *Forbes* (September 26, 1995), 84.

24. Cyndee Miller, "King of Licensing Takes Cat Nap; Back for Holidays," *Marketing News* (September 26, 1994), 2, 14.

25. Brigid McMenamin, "Grunge Is Out, Licensing Is In," *Forbes* (May 23, 1994), 46.

26. Joshua Levine, "Anemic Crocodile," *Forbes* (August 15, 1994), 116.

27. Phyllis Berman, "We Don't Do an Exact Copy," *Forbes* (October 10, 1994), 78.

28. Chad Rubel, "Price, Quality Important for Private Label Goods," *Marketing News* (January 2, 1995), 24.

29. Cyndee Miller, "Big Brands Fight Back against Private Labels," *Marketing News* (January 16, 1995), 1.

30. Howard Schlossberg, "Marketers Told to Get Customers Involved and Take Back the Store," *Marketing News* (April 13, 1992), 5.

31. See Ian Murphy, "Perfume Bottles Make a Fashion Statement," *Marketing News* (December 4, 1994), 6–7.

32. See Marc E. Babej, "How about a Nice Box of Warm Milk," *Forbes* (August 29, 1994), 86.

33. Cyndee Miller, "What's Cool and Delicious and RED All Over?" *Marketing News* (November 7, 1994), 2.

34. Judy Ward, "Marriott: The Sequel," *Financial World* (August 2, 1994), 28–29. Also see Rita Koselka, "Marriott, Meet Marriott," *Forbes* (March 13, 1995), 48.

35. Zachary Schiller. "Ed Artzt's Elbow Grease Has P&G Shining," *Business Week* (October 10, 1994), 86.

36. See Richard Phalon, "A Bold Gamble," *Forbes* (February 28, 1994), 90–91. Also see William M. Stern, "Southern Fried Reading," *Forbes* (June 20, 1994), 91–92.

37. This discussion adapted from C. Merle Crawford, *New Products Management*, Fourth Edition (Burr Ridge, IL: Irwin, 1994), 11.

38. Rita Koselka, "It's My Favorite Statistic," *Forbes* (September 12, 1994), 166.

39. Robert D. Hof, "Hewlett-Packard," *Business Week* (February 13, 1995), 67.

40. This discussion is based on the material found in Appendix A, "Other Techniques of Concept Generation," by C. Merle Crawford, *New Products Management*, Fourth Edition (Burr Ridge, IL: Irwin, 1994), 444–51.

41. Ibid, 477.

42. Susan Caminiti, "Can The Limited Fix Itself?" *Fortune* (October 17, 1994), 172.

43. Christopher Palmeri, "Kombat Marketing," *Forbes* (February 28, 1994), 102.

DISTRIBUTION DECISIONS

CHAPTER OUTLINE

- **INTRODUCTION**
- **MARKETING CHANNELS**
    - CHANNEL SYSTEMS: AN INTERCOMPANY NETWORK
    - CHANNEL INSTITUTIONS: THE MARKETING TEAM
    - CHANNEL INTERACTIONS: A COOPERATIVE EFFORT
    - CHANNEL FLOWS: A DISTRIBUTIVE PATHWAY
- **THE DESIGN OF MARKETING CHANNELS**
    - RECOGNIZING DISTRIBUTION NEEDS
    - ESTABLISHING DISTRIBUTION OBJECTIVES
    - IDENTIFYING DISTRIBUTION ALTERNATIVES
    - EVALUATING DISTRIBUTION ALTERNATIVES
    - SELECTING DISTRIBUTION ALTERNATIVES
- **THE MANAGEMENT OF MARKETING CHANNELS**
    - CHANNEL CONFLICT
    - CHANNEL CONTROL
    - CHANNEL COOPERATION
- **CONCLUDING REMARKS**

Introduction

In recent years, as markets have fragmented and competition intensified, the role of distribution has become an increasingly important and vital element in the success of any marketing program. The success of such retail Goliaths as Wal-Mart and Home Depot is predicated on their ability to forge close alliances with key vendors. "For instance, VF Corp., maker of Lee and Wrangler jeans, has linked its computers to those of its retailers. Now it can track daily sales and replenish stocks automatically, without cumbersome order forms. That makes for happy customers and bigger sales."[1] IBM, on the other hand, not only remained wedded to the mainframe long after the emergence of the lucrative personal computer, but the firm also failed to recognize and react to the competitive threat posed by a new and viable channel of distribution for personal computers—the direct marketing channel employed by such computer firms as Dell and Gateway.

The very nature of marketing and the exchange process suggests that a key task for the marketing manager is to arrange for the efficient distribution of the organization's products. Having the right products in the right place at the right time are basic tasks of the organization's **marketing channel of distribution**—an intercompany network of marketing institutions that cooperate in the operation and management of distributive pathways. This network directs channel flows and facilitates channel exchanges among processors, producers, resellers, and consumers. Marketing channel networks are viewed as operating systems because their structures and designs satisfy system requirements of sequential linkages, nonrandom organizations, and goal orientation. The links in a distribution channel are the channel participants (marketing institutions and facilitating agencies), which are organized to perform certain tasks at certain times and places. This interdependency among channel participants necessitates commonly agreed upon goals, which serve as a focus for the distributive and operational activities of each participant.

Marketing Channels

Channel Systems: An Intercompany Network

The market channel system is composed of two subsystems—the industrial channel and the consumer channel (see Figure 11-1). The **industrial channel** originates with the raw-resource supplier and terminates with the manufacturer, who processes the product into its final form. This intercompany network includes some combination of raw-resource producers, jobbers, semiprocessors, industrial distributors, and final manufacturers.

FIGURE 11–1

MARKETING-CHANNEL SUBSYSTEMS

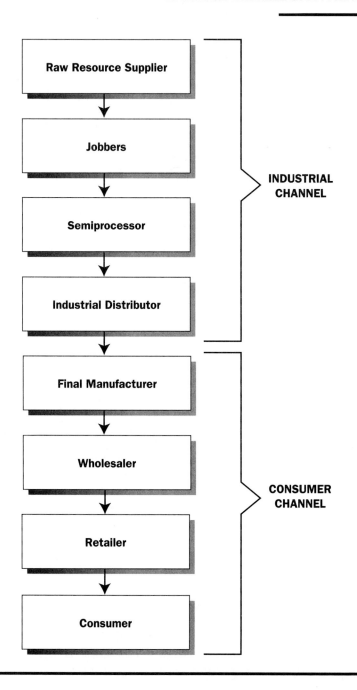

A **consumer channel** is concerned with moving products from the final manufacturer to the ultimate consumer. The composition of the consumer channels includes a number of different arrangements involving final manufacturers, wholesalers, retailers, and final consumers.

Channel Institutions: The Marketing Team

Distribution is a team effort. Channel team membership is based on the nature of an institution's transactional involvement and whether or not members assume title to the goods involved in the transaction. Channels of distribution are comprised of both full- and limited-member institutions, which are supported by a wide range of facilitating nonmember agencies. A **full-member institution** is a marketing intermediary who is directly involved in the purchase and/or sale of products and who takes title to the products involved in a transaction. Raw-resource producers, final manufacturers, merchant wholesalers, and most retailers have full membership in consumer channels.

Marketing middlemen who are directly involved in the sale and/or purchase of products but who do *not* take title to those products are **limited-member institutions.** Marketing firms that have limited membership status usually work on commission; many jobbers, distributors, agent wholesalers, and consignment retailers operate in such a fashion. Firms that perform or assist in the performance of one or a limited number of marketing functions, and who neither take title to the product involved in a transaction nor become directly involved in negotiating sales and purchases, are termed **facilitating agents.** These nonmember institutions are typified by transportation companies, advertising agencies, marketing research firms, and financial institutions that support and facilitate the distributive activities of full- or limited-member institutions.

Channel Interactions: A Cooperative Effort

In the normal course of marketing-channel operations, a large number of different types of interactions among different channel members are necessary if distribution is to be completed efficiently and effectively. For example,

> [M]any wholesalers define their companies as being in the "marketing support business." These wholesalers view themselves as *marketing with* their suppliers and customers and not *distributing from and to* them. They recognize their primary purpose is to help both suppliers and customers develop effective marketing programs.[2]

These cooperative interactions include the following:

❑ *Buying*—channel members create product assortments by purchasing products from several different channel members

- *Stocking*—channel members carry product inventories and make them available to members as needed

- *Informing*—channel members provide each other with useful information that is mutually beneficial to each party

- *Financing*—channel members extend credit or provide loans to other channel participants

- *Transporting*—channel members arrange for the transfer of products from one channel member to another

- *Selling*—channel members establish terms and conditions of sale under which they are willing to participate in an exchange with other channel members

- *Transferring*—channel members exchange a free-and-clear title to the product for the appropriate payment

- *Promoting*—channel members engage in persuasive communications with each other concerning products, prices, and services

Channel Flows: A Distributive Pathway

The marketing channel of distribution is concerned with delivering the firm's entire program to chosen market segments. **Channel flows** are movements among channel participants within a given marketing channel. These movements consist of several different types of flows, which travel over different routes in various directions at different speeds. Five major types of flows pass through a channel of distribution: physical, ownership, payment, information, and promotion flows. Each flow is vital to the successful completion of a firm's marketing program.

Physical Flow The **physical flow** involves the actual movement of a physical product from one channel participant to another. Tasks associated with the physical flow include order processing, materials handling, warehousing, inventory control, packaging, and transporting activities. In addition to channel members who take possession and are directly involved in the buying and selling process, the physical flow often involves facilitating agencies (common carriers and public warehouses). These facilitators assist in the movement of products by providing one or more specialized tasks. The typical direction of the physical flow is down the channel from producer to resellers to consumers. On occasion, however, the physical flow moves *up* the channel. This reverse physical flow might consist of customer returns of goods deemed unsatisfactory for some reason or recycling of reusable materials such as aluminum cans, returnable bottles, or rebuildable auto parts.

OWNERSHIP FLOW With the exception of a few major purchases such as homes and automobiles, consumers purchase most products without ever giving any thought to the right of ownership and obtaining a certificate of title. Why? Past experience has taught consumers that it is not an issue of concern; they assume that full payment ensures a free-and-clear title to their purchases. And, because of the Uniform Commercial Code, the consumer assumption is generally valid. Under this code, every sale is subject to an implied warranty known as the "warranty of title." It states that every legitimate seller makes an intended promise that he or she has offered the buyer a free-and-clear title to the product and that consumers have the right to assume that they own the product and have full use of it without fear of repossession. The fact that most of us have seldom experienced the problem of a questionable title attests to the tremendous success of the marketing channel in managing the **ownership flow**—the transferring of title (the right of ownership and usage) from one channel participant to the next.

Participants in the ownership flow include those who engage in the buying process for purposes of reselling or consumption and those who facilitate the ownership flow by offering financial services (such as banks). Financial institutions often retain a claim to the title until they have been compensated for their services (repayment of a loan). For example, **conditioning financing agreements** involve credit arrangements in which the passage of title is conditioned upon full payment; nonpayment results in title repossession. Like the physical flow, the primary direction of the ownership flow is down the channel; however, title can move up the channel, as in the case of title repossessions for nonpayment or product returns due to unsatisfactory performance.

PAYMENT FLOW Buying and procurement lead to compensation and payment. The **payment flow** consists of the transfer of monies from one channel participant to another as compensation for services rendered or goods delivered. In other words, the payment flow involves remuneration for value received. Channel participants enhance a product's value in the following ways:

1. Making products more readily available—time and place utility

2. Improving product composition and structure—form utility

3. Transferring the right of product ownership—possession utility

4. Communicating the various elements of the firm's marketing program—information utility

5. Providing product choice situations—assortment creation

The directional flow of payments has a percolator character in that payments percolate up from consumers through most participating channel members and facilitators. A return payment flow is also present; rebates, refunds, allowances, and coupons are all examples of payments that flow down the channel.

INFORMATION FLOW Meaningful interactions among channel participants depend on transmission of useful data. The **information flow** is a two-way communication of useful data among channel participants. Information on the availability and character of each channel member's marketing program flows down the channel. Prior to any purchase decision, potential buyers require information on the product, place, and price offerings of various sellers. Information also flows up the channel. Basic market information on consumer acceptance of a marketing program is essential since firms must constantly make adjustments in their programs if they are to remain competitive in the dynamic marketplace. Equally important is the exchange of essential operating information among channel participants attempting to achieve a coordinated distribution effort.

PROMOTION FLOW Marketing involves the art of influence. The **promotion flow** is a firm's flow of persuasive communications directed at influencing the decisions of consumers (consumer promotion) and other channel participants (trade promotion). The promotion flow involves the use of advertising, personal selling, merchandise incentives, and publicity. Each of these promotional methods may be used under different conditions and in various ways to influence the actions of consumers and the behavior of participating channel members. Promotional methodology is discussed in Chapter 12, "Promotion Decisions."

RATES OF FLOW The rate of movement through a distribution channel depends on the marketing philosophies of channel members and the demand characteristics of the marketplace. Channels that operate under a "low margin–high turnover" philosophy tend to move products more rapidly than channels that follow a "high margin–low turnover" strategy. By keeping operating expenses low, the low margin–high turnover channel can offer lower prices in hopes of generating higher sales levels—the volume strategy. The high margin–low turnover channel is willing to forego higher sales volumes in anticipation of lower sales volumes at higher per-unit profits.

The rate at which products travel through the channel is also influenced by the ultimate consumer. Products that are characterized by high and steady marketplace demand move through the channel at a faster and more continuous rate of flow. Low or seasonal product demand promotes slower and uneven channel flows.

THE DESIGN OF MARKETING CHANNELS

Designing a distribution system is a complex process due to the marketing system's need to develop different channels for different markets at different times. We define **marketing-channel design** as "those decisions involving the development of new marketing channels where none had existed before or the modification of existing channels."[3]

Successful channel designs are the result of a careful planning process involving the following steps:

1. Recognizing distribution needs
2. Establishing distribution objectives
3. Identifying distribution alternatives
4. Evaluating distribution alternatives
5. Selecting distribution alternatives

The five steps in the marketing-channel design process also are shown in Figure 11-2. This channel paradigm will serve as the organizational framework for our discussion on channel design.

RECOGNIZING DISTRIBUTION NEEDS

The need for developing new channels or modifying existing channels stems from a wide variety of internal and external situations. Internally, channel-design changes may be necessary to overcome conflict among channel participants, to control the behavior of another channel member, or to better coordinate the efforts of individual channel participants. For example, Quaker Oats had to rework its distribution system for Gatorade because it had reached the limits of its wholesale delivery system. The new strategy involved expanding Gatorade's distribution beyond its traditional grocery channel via wholesalers. The goal was to move into "direct-store deliveries, vending machines, and fountain service... to go after food outlets and point-of-sweat locations such as golf courses."[4] The issues surrounding channel conflict, power, control, and coordination are numerous and will be treated later in this chapter.

Externally, environmental dynamics require constant development and modification of channel designs in order to adapt to new market opportunities and to meet new competitive threats. Based on marketplace conditions, a firm's management may recognize the need for a number of different market and channel-design strategies. Market penetration and channel integration necessitate considerable modification of existing channel structures. Other marketing strategies, such as product development, diversification, differentiation, and market positioning, would require decisions concerning new channel development as well as existing channel modification. See Chapters 2 and 3 for a discussion of these strategies.

FIGURE 11-2

The Marketing-Channel Design Process

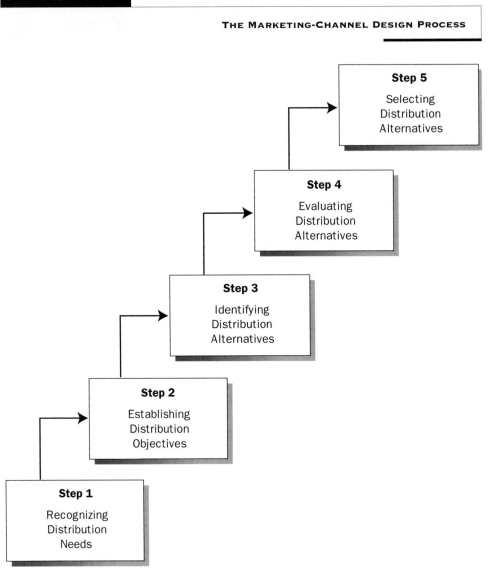

Establishing Distribution Objectives

Channel-design decisions are guided by carefully considered objectives. The potential number of distribution objectives is large; however, the following statements tend to be representative of the type of objectives used to direct channel-design decisions.[5]

1. *Coverage of Important Resellers*—having the firm's products available in most of the retail outlets where consumers expect to find them.

Toothpaste is a product that most consumers purchase in either a supermarket, discount store, or drugstore. Therefore, a toothpaste manufacturer could establish an objective of having its brands of toothpaste available in 80 percent of all supermarkets, discount stores, and drugstores within each of the company's market areas.

2. *Coverage of Geographic Markets*—being able to make a delivery within a given amount of time. Quick and reliable delivery of the firm's products is a service standard valued by both industrial buyers and resellers of consumer goods. For example, a firm may establish an objective of being able to meet a one-week delivery standard for 60 percent of its markets and a two-week delivery standard for the remaining 40 percent.

3. *Amount and Location of Sales Space*—gaining reseller cooperation in providing a desired level of product exposure. Customer purchases are influenced by the visibility and accessibility of a product within a store; people purchase what they can see and find. In-store product exposure is a function of the amount of space (sales-floor square footage and linear feet of shelf space) devoted to the product and the location (end-of-aisle or eye-level position) of that space. A specific objective might be stated as gaining the cooperation of 80 percent of all resellers in providing display areas of one linear foot of eye-level shelf space for each of the company's major brands.

4. *Level of Inventory Investment*—gaining ample marketplace representation of the firm's product lines and securing adequate stock support levels for each item within each product line. Ample inventory investment levels of a firm's product variety and assortment is essential if the firm is to gain acceptable sales volumes for all of its lines and avoid losing sales due to stock-outs. Specifically, this objective could be stated as obtaining commitments from all resellers to stock 75 percent of the firm's full line of products and to support each product item with a maximum inventory sufficient to cover expected sales for a three-week period.

5. *Personal Selling Support*—obtaining sufficient personal selling effort from resellers to generate a desired level of sales. Personal selling attention is crucial to the success of some products and brands. A company may have as an objective that the sales personnel of any retailer stocking the company's products will attempt suggestive selling of the firm's products in 80 percent of those selling situations in which the customer has not indicated a specific product or brand preference.

6. *Effective Sales Promotion*—enticing resellers to participate in the firm's sales promotion programs. Such merchandising incentives as coupons and premiums are of no value to consumers if local retailers do not support such activities. Hence, a goal of having 75-percent reseller participation in each sales promotion program is a specific enough statement to direct the actions of the channel planner.

Based on these and other relevant objectives, the channel planner must select channel participants that are willing and able to support these operational guidelines. When such guidelines are in place, the channel manager possesses the means to identify distribution alternatives.

IDENTIFYING DISTRIBUTION ALTERNATIVES

Marketing channels can be characterized by a number of different structural designs. The term **channel structure** refers to the arrangement or positioning of channel members within a distribution system and to how various distribution tasks are allocated among them. As shown in Figure 11-3, the number of alternative channel structures is a function of channel length, width, complexity, and multiplicity of dimensions.

CHANNEL LENGTH DECISIONS Channel length is concerned with the vertical dimensions of a distribution system. Channel length decisions involve determining how many independent intermediaries (in terms of ownership and operations) are to be positioned between the producer and the consumer. **Short channels** are channel structures containing few if any independent intermediaries between the producer and the consumer. Short channels suggest a more direct marketing approach in that the producer in certain circumstances might sell directly to the consumer. **Long channels** are indirect channel structures in that several independent intermediaries are positioned between the producer and consumer. In point of fact, channel length is a relative term; marketers tend to think of channel structures as being longer or shorter and more direct or indirect distribution systems.

Figure 11–4 depicts relative channel length from the perspective of the number of levels that comprise a given channel structure. A **two-level** channel is a short channel consisting of two levels—a producer-to-consumer channel. This direct channel contains no independent middlemen; factory outlet stores and farmers' markets exemplify this two-level channel. Some consumer-products manufacturers also go directly to the consumer via door-to-door, mail-order, and television or radio selling.

FIGURE 11-3

THE DIMENSIONS OF CHANNEL STRUCTURE

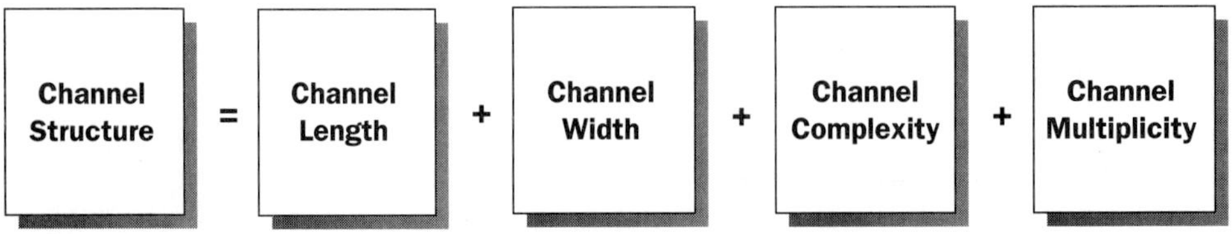

Channel Structure = Channel Length + Channel Width + Channel Complexity + Channel Multiplicity

FIGURE 11-4

TYPES OF MARKETING CHANNELS BASED ON CHANNEL LENGTH

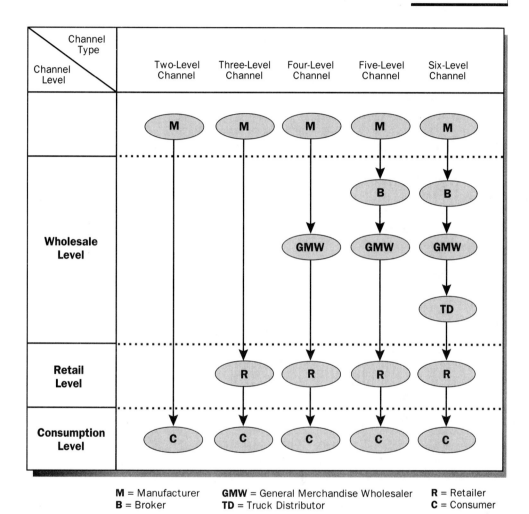

M = Manufacturer   GMW = General Merchandise Wholesaler   R = Retailer
B = Broker   TD = Truck Distributor   C = Consumer

A **three-level channel** contains three channel participants situated at different levels. The most common example is the manufacturer-to-retailer-to-consumer channel, with the retailer being the independent intermediary. Large retailing firms such as Sears, JCPenney, and Kmart have the operating economies of scale to successfully utilize this type of channel structure.

Typically a **four-level channel** includes participants at both the manufacturing and consuming levels with two independent middlemen—one each at the wholesale and retail levels. These indirect marketing channel structures are commonly associated with accessing the marketplace through small, independent retailers.

Five- and **six-level channels** are extended structures that incorporate three and four independent intermediaries, respectively. As seen in Figure 11-4, these multilevel channels are lengthened considerably by the inclusion of several wholesaling intermediaries—brokers, general merchandise wholesalers, and truck jobbers. Convenience products that require intensive distribution over extended geographic areas are perhaps the best examples of products requiring lengthy channels. Five- and six-level channels are not commonly encountered in the United States and tend to be employed far less frequently than shorter channels.

Up to this point we have discussed channel length with respect to consumer channels. Industrial channels are also characterized by different channel structures based on channel length and the number of levels. Typically, industrial channels tend to be somewhat shorter than consumer channels. A more direct marketing approach is possible because industrial markets tend to be made up of large-volume buyers that are more geographically concentrated than consumer markets. In general, shorter industrial channels are used to market major facility and equipment purchases while somewhat longer channels are used to distribute standardized maintenance and supply items.

CHANNEL WIDTH DECISIONS Channel width decisions focus on the intensity of market coverage. The desired intensity of distribution is a crucial factor in determining the exposure and perhaps the success a product enjoys in the marketplace. **Channel width** decisions involve determining how many middlemen will be required at each channel level in order to achieve the desired intensity of market coverage. Figure 11-5 illustrates the three channel width and market coverage strategies—intensive, selective, and exclusive.

Intensive Distribution The strategy of achieving maximum market coverage and product exposure in all market segments by stocking the product in as many outlets as possible is known as **intensive distribution.** In the extreme, this strategy requires that the product be readily available wherever potential consumers desire to purchase it. The marketer who employs an intensive strategy is attempting to serve all customers within a given market by obtaining a "blanket" coverage of that market. To achieve this blanket coverage, a wide channel structure involving many different types of wholesalers and retailers is necessary (see Figure 11-5).

In addition to excellent market coverage and product exposure, this "everyplace" distribution strategy has the following advantages:

❑ Creating wide consumer recognition of the company's brands

❑ Preserving sales on company brands that consumers prefer but will not search for if they are not readily available

THE DESIGN OF MARKETING CHANNELS

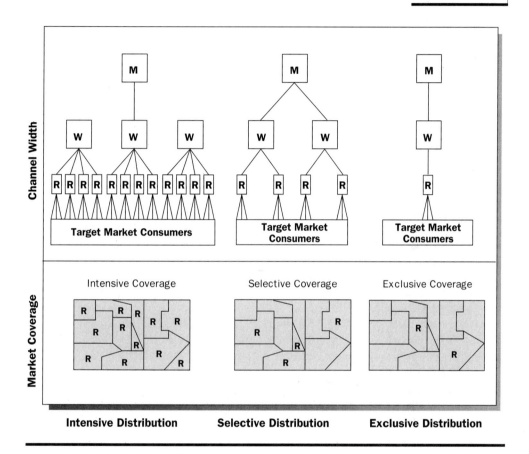

FIGURE 11-5

CHANNEL WIDTH AND MARKET COVERAGE STRATEGIES

❑ Promoting considerable impulse purchases of company products, which represent additional sales that would not have been made if the product were not so conveniently available

The principal limitations of an intensive strategy are the loss of some management control over the distribution process and the number of problems associated with operating such an extensive flow of products. Convenience products are typically marketed through intensive channels of distribution.

Exclusive Distribution The marketer can focus on a single market segment and exclusive market coverage by structuring a narrow marketing channel (see Figure 11-5). **Exclusive distribution** is the strategy of limiting product distribution to a single outlet per targeted market segment. It is directed at market segment penetration and not at maximizing the coverage of all market segments; in other words, exclusive distribution focuses on a quality—not quantity—market coverage.

The benefits of exclusive distribution to the manufacturer are inviting. First, it allows more direct control over the marketing effort for company products. The pricing, promoting, and service practices of resellers can be managed more closely and efficiently due to their limited numbers. Second, by giving a reseller an "exclusive," the manufacturer can expect that reseller to stock the manufacturer's complete product line and to provide an aggressive selling effort in merchandising each line. Third, exclusive distribution enhances the prestige and image of the manufacturer's products; it promotes an individualistic image and helps to attract the consumer who is looking for unique and distinctive products. In contrast to the maximum product exposure tactic of intensive distribution, the strategy of exclusive distribution helps to avoid overexposure of company products and brands and to promote an image of "specialness." TAG Heuer eliminated more than 1,500 of the 3,000 retailers in its strategy to make its watches more exclusive. In a similar vein, Cartier and Gucci pulled their products (expensive jewelry and fine leather goods, respectively) out of hundreds of stores in the United States in an effort to stop discounting by cash-strapped department stores and to preserve the more exclusive image of their brands.[6] Finally, exclusively distributed products usually command higher prices and per-unit profit margins. If the right target markets are selected, consumers are willing to pay for the exclusiveness of their shopping preferences.

The principal limitation of exclusive distribution is its concentration of risk. By restricting distribution to one outlet per market, the manufacturer becomes dependent on that outlet and, should it prove to be ineffective in merchandising the company's products, there are no backup outlets to cover that market. An exclusive strategy is suited to the specialty products marketer. Exclusive distribution enhances the "special" character and image of specialty products.

Selective Distribution An intermediate distribution arrangement between intensive and exclusive channels is **selective distribution**—restricting the distribution of company products to a select few resellers. Using a channel of intermediate width, the marketer achieves a select product exposure in each targeted market segment. The number of targeted markets served depends on a number of factors:

1. How many market segments contain the desired type of consumer

2. The expected sales volume for each segment

3. The degree of representation the marketer wants in the total market in order to create a desired image and exposure level

Selective distribution offers a balance between the advantages and disadvantages of intensive and exclusive distribution. Selective channels of distribution allow reasonable control over the firm's marketing effort, promote an average or better sales effort, and provide acceptable coverage of markets. Selective channel structures also permit comparison shopping behavior at selected outlets and strike a balance between overexposure and underexposure of the firm's products. Both new and established companies utilize selective strategies for their shopping products since these products require that consumers be given the opportunity to compare one product with another. Marketing managers use selective distribution in order to induce resellers to stock their products. They also like selective channel arrangements because they retain a reasonable amount of control over the marketing of their products.

CHANNEL COMPLEXITY AND MULTIPLICITY Realistically, the number of feasible alternative channel arrangements is limited by practical considerations, which will be discussed in the next section on channel design. Nevertheless, the complexity and multiplicity of channel arrangements varies from simple/single to complex/multiple structures. **Channel complexity** refers to how complicated the relationships are among various participants within a marketing channel. **Channel multiplicity** relates to the practice of developing several channel alternatives in an effort to reach the same or different market segments. Talbots, the stylish women's apparel retailer, employs a dual distribution system in reaching its customer niche of women who prefer a classic look to a trendy look. The firm operates both retail outlets and catalog operations.[7] Sherwin-Williams repositioned its four main brands so that each brand has a different and focused channel of distribution. The 2,030 Sherwin-Williams stores sell only Sherwin-Williams paint. Mass merchants carry Dutch Boy. Independent paint and hardware stores get the Martin Senour brand while discount stores sell the Kem-Tone label. Sherwin-Williams is also the largest private-label paint maker (Sears' Weatherbeater and Easy Living).[8] Figure 11-6 illustrates both a simple/single and a complex/multiple channel structure that might be used by a stationery manufacturer in targeting one or more market segments.

EVALUATING DISTRIBUTION ALTERNATIVES

The Franklin Mint markets its collectibles directly to the consumer by mail-order retailing. Avon uses door-to-door selling in its direct marketing efforts. Sherwin-Williams, the paint company, owns and operates a chain of home decorating centers. General Motors utilizes a network of franchised dealers to merchandise its many lines of automobiles. In marketing its numerous personal care products, Bristol-Myers uses a company sales force to call on wholesalers and large chain accounts. PepsiCo distributes its soft drinks in as many outlets as possible. Liz Claiborne, a maker of women's apparel, limits the distribution of its products in order to achieve a selective coverage of retail markets. Louis Vuitton handbags are sold through an exclusive network of stores.

Why did each of these firms select their particular mode of distribution? The reasons are many and suggest a complex decision involving several

FIGURE 11-6

THE COMPLEXITY AND MULTIPLICITY OF CHANNEL STRUCTURES

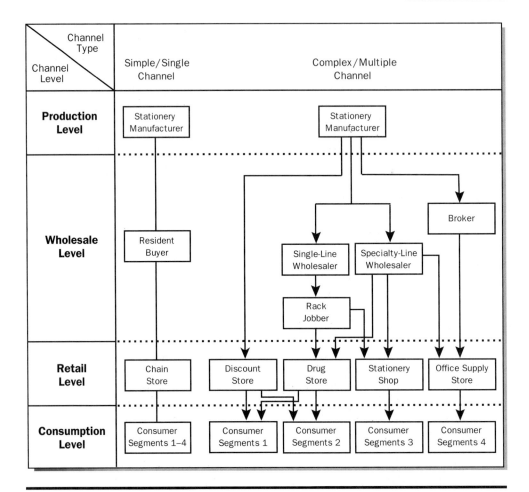

interacting elements. At this stage of the channel design process, we examine a number of factors on an individual basis to discern how long or short or wide or narrow a channel should be. You should keep in mind that the following discussion is from the perspective of the manufacturer.

CHANNEL LENGTH INFLUENCERS The distribution manager is not totally free in making channel-design decisions. Channel length is influenced by a number of interrelated factors, including the markets to be served, the products to be marketed, the company's mode of operation, and the environmental conditions surrounding the firm's marketing efforts. The influence of market, product, company, and environmental factors on the tendency to use longer or shorter channel structures is shown in Figure 11-7. When reviewing Figure 11-7, keep in mind that the expressed relationships are general rules of thumb and not absolute determinants of channel length. However, the final decision on channel length will be based on some composite of these factors.

Market Characteristics   Smaller concentrated markets located in close proximity to the manufacturer's production facilities are suitable targets for shorter distribution channels. The tendency to use longer channels is increased when the firm's markets are large or dispersed and located some distance from production points. This need for longer channels and the use of additional intermediaries is obvious when one considers the difficulties involved in reaching consumers of a product like candy bars. The number of sales contacts required to reach such a large number of widely dispersed customers and the problems of physically distributing the firm's products to such a market makes the task of reaching those buyers impossible without the use of many intermediaries. Also, markets of a large, distant, and dispersed nature incorporate a more diversified group of consumers. By including intermediaries who have expertise on the local character of a market, the channel manager has substantially increased the likelihood of being able to tailor the marketing program to the specific needs of that market.

Product Characteristics   Bulky products such as building materials require short channels (see Figure 11-7) because they are heavy or large in relationship to their value and cannot support the expense of unnecessary handling. A direct flow from production to consumption points keeps handling costs to a minimum. Products that are perishable, fashionable, or seasonal are also distributed through shorter channels because of the urgency associated with these products. The loss of marketability due to physical deterioration or fashion and seasonal obsolescence requires rapid distribution. Shorter channels are faster because fewer channel participants are involved. Also, security and care-in-handling considerations may lead marketers of products such as jewelry or delicate equipment to select channels that employ as few intermediaries as possible.

Shorter channels are also more appropriate for products that require a personal selling effort; with fewer participants, the manufacturer is better able to successfully employ sales motivation programs and to influence the amount of personal selling attention devoted to the company's products. But, when products are purchased in small quantities and on a frequent basis, the investment costs and the lack of economies of scale typically prohibit most attempts at direct marketing. Longer channels with a multitude of intermediaries are better suited to handling the frequent individual purchases of ultimate consumers.

Company Characteristics   Short, direct channels of distribution require considerable strength on the part of the manufacturer who elects to use this type of structure. This strength stems from the firm's financial resources, managerial expertise, and practical experience in operating a distribution system. Maintenance of control is the reason strong companies prefer to

FIGURE 11-7

FACTORS INFLUENCING CHANNEL LENGTH

Factor	Factor Definition	Channel Length Tendency	
		Longer Channels	**Shorter Channels**
Market Characteristics			
•Market Size	•The number of customers making up a market	•Larger Markets	•Smaller Markets
•Market Dispersion	•The number of customers per unit of land	•Dispersed Markets	•Concentrated Markets
•Customer Location	•The proximity of customers to production points	•Distant Locations	•Close Locations
Product Characteristics			
•Product Bulk	•The largeness or weight of a product relative to its value	———	•Bulky Products
•Physical Perishability	•The loss of marketability due to physical deterioration	———	•Perishable Products
•Fashion Perishability	•The loss of marketability as a result of style or fashion obsolescence	———	•Fashionable Products
•Seasonal Perishability	•The loss of marketability because the product is out of season	———	•Seasonal Products
•Product Value	•The per-unit market value of a product	———	•Expensive Products
•Product Standardization	•The degree to which a product fits standard operating procedures	•Standardized Products	•Customized Products
•Product Complexity	•The degree of technical sophistication of a product	———	•Highly Technical Products
•Product Age	•The product's stage in the product life cycle	•Mature Products	•New Products
•Product Type	•The type of product based on type of end user	•Consumer Products	•Industrial Products
•Product Type	•The type of product based on the final consumer's willingness to spend time, money, and effort	•Convenience Products	•Specialty Products
•Product Service	•The level of service required for effective marketing	———	•Extensive Service Products

continued

utilize a short channel. By maintaining tighter control over their distribution system and other marketing activities, these firms are better able to tailor their efforts to the specific needs of their markets.

FIGURE 11-7

CONTINUED

Factor	Factor Definition	Channel Length Tendency	
		Longer Channels	Shorter Channels
• Selling Method	• The most appropriate selling method for a product	• Self-Service Products	• Personal Selling Products
• Purchase Quantity	• The typical order size of the ultimate consumer	• Small-Order Products	• Large-Order Products
• Purchase Frequency	• The average number of times a consumer buys a product within a given time frame	• Frequently Purchased Products	
Company Characteristics			
• Company Resources	• The composite strength of a firm based on finances, marketing programs, and other resources	• Weak Company	• Strong Company
• Company Control	• The degree to which a firm needs to control its marketing programs		• Extensive Control
• Company Experience	• The amount of distribution experience possessed by the firm's management team	• Inexperienced Company	• Experienced Company
• Market Coverage	• The desired number of outlets in each market area	• Intensive Coverage	• Exclusive Coverage
• Product Selection	• The nature of the firm's product variety and assortment	• Narrow Variety—Shallow Assortment	• Wide Variety—Deep Assortment
• Product Consistency	• The degree to which a firm's product lines are related	• Heterogeneous Product Line	• Homogeneous Product Line
Environmental Characteristics			
• Economic Conditions	• The inflationary nature of the economy	• Boom Conditions	• Recessionary Conditions
• Competitive Conditions	• The number of competitors in the market area	• Many Competitors	• Few Competitors
• Social Conditions	• The degree of social acceptability of the firm's product line	• Socially Acceptable Products	• Socially Unacceptable Product

The support of intermediaries is essential if a company wants to obtain intensive coverage of the marketplace. No matter how strong or big the company is, it will need the cooperation of a wide variety of resellers within a longer channel structure if the product is to be conveniently located and available to all consumer groups. Finally, a company characterized by a wide variety of homogeneous product lines with a deep assortment of items within each line has a product offering that is extensive enough to make a direct-marketing effort feasible. The probability of successfully establishing a direct sales relationship with retailers and consumers is substantially increased when the manufacturer offers an extensive choice situation.

Environmental Characteristics Longer, more direct methods of distribution are used when economic conditions are good. An attitude of "share the wealth" often prevails. During recessionary times cost cutting is likely and channels are trimmed to include only those participants who are essential to channel operations and who accomplish their tasks in the most efficient manner possible.

A highly competitive market environment often necessitates a longer channel. To remain competitive, additional intermediaries may be required to meet or better the product exposure and availability of competitors' products. Finally, freedom of channel design can be influenced by the social acceptability of the firm's products. The more socially unacceptable the firm's products, the more limited the channel manager is in finding middlemen who are willing to handle the product. The questionable character of pornographic materials restricts the options for channel design.

CHANNEL WIDTH INFLUENCERS Channel width alternatives can be identified along a continuum ranging from wide channels resulting in intensive distribution to narrow channels for exclusive distribution. Figure 11-8 illustrates the relationship between several influencing factors and the desired type of market coverage.

Intensively Distributed Products Products that are distributed through an intensive channel system tend to be frequently purchased, lower priced products for which consumers are not willing to make an exerted shopping effort (convenience products). Intensively distributed products also tend to be common, "everyday" products of a nontechnical nature, which can be sold on a self-service basis with limited service support. Given the widely distributed nature of these products, resellers usually try to limit their investment in such products by stocking the best-sellers.

Exclusively Distributed Products In contrast, exclusively distributed products tend to be of a specialty and distinctive nature and have a higher price tag. Typically, these products are purchased on a less-frequent basis and require a salesperson's support for effective merchandising. Also, exclusively distributed products tend to be new or technical products with extensive service requirements. Because of the exclusivity of distribution, which eliminates direct brand competition, resellers are more willing to stock the seller's full line of products.

FIGURE 11-8

FACTORS INFLUENCING CHANNEL WIDTH

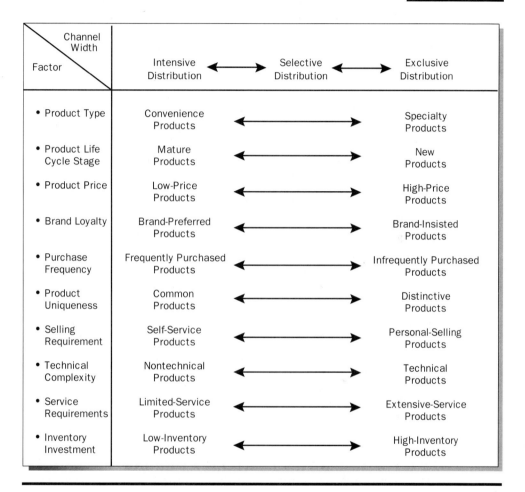

Selecting Distribution Alternatives

The last step in the channel design process is the selection of a distribution alternative. The channel manager is directed in this step by the firm's distribution needs and the corresponding distribution objectives. Within the constraints established by these needs and objectives, the marketing channel choice must take into account the issues of availability, suitability, feasibility, controllability, and flexibility. Each channel alternative should be screened with respect to each of the above criteria before any channel decision is made.

Not all channel alternatives are available to the marketing manager. Some wholesalers and retailers are simply not in the firm's choice field because they have entered into exclusive distribution arrangements with other firms, or they are currently satisfied with their present suppliers and do not wish to stock additional product lines.

Nor are all channel alternatives suitable. A firm's distribution requirements may not coincide with a potential reseller's mode of operation, thereby eliminating any channel alternative containing such a reseller. Suitability can be judged on a wide variety of criteria. Product assortment, product quality, promotional support, delivery requirements, pricing programs, service levels, inventory practices, and cooperative spirit comprise a short list of criteria used by one channel member in judging the suitability of possible channel partners.

The economic feasibility of each channel alternative is also a primary factor in selecting viable channel partners. Each channel alternative and the intermediaries that comprise it must be evaluated in terms of the cost of services provided relative to the level of sales generated. The major difficulty with applying this criterion is the problem associated with obtaining accurate sales and cost estimates for each alternative channel structure. Typically, direct channels are more costly to the manufacturer than longer channels because all marketing costs must be borne singlehandedly. However, many experts feel that a company sales force is more effective in securing higher sales levels. If this is true, the additional cost associated with a company sales force may be justified and create a more profitable situation. If not, longer channels with lower capital outlay, and possibly lower sales, might be the best choice.

Not all channel alternatives are equally controllable. Shorter channels are more controllable than longer channels. Exclusive distribution systems are more controllable than intensive channel structures. If the firm's management deems it necessary to have tight control over all aspects of the marketing mix, then shorter and more exclusive channel structures should be selected.

Channel alternatives are not all equally adaptable. The marketplace changes rapidly; therefore, a desired structural attribute is sufficient flexibility to make whatever adaptations are necessary. Channel structures and relationships should be developed with the expectation that change is not only necessary but desirable. The big-three card companies, Hallmark, American Greetings, and Gibson, each favor a different channel of distribution. Hallmark is number one in specialty stores, American Greetings is the leader in mass retail chains, and Gibson heads up deep-discount stores. This works out well for American Greetings because changing card-buying patterns favor the one-stop shopping associated with mass merchants. With declining market share, Hallmark has entered the drugstore market by selling the Hallmark label to Walgreen and Osco.[9] Successful market channels are adaptive organisms that welcome change.

THE MANAGEMENT OF MARKETING CHANNELS

The distribution marketing channel is an interactive system of participating members. As such, it is subject to the behavioral processes inherent in all social systems. Each channel participant's actions impact on the whole system. The entire system benefits when individual actions are directed at cooperative behavior. Channel disruption and disharmony occur when individual behavior conflicts with the norms of the channel social system. Whether the marketing channel is in a state of conflict or cooperation, it must be managed and controlled. The elements of marketing-channel management are shown in Figure 11-9. Because the relationship among these elements may lead to channel conflict, channel control is needed if channel cooperation is to be maintained.

FIGURE 11-9

THE ELEMENTS OF MARKETING-CHANNEL MANAGEMENT

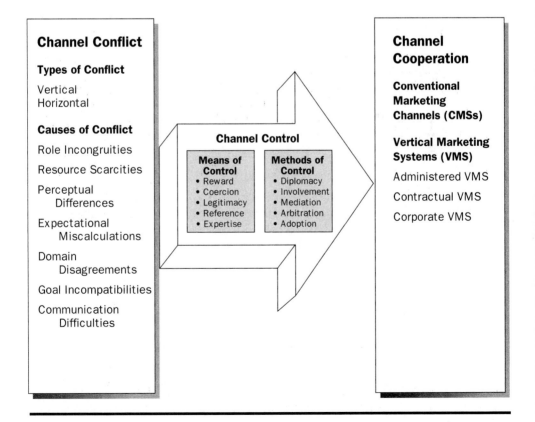

Channel Conflict

The very nature of a marketing channel creates an environment wherein conflict is likely to develop. Disagreement should be anticipated given the variety of channel participants and the complexity and multiplicity of channel relationships. **Channel conflict** is a "situation in which one channel member perceives another channel member(s) to be engaged in behavior that is preventing or impeding him from achieving his goals."[10] Channel conflict can also be viewed as a state of frustration felt by one channel participant when another participant restricts its role performance.[11] Suppose, for example, that a manufacturer perceives that a retailer is unduly restricting the amount of shelf space that the firm believes is required for proper product exposure. An adversarial relationship might emerge wherein the manufacturer feels it is necessary to gain product exposure forcibly by threatening unfavorable adjustments in trade allowances. In turn, retailers may counter by further reducing the shelf space allocated to the manufacturer's products and increasing the stock levels of competitive products. The injurious nature of this type of conflict not only impacts on the conflicting parties but also disrupts the operations of the entire marketing channel. This spillover has the net result of reducing channel efficiency and retarding business operations among all channel participants.

TYPES OF CONFLICT Channel conflict can be classified as either vertical or horizontal confrontation. **Vertical conflict** occurs among channel participants at different levels within a marketing channel. Serious disagreements among manufacturers, wholesalers, and retailers are examples of vertical conflict. This type of conflict may stem from different situations.

- *Branding issues*—retailers develop private house brands to compete with the manufacturer's national brands
- *Pricing issues*—a manufacturer insists on a price maintenance agreement which requires the retailer to set prices at a certain level or above
- *Order issues*—a manufacturer's minimum order quantity exceeds the retailer's desired stock levels
- *Display issues*—a retailer requires that the manufacturer's local advertising expenditures exceed a certain level before preferred display space will be granted
- *Assortment issues*—the manufacturer interferes with the retailer's desired product assortment plan by following a full-line forcing policy

Nike's inventory-control system, called Futures,

> forces retailers to order up to 80 percent of their purchases six to eight months in advance in return for guaranteed delivery times and a discount

of up to 10 percent. ... Retailers hate it because if they guess wrong about the market, they get stuck with the shoes. But Nike's market pull lets it call the shots.[12]

The list of issues resulting in vertical conflict is almost endless. Conflict issues between franchisers and franchisees are quite common. For example, General Nutrition Company (GNC) franchisees charge that the management favors company-held stores by supplying products to them more often, while franchisees wait for order fulfillment. Franchisees also charge that GNC's distribution system is overtaxed, resulting in stock-outs. And that in oversaturated markets, company-owned stores launch price wars and put franchised outlets at a disadvantage.[13]

Horizontal conflict is a serious disagreement among channel members at the same level within the marketing channel. Conflict between two or more wholesalers or two or more retailers constitutes horizontal conflict. This type of conflict takes one of two forms: conflict among different intermediaries at the same level (discount store versus supermarket retailer) or conflict among similar intermediaries at the same level (department store versus department store). Potential horizontal issues of conflict include destructive price wars and unfair comparative advertisements.

CAUSES OF CONFLICT The reasons for vertical and horizontal conflict are many. A number of traceable and explainable causes of channel conflict have been identified; they include role incongruities, resource scarcities, perceptual differences, expectational miscalculations, decision domain disagreements, goal incompatibilities, and communication difficulties.

The role of each channel participant is clearly defined in well-established channels. A **role** is the behavior expected of a particular channel member who occupies a certain level within the channel system. Given the relative channel positions of raw-resource producers, industrial distributors, final manufacturers, wholesalers, and retailers within the distribution channel, each is expected to perform certain tasks at certain times in prescribed places. **Role incongruities** occur when channel participants do not behave as expected; that is, when they do not live up to their prescribed role. For example, a franchised Ford auto dealer is expected to have a service department that is capable of supporting the warranty programs of the Ford Motor Company. If the dealer fails to stock sufficient parts or to employ qualified mechanics, the dealer is not meeting the prescribed role established in the franchise agreement.

Resources are essential to goal attainment. **Resource scarcities** refers to "conflict stemming from a disagreement between channel members over the allocation of some valuable resources needed to achieve their respective goals."[14] Eye-level shelf space is an example of a limited resource that must be carefully allocated. A retailer may feel that in-store eye-level merchandising space should be restricted to high-margin items that have proven sales capabilities. But the manufacturer may need desired display space to gain the exposure essential to the successful introduction of a new product. Advertising dollars are also scarce resources. Different channel members are likely to disagree as to the most effective budget allocation among different advertising media, time slots, and product lines.

Each channel participant views channel operations from its own unique perspective or position within that channel. A retailer "looking up" the channel will have a different view than a manufacturer "looking down" the channel. **Perceptual differences** are a logical outcome of the many vertical positions occupied by channel participants. A manufacturer who is concerned with gaining entry and representation in the marketplace will view many distribution problems in a different light than a retailer who views similar problems from the perspective of securing supportive sources of supply. Consider, for example, the issue of inventory investment at different levels in the channel. Both the manufacturer and the retailer want sufficient product inventory readily available in order to gain product exposure and new sales, as well as to avoid stock-outs and lost sales. To meet this objective, the manufacturer sees the solution as moving as much inventory as possible on to the retailer's shelves. The retailer, who is concerned with overstocking and high inventory carrying costs, might view the situation from the perspective of delivery time. A manufacturer's delivery standard of one or two days is far more preferable to retailers than having inventory pushed into their stockrooms.

Marketing success requires that the marketer anticipate the future behavior of both organizational and ultimate consumers. In planning marketing-channel operations, the manager forecasts the behavioral intentions of channel participants and takes actions based on these predicted outcomes. For example, in negotiating terms and conditions of a sales contract, one party may anticipate that the other party will assume a hard bargaining position. And, sure enough, based on the first party's position, the second party does take a hard negotiating stand even though it was not its original intention to do so. These **expectational miscalculations** lead to channel conflict due to the self-fulfilling-prophecy syndrome of creating a predicted outcome by engaging in certain actions that would normally lead to the expected future behavior.

Channel conflict also occurs when two or more channel members believe that they have the exclusive or primary right to make certain decisions. Who determines the retail selling price? What types of displays are necessary to properly merchandise the product line? When and where should cooperative advertising be used? These are but a few of the potential **decision domain disagreements** among channel members. Who has the right to make what decisions? These rights need to be clearly specified. While highly integrated channel systems have clearly defined each member's decision domain, many loosely structured channels have failed to spell out each member's decision rights. The result is more conflict.

Channel conflict often stems from incompatible goals of channel members. **Goal incompatibilities** are of two types:

1. Those between two or more members of the marketing channel

2. Those that occur between an individual member and the entire channel system

A wholesaler's goal of profit maximization (buy low, sell high) would obviously be achieved at the expense of the manufacturer (supplier) and the retailer (customer). If the overall goal of the channel system is to increase sales and market share while an individual channel member is concerned with minimizing costs, a conflict situation is likely to occur between the individual and the system. Efficient channel operations are a team effort, and team effort requires compatible goals. Benetton, the Italian apparel company, pursued a goal of creating awareness of social issues through highly controversial ad campaigns featuring photos of dying AIDS patients and Palestinian refugees. Independent Benetton store owners have filed suits charging that the ads were inappropriate and have turned shoppers away in droves.[15]

Written, verbal, and electronic communications are vital to effective interaction among channel participants. **Communication difficulties** can result from any of the following problems:

❏ *Encoding and decoding messages*—misinterpretation of terms and expressions by either the sender or receiver

❏ *Transmitting messages*—misplacement of a message by a transmitter

❏ *Interfering noise*—distortion or delay of a message caused by internal or external sources

A misplaced order, a misprinted expression of a discount term, a failure to communicate new warranty conditions, and a false rumor concerning a channel member's actions or intentions are all examples of breakdowns in marketing channel communications that can lead to internal channel strife.

CHANNEL CONTROL

Channel conflict must be resolved and converted to channel cooperation. This resolution and conversion process becomes the responsibility of the **channel captain**—the most powerful and controlling member of the channel. It is through leadership that cooperative channel effort is achieved (see Figure 11-9). Any channel member (manufacturer, wholesaler, or retailer) can assume the role of channel captain providing it possesses the means and methods of control.

MEANS OF CONTROL The means of control is the basis of the power of the channel captain. **Channel power** is the ability of the captain to influence the decisions and actions of other channel members. The bases of power are also shown in Figure 11-9.

- *Reward power*—the captain's ability to enhance a channel member's operation by compensating the cooperative member in the form of financial rewards (wider margins and extended credit terms) or operational rewards (exclusive territories and preferred delivery arrangements)

- *Coercive power*—the captain's ability to punish a noncooperative channel member by refusing to deal, delaying shipments, withdrawing service support, reducing margins, and other similar punishments

- *Legitimate power*—each channel member's recognition and acceptance of the captain's legitimate right to lead the channel; this legitimacy may stem from financial strength, contractual arrangements, a successful marketing program, consumer product loyalty, or a host of other factors, for example, Philip Morris's food empire consisting of Kraft, General Foods, Oscar Meyer Foods, and Maxwell House.[16]

- *Referent power*—each channel member's desire to be identified or associated with the channel captain, who has achieved a position of status and a prestige image in the marketplace

- *Expert power*—the captain's perceived expertise (skills and information) in marketing and other business functions

By carefully cultivating each of the power bases, the channel captain is in a position to encourage, or even force, the cooperation of individual members of the channel system. The better developed each of the power bases is, the more effective the channel captain is in controlling membership behavior.

METHOD OF CONTROL Having means of control and knowing how to use them are two different issues. The task of channel leadership is to skillfully use appropriate bases of power to convert conflicting situations into cooperative effort. The channel captain has the following methods of control from which to choose—diplomacy, involvement, mediation, arbitration, and adoption.[17]

Diplomacy is the art and practice of conducting negotiations among channel members. It involves settling conflict without arousing additional hostility. Channel leadership uses "ambassadors" in their diplomatic efforts to overcome hostilities and to reduce tension. The responsibilities of the ambassadors are to:

1. Gather information relevant to the conflict situation
2. Study the problem from each channel member's perspective
3. Identify possible alternative solutions
4. Explore the acceptability of each alternative solution with conflicting parties
5. Gain agreement as to the most acceptable alternative
6. Initiate the actions required to implement the agreed-upon solution

Diplomacy is one of the more preferred methods of conflict resolution because it represents a joint, voluntary, and cooperative effort at problem solving.

Involvement is the method of having conflicting parties become participants in various conflict-resolution structures. This method is utilized in the belief that personal interaction and association promotes a better appreciation of the channel member's position. Involvement can take any of the following forms:

1. *Joint membership in trade associations*—for example, when manufacturers belong to the National Retail Merchants Association
2. *Personnel exchange*—trading personnel among channel members (role reversal) for a specific time period
3. *Co-optation*—"the process of absorbing new elements into the leadership or policy determining structure of an organization as a means of averting threats to its stability or existence."[18]

Mediation involves the active intervention of a third party between conflicting channel members to promote reconciliation, settlement, or compromise. The tasks of the mediator are the same as those of the channel ambassador. Mediators are individuals who have the confidence of both conflicting parties. They may be supplied by government agencies or trade associations or selected from the private sector (such as a respected consultant or professor).

Arbitration is the hearing and settlement of a conflict by a third party chosen by the disagreeing parties (voluntary arbitration) or appointed under statutory authority (compulsory arbitration). The decision of the arbitrator is final and binding for both parties. The potential advantages of this method of resolving channel conflict are that arbitration (1) is fast, (2) can preserve secrecy, (3) is less expensive than litigation, (4) can lead to easier solutions because the problem is confronted in its earlier stages, and (5) is conducted by industrial experts who have a good understanding of the complex issues.

Adoption is the strategy of securing agreement on common channel goals that are in the best interest of all channel members, including those members who find themselves in conflict with other members. These goals tend to be of such an extensive nature that they are beyond the reach of any individual channel member and require the cooperative effort of the entire channel membership. The principal limitation of this conflict control method is the difficulty of finding such an encompassing goal. Competitive channel action that threatens the existence of the channel is an obvious reason for developing such a goal. Survival is a goal that most individuals will support.

Channel Cooperation

The goal of channel management is channel cooperation (see Figure 11-9). Sometimes, getting channel participants to work together for their own mutual benefit can be a difficult task. Nevertheless, harmonious and cooperative relationships are essential to efficient and effective channel operations. Baxter International, a drug wholesaler and medical supply distributor, has entered into long-term contracts with hospitals in which it assumes management of the hospital's purchasing function. This cooperative arrangement results in Baxter becoming the sole supplier for many medical and other products while the hospital focuses on its health care services.[19]

Channel integration is the major management strategy used to foster channel cooperation. **Channel integration** is the process of incorporating all channel members into one channel system and uniting them under one leadership and one set of goals. The integration of the marketing channel can be accomplished through:

1. *Vertical integration*—seeking control of intermediaries at different levels of the channel

2. *Horizontal integration*—seeking control of competitive intermediaries at the same level of the channel

3. *A combination of vertical and horizontal integration*

The purpose of this unifying process is to end the segregation of intermediary operations and their functional tasks. Figure 11-10 illustrates the concept of vertical integration by showing a comparison between Conventional Marketing Channels (CMCs) and Vertical Marketing Systems (VMSs).

Conventional Marketing Channels A **conventional marketing channel** is a loosely aligned organization of manufacturers, wholesalers, retailers, and facilitators that are independently owned and operated. In comparison to the VMS, the CMC is characterized by a low degree of channel member cooperation, coordination, and control (see Figure 11-11). Additional structural and operational comparisons between these two

FIGURE 11-10

MARKETING-CHANNEL INTEGRATION

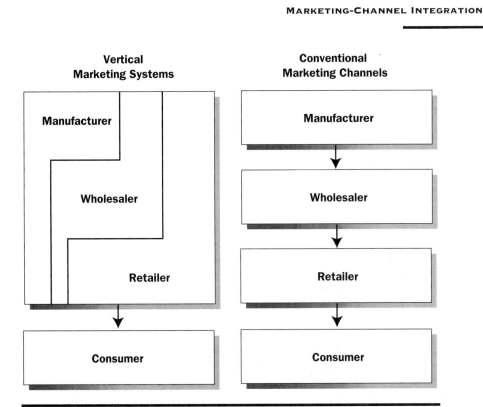

channel organizations are presented in Figure 11-12. The limitations of conventional marketing channels and the operational uncertainty they represent have hastened the decline of their importance and fostered the growth of the more viable vertically integrated channel structure.

VERTICAL MARKETING SYSTEMS Unlike conventional channels, with a vertically integrated marketing system the channel captain is able to achieve a high degree of cooperation, coordination, and control in the distribution process. A **vertical marketing system** is "a professionally managed and centrally programmed network, pre-engineered to achieve operating economies and maximum market impact."[20] The capital-intensive system is designed to achieve technological, managerial, and promotional advantages through the integration and synchronization of the various channel flows.[21] Additional strengths of the VMS over the CMC are shown in Figure 11-12.

If integration is the cornerstone of the VMS, then how does the channel captain achieve this integration? Vertical integration is accomplished through persuasion, contracts, and ownership.

FIGURE 11-11

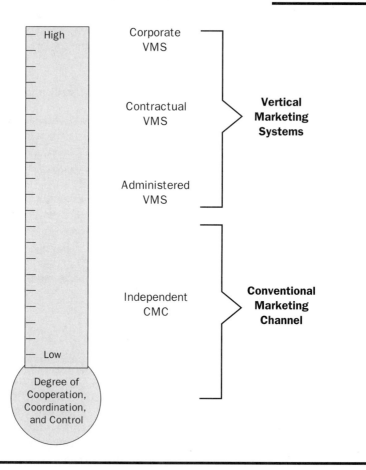

THE DEGREE OF COOPERATION, COORDINATION, AND CONTROL BY TYPE OF CHANNEL ORGANIZATION

Administered VMSs An **administered vertical marketing system** is a channel organization that achieves an integrated channel effort through the persuasive administrative powers of the channel captain. The channel captain's administrative power is derived from any one or more of the power bases previously discussed. A typical administrative VMS involves the channel captain developing a comprehensive marketing program that resellers find attractive and voluntarily agree to support. Cooperation and coordination among channel members is based on mutual respect and benefits. While individual members of an administered system retain authority over their own operations, they are willing to collaborate with the channel captain because of the actual or potential success that collaboration brings to their marketing program. Examples of companies that

FIGURE 11-12

THE CONVENTIONAL MARKETING CHANNEL AND THE VERTICAL MARKETING SYSTEM—STRUCTURAL AND OPERATIONAL COMPARISONS

Conventional Marketing Channel	Vertical Marketing System
• Channel composition consists of isolated and autonomous participating units	• Channel composition consists of integrated participating units
• Channel coordination is achieved through bargaining and negotiation	• Channel coordination is achieved through detailed plans and comprehensive programs
• Channel member responsibilities are based on a traditionally defined set of marketing functions	• Channel member responsibilities are based on the most desired combination of marketing functions
• Channel operations often fail to achieve economies of scale	• Channel operations frequently achieve economies of scale
• Channel stability is low due to low member loyalty and ease of channel entry and exit	• Channel stability is high due to assured member loyalty stemming from long-term commitments
• Channel decisions are the result of judgmental processes of a large number of decision makers	• Channel decisions are the result of scientific processes of a limited number of decision makers
• Channel goals are individualistic in that they are concerned with desired outcomes from a single member at one level in the channel of distribution	• Channel goals are systems oriented in that they are concerned with desired outcomes for all members at all levels in the channel of distribution

have been able to establish and manage administered VMSs based on successful product marketing programs include Campbell's soups, Kellogg's cereals, Kraft's food products, Scott's lawn products, Magnavox's electronic products, and General Electric's household appliances.

Contractual VMSs To achieve a higher level of cooperation, coordination, and control than is possible with an administrative VMS, the channel captain may elect to use a **contractual vertical marketing system**—a channel organization that achieves channel integration through the use of a business contact. In the contractual VMS, the rights and obligations of each channel member are formalized by a legally binding written agreement. The different forms of contractual VMSs include retailer-sponsored cooperative groups, wholesaler-sponsored voluntary chains, and manufacturer-, wholesaler- and service firm-sponsored franchise systems.

Corporate VMSs The most highly integrated vertical marketing system is the **corporate vertical marketing system**—an integrated channel organization in which the channel captain owns and operates two or more stages of the distribution system. A fully integrated corporate VMS is one in which the entire system is owned and operated by the channel captain. The corporate VMS represents the channel organization with the highest level of cooperation, coordination, and control (see Figure 11-11). The principal limitation of this organization arrangement is its cost; channel ownership necessitates large capital investments on the part of the channel captain.

Channel integration through ownership can take two forms. **Forward integration** is the process of seeking ownership and control of a market distribution system, as when a manufacturer owns and operates businesses at the wholesale and retail levels of the channel. Goodyear (tire and rubber products) and Sherwin-Williams (home decorating products) are examples of manufacturers who operate forward-integrated channels of distribution. **Backward integration** is the ownership and control of supply distribution systems. Retailers like Sears, Safeway, and Kmart have sought to ensure reliability of supply by securing ownership of wholesale and production facilities.

Concluding Remarks

As an intercompany network of marketing institutions, the distribution marketing channel is a cooperative effort in which various channel flows are exchanged among various processors, distributors, producers, resellers, and consumers. The marketing-channel design process involves the five steps of recognizing distribution needs, establishing distribution objectives, identifying distribution alternatives, evaluating distribution alternatives, and selecting distribution alternatives. The basic elements of marketing channel management include resolving channel conflict, maintaining channel control, and gaining channel cooperation.

Endnotes

1. Wendy Zellner, "Go-Go Goliaths," *Business Week* (February 13, 1995), 68. Also see Joseph Weber, "Just Get It to the Stores on Time," *Business Week* (March 6, 1995).

2. Robert F. Lusch, Deborah Zizzo, and James M. Kenderdine, "Strategic Renewal in Distribution," *Marketing Management*, Vol. 2, No. 2. (1993), 25.

3. Bert Rosenbloom, *Marketing Channels—A Management View*, 2nd ed. (Hinsdale, IL: The Dryden Press, 1983).

4. Greg Burns, "Gatorade Is Starting to Pant," *Business Week* (April 18, 1994), 98.

5. This discussion is based on J. Taylor Sims, J. Robert Foster, and Arch G. Woodside, *Marketing Channels—Systems and Strategies* (New York: Harper and Row, 1977), 132-34.

6. William Echikson, "Luxury Steals Back," *Fortune* (January 16, 1995), 119.

7. Amy Feldman, "Basics for the Nineties," *Forbes* (May 9, 1994), 55.

8. Amy Feldman, "The House That Jack Built," *Forbes* (April 25, 1994), 92.

9. William M. Stern, "Loyal to a Fault," *Forbes* (March 14, 1994), 58-59. Also see Debra Sparks, "The Card Game," *Financial World* (July 5, 1994), 28-29.

10. Louis W. Stern and Adel I. El-Ansary, *Marketing Channels*, 4th ed. (Englewood Cliffs, NJ: Prentice-Hall, 1992), 289.

11. Ibid.

12. Dori Jones Yang and Michael Oneal, "Can Nike Just Do It?" *Business Week* (April 18, 1994), 86.

13. Rosenbloom, *Marketing Channels*, 124.

14. Stephen Baker and Keith L. Alexander, "Is General Nutrition Headed for Civil War?" *Business Week* (November 21, 1994), 59.

15. John Rossant, "The Faded Colors of Benetton," *Business Week* (April 10, 1995), 87, 90.

16. See Greg Burns, "Will So Many Ingredients Work Together?" *Business Week* (March 27, 1995), 188, 191.

17. See Louis W. Stern and Adel I. El-Ansary, *Marketing Channels*, 300-09.

18. Ibid., 303

19. See Robert F. Lusch, Deborah Zizzo, and James M. Kenderdine, "Strategic Renewal in Distribution," 27.

20. Bert C. McCammon, Jr., "Perspectives for Distribution Programming," *Vertical Marketing Systems* (Glenview, IL: Scott, Foresman and Co., 1970), 43.

21. Ibid.

PROMOTION DECISIONS

CHAPTER OUTLINE

- **INTRODUCTION**
- **THE MARKETING COMMUNICATIONS PROCESS**
    - THE BASIC COMMUNICATION MODEL
    - THE AIDA AND HIERARCHY OF EFFECTS MODELS
- **THE MARKETING COMMUNICATIONS MIX**
    - INDIVIDUAL MARKETING COMMUNICATIONS MIX COMPONENTS
    - INTEGRATIVE MARKETING COMMUNICATIONS
- **THE PROMOTION MANAGEMENT PROCESS**
    - REVIEW ANNUAL MARKETING PLAN
    - ESTABLISH PROMOTION OBJECTIVES
    - ORGANIZE PROMOTION CAMPAIGN
    - PREPARE PROMOTION BUDGET
    - IMPLEMENT PROMOTION CAMPAIGN

Introduction

- **The Advertising Component**
  - Types of Advertising
  - The Creative Advertising Campaign
  - Advertising Management
- **The Personal Selling Component**
  - Types of Personal Selling
  - The Personal Selling Process
  - Sales Management
- **The Direct-Marketing Component**
  - Direct-Mail Marketing
  - Mail-Order Marketing
  - Direct-Response Marketing
- **The Sales Promotion Component**
- **Concluding Remarks**

Introduction

Promotion is defined as effective marketing communication. **Communication** is the exchange of ideas, the sharing of feelings, and the trading of information. **Marketing communication** is a two-way exchange process in which consumers disclose their needs and desires while marketing organizations communicate how they might satisfy those needs and desires. Effective marketing communication accomplishes three major tasks. First, it **informs** current and potential customers about the organization and its products, prices, and channels of distribution. Second, it **persuades** targeted consumers that the organization's market offerings are highly suited to their specific needs. The final task of marketing communication is to **remind**—the continuous reinforcement of previous messages and the enhancement of customer loyalty. The overall goal of marketing communications is to impact consumer behavior in favor of the organization.

THE MARKETING COMMUNICATIONS PROCESS

Given that the typical consumer regularly encounters thousands of marketing messages, communicating effectively can be an extremely difficult and challenging task.[1] A number of different models have been proposed that attempt to explain the communication process and to suggest ways that it can be accomplished more successfully. In this section, we examine three models of marketing communication.

THE BASIC COMMUNICATION MODEL

The communication process can be modeled as a meaningful message exchanged between a source (the marketer) and a receiver (the consumer) using specific communication and feedback channels. This basic communication model is illustrated in Figure 12-1.

FIGURE 12-1

THE BASIC COMMUNICATION MODEL

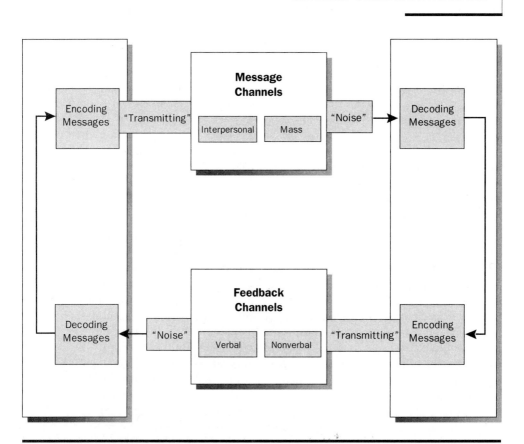

The **source** of the communication process is the marketing organization that wants to inform a select group of consumers **(receivers)** of the superior benefits **(messages)** of its market offering (such as better quality products, a greater selection of product features, a higher level of customer services, or a larger number of customer conveniences). Messages are **encoded** using words, displays, pictures, gestures, or other sensory devices that convey meaning, promote understanding, attract attention, stimulate reaction, and suggest a course of action.

Having encoded the desired message, the marketer must then select the most appropriate **channel** for **transmitting** the message to the targeted receivers. Channel choices include **interpersonal message channels** (face-to-face communication between source and receiver—personal selling and word-of-mouth communications) and **mass message channels** (indirect communication to a large audience through a mass medium—television, radio, newspaper, magazine, or outdoor signs).

The receiver is the intended recipient or audience of the source's messages. The receiver **decodes** the message by interpreting and assigning meaning to the words, symbols, and pictures. The decoding of the message may be correct (interpreting the message as intended by the marketer) or incorrect (assigning an unintended meaning to the message). In either case, the receiver's reactions, or lack thereof, are transmitted back to the source. **Feedback** can be transmitted directly through **verbal feedback channels,** as in the case of an objection made during a personal sales presentation, or **nonverbal feedback channels,** such as by not buying the product. By carefully decoding feedback, the organization can gain valuable information on the acceptability of the market offering and on how well that offer was communicated.

A significant barrier to effective marketing communication is **noise**—any distraction (such as a telephone call) or distortion (an unusual choice of words) that occurs during the communication process and interferes with the correct coding or decoding of the message or feedback and its transmission between the two communicating parties.

The AIDA and Hierarchy of Effects Models

The goal of communications is to gain a response. That response may be to purchase a good, try a service, accept an idea, make a contribution, or a host of other physical actions or mental states. A number of communications paradigms have been developed to model effective communications as a sequential series of steps that guide consumers to the intended outcome. Two such paradigms are the AIDA and the Hierarchy of Effects models. Figure 12-2 is a comparative illustration of both of these response models.

The **AIDA model** is a four-stage consumer-response process in which consumers go through the sequential stages of attention, interest, desire,

FIGURE 12-2

A Comparative View of the AIDA and the Hierarchy of Effects Models of Communication

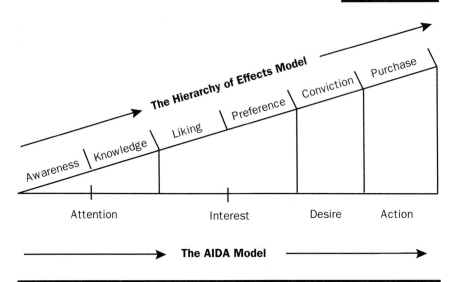

and action (see Figure 12-2). During the **attention** stage, the communicator's goal is to create awareness and build knowledge by grabbing and holding the receiver's attention. In the second stage, the marketer must arouse and build the consumer's **interest** by effectively communicating the offer's benefits. Interest is transformed to **desire** by convincing the consumer of the usefulness of the offer and its superiority to other offers. The final stage in the AIDA model is **action.** An effective communicator suggests appropriate courses of action (asks for the sale) and provides the means for successfully completing the exchange process. Effective communication has occurred when the communication process has come full circle and the marketer has received favorable feedback from the customer.

The **Hierarchy of Effects Model** is a more elaborate model than the AIDA process in that it proposes six response stages. The basic premise of this model is that effective marketing communication is capable of propelling the consumer through a sequence of effects (conclusions or outcomes) that include the following:

- ❏ *Awareness*—the initial exposure to the offer and the recognition of its existence
- ❏ *Knowledge*—an understanding of the offer and a heightened consciousness of its attributes
- ❏ *Liking*—a favorable attitude toward the offer and an appreciation of its attributes

❏ *Preference*—the favorite choice in terms of offers and the willingness to consider it as a viable alternative

❏ *Intention*—the inclination to accept the offer and to proceed with a trial purchase

❏ *Purchase*—the acceptance of the offer and the completion of an exchange process

As a hierarchical model, it recognizes the progressive nature of the communication response process. Knowledge precedes liking which precedes preference which precedes intention which leads to making a purchase. Effective marketing communication helps to guide the consumer through this adoption process. Consciously or unconsciously, consumers go through a process similar to this each time a purchase decision is made. As suggested in Chapter 7, the decision may be made routinely or involve extensive deliberation at each stage, depending on the circumstances surrounding the purchase.

The Marketing Communications Mix

Effective marketing communication uses several individual promotional tools, which are integrated into the **marketing communications mix,** also referred to as the promotion mix. It is a blend of mass communication and personal communication elements. First we must identify the individual components of the mix and then discuss how they are integrated.

Individual Marketing Communications Mix Components

The components that make up the marketing communications mix include advertising, personal selling, direct marketing, sales promotion, public relations, and publicity. Each component has its unique qualities that allow it to make an important contribution in the marketer's efforts to successfully communicate the organization's market offering.

Advertising Advertising is an indirect, one-way, impersonal form of communication carried by a mass medium and paid for by an identified sponsor. Television, radio, newspapers, magazines, billboards, and transit signs are the most commonly used media for transmitting advertising messages to potential and existing customers. Advertising offers the advantages of reaching large audiences for a relatively low cost per exposure, using a wide variety of channels to reach different target markets, providing a great deal of control over the delivery of the message, and providing quick access to large market audiences. The lack of fast and accurate feedback, its nonpersonal nature, high total costs, and the inability to tailor the message to individual customers are all weaknesses that limit the effectiveness of advertising.

PERSONAL SELLING **Personal selling** is a personal form of communication involving person-to-person interactions (either face-to-face or over the telephone) between buyers and sellers. The individual and two-way nature of personal selling encourages messages to be tailored to the interest of each potential customer, allows immediate and direct feedback, and permits a more direct assessment of effectiveness. Shortcomings include a very high cost per customer contact and a high level of dependence on the communication abilities of the salesperson.

DIRECT MARKETING As defined by *Direct Marketing* magazine, **direct marketing** is an interactive system (between buyer and seller) of marketing that uses one or more advertising media (for customer exposure) to effect a measurable response (inquiry) or transaction (an order). The direct marketer uses a database to identify target markets and to tailor marketing programs, which are communicated to the consumer through such nonpersonal media as television, radio, newspapers, magazines, and direct mail. Consumers respond via the telephone, mail, or cable. Direct marketing offers the advantages of being able to precisely define target markets, to solicit immediate responses from the customer, and to accurately measure the response to the direct marketer's offer.

SALES PROMOTION **Sales promotions** are direct or indirect, impersonal inducements that offer extra value to the targeted audience. Some sales incentives, such as coupons, samples, premiums, contests, sweepstakes, rebates, specialties, and tie-ins, are directed at the final consumers. Trade promotions are sales incentives such as trade shows, sales contests, dealer loaders, push money, allowances, demonstrations, and sales training that attempt to induce desired behavior from distribution marketing channel members. Sales promotions offer a choice from a wide variety of activities that can be used in communicating the enhanced benefits being offered to the buyer and in soliciting an immediate response to that offer. Sales promotion shortcomings include the difficulty and expense of creating programs distinct from those of competitors and the limited amount of feedback on the promotion's effectiveness.

PUBLIC RELATIONS AND PUBLICITY **Public relations** incorporates the firm's marketing communications, which are designed to manage the relationship between the organization and its many publics (general public, shareholders, governments, vendors, customers, and employees). The central focus of this form of marketing communication is to build a favorable public image and to foster goodwill by providing information about the organization and its products. Cobra Golf builds sales and generates goodwill by lending sets of King Cobra clubs to pro shops, asking club pros to try the clubs and lend them to customers.[2] **Publicity** is indirect, impersonal communication carried by a mass medium that is neither paid for nor credited to an identified sponsor. Publicity can be either positive or negative news about the organization, which must be managed to gain the full benefit of favorable stories and to limit the damage that could result from unfavorable news items. The R.J. Reynolds Tobacco Company used several tactics to defend the Joe Camel advertising campaign against charges that it was pushing cigarettes to kids. Specific tactics included undermining the credibility of its opponents' research by attacking the methodology, undertaking its own research on Joe Camel's popularity with kids to counter its opponents' findings, and spinning publicity in its direction with a public-service campaign discouraging underage smoking.[3] Public relations is controlled by the firm while publicity is beyond the direct control of the firm.

INTEGRATIVE MARKETING COMMUNICATIONS

Mixed sales messages, blurred brand images, and confused market positions are some of the results that emerge from a marketing communications program that treats each of its promotion components as isolated activities. **Integrated marketing communication (IMC)** is the strategic integration and coordination of all messages and media used by an organization in order to develop a comprehensive and consistent communications plan. The idea behind IMC is to "speak to consumers with one voice."[4] This unified effort is directed at gaining synergistic effects among all of the components of the communications mix. The IMC process proceeds through the following steps:

1. Starts with the customer or prospect and works backward to determine which communication mix components to use in developing effective messages

2. Considers any contact with the brand, product, or company as a potential communications channel for future messages

3. Uses all forms of communication that are relevant to the customer to deliver the company's messages in a variety of ways

4. Coordinates the activities of all functional communication groups within and outside the organization[5]

Coca-Cola, one of the world's biggest advertisers, is placing less emphasis on traditional print and television ads and using interactive in-store promotions, checkout-lane merchandisers offering ice-cold Coke, and toll-free numbers that allow callers to hear a local sports hero.[6]

THE PROMOTION MANAGEMENT PROCESS

Integrative marketing communication leads to the promotion management process and its emphasis on planning and controlling all phases of the marketing communications program. The five stages of the promotion management process are identified in Figure 12-3. This process outlines the basic blueprint for implementing any individual advertising, personal selling, direct marketing, sales promotion, or public relations campaign. It is also the structural framework for implementing a campaign involving two or more promotion-mix elements. The overall goal of the promotion management process is to ensure that all elements of the promotion mix work in harmony with each other.

REVIEW ANNUAL MARKETING PLAN

The integrated marketing communications program must, in turn, be integrated with the organization's broader marketing plans. The strategies and

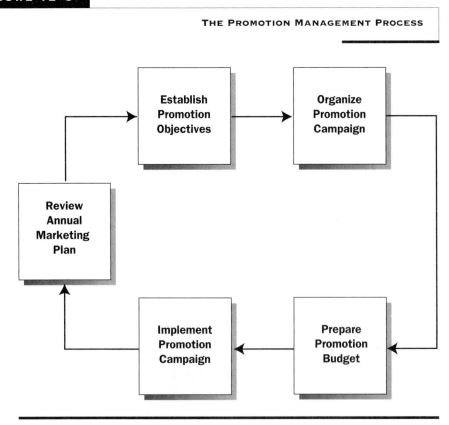

FIGURE 12-3

THE PROMOTION MANAGEMENT PROCESS

objectives outlined in the annual marketing plan (see Chapter 4) provide the focus for developing and implementing promotional strategies and objectives. Hence, the first stage in managing the firm's efforts to effectively communicate with its customers and other interested parties is to conduct a review of the annual marketing plan and identify the role that marketing communication is to play in achieving the overall mission of the organization.

ESTABLISH PROMOTION OBJECTIVES

The entire marketing communications process is directed at achieving a desired response from the targeted audience; that outcome should be expressed as a promotion objective. Objectives establish the criteria by which a promotion is judged a success or failure. To be useful, objectives need to be realistic, specific, and measurable. Figure 12-4 lists selective examples of commonly stated promotion objectives.

ORGANIZE PROMOTION CAMPAIGN

A **promotion campaign** is an integrative mix of marketing communication activities directed toward accomplishing one or more promotion objectives. Most larger organizations launch and manage several different campaigns directed at different but coordinated objectives. In creating the right communication mix for a promotion campaign, the marketing manager can elect to go with a push strategy, a pull strategy, or some combination of the two.

FIGURE 12-4

SELECTIVE EXAMPLES OF PROMOTION OBJECTIVES

• Create consumer awareness	• Enhance firm image
• Provide pertinent information	• Increase sales volume
• Improve customer understanding	• Change consumer attitudes
• Induce product trial	• Alter customer behavior
• Increase usage rate	• Introduce new products
• Retain customer loyalty	• Establish market position
• Build customer relationship	• Develop brand recognition
• Create positive associations	• Increase customer demand
• Explain company viewpoint	• Generate sales leads
• Counter competitive actions	• Increase store traffic
• Improve purchase frequency	• Differentiate market offer
• Stabilize sales volume	• Accentuate product value

A **push strategy** involves gaining the marketing support of each level of the distribution channel by directing the organization's marketing communication effort at channel members rather than final consumers. By aggressively promoting and selling the product from the manufacturer to the wholesaler to the retailer, the product is shoved through the channel. A push strategy dictates a promotion mix that relies heavily on personal selling as the primary element. Trade promotions (sales contests) and advertising (in trade publications) play a secondary role in convincing intermediary channel members to participate in a top-down marketing effort.

The ultimate consumer is the focus of a **pull strategy**—the practice of communicating directly with the final consumer in an effort to stimulate demand for the seller's products and to create pressure on intermediaries to participate in the distribution of the product. In theory, the pull strategy encourages consumers to pressure retailers to stock and sell the product. Retailers, in turn, put pressure on vendors to supply the product, who then cooperate with the producer in distributing the product. A sufficient level of consumer demand can draw the product through the channel. A pull strategy is accomplished by constructing a promotion mix that emphasizes advertising and sales promotion. To get shelf space for its Chantilly brand of women's fragrance, Renaissance Cosmetics advertised so extensively that buyers asked for it by name, thereby forcing stores to stock the item.[7]

By directing advertisements at final consumers and using personal selling to gain the cooperation of intermediaries, some marketing managers employ a **combination strategy** that pulls and pushes the product through the channel. Sales promotion, direct marketing, and public relations are used to enhance the total communications effect. A combination strategy allows the organization to take full advantage of the communication effectiveness that comes with an integrated promotion mix.

Other factors are also influential in determining the promotion mix. Complex and technical products that require demonstration and customization usually rely on personal selling as the core element of the promotion mix. Products that have a high per-unit value also tend to need a promotion mix that is heavy on personal selling. Products that are in the introductory and growth stages of the product life cycle rely on advertising to stimulate consumer demand and personal selling and trade promotions to gain the support of the dealer network.

Organizations that pursue individual brand identities require a greater advertising effort to build awareness than companies that follow a family branding strategy. Advertising is more economical and feasible when the target market consists of a large number of buyers who are geographically dispersed over an extensive area. Limited financial resources strongly influence the composition of the communications mix for any given promotion campaign. Finally, the structure of a competitor's promotion mix has to be considered when determining the type and level of promotion efforts to be directed at contested market segments. And these examples are but representative of the numerous and complex influences that must be considered in organizing a campaign to promote the organization and its products.

PREPARE PROMOTION BUDGET

Determining how much the organization should spend on promotion and how those financial resources should be allocated among various promotion elements are the two key decisions to be made in preparing promotion budgets.[8] Promotion budgets are determined by using one of the several approaches described in Figure 12-5. Once the budget has been determined, the promotion manager allocates the available funds among those elements of the mix in such a fashion that the stated objectives are achieved in the most cost-effective way. It is impossible to achieve an optimally allocated budget because it is inherently impossible to accurately measure the effectiveness of many promotional efforts. Nevertheless, a careful and practical examination of the factors that impact the makeup of the promotion mix can yield useful guidelines for budget allocation.

IMPLEMENT PROMOTION CAMPAIGN

The final stage in the promotion management process is to implement the promotional campaign. The following two discussions of the advertising component and the personal selling component will illustrate how promotional campaigns are created and executed. The creative advertising campaign will be discussed first, followed by a review of the personal selling process. In addition, a section on direct marketing and another on sales promotion round out the detailed review of each of the components that make up the marketing communications mix.

THE ADVERTISING COMPONENT

Advertising includes all paid forms of nonpersonal communications about the organization, its goods, services, or ideas, in which the sponsor is identified. Advertising is considered impersonal because the message is delivered through mass media to many consumers simultaneously.

TYPES OF ADVERTISING

It is important to understand what type of advertising is needed to accomplish a particular marketing communication objective. There are several different ways in which advertising can be classified. In this discussion, we will classify advertising approaches on the basis of the extent of the advertisement's purpose. Hence, the two categories of advertising are general-purpose and specific-purpose advertising.

FIGURE 12-5

METHODS USED IN DETERMINING THE PROMOTION BUDGET

Educated-Guess Method	This is the use of intuitive feelings and practical experience to establish an annual expenditure level for promotion. The marketing manager reviews promotion expenditures and sales records from previous years and makes subjective judgments as to how much is needed to reach sales projections or to support some other objective for the coming year.
Arbitrary Amount Method	The marketing manager capriciously determines how much money should be spent or arbitrarily ascertains how much the organization is willing to spend on promotional activities for some determined period of time. The subjectivity of this method frequently results in promotional allocations that are inconsistent with stated promotion objectives.
Available Funds Method	The marketing manager identifies an amount that the organization can afford to spend on promotions. Usually, the affordable amount is what is left over after other expenditures and profit margins have been covered. Under this method, promotion is something that is funded when extra funds are available. Promotion is typically viewed as an expense rather than an investment.
Percentage-of-Sales Method	To calculate the promotion budget using this method, the marketing manager takes a predetermined percentage of either the previous year's sales or estimated sales for the upcoming year. The percentage used can be based on some traditional amount used in the past, the judgment of the marketing management team, the dictates of senior management officials, the legal requirements of a franchise contract, or an industrial norm. The simplicity of the method accounts for its popularity.
Competitive Parity Method	The amount spent on promotion is equal to the promotional expenditures of one or more key competitors. Organizations can usually monitor the promotional activities of their competitors closely enough to gain a fairly reliable estimate of their past expenditures but not current and future funding. Hence, the competitive parity method might result in a budget whose equity is based on last year's standard.
Objective and Task Method	Promotion budgets are set at an amount that is necessary to successfully complete all of the tasks required to meet an established promotion objective. Using this method the marketing manager must understand the effectiveness of each promotion element in achieving specific communication objectives. Because the productivity of each dollar invested in promotion must be measured, each communication method must be clearly stated in quantified terms.

GENERAL-PURPOSE ADVERTISING General-purpose advertising is based on what is advertised. Using this criteria, advertising can be broken down into product and institutional advertising.

Product advertising focuses on promoting individual goods and services that the organization is offering for sale. Product ads are directed at informing the consumer of special and unique aspects of the product offering and attempt to persuade the consumer that the advertised product is the best solution for the consumer's need. A product ad can center its message on a certain product feature, user benefit, or usage characteristic. Product advertisement can also be directed at creating and enhancing the overall image of the good or service.

Institutional advertising centers on the organization and its attributes and activities. Creating greater awareness, understanding, and appreciation of the organization are three of the more important roles of institutional advertising. Institutional ads are directed at influencing the perceptions and opinions of customers, investors, competitors, employees, and the general public. Creating and maintaining a positive image and reputation for the company and its products is the central goal of most institutional ads.

SPECIFIC-PURPOSE ADVERTISING Specific-purpose advertising is directed at accomplishing a limited and specialized objective. These more focused forms of marketing communications include pioneering, competitive, comparative, advocacy, cooperative, and reminder advertising.

Pioneering advertising is intended to build awareness and acceptance of a new product or product category. Its specific purpose or goal is to build primary demand (product) rather than selective (brand) demand. Hence, pioneering advertising tends to be more informative than competitive. In an attempt to build primary demand and enhance church attendance, many mainline denominations, such as Southern Baptists, Lutherans, and Roman Catholics, are using promotion themes centered around the concerns of the family instead of specific religious messages or church doctrine.[9] When products enter the growth stage of the product life cycle, advertising becomes more competitive and specific.

Competitive advertising attempts to build demand for a specific brand of good or service. To direct consumer attention to its new Homelife Store, and to take advantage of the flourishing home furnishings business, Sears used a major television campaign with the advertising theme of "It's everything you need to bring your home to life."[10] Competitive advertising is more persuasive in character and strives to differentiate the sponsoring organization and its products by promoting their superior features and benefits. In mature markets, competitors often resort to making comparisons between their products and those of their competitors.

Comparative advertising is a somewhat controversial form of advertising in which the brand or promotion manager decides to directly compare the more favorable features of his or her brand to those of a rival brand. The rival brand name, logo, or package is shown and identified as having less desirable features or qualities when equated with those products of the ads' sponsor. Comparative advertising is controversial because research has shown that it facilitates the mental recall of the rival brand, thereby helping to build awareness of competing brands. Also, there are strict regulations against making a false claim about either the competitor's product or the advertiser's product within the context of a comparative advertisement. Retailers also use comparative advertising. Pancho's Mexican Buffet uses an aggressive television advertising campaign that stresses that "an all-you-can-eat meal at Pancho's costs little more than dinner at Taco Bell."[11]

Advocacy advertising is a form of institutional advertising in which the organization expresses a specific viewpoint or takes a specific stand for or against a particular issue. Frequently, these advertisements involve such controversial issues as the environment, governmental actions, social problems, political positions, economic programs, and cultural trends. The variety of approaches to advocacy advertising is well illustrated by the following examples. "Avon supports breast-cancer research, Timberland says it wants to 'give racism the boot'; Adolph Coors promotes literacy; Kraft General Foods donates 25 cents for scholarships for African American college students; American Express stirred marketers' interest in cause marketing . . . with a campaign supporting the Statue of Liberty restoration."[12] Advocacy advertising can be a reaction to public criticism, taking the initative in response to a possible threat, the championing of a particular cause, or reacting to a media attack.

Cooperative advertising involves sharing the cost of an advertisement between two or more parties. Within a distribution channel, vertical cooperation might involve the manufacturer preparing a print ad of its own product, allowing a retailer to insert its name in the ad, and then both parties sharing the cost of running the ad in the local newspaper. An example of horizontal cooperation is the practice of several retailers located in close proximity to one another (such as a shopping mall or a cluster of automobile dealerships) jointly advertising the amenities of their business location. Stretching the advertising budget is the single most important purpose of cooperative advertising.

The specific purpose of **reminder advertising** is to keep the organization's name and its products' labels in front of current customers. Retaining customer loyalty and encouraging repeat purchases is accomplished through communication messages that remind customers of the benefits of buying the organization's products and provide positive reinforcement of the customer's decision to buy those products.

THE CREATIVE ADVERTISING CAMPAIGN

The creative advertising campaign is an extension of the organization's overall promotional campaign and its communication goals. To be creative, advertisements are envisioned as having the originality to attract and hold the consumer's attention as well as the ingenuity to foster and reinforce consumer comprehension of the offer while being both believable and memorable.[13] Creative advertising, however, does not involve gimmicks, cleverness, or tricky attention-getting devices. Rather, creative, effective advertisements use simple language, messages, and presentations that are understood, appreciated, and direct.[14] In a similar vein, "it is doubtful that ads relying on crude language do much for the advertiser, no matter how many heads they might turn. Studies show that people do tend to remember outrageous ads but often forget what product is being flogged."[15] To accomplish this formidable task of attracting and holding consumers without crossing the line into gimmicks or crudity, the marketing manager might follow the process described in Figure 12-6.

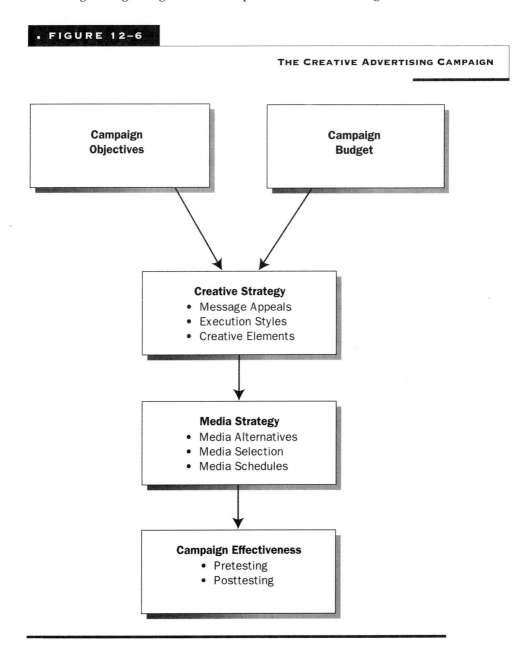

FIGURE 12-6

THE CREATIVE ADVERTISING CAMPAIGN

CAMPAIGN OBJECTIVES Advertising objectives for any specific campaign are derived from the promotion objectives that guide the firm's total marketing communications effort (review the objectives in Figure 12-4). For example, the decision to launch a new product will require the promotion effort to create consumer awareness. Given the effectiveness and efficiency of advertising in accomplishing this task, a creative advertising campaign is developed with this objective in mind.

CAMPAIGN BUDGET Any of the budget determination methods described in Figure 12-5 can be used to set the budget for an advertising campaign. For instance, using the objective-and-task method of budgeting, the promotions manager confirms the amount of resources that will be needed to achieve the type and/or level of response called for by the stated objective.

CREATIVE STRATEGY Creative strategy develops around the issues of identifying the right message appeal, selecting the right execution style, and employing the right creative elements. Figure 12-7 describes each of these issues in terms of choices to make or tasks to accomplish.

Message Appeals The appeal is concerned with the content (what to say) of advertisement. A **message appeal** is the advertisement's central theme or basic idea being proposed to the consumer. It provides the reason or justification for accepting the seller's product offering. The message can be either direct-action or indirect-action appeals. **Direct-action appeals** are messages that urge the consumer to act now. They are directed at soliciting immediate reaction to the advertisement. **Indirect-action appeals** are directed at the long-run goal of building an image for the advertiser or a product. These indirect messages are attempts at changing consumer perceptions and attitudes.

FIGURE 12-7

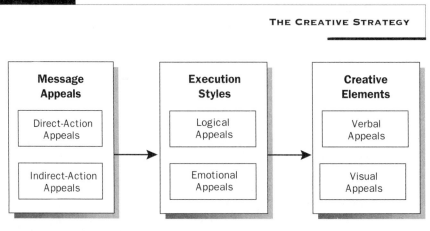

THE CREATIVE STRATEGY

Message appeals are commonly centered on such themes as love and belongingness, fear and security, health and wellness, fun and enjoyment, time and convenience, acceptance and association, value and quality, price and economy, or any other reason that might motivate consumers. An effective message appeal emphasizes what consumers are most concerned about and explains how the marketer's offering can meet those concerns. To be effective, message appeals should emphasize product benefits, not product attributes. While an advertising campaign may make multiple appeals, most campaigns have a signature or dominant message appeal referred to as the **unique selling proposition.** This proposition can usually be identified as the campaign's principal advertising slogan. Some unique selling propositions include "The Best-Selling Trucks Are Built Ford Tough," "Samsonite, Our Strengths Are Legendary," "MassMutual, We Help You Keep Your Promises," "Take Stock In America, U.S. Savings Bonds," and "Lotus, Working Together." To emphasize the fact that its stores are the only full-line (hard and soft goods) department store left in the regional shopping mall, Sears advertises itself as a "whole store."[16]

Execution Styles The marketer must not only present the right message appeal but also deliver the message in the right manner. **Execution style** is the way or form in which the message is presented. How one delivers a message can be as important as the message itself. Logical and emotional appeals are the two broad approaches to presenting the marketer's advertising message. A **logical appeal** is a factual presentation of product attributes and benefits that is meant to convince the consumer that the advertiser's offer is the best choice. An advertisement that offers the lowest price on a good or service is to a large extent a logical appeal. **Emotional appeals** do not speak to what consumers think but to what they feel. Advertisements that appeal to love and belongingness needs or use hope and fear as marketing appeals tend to be emotional appeals that speak to the consumer's feelings.[17] Advertisers have developed a number of execution styles for delivering logical and emotional appeals. Figure 12-8 provides a brief description of some of the more commonly used execution styles.

Creative Elements After the decision of what to say and how to say it, the next step is creating the advertisement. The **creative elements** are those features of an advertisement that create sensory appeals that attract attention, stimulate interest, heighten desire, and encourage action. An advertisement might use cues to appeal to the consumer's sense of sight, hearing, smell, and touch. The selection of which creative elements to use depends on the media selected for delivering the message. Nevertheless, two fundamental elements comprise any advertisement: the advertisement's copy and artwork. **Copy** is the verbal part of the ad. Copy can be spoken (broadcast media) or written (print media). Headlines, subheadings, body copy, and signature are elements that make up the copy in a

FIGURE 12-8

EXECUTION STYLES

Testimonial	A spokesperson, authority figure, celebrity, company official, or typical consumer offers a testimonial to the merits of the offering or provides an endorsement of the product.
Slice-of-Life	Ordinary people are depicted in traditional life situations buying and using the advertised product.
Demonstration	Product attributes and features are presented and illustrated together with the benefits of using the product.
Lifestyle	The product is portrayed as essential to and compatible with the way a particular consumer group lives and behaves.
Associative	The product and its use are shown with respect to a highly desirable situation, a positive relationship, or an exciting fantasy.
Humor	Humorous stories, comical happenings, and fun situations are used to draw attention to the product and its benefits.
Symbolism	A symbol that is widely recognized, highly symbolic, uniquely suggestive, or greatly respected is used to represent the product and its benefits.
Musical	Songs, jingles, and other musical formats are used to gain attention and convey information about the product and its uses.
Comparison	Product attributes and benefits between competing market offerings are compared directly.

print ad. Copy is important because it helps to build interest in and desire for the advertiser's offer.[18] **Art** is the visual part of the advertisement; it incorporates both the ad's illustrations—the types of visuals used, such as photos, drawings, graphs, tables, and charts—and layout, the physical composition of the illustrations or the arrangement of copy elements within the ad. Art is important in getting and holding the consumer's attention. By using distinctive art in its advertisements, which featured artists' depictions of the Absolut bottle, an obscure Swedish vodka was turned into one of the hottest brands of the 1980s.[19] Art also contributes to building comprehension of the advertiser's offering.

The importance of a good creative strategy has increased as the competition for the consuming public's attention intensifies. Creative strategies are unusual but relevant, different yet understandable, and imaginative and informative.

MEDIA STRATEGY Media strategy is concerned with the selection of the communications channels that will carry the advertiser's messages to the targeted audiences. As illustrated in Figure 12-9, the media strategy requires that the advertising manager select the most appropriate media

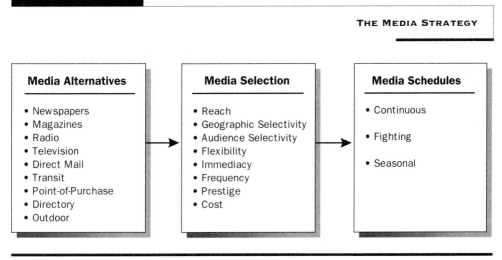

FIGURE 12-9

THE MEDIA STRATEGY

alternative relative to one or more media selection criteria and consistent with media scheduling parameters.

Media Alternatives Traditionally, media alternatives have been classified into the following categories:

❑ *Print media*—newspaper and magazine advertising

❑ *Broadcast media*—radio and television advertising

❑ *Out-of-home media*—outdoor, transit, in-store advertising

❑ *Direct response*—direct mail

❑ *Specialty media*—telephone and other directories

Figure 12-10 outlines the more important advantages and disadvantages of various media alternatives. When traditional media become saturated and cluttered with advertising messages, the creative advertising strategy for many organizations is to use less-traditional and more innovative methods of reaching selective consumer groups. Fax advertisements, electronic mail, bill inserts, telemarketing, and sponsorships are but a few of the less-traditional approaches to communicating the firm's promotional messages. Sponsorship of NASCAR (National Association for Stock Car Auto Racing) drivers [20] or the expanded use of blimps (Goodyear, Fuji, Gulf, and Sea World)[21] are two good examples of nontraditional advertising methods.

Media Selection Advertisers use a number of different criteria in deciding which media to use to deliver a specific message to the desired audience. Certain media alternatives lend themselves to one set of tasks while others are more suited to different tasks and objectives. In evaluating

FIGURE 12-10

ADVANTAGES AND DISADVANTAGES OF SELECTED MEDIA ALTERNATIVES

Newspapers		Transit		Magazines	
Advantages	**Disadvantages**	**Advantages**	**Disadvantages**	**Advantages**	**Disadvantages**
geographic market selectivity Flexibility—ease of ad insertion and change Editorial support	Lack of permanence of advertising message Poor quality of printing production Limited demographic orientation	High reach and frequency potential Impact—total bus may be ad Geographic market selectivity Inexpensive on a relative basis	Limited demographic selectivity Limited availability—does not exist in many markets Image is thought to be poor for certain markets	Demographic market selectivity Long-life ad capability Good-quality print production Editorial support	Lack of flexibility—difficult to make last-minute changes Limited availability Expensive—especially for color
Point-of-Purchase		**Radio**		**Directory**	
Advantages	**Disadvantages**	**Advantages**	**Disadvantages**	**Advantages**	**Disadvantages**
Promotes impulsive buying "Sells" in non-personal selling environment Ties together product and ad	Difficult to obtain desired placements Clutter Limited creative possibilities	Geographic and demographic market selectivity Flexibility Inexpensive on a relative basis	Lack of permanence—perishability Clutter Lack of visual support Limited impact—background medium	Permanence—long-life High reach and frequency potential	Limited customer usage Market coverage limited to phone customers
Television		**Outdoor**		**Direct Mail**	
Advantages	**Disadvantages**	**Advantages**	**Disadvantages**	**Advantages**	**Disadvantages**
Show and tell—demonstration is possible Geographic market selectivity Market penetration due to large viewing audience	Perishable ad message unless repeated Expensive on a relative basis Clutter—message may become lost in group advertisements	High reach and frequency potential Market selectivity High impact due to size Inexpensive on a relative basis	Brevity of message Image is thought to be poor for certain markets Clutter is often present Location choices may be limited	High selectivity Easy to measure results Lengthy copy possible Reader governs exposure	Expensive—especially on a cost-per-person basis Little or no editorial support Limited reader interest

SOURCE: Reprinted by permission of the authors from William H. Bolen, *Advertising*, 2nd ed. (New York: John Wiley & Sons, 1984), 601–02

media alternatives, both their effectiveness and their efficiency must be taken into consideration. Media selections are made by considering the following criteria.

❏ *Reach*—a medium's ability to expose a certain number of people to an advertisement during a defined time period

❏ *Geographic selectivity*—a medium's ability to hone in on a specific geographic area such as a city or state

- *Audience selectivity*—a medium's ability to present a tailored message to a selected target audience within a population

- *Flexibility*—a medium's ability to use more than one sensory appeal in delivering the advertiser's message

- *Immediacy*—a medium's ability to present a timely message by permitting short lead times for preparing and delivering advertisements

- *Frequency*—the ability of the medium to generate multiple exposures to the same advertisement

- *Prestige*—the medium's ability to enhance the status of an advertisement based on its own creditability and stature

- *Cost*—the ability to deliver the advertisement with acceptable cost structures in terms of both absolute cost (total dollar amount) and relative cost (number of dollars to reach a specific number of people)

In addition to these criteria, there are several other factors that greatly impact media selection. Some of the more important factors include the creative content of the advertisement, the size of the intended audience, and the structure of the targeted market.

Media Schedules Once the appropriate media have been selected, the final step in executing the media strategy is to determine when and how often the advertisement is to run, that is, to develop a media schedule. In creating the media schedule, the advertising manager selects the media alternative, specifies the media vehicle (a particular program or publication), and identifies when the advertisement will run. Media schedules are greatly impacted by any seasonal demand for the advertised product, the type and level of advertising by competitors, and the size of the firm's advertising budget.

Media schedules typically take one of three forms—continuous, fighting, and seasonal schedules. The **continuous media schedule** calls for a strategy of spreading out the advertisements over the entire period of time designed for the advertising campaign. This reminder strategy is appropriate when demand is fairly constant and competitive ads are being run on a regular basis. A **fighting media schedule** is a scheduling strategy in which ads are concentrated during specific times (days, weeks, or months) with modest amounts of advertising between these times of concentration. Peak product demand periods usually call for a fighting media schedule. By combining continuous advertising activities with short bursts of heavy advertising during peak demand periods, a **pulsing media schedule** is created. A **seasonal media schedule** concentrates all or most of its advertising effort during one or more specific time periods with little or no advertising at any other time (such as antifreeze during the winter, eggnog at Christmas, or charcoal during the summer).

Campaign Effectiveness The final stage in the creative advertising process is to determine the effectiveness of the campaign (see Figure 12-6). The dynamic nature of the marketplace makes it difficult to accurately measure whether or not a particular advertisement has met its objective. Everything from bad weather conditions to new product introductions could easily distort the impact of an advertising campaign. Nevertheless, advertising researchers have developed numerous procedures for judging the effectiveness of advertising. These procedures are typically grouped into two testing categories—pretesting and posttesting.

Pretesting When advertising researchers want to obtain an assessment of an advertisement's effectiveness before it is run, they conduct a **pretest**. Commonly employed pretesting procedures involve seeking customer reactions to proposed commercials or print ads using focus groups, consumer juries, or direct questioning of a representative sample of the target audience. Pretests seek to evaluate information recall, message suitability, consumer reactions and response levels, attention-getting capabilities, or any number of additional measures of effectiveness.

Posttesting A **posttest** is an evaluation of the effectiveness of an advertisement after it has run. It seeks to measure the actual audience reaction and response to an advertisement. An **unaided recall test** asks qualified respondents (those who can demonstrate that they have seen a particular television program or read a particular newspaper in which the advertisement had been placed) if they recall the advertisement and what particular details about the advertisement they recalled. An **aided recall test** shows respondents an advertisement and asks if they remember seeing it. An **inquiry test** incorporates an invitation within the advertisement to call or write the sponsor (for additional information, to redeem a coupon, or to receive a free sample) and measures the number of responses to the invitation.

Advertising Management

There are three basic options for managing advertising functions and activities. Advertising can be handled by an in-house advertising department, an outside advertising agency, or some combination of the two.

In-House Advertising Department Advertising can be managed internally by an in-house advertising department that both produces and places advertisements in the appropriate media. The firm's advertising manager assumes the following responsibilities:

    1. Supervises artists, copywriters, and production specialists who produce the advertisement

    2. Interacts with media representatives in the placement of the advertisement

3. Outsources specialized advertising functions to various advertising agencies and specialists

With the downsizing and right-sizing of many organizations, the in-house advertising department is slowly being replaced by outside agencies.

OUTSIDE ADVERTISING AGENCIES An advertising agency is a firm that specializes in offering advertising and other marketing communication services to its clients.[22] These agencies range from full-service, international organizations like Young & Rubicam and Ogilvy & Mather Worldwide to local, one-person shops that provide a limited number of specialized advertising functions. Advertising planning, marketing research, creative services, production department, and media services are the principal functional areas of an agency. These comprehensive service organizations are capable of planning and managing the entire advertising process from campaign planning to audience assessment to message creation to media selection to program evaluation.

THE PERSONAL SELLING COMPONENT

As a direct and personal form of marketing communication, the personal selling component is the most appropriate communications tool when an organization is marketing products that might be classified as either:

1. a highly technical and complex good,
2. a custom-made good,
3. a high-fashion merchandise item,
4. an expensive good or service, or
5. a specialty good or service.

A personal selling effort is needed to market any product in which the potential buyer requires additional information, persuasive arguments, and personalized service.

TYPES OF PERSONAL SELLING

Not all salespeople are the same. They vary depending on the nature of their role within the organization, the extent of their responsibilities within the selling process, the type of consumer they interact with, and the type of product they sell. One of the more common ways to categorize sales personnel is to group them into two categories based on the nature of their customer base. Using this basis, salespeople are in either organizational sales or consumer sales.

ORGANIZATIONAL SALES The organizational sales force is concerned with business-to-business sales and is grouped according to the sales tasks each salesperson performs. **Order takers** are salespeople whose primary responsibilities are to take and process orders from existing customers. The order taker typically is not involved with the creative selling process (gaining additional orders from existing customers or securing new orders from new customers). **Order getters** are sales personnel actively involved in finding new customers and obtaining new orders as well as generating additional orders from current customers. Order getters are actively involved in the creative selling process by prospecting for new customers, determining customer needs, developing presentations that explain how the firm's products meet those needs, handling customer objections, closing the sales, and engaging in follow-up activities.

Part of an organization's sales force is devoted to providing backup support for order getters. Although sales support personnel are not directly involved with closing the sale, they help the selling process by providing a variety of services. Sales support personnel include missionary salespeople and technical support personnel. **Missionary salespeople** provide current and potential customers with information about the company and its products. It is their responsibility to "convert the customer" by instilling a favorable image and goodwill toward the company and its market offering. Sales missionaries tend to be most active with promoting new products. **Technical specialists** are support personnel who have expertise in some area that is needed by both the order getter and the customer. Common areas of expertise have traditionally included engineering, chemistry, biology, physics, computer technologies, or some other hard science. Social science, specialized business functions, and fine arts expertise are becoming more common areas in service sales.

THE PERSONAL SELLING PROCESS

The creative **personal selling process** is both a series of procedural steps designed to complete a transaction by closing a sale and the means by which the firm develops and builds long-term, mutually satisfying relationships with its customers and clients. As illustrated in Figure 12-11, the personal selling process consists of six steps: prospecting for a sales opportunity, approaching the sales prospect, making the sales presentation, handling the sales objection, closing the sale, and following up the sale.

PROSPECTING FOR A SALES OPPORTUNITY Prospecting is searching for and locating potential customers. In this first step of the selling process, the salesperson is expected to identify sales leads and qualify sales prospects. A sales **lead** is an individual or organization that might be interested in the firm's products and therefore is a potential customer. Sales leads are generated from a number of different sources, including personal

FIGURE 12-11

THE PERSONAL SELLING PROCESS

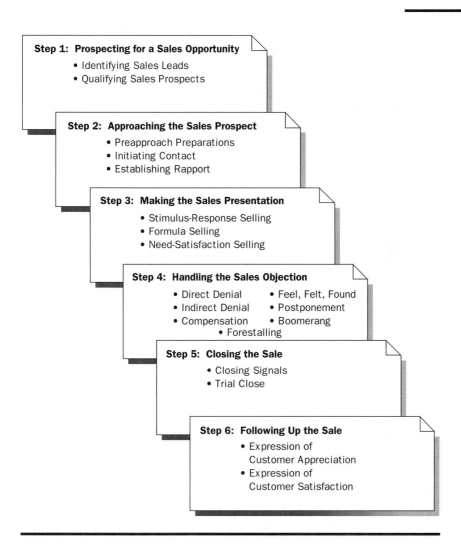

contacts, mailing lists, current customers, former customers, trade shows, trade publications, databases, directories, suppliers, advertisement inquiries, and telemarketing activities.

Not all prospects will become customers. Sales leads must be willing to buy, as well as have the ability and authority to buy. Qualifying sales prospects involves (1) determining if the sales lead can benefit from using the firm's products and participating in its marketing program, (2) resolving whether or not the sales lead can afford the firm's goods and services, and (3) discovering who has the authority to make the buying decision. Once leads have been qualified, they are approached with the company's sales message.[23]

APPROACHING THE SALES PROSPECT **Approaching** is gaining access to and developing the initial relationship with qualified sales leads. A successful approach entails making preapproach preparations, initiating contact, and establishing rapport with the sales prospect.

Preapproach preparations involve learning as much as possible about the prospect prior to the initial contact. Effective salespeople gather specific information about the company and its needs, the problems that face the company and management's typical approach to problem solving, the personal characteristics of those individuals who might be involved with the purchase decision, and any other information that might be useful in making the initial contact and establishing the needed rapport.

First impressions can be vital to long-term business relationships, hence the importance of beginning the relationship on the right note. At the **initial contact** salespeople are expected to do the following:

❑ Use professional etiquette in scheduling and meeting appointments

❑ Employ sales openers that gain the prospect's attention and hold interest

❑ Ask relevant questions that secure information that will be useful in making the sales presentation

❑ Discover common interests and concerns that might be valuable in creating a lasting relationship with the prospect

The most effective approach for **establishing rapport** with prospective customers is by being genuinely interested in their needs and working diligently to meet those needs. Most organizations are willing to establish long-term relationships with practical problem solvers. Good people skills and business etiquette, personal characteristics and mannerisms, and selling talents and abilities are all part of the chemistry for building rapport between sellers and buyers.

MAKING THE SALES PRESENTATION In **presenting,** the third step in the selling process, the salesperson makes an informative and persuasive presentation of the firm's products and marketing program. A strong sales presentation attempts to identify needs and discover problems, reduce risks and eliminate uncertainties, show product attributes and demonstrate product features, sell the benefits of the product and the salesperson's problem-solving capabilities, and motivate prospective customers by invoking their feelings and stimulating their senses, as well as enhance better understanding and promote greater appreciation for the firm's products and programs. Effective sales presentations are two-way communications. The effective salesperson is one who listens as well as talks. Based on how much and when salespeople talk and listen, sales presentations are classified as stimulus-response selling, formula selling, or need-satisfaction selling.

Stimulus-response selling is a canned approach to selling in which the salesperson presents a series of sales pitches (faster inventory turnover, lower cost structures, or more promotional support) in hopes of achieving the desired response (product trial, new sales order, or larger order quantity). The assumption behind this presentation method is that there is a right button (or buying motive) to press in order to obtain the sale and that it is the salesperson's job to keep pushing the buttons until the right one is found. For standardized products that are purchased in a routine fashion based on one or a limited number of motives, the stimulus-response selling system is adequate in making one-time sales but not conducive to building customer relations.

Formula selling is a method in which the salesperson follows a predetermined script and a standardized procedure in making a sales presentation. A commonly used format in formula selling involves a series of question/answer/message sequences in which salespeople ask prospects a certain question and deliver a canned sales message depending on the prospect's answers. While this method tends to be highly structured, it is somewhat adaptive in that the sales message is individually matched to the expressed concerns of the prospective buyer. Given the more personal nature of this method, it is somewhat more effective in building customer relations than the stimulus-response method.

As suggested by its name, **need-satisfaction selling** is based on the idea that the salesperson should first clearly identify the needs of the sales prospect prior to the development and delivery of the sales message. Using this totally adaptive selling approach, the salesperson asks several probing questions of the prospective buyer during the initial stages of the presentation. When sufficient information has been gathered, the salesperson then tailors the sale presentation to fit the specific needs, concerns, and problems of the prospective buyer. By listening first and talking later, salespeople who use need-satisfaction selling are able to build long-term relationships that result in a highly loyal customer base that is easier to retain and expand upon.

HANDLING THE SALES OBJECTION Sales objections are expressed doubts or concerns about any number of issues that might arise during the sales presentation; they are perceived "stumbling blocks" to buying the product and patronizing the company. Potential customers voice objections relative to product design and features, product quality and image, product price and value, terms and conditions of sale, company policies and practices, and personal reasons and circumstances, as well as a host of other real and perceived problems. It is one of the responsibilities of the sales force to overcome a prospect's resistance to making a purchase. Salespeople should welcome questions and encourage sales prospects to voice concerns. These objections should be viewed as additional information that can be used to make a more effective sales presentation.

Sales objections are handled on an individual basis as they arise within the sales presentation. Nevertheless, following are some common means employed by salespeople in handling objections:

❑ *Direct denial*—used when sales prospect has incorrect information. For example, "No, our price has not increased since the first of the year."

❑ *Indirect denial*—used when sales prospect has incorrect information. For example, "I can understand why you believe that we have had a price increase this year since almost all of our competitors have experienced price increases."

❑ *Compensation*—used when objection is valid but there are extenuating circumstances. For example, "Yes, there has been an increase in the base price, but the current price includes several additional standard features that the previous price did not include."

❑ *Feel, felt, found*—used with emotional objections. For example, "I know how you feel about the increase in price. I also felt that it was a bit excessive until I found out that the overall value created by the addition of several important safety features more than justifies the price increase."

❑ *Postponement*—used with valid and emotional objections. For example, "That's a valid concern, but I would like to discuss the price after we have had a chance to fully review all of the new features that are a standard part of this year's model."

❑ *Boomerang*—used when an objection can be turned into a positive factor. For example, "Yes, there has been an increase in price since the first of the year. And we expect another price increase later this year. I do not think we will ever see prices this low again."

❑ *Forestalling*—used with an anticipated objection. For example, "I'm sure you've noticed the increase in the base price. Rather than charge separate prices for a whole list of commonly bought accessories, we have simply included them as standard items and not charged for these desirable options. The base price with these options is much lower than if you were to buy them separately."

CLOSING THE SALE **Closing** is an attempt on the part of the salesperson to secure a purchase commitment from the prospect. In other words, closing the sale is asking for the sale. Frequently, sales prospects provide such **closing signals** as friendly nonverbal signs (smiling or nodding agreement), positive verbal comments (this product seems to be the solution to our problem), or affirmative action (examines the order form or takes out a credit card). When salespeople receive mixed signals regarding the prospect's willingness to buy, they often attempt a **trial close**—a sales tactic that solicits information concerning the prospect's buying intentions. For example, the salesperson may ask about the preferred product features, methods of payment, or delivery times. Trial closes seek some additional commitments and bring the prospect closer to the final sales agreement. Skilled salespeople have developed a variety of closing techniques that move the prospect closer to the final purchase commitment. Figure 12-12 identifies and defines several customer closing techniques.

FOLLOWING UP THE SALE A good salesperson follows up each sale by ensuring that the essential administrative tasks (the order form is correctly filled out, the terms and conditions of the sale are completely understood and agreed to by both parties, and the delivery arrangements are satisfactory) are completed. The selling process continues after the sale has been made. An expression of appreciation for the business, a verification that the order was filled correctly, a confirmation of the product performance, and an assessment of customer satisfaction are all follow-up activities that develop goodwill and build strong customer relationships.

SALES MANAGEMENT

While many sales activities tend to be conducted on an individual basis, the salesperson is part of a much larger marketing communications team that requires a coordinated effort in reaching and servicing target groups of qualified buyers. Sales force organization and development are two central issues facing the sales manager.

SALES FORCE ORGANIZATION The size and structure of the marketplace, the type and level of competition, the nature and character of the product line, the preferences and expectations of company management, and the buying behavior of existing and potential customers are some of the factors that the sales manager considers in organizing the sales force. The sale force is commonly organized by geographic territory, product line, or customer or market type.

Sales force organization based on **geographic territory** involves assigning each salesperson a specific geographic area in which the individual sells all of the firm's products to all customers located within that area. This approach offers spatial efficiency in that the salesperson can locate within the area in such a fashion as to reduce travel time and expense. A high level of familiarity with the area allows salespeople to build closer relations with customers and identify potential opportunities for new business. Geographic sales territories range from limited

FIGURE 12-12

CLOSING TECHNIQUES

Technique	Definition	Example
Direct Close	The salesperson asks the customer directly for the order.	"Can I write this order up for you?"
Assumptive Close	The salesperson assumes the customer is going to buy and proceeds with completing the sales transaction.	"Would you like to have this gift wrapped?"
Alternative Close	The salesperson asks the customer to make a choice in which the alternative is favorable to the retailer.	"Will this be cash or charge?"
Summary/ Agreement Close	The salesperson closes by summarizing the major features, benefits, and advantages of the product and obtains an affirmative agreement from the customer on each point.	"This dishwasher has features you were looking for."—YES "You want free home delivery."—YES "It is in your price range."—YES "Let's write up the sale."
Balance-Sheet Close	The salesperson starts by listing the advantages and disadvantages of making the purchase and closes by pointing out how the advantages outweigh the disadvantages.	"This dishwasher is on sale; it has all the features you asked for; you have 90 days to pay for it without any financial charges; and we will deliver it free. Even though we cannot deliver it until next week, now is the time to buy."
Emotional Close	The salesperson attempts to close the sale by appealing to the customer's emotions (love, fear, acceptance, recognition).	"The safety of your children could well depend on this smoke alarm. Now is the time to get it installed."
Standing-Room-Only Close	The salesperson tries to get the customer to act immediately by stressing that the offer is limited.	"The sale ends today." "This is the last one we have in stock."

SOURCE: Reprinted by permission of the author, Dale M. Lewison, *Retailing,* 5th ed. (New York: Macmillan College Publishing, 1994), 565.

sections of some cities to entire states or countries, depending on the needs and resources of the company.

Organizing the sales force by **product line** entails making each salesperson responsible for selling a specific product item, product line, or brand to existing and potential customers within a market area. Because it allows the salesperson to develop extensive product knowledge, this form of sales force organization is used when the product line is highly technical or requires customization in order to meet the customer needs. A common problem associated with this form of organization is that several members of the firm's sales force may be calling on the same company selling different product lines. Customer confusion and irritation are dangers connected with overlapping territories.

When the sales force is organized on the basis of **market** or **customer type,** the salesperson is required to focus on a single customer or type of customer within a designated market area. Kraft Foods reorganized its sales force in such a fashion that one sales representative calls each store and sells all of the firm's brands. This is a considerable change from the previous practice of having several salespeople call on each store representing a single product line or brand.[24] This form of organization is highly suited to meeting the individualistic needs of a particular firm. Excellent customer knowledge is combined with good product and market knowledge to greatly enhance the effectiveness of the sales force. The high cost associated with this approach to sales force organization is its chief limitation.

SALES FORCE DEVELOPMENT Sales force development is centered on recruiting individuals who have the talent to become effective salespeople, offering training programs that develop new skills and enhance existing competencies, providing the type of supervision that both motivates and coordinates the efforts of a group of individualistic people, and providing a compensation program that is equitable and manageable.

Recruiting the Sales Force **Recruiting** is the active search for and careful selection of qualified sales personnel. The **employee search** process starts with a well-defined and clearly stated **job description** that identifies the tasks, duties, and responsibilities of the position, the level of performance expected of the employee, and the minimum qualifications required to obtain the position. Once the sales manager has articulated what type of individual is needed, the next step is to initiate the **employee search.** The typical procedure is to explore both internal and external sources for prospective employees. Internal sources include referrals from current employees, consideration of past employees, and transfers from other divisions and functional areas within the organization. Advertisements, employment agencies, educational placement centers, and unsolicited applications serve as the primary external sources of qualified prospects.

Personnel selection is accomplished using several methods of reviewing and assessing the qualifications of potential salespeople. Application forms, references, candidate interviews, psychological and achievement tests, and physical examinations are all used to find individuals who have the attributes and skills to succeed at sales.

Training the Sales Force   The high cost associated with personal selling necessitates a well-trained sales force in order to justify this approach to the organization's marketing communication effort. **Training** is the development and improvement of the salesperson's capabilities. **Functional training** is a program designed to develop and improve basic skills and competencies that are needed to be a successful salesperson. Functional training areas include the application of sales techniques, the building of customer relationships, the use of effective communication, and the management of time and resources. **Organization training** revolves around educating the employee about the organization's structure (organizational chart and reporting relationships) and operations (policies, procedures, rules, and regulations), as well as the organization's marketing programs (product lines, pricing strategies, distribution practices, and promotional programs). Training methods range from individual "do-it-yourself" programs to sponsoring (mentoring by an experienced employee) and group activities (lectures, demonstrations, case studies, role playing, and interactive computer exercises).

Supervising the Sales Force   **Supervising** involves directing, coordinating, and managing the efforts of the sales force to achieve both company and individual goals. The very nature of the selling process suggests that a considerable amount of autonomy is needed by the sales force in order to perform effectively.[25] This is particularly true with the outside sales force, which tends to be entrepreneurial in character. By recruiting self-starters who both enjoy the "freedom of the road" and assume the responsibilities that come with that freedom, the sales manager can focus on motivating the sales force and coordinating their individual efforts. In addition to the psychic nature (freedom and individualism) and perks (company car and expense account) associated with a sales position, sales managers rely heavily on sales quotas and sales incentives to motivate and coordinate the efforts of this diverse group of employees. **Sales quotas** are dollar- or unit-sales goals that each salesperson must achieve to receive a favorable performance review and to qualify for various incentive programs. The number of sales calls, the number of new accounts, and the amount of sales expenses can also be incorporated into the salesperson's performance quota. **Sales incentives** in the form of prizes or rewards are used to direct the efforts of salespeople toward a particular product line and are intended to increase sales of certain products during specific time periods.

Compensating the Sales Force   Equitable compensation methods are an integral part of the sales manager's efforts to recruit and retain a highly motivated sales force. Straight salary, straight commission, and combinations of the two are the principal sales compensation plans. **Straight salary plans** give the salesperson a fixed amount of compensation for a specific work period (such as $4,000 per month). Easier administration and greater control over the actions of salespeople accrue to the sales manager who uses the straight salary method. In sales positions that involve significant amounts of nonselling activities and customer relations, this form of compensation can be the more appropriate method. At the opposite end of the continuum is commission selling. The **straight commission plan** usually compensates salespeople by paying them a flat percentage of the sales or gross profits they generate. The commission percentage can be either fixed (the same percentage for all sales) or variable (different percentages for different product lines or a variable percentage that reflects different sales level goals). The straight commission plan rewards sales productivity; hence, it is a strong motivator for the salesperson to achieve and exceed sales goals. Because short-term sales and profits are the focus of the salesperson's attention, such long-term goals as building customer relationships often get slighted.

The Direct-Marketing Component

Direct marketing is a form of marketing communications in which the marketer uses a customer database (a list and profile of current and potential customers) and an advertising medium to identify and communicate with a target market that is highly likely to respond immediately to the marketer's offering with a measurable action (a request for additional information, a complaint about a past transaction, or an acceptance of the current offer—a sale). Direct marketers Gateway 2000, Inc. and Dell Computer Corp. racked up record sales when they appealed to businesses and consumers who knew what they wanted (cutting-edge machines at the best possible price) and did not need the hand-holding required by neophytes in the stores.[26] Figure 12-13a illustrates the direct-marketing process.[27] Also shown in Figure 12-13 is a classification and profile of the various methods employed by the direct marketer.

Direct-Mail Marketing

In **direct-mail marketing,** the marketer uses only the postal service to communicate the offer to the consumer, who then responds by mail or telephone (see Figure 12-13b). The direct marketer's promotional message (the offer) is presented in one of the the following forms:

- *Letters*—a direct-mail piece that typically consists of a letter that presents the selling proposition to the customer, a brochure that illustrates the product and promotes its benefits, and an order form that asks for the sale

FIGURE 12–13

A Classification and Profile of Direct Marketers

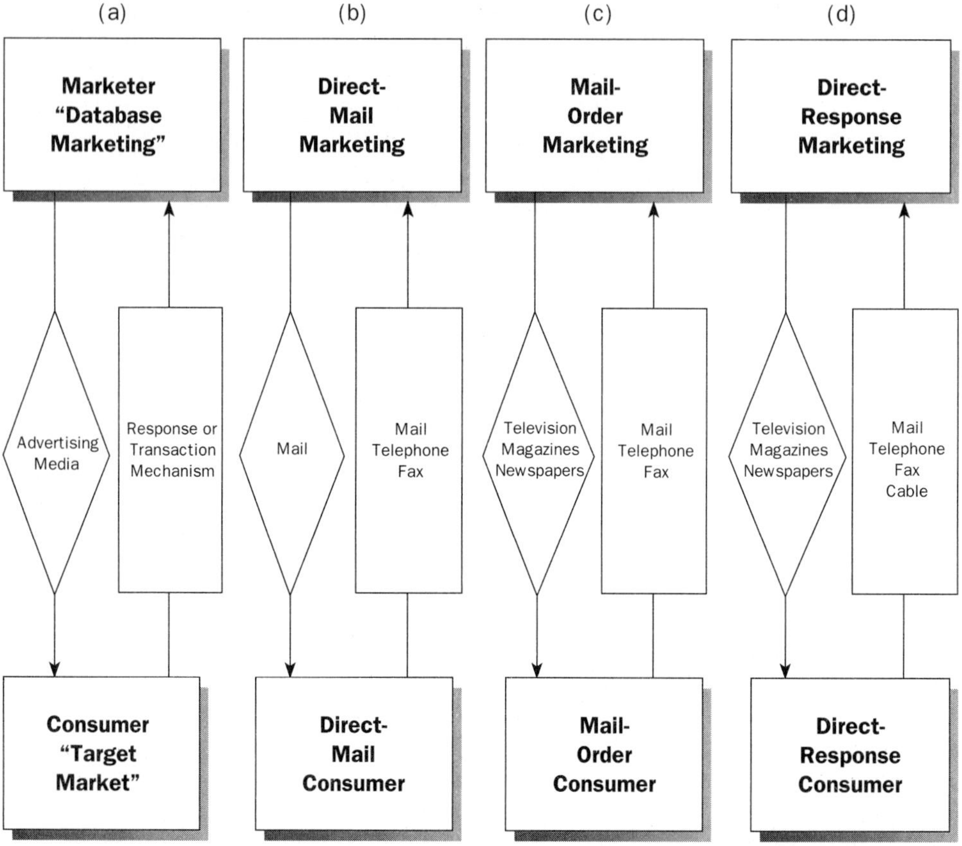

(a)	(b)	(c)	(d)
Marketer "Database Marketing"	Direct-Mail Marketing	Mail-Order Marketing	Direct-Response Marketing

Media/mechanisms:
- (a) Advertising Media; Response or Transaction Mechanism
- (b) Mail; Mail, Telephone, Fax
- (c) Television, Magazines, Newspapers; Mail, Telephone, Fax
- (d) Television, Magazines, Newspapers; Mail, Telephone, Fax, Cable

Consumer "Target Market"	Direct-Mail Consumer	Mail-Order Consumer	Direct-Response Consumer

❑ *Catalogs*—a specially prepared booklet consisting of a collection of pictures, drawings, and words that describe product features and benefits, pricing information, and ordering instructions. Catalogs are direct-marketing tools used in both retail and business-to-business markets.

❑ *Videologs*—shop-at-home or shop-at-office videotapes that present the marketer's selling proposition. Because both sound and sight are used in presenting products, this direct form of marketing is enjoying increased use.[28]

Mail-Order Marketing

Mail-order marketing differs from direct-mail marketing in that it uses television, radio, newspaper, and magazine advertisements to communicate the offer. Like direct mail, mail order marketing requires that the consumer respond to the offer by mail or telephone (see Figure 12-13c). A traditional method of mail-order marketing has been **response coupons**, which are inserted in newspaper or magazine advertisements featuring a particular good or service. The coupon serves as an order form and is the principal means to close the sale. **Home shopping** is a newer form of mail-order marketing in which products are presented on commercial television programs totally devoted to communicating the marketing offerings of one or more sellers. Figure 12-14 describes the home shopping business format. **Infomercials** are typically half-hour television advertisements that mix information and entertainment with a sales presentation. This format has traditionally been the marketing vehicle for a wide range of personal services, health programs, professional development, and home care products. In recent years infomercials have been used by more mainstream companies.[29] Orders are placed by mail, telephone, or fax, and products are delivered parcel post.

Direct-Response Marketing

Using both broadcast and print media to communicate the firm's offer, **direct-response marketing** differs from other direct-marketing methods in that consumers can use cable as an additional response mechanism to place orders and make inquiries (see Figure 12-13d). The two most common forms of direct-response marketing are videotex and interactive television. **Videotex** is an "interactive electronic system in which data and graphics are transmitted from a computer network over telephone or cable lines and displayed on a subscriber's television or computer-terminal screen."[30] CompuServe, Genie, and Prodigy are three of the larger videotex operators. **Interactive television** permits viewers to shop and buy goods and services that are displayed on a television screen and pay for

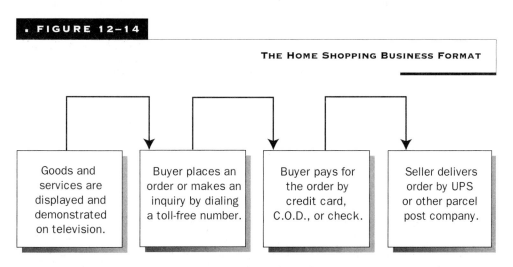

FIGURE 12-14

The Home Shopping Business Format

| Goods and services are displayed and demonstrated on television. | Buyer places an order or makes an inquiry by dialing a toll-free number. | Buyer pays for the order by credit card, C.O.D., or check. | Seller delivers order by UPS or other parcel post company. |

products using a computerized payment system that bills the purchase to a credit card or bank account after the consumer simply punches the right key on the keypad. Described as the next technological revolution, interactive television could "transform the humble television set into a powerful new medium, through which viewers sitting at home could order videos, pick their own camera angle for TV sports, play games with other viewers, buy and sell products—and train the set to pick only the fare they want and air it when they feel like watching."[31]

THE SALES PROMOTION COMPONENT

Anytime something extra is offered as an inducement for the customer to buy or respond in some fashion it is considered a **sales promotion**. Typically, a sales promotion is a short-term offer that seeks to gain an immediate response from the targeted consumer group by adding extra value to the offer. This extra value usually takes the form of an add-on that goes beyond the features and benefits provided by the product itself. The two forms of sales promotion are consumer and trade promotions.

Consumer promotions are extra-value incentives directed at the final consumer in an attempt to encourage a positive buying decision. The major forms of consumer promotions are coupons, samples, premiums, contests, sweepstakes, rebates, specialties, and tie-ins. **Trade promotions** are directed at providing members of the distribution channel (wholesalers and retailers) an incentive to cooperate with the manufacturer in promoting and selling its products. Trade shows, point-of-purchase displays, trade contests, dealer loaders, push money, trade allowances, product demonstrations, and sales training are sales promotion tools that offer additional incentive for a cooperative effort in selling and promoting the sponsor's products. Figure 12-15 briefly describes each of the consumer and trade promotion methods.

CONCLUDING REMARKS

Promotion is an effective marketing communications tool in which marketers and consumers exchange ideas, share feelings, trade information, and complete transactions. Effective marketing communications inform, persuade, and remind customers about the benefits of the marketer's offerings. The marketing communications process can be modeled as a meaningful message exchange process between the marketer (the source) and a customer (the receiver) using various communication and feedback channels.

The marketing communications mix is a blend of mass and personal communication components. Advertising, personal selling, direct marketing, sales promotion, public relations, and publicity are the principal components

CONCLUDING REMARKS

FIGURE 12-15

SALES PROMOTION METHODS

Consumer Promotions	
Coupons	Manufacturer or retailer certificates that offer a reduction in price on a particular product for a specific time period when presented at the point of purchase
Samples	Trial sizes or samples of products that allow the customer to experience the product at no cost or a sharply reduced price
Premiums	Merchandise items given to consumers free of charge or at a substantial price reduction as an inducement to purchase another product or participate in an activity or both; it is an extra bonus or gift given to a qualified individual
Contests	Promotion activities in which contestants compete for prizes and rewards by applying their skills in order to successfully complete a particular task
Sweepstakes	Promotion activities in which contestants win prizes and gifts based on chance
Rebates	Cash refund offers from manufacturers or other distributors that consumers can receive when they mail in proofs-of-purchase
Specialties	Useful articles of merchandise imprinted with an advertisement and given to consumers as gifts
Tie-ins	Merchandise offers that are associated with a special event, person, place, or thing and capitalize on the excitement and recognition that association brings to the firm's marketing program
Trade Shows	Periodic national, regional, and local occasions sponsored by trade and professional associations wherein manufacturers and other vendors market and display their products
Point-of-Purchase Displays	Display kits and fixtures that are given to retailers to assist them in displaying and featuring the vendor's products
Trade Contests	Sales incentive programs that reward salespeople for meeting or exceeding sales goals and for providing other promotional support for the sponsor's products and marketing programs
Dealer Loaders	Special incentives or gifts given to resellers for allowing the vendor to create a special display of the products
Push Money	Payments made by manufacturers to the reseller's salespeople for promoting and pushing the product over competitive brands
Trade Allowances	Payments or other incentives granted to buyers who agree to provide special support for the seller's products by advertising, displaying, selling, or servicing them
Product Demonstrations	In-store presentations and exhibits of the manufacturer's goods and services created and paid for by the manufacturer
Sales Training	Instructional programs sponsored by the manufacturer that help train the reseller's sales force with special focus on the sponsor's products

of the communications mix. It is the promotion manager's responsibility to incorporate these components into a marketing communications program by integrating and coordinating all the messages and media used to develop a comprehensive and consistent communications plan.

The promotion management process is the means by which the promotion manager achieves an integrated marketing communications program. It consists of the five stages of reviewing the annual marketing plan, establishing promotion objectives, organizing promotion campaigns, preparing promotion budgets, and implementing promotion programs.

ENDNOTES

1. Erik Larson, "Attention Shoppers: Don't Look Now but You Are Being Tailed," *Smithsonian* (January 1993), 71.

2. Damon Darlin, "Borrow from Thy Neighbor," *Forbes* (November 7, 1994), 215.

3. Maria Mallory, "That's One Angry Camel," *Business Week* (March 7, 1994), 94.

4. Jonathan Berry, "Wilma! What Happened to the Plain Old Ad?" *Business Week* (June 6, 1994), 54.

5. See Don E. Schultz, "Integrated Marketing Communications: Maybe Definition Is in the Point of View," *Marketing News* (January 18, 1993), 17. Also see Don E. Schultz, "Integration Helps You Plan Communications from Outside-In," *MarketingNews* (March 15, 1993), 12, and Don E. Schultz, "Objectives Drive Tactics in IMC Approach," *Marketing News* (March 22, 1994), 3.

6. Maria Mallory, "At Coke, Marketing Is It," *Business Week* (February 21, 1994), 39. Also see Maria Mallory, "Behemoth on a Tear," *Business Week* (October 3, 1994), 54–55.

7. Phyllis Berman, "The Spray Lingerie," *Forbes* (November 7, 1994), 108.

8. See Joel Dean, "Does Advertising Belong in the Capital Budget?" *Marketing Management*, Vol. 2, No. 2 (1994), 52–56.

9. Fara Warner, "Churches Develop Marketing Campaigns," *Wall Street Journal* (April 17, 1995), B4.

10. Jeanne Whalen, "Sears Polishes Efforts in Furniture," *Advertising Age* (March 6, 1995), 3.

11. R. Lee Sullivan, "Raise the Flag," *Forbes* (April 25, 1994), 88.

12. Geoffrey Smith and Ron Stodghill II, "Are Good Causes Good Marketing?" *Business Week* (March 21, 1994), 64.

13. See John C. Maloney, "Is Advertising Believability Really Important?" *Marketing Management*, Vol. 3, No. 1 (1994), 47–52.

14. See Alfred Politz, "The Dilemma of Creative Advertising," *Marketing Management*, Vol. 2, No. 2, (1993), 55–58.

15. R. Lee Sullivan, "Crude Doesn't Sell," *Forbes* (October 24, 1994), 84.

16. Robert Stowe England, "Penney-Wise?" *Financial World* (April 26, 1995), 37.

17. See Rita Koselka, "Hope and Fear as Marketing Tools," *Forbes* (August 29, 1994), 78–79.

18. See Joshua Levine, "Gutenberg's Revenge," *Forbes* (May 9, 1994), 166–67.

19. Julia Flynn, "Skol, Dude: Spirits Get Hip," *Business Week* (May 30, 1994), 95.

20. See Chris Roush, "Red Necks, White Socks, and Blue-Chip Sponsors," *Business Week* (August 15, 1995), 74. Also see Nanette Byrnes, "Rolling Billboards," *Financial World* (April 12, 1994), 46–56.

21. Joshua Levine, "Lighter than Air," *Forbes* (October 10, 1994), 120, 122.

22. See Joshua Levine, "Makeovers on Madison Avenue," *Forbes* (March 27, 1995), 110–11.

23. See Bob Donath, James W. Obermayer, Carolyn K. Dixon, and Richard A. Crocker, "When Your Prospect Calls," *Marketing Management*, Vol. 3, No. 2. (1994), 27–37.

24. Greg Burns, "Will So Many Ingredients Work Together?" *Business Week* (March 27, 1995), 188.

25. See Michael Kelly, "Replace Sales Management with Sales Leadership," *Marketing News* (June 19, 1995), 10.

26. Peter Burrows, "The Computer Is in the Mail (Really)," *Business Week* (January 23, 1995), 76.

27. See Debra Aho Williamson, "Building a New Industry," *Advertising Age* (March 13, 1995), S3–S8.

28. See Junu Bryan Kim, "Marketing with Video," *Advertising Age* (May 22, 1995), S1, S4.

29. See Chad Rubel, "Informercials Evolve as Major Firms Join Successful Format," *Advertising Age* (January 2, 1995), 1, 36.

30. *Marketing News*, "Videotex: What It's All About," (November 1983), 16.

31. *Wall Street Journal*, "Age of Interactive TV May Be Nearer as IBM and Warner Talk Deal" (May 21, 1992), A1.

PRICING DECISIONS

Chapter Outline

- **Introduction**
- **Pricing Perspectives**
    - Price and the Exchange Process
    - Price and the Value Concept
- **Pricing Determinants**
    - Demand Characteristics
    - Cost Structures
    - Customer Expectations
    - Competitive Conditions
    - Legal Constraints
- **Pricing Objectives**
    - Competition-Based Objectives
    - Sales-Oriented Objectives
    - Profit-Directed Objectives
- **Pricing Methods**
    - Cost-Based Pricing
    - Profit-Based Pricing
    - Customer-Based Pricing
    - Competition-Based Pricing
    - Vendor-Based Pricing
- **Pricing Strategies**
    - Differential Pricing
    - Competitive Pricing
    - Geographic Pricing
    - Product-Line Pricing
    - Psychological Pricing
    - Promotional Pricing
- **Concluding Remarks**

INTRODUCTION

Price is a powerful weapon in the marketing manager's toolbox of marketing strategies. Creatively applied, price decisions can help the organization promote consumer awareness of its market offerings by attracting attention to its value proposition. Price is also used to stimulate consumer trial of its goods and services by reducing the risks associated with new product adoption, to enhance consumer satisfaction and loyalty by creating greater perceived value, and to sustain a competitive advantage by providing superior value on a continuous basis. Effective pricing decisions are accomplished through adherence to a fairly structured four-stage process as shown in Figure 13-1. The pricing process requires the marketing manager to review pertinent pricing determinants, establish relevant pricing objectives, select appropriate pricing methods, and implement applicable pricing strategies. Before discussing the pricing process, we must first examine the nature of price from the perspectives of the exchange process and the value concept.

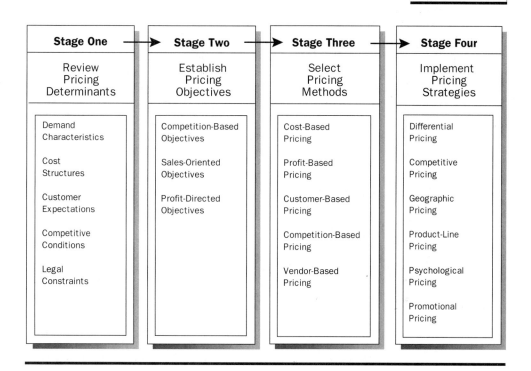

FIGURE 13-1

THE PRICING PROCESS

PRICING PERSPECTIVES

Historically, price has played a key role in promoting exchanges and determining value. Price helps buyers decide how to allocate their buying power among various market offerings. It also provides a means of communicating the relative worth of a product between buyers and sellers.

PRICE AND THE EXCHANGE PROCESS

In most modern-day transactions, price is a monetary expression of what it takes to successfully complete an exchange. **Price** represents the value of goods or services within a particular exchange process. From the perspective of the buyer, price is the economic sacrifice that the buyer is willing and able to make in order to acquire a particular product. For the seller, price represents an amount of money viewed as an acceptable payment for goods provided or services rendered.

The price, or value, of goods and services is expressed by using many different terms or labels. Charges for the professional services of doctors, consultants, and lawyers are referred to as *fees*. Schools and universities charge *tuition*. Organizations levy membership *dues;* landlords charge *rents* while airline prices are expressed as *fares*. The turnpike charges *tolls*, and insurance companies require payment of *premiums*. Charitable organizations accept *donations*, and violators are charged *fines* for improper behavior. For the use of their money, banks charge *interest*. These are but some of the more common expressions of price that are used to indicate the value of a good and service within different industry groupings.

Price is not always expressed in monetary terms. **Barter,** the oldest form of exchange, involves trading goods for goods or goods for services. The plumber who fixes the nursery's irrigation system in exchange for several shrubs and trees is engaging in the time-honored practice of bartering. The opportunity to make a good trade can be as important a part of the weekend flea-market culture as the successful completion of a sale.

PRICE AND THE VALUE CONCEPT

The concepts of price and value are inseparable. Price is an expression of value. What constitutes value is something that has different meaning for different individuals during different exchange situations. While there is no single, agreed-on definition of value, one possible description of **value** is that it is an interactive and changing relationship among the elements of product utility, product quality, product price, customer service, customer convenience, and intangible benefits. Figure 13-2 describes each of these six value elements and illustrates their interrelationships. In defining value for a particular purchase situation, the buyer combines and emphasizes different value elements in order to obtain a value proposition that is appropriate for that shopping experience. The

FIGURE 13-2

THE DETERMINANTS OF VALUE

Product Utility
the functional benefits derived from good product design and enhanced product feature

Product Quality
the utilitarian benefits that are associated with good materials and superior workmanship

Product Price
the absolute dollar cost of the goods and services and their comparable cost relative to competition

Customer Service
the benefits secured as a result of the types of services offered and the manner in which the customer is treated and assisted

Customer Convenience
the benefits affiliated with the time and place offered by the seller's place of business

Intangible Benefits
the perceived gain derived from the image of the seller or the products

---

composition and emphasis of value elements will vary from one purchase decision to another.

> Customers today want more of those things they value. If they value low cost, they want it lower. If they value convenience or speed when they buy, they want it easier and faster. If they look for state-of-the-art design, they want to see the art pushed forward. If they need expert advice, they want companies to give them more depth, more time, and more of a feeling that they're the only customer.[1]

One explanation for Papa John's pizza restaurants' success is their appeal to value-conscious households by including "a small tub of garlic butter and two hot peppers with each pie—little lagniappe that helps give the perception of more bang for the buck."[2]

Pricing Determinants

The first stage of the pricing process is to understand the multitude of influences that have a direct impact on setting and adjusting prices. In this section, we review some of the more compelling determinants of price (see Figure 13-1).

Demand Characteristics

How much are consumers willing and able to buy? It often depends on the price. **Demand** is the quantity of a good or service that will be sold at a given price for a specific time period. This relationship between price and quantity demanded is often expressed as the **law of demand** or shown in the form of a **demand curve.** Simply stated, lower prices result in higher demand levels while higher prices will restrict the quantity of goods or services sold. The common "airfare wars" among major U.S. carriers suggest that there is a strong relationship between price and the number of air travelers. This relationship is usually stronger for the nonbusiness traveler (family and leisure segment) than for the business traveler.

Marketing managers must consider the effect of different price levels on consumer demand for each of their products. This effect is called **price elasticity of demand**—the degree of consumer sensitivity to price changes. **Elastic demand** is a price-sensitive situation in which a change in price will strongly influence consumer demand. In these situations, consumer responsiveness to price increases and decreases is usually pronounced and timely. Under conditions of **inelastic demand,** price changes have little or no effect on demand. Inelastic demand suggests that consumers are relatively insensitive to price changes and do not alter their buying behavior significantly when price is altered.

Cost Structures

If demand conditions establish price ceilings, or the highest price a marketer can charge, then cost structures determine the lowest price that should be charged—the price floor. Normally, the price of a good or service should be set high enough to cover the total costs associated with production/procurement and marketing/merchandising of the product plus a profit margin. How total cost structures are expressed depends on the location of the organization within the distribution channel.

Manufacturers view **total costs** as the sum of fixed and variable costs. **Fixed costs,** such as rent, property taxes, insurance, and executive salaries, are costs that remain unchanged regardless of production levels. **Variable** costs change with the level of production. Labor and raw-materials costs typically increase as unit production increases. To obtain the **average total cost** of producing a product, total variable costs plus total fixed costs are divided by the number of units produced. Manufacturers are also interested in **marginal costs**—the change in cost that results from increasing production by one more unit. Marginal costs are calculated by dividing *change in total costs* by *change in quantity sold.*

Another view of cost structures can be obtained by examining a retailer's merchandise cost. To gain an accurate and complete picture of the retailer's merchandise cost structures, it is important to include both the actual cost of the merchandise and the costs associated with getting the goods into the store and ready for sale. From the retailer's perspective, **merchandise cost** equals net invoice price (gross invoice price minus trade discounts, quantity discounts, seasonal discounts, and promotional allowances) minus cash discounts plus transportation charges plus workroom expenses. Merchandise costs serve as a reference and starting point for several different methods of cost pricing.

Customer Expectations

Customers' feelings and beliefs regarding prices must be taken into account in making price decisions. Both final consumers and organizational buyers hold a large number of opinions regarding price and its role in purchase decisions. These opinions may be correct or incorrect, logical or illogical, or practical or impractical. Nevertheless, these expectations direct the consumer's buying activities. If the consumer believes that the lowest price is the best value or the highest price represents the best quality, the buyer's selective perception mechanisms will reinforce that opinion. It is the marketing manager's responsibility to discover the relevant price opinions of targeted consumers, then set and adjust prices in order to meet those expectations. Most of the pricing strategies discussed later in this chapter take into account consumers' feelings and beliefs concerning price and their role in the value equation.

Competitive Conditions

Consumers compare prices. For this reason alone, marketers must consider the prices charged by competitors and how they are going to position their organization and its products against those competitors. Each marketer's prices must be competitive. That does not mean that they must be the same. Consumers will accept price differentials if they are justified. For example, higher prices are acceptable if greater value is offered and considered important enough to justify the higher price. In the highly competitive personal computer market, any price difference must be justified on the basis of hardware capabilities or the additional value delivered by the software bundle.[3]

Competitive market structures of the industry within which the organization operates can have a significant impact on pricing strategies. They greatly affect the flexibility of the organization in setting prices. Under a **monopoly** an organization has considerable latitude in setting prices. With no competition, the organization has the freedom to set prices at any level the market will bear. With **oligopolistic** market structures, organizations usually raise prices in the anticipation that the competitors also will increase prices. With a small number of sellers dominating the market, there is little incentive to lower prices. Product differentiation and other forms of nonprice competition are practiced by organizations engaged in **monopolistic competition**—market structures in which a large number of sellers are marketing similar product lines. Marketers have no leeway in setting prices in markets characterized by **pure competition;** the large number of buyers and sellers prohibits any attempt at controlling prices.

Legal Constraints

Pricing is the most regulated element of the marketing mix. There are government regulations that address such issues as price discrimination, price fixing, predatory pricing, deceptive pricing, and dumping. Offering the right price requires that the marketer offer it in the right way.

Price discrimination involves charging different customers different prices for the same good or service. This practice is illegal if the difference in price cannot be defended on the basis of **cost justification** (the cost of doing business is higher for the customer being charged a higher price) or as an article of **good-faith justification** (the need to meet an equally low price of a competitor in one market and not another). In short, sellers must treat all buyers equally under the same transactional circumstances.

Price fixing is any agreement among all or most of the organizations within a market to set prices for a good or service at an agreed-upon level. These conspiracies to set prices have been declared illegal. **Vertical price fixing** is an illegal collaboration among various members of the same marketing channel (such as a manufacturer and a retailer) to set retail prices. **Horizontal price fixing** involves verbal or written agreements between members in one marketing channel and competitors in a different distribution channel to establish and charge a fixed retail price for one or more product lines.

The pricing practice of charging artificially lower prices in one targeted market than those charged in other markets in order to restrict competition in the targeted market or eliminate competitors from that market is termed **predatory pricing.** Price differences among markets must be cost justified in order to be legal.

Deceptive pricing practices involve expressing prices in confusing and misleading ways. The Federal Trade Commission (FTC) has established guidelines as to what constitutes deceptive pricing. For example, in making **former price comparisons,** a seller who promotes a price as a price reduction from a former price must first establish that the former price was the original, usual, or regular selling price. In other words, the former higher price was offered for a reasonable length of time, not simply inflated to make the new price more attractive. Another example involves **competitive price comparisons,** which require that the seller first establish, before making price comparisons, that the competitor's price is, in fact, the one that is regularly and typically charged by the competitor. The FTC also regulates free merchandise offerings, cents-off pricing, suggested-retail-price comparisons, and a host of other potentially deceptive price techniques.

Dumping is the practice of selling products in foreign markets at prices below those charged in the seller's domestic market. Dumping often involves selling products below cost in order to gain an initial foothold or additional market share in foreign markets. The governments of most countries have established antidumping regulations in an attempt to protect domestic industries from unfair pricing practices of foreign competitors.

Pricing Objectives

In this second stage of the pricing process, the marketer needs to establish clearly what is to be accomplished by the price element of the marketing mix. Which pricing method is selected and which pricing strategy is implemented will depend on what objectives are to be achieved by the firm's pricing program. Pricing objectives can be competition based, sales oriented, or profit directed.

Competition-Based Objectives

Competition-based price objectives range from **market survival** (setting prices to ensure the organization's short-term survival) to **price leadership** (taking the lead in establishing price levels for selected product lines). To stay in business, organizations may have to adjust prices upward or downward in response to internal (excessive inventory) or external (an economic downturn) circumstances. To remain competitive in low-end photographic markets, Kodak introduced its low-price Funtime film.[4] To survive and fill seats, some airlines have engaged in airfare wars that are quite shortsighted.

Price leaders are usually organizations that have operating strengths (low-cost producers) and marketing advantages (high brand loyalty) that allow them to dictate going market prices in particular product categories. Medco has become a price leader in the pharmaceutical industry and one of the nation's largest providers of pills by efficiently selling and distributing drugs at cut-rate prices using a direct-mail distribution channel.[5] Many firms simply elect not to compete on the basis of price. **Nonprice competition** involves competing on the basis of better products, faster service, more convenience, or a host of other value-enhancement factors.

SALES-ORIENTED OBJECTIVES

Sales-oriented objectives are usually expressed in terms of sales volume and market share goals. To achieve future sales growth or to maintain current sales levels are two **sales volume** objectives commonly used in establishing prices. In either case, the ultimate goal in price setting is to generate profitable sales volume. Like sales volume objectives, **market share** (the percentage share of the total market captured by a particular product or organization) objectives are directed at setting prices to increase or maintain market-share. Price-setting objectives directed at increasing market share are most appropriate for new and expanding markets in which sales are increasing for all or most competing firms. In established and stable markets, a market-share growth objective is likely to attract retaliatory pricing actions (price wars) as competitors seek to protect their market share at all costs. Hence, market-share maintenance is typically the more appropriate pricing objective for mature markets. To maintain its 44-percent share of the mature $20-billion minivan market, Chrysler offered discounts of up to $1,500 in order to make it tough for Ford to gain market share when it introduced its new Windstar model.[6]

PROFIT-DIRECTED OBJECTIVES

Prices must be set at a level high enough to cover all of the costs associated with producing and marketing the product. In addition, the price must provide a fair return for the organization's efforts. **Profit maximization** is the profit objective of obtaining the highest possible profit margins through pricing and other marketing activities. This "buy-low, sell-high" strategy is difficult to implement because it requires a complete understanding of the price determinants. Given the limited amount of information available for making a price determination, profit maximization is usually more of a promotional statement than a pricing objective. Profit maximization objectives often create channel conflict because achievement of such objectives often comes at the expense of other members of the marketing channel. **Target return** objectives are expressed as a percentage return on the organization's investments or sales. **Return on investments (ROI)** is the ratio of profits to capital investments (land, building, equipment, and inventory). **Return on net sales (ROS)** is obtained by dividing dollar profit by net sales. Target return objectives permit price setting consistent with financial performance goals and high customer satisfaction.

PRICING METHODS

The third stage of the price-setting process is the selection of one or more pricing methods. While some marketing managers tend to rely on a single pricing method in their initial price-setting efforts, others use a combination of methods to arrive at an initial asking price. The marketing manager has a choice of cost-, profit-, customer-, competition-, and vendor-based pricing

FIGURE 13-3

SELECTING PRICING METHOD

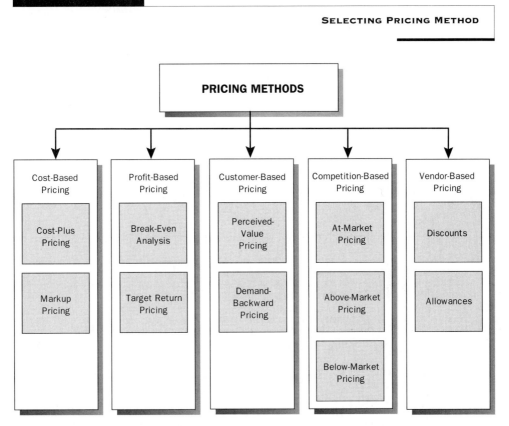

methodologies. Figure 13-3 identifies specific practices employed in each of these price-setting methods. Prices set in this third stage of the pricing process will undergo adjustments in order to accommodate one or more of the pricing strategies outlined in the final stage of the pricing process.

COST-BASED PRICING

In cost-based pricing the marketing manager adds a profit margin (dollar or percentage) to the cost of a product to arrive at the selling price. This basic form of price setting is easy to understand, calculate, and implement. Cost-plus and markup pricing are the most commonly used cost-based pricing methods.

In **cost-plus pricing** the marketing manager

1. ascertains total product costs,
2. determines an appropriate dollar or percentage profit figure, and
3. calculates the selling price by combining cost and profit figures.

This method is frequently used by the government when cost structures (such as some defense contracts) are difficult to determine.

Retailers use a form of cost-based pricing known as **markup pricing.** In determining **dollar markup,** the retailer adds to the cost of merchandise a dollar amount large enough to cover operating expense and provide an acceptable profit. Dollar markups are used with big-ticket items (automobiles or jewelry) because they are more realistic and easier to use. **Percentage markups** are used to set prices for most merchandise lines because they facilitate price comparisons among different product lines. Percentage markups are calculated and expressed using either merchandise cost or retail price as the base:

$$\text{Markup Percentage (at cost)} = \frac{\text{Retail Price} - \text{Merchandise Cost}}{\text{Merchandise Cost}}$$

$$\text{Markup Percentage (at retail)} = \frac{\text{Retail Price} - \text{Merchandise Cost}}{\text{Retail Price}}$$

Profit-Based Pricing

The most common forms of profit-based pricing are break-even analysis and target return pricing. **Break-even analysis** allows the marketer to consider both demand and cost structures in setting prices. It involves calculating the **break-even point**—the number of units that must be sold at a certain price in order for the firm to cover all costs. At the break-even point, total revenues equal total costs. It represents the minimum quantity of goods that must be sold at a stated price before the company will make a profit. If sales fall below the break-even point, a loss is incurred. Unit sales above the break-even generate profit. The break-even point in units is calculated using the following formula:

$$\text{Break-Even Point (in units)} = \frac{\text{Total Fixed Costs}}{\text{Selling Price} - \text{Average Variable Costs}}$$

The usefulness of break-even analysis depends on marketing management's ability to obtain reliable cost information.

Target return pricing attempts to establish a price that will result in a desired rate of return on the firm's investments. It is an extension of the break-even point method in which a desired profit is added to fixed costs and a **break-even point return on investment** is calculated by the following formula:

$$\text{Break-Even Point Return on Investment} = \frac{\text{Total Fixed Costs} + \text{Desired Profit}}{\text{Selling Price} - \text{Average Variable Costs}}$$

By inserting different selling prices into the equation, the marketing manager can determine how many units must be sold in order to attain the desired return on investment.

Customer-Based Pricing

Perceived-value and demand-backward pricing are two commonly employed customer-based pricing methods. **Perceived-value pricing** involves setting prices based on the customer's perceived value of the product. Perceived value is based on one or more of the nonprice factors outlined in Figure 13-2. Product quality, product utility, customer service, customer convenience, and other nontangible benefits are used to enhance the perceived value in the customer's mind and to increase the price at which the product can be sold.

In **demand-backward pricing,** the marketing manager starts with a reliable estimate of what the consumer is willing to pay for a product and works back from the selling price to determine if there is sufficient profit margin by subtracting estimates of per-unit costs from the estimated per-unit selling price. If profit margins are adequate and reasonable, the demand-backward selling price is established. If the calculated profit margin is unacceptable, the marketing manager needs to explore ways to lower costs (such as more efficient production and distribution methods).

Competition-Based Pricing

In using a competition-based pricing scheme, the marketer sets prices in relation to competitors' prices. In this judgmental pricing method, prices charged by competitors are used as benchmarks for price-setting decisions. At-market, above-market, and below-market pricing are the three basic alternatives when using a competition-based pricing method.

At-market pricing is the practice of setting prices at the going, or traditional, market price. In pursuing an at-market pricing scheme, the marketing manager has elected to de-emphasize the price factor and to emphasize nonprice elements of the marketing mix. This price follower, middle-of-the-road strategy involves setting prices within an acceptable range of the competitive standard for a given market area.

In **above-market pricing,** the marketer sets the price at a level that is above the going market price. To justify higher prices, the marketer must carefully communicate to consumers what extra benefits they can expect to receive in return for paying a premium. Prestige prices can be justified on the basis of such extras as better quality and more exclusive merchandise, higher service levels and more personalized attention, a more prestigious image and more customer conveniences, or any other benefit that would enhance the customer's enjoyment in buying, using, and possessing the product.

Underselling competitors is the goal of **below-market pricing.** By selling below going market prices, the marketer is hoping to increase total sales revenues with an acceptable profit margin. To enjoy long-term success with this low-price, high-volume, high-turnover strategy, the organization must be in a cost-leadership position wherein cost structures are tightly controlled and managed. In contrast to the at-market method of price setting, in below-market pricing the price factor assumes center stage in determining the customer's value equation.

A pricing approach that attempts to neutralize the competitive price factor is **price matching.** A price matching policy is a price insurance policy that promises to match (and in some cases beat) the competitor's lowest price. Automobile dealers often advertise that they will meet the lowest advertised price of any competitor. Best Buy, a Minneapolis-based home electronics retailer, offers a thirty-day, 110-percent guarantee if the consumer finds a lower price on a compact disc.[7]

VENDOR-BASED PRICING

Business-to-business pricing within the marketing distribution channel usually takes the form of **vendor-based pricing**—the pricing practice of establishing a basic **list price,** which is adjusted for each customer. **Discounts** and **allowances** are reductions from the list price given to customers depending on the circumstances of a particular transaction. This price discounting system allows the marketer to adjust price without revising the basic price list. While there are many forms of discounts and allowances, the most common discounts are trade, quantity, cash, and seasonal. Common allowances include promotion, brokerage, and slotting allowances, and accepting trade-ins. Figure 13-4 provides a brief description of each of these discounts and allowances.

PRICING STRATEGIES

The fourth and final stage of the pricing process is the implementation of various pricing strategies. These pricing strategies are used to supplement and to modify the price structures created by the price-setting methods described in stage three. As shown in Figure 13-5, price strategies can be classified into six different categories—differential, competitive, geographical, product-line, psychological, and promotional. In reviewing these strategies, it is essential to keep in mind that these strategies are not mutually exclusive; they are commonly employed in conjunction with one another, and they can often come into conflict with one another.

DIFFERENTIAL PRICING

Differential pricing is the practice of selling the same product to different markets for different prices. Because consumer reactions to price vary from one market segment to another, marketers can successfully practice price

FIGURE 13-4

TYPES OF DISCOUNTS AND ALLOWANCES

Promotional Allowances	Reductions from list price that compensate the buyer for assisting the seller in various promotional activities (participating in local advertising campaigns, setting up special in-store displays, or distribution of sales literature)
Slotting Allowances	Payments made by the vendor to the buyer to get special consideration in the allocation of store space to the vendor's products. Essentially, slotting allowances are admission fees paid by the manufacturers and other suppliers to get their products onto crowded retail shelves. Preferred sales areas include free-standing displays in high-traffic aisles, end-of-aisle displays, and checkout counter displays.
Brokerage Allowances	Payments granted to a broker for providing value-added services and functions. These allowances are essentially trade discounts that are granted to outside independent-agent middlemen who provide many of the same functions and services as intermediaries who are members of the marketing channel.
Trade-in Allowances	Reductions in the selling price granted to buyers who trade in used products when purchasing a new product
Trade Discount	Often referred to as a functional discount because it is a reduction from list price given to buyers as compensation for services that are essential to the successful marketing of a product. Trade discounts are expressed as a percentage or a series of percentages off list price.
Quantity Discount	Inducements given to encourage large purchase quantities and to reward buyers for being loyal customers. Larger order quantities result in economies of scale in production, distribution, and marketing. These reductions are expressed as percentages off list price or as schedules with unit or dollar sales corresponding to a particular dollar discount amount. Quantity discounts can be either *noncumulative* (based on a single order) or *cumulative* (based on several orders).
Cash Discount	A price reduction given for making prompt payment of the invoice. Cash discounts are expressed as a percentage reduction from net invoice price. The terms and conditions of cash discounts vary in terms of the discount amount and the amount of time (dating terms) allowed to take advantage of the discount.
Seasonal Discount	Price reductions off list price given to buyers who are willing to order, take delivery, and pay for goods during the off-season. Seasonal discounts reimburse buyers for incurring additional operating expense (inventory carrying costs) and for assuming the additional risks of buying before the season starts.

discrimination by charging one market higher or lower prices than those charged in other settings. *U.S. News & World Report* has used different prices in different parts of the country in order to boost declining single-copy sales.[8] As related in Figure 13-5, there are several variations of differential pricing; they include flexible pricing, second-market discounting, periodic discounting, and random discounting.

Flexible pricing allows and encourages retail consumers to negotiate the final selling price. The purchase of an automobile and other large-ticket

FIGURE 13-5

IMPLEMENTING A PRICING STRATEGY

Differential Pricing

Flexible Pricing
Second-Market Discounting
Periodic Discounting
Random Discounting

Competitive Pricing

Penetration Pricing
Price Signaling
Reference Pricing

Geographic Pricing

F.O.B. Origin Pricing
Uniform Delivery Pricing
Zone Pricing
Freight Absorption
Basing-Point Pricing

Product-Line Pricing

Price Bundling
Captive Pricing
Concept Selling
Price Lining
Bridge Pricing

Psychological Pricing

Odd Pricing
Even Pricing
Multiple Pricing
Customary Pricing

Promotional Pricing

Leader Pricing
Everyday Low Pricing
High-Low Pricing

items often involves price haggling. However, as a contrary strategy some automobile companies, such as Saturn and Oldsmobile, are successfully employing simplified pricing without price haggling.[9] Flexible pricing allows the seller to adjust prices to meet the needs of individual consumers. **Second-market discounting** is the strategy of offering a special discounted price to a secondary market. A manufacturer might elect to sell overruns of a product in a foreign market at a discounted price in order to get rid of excess inventory. Apparel manufacturers, for example, market their overruns and packaways from the previous season to off-price retailers at a substantial discount. Finally, many retailers offer senior citizens a special discount in recognition of their status as mature consumers.

Periodic discounting, also referred to as price skimming, is the practice of setting a high market-entry price on a new or unique product in order to take advantage of the relative price insensitivity of the market segment known as early adopters. As the product matures, it is systematically discounted through a series of price reductions, which attract new and more price-sensitive adopter segments. **Random discounting** involves unscheduled price reductions (unadvertised specials, unannounced specials, and in-store couponing) that encourage customers who just happen to be available to make an immediate purchase.

COMPETITIVE PRICING

Competitive pricing incorporates several pricing strategies that attempt to position an organization's prices relative to its competitors. Given that consumers tend to gather information by comparison shopping, an organization's competitive price position is vital to fostering an image of competitiveness. Penetration pricing, price signaling, and reference pricing are all commonly employed competitive pricing strategies.

In implementing a **penetration pricing** strategy, the organization attempts to gain market share or maximize sales growth by entering the market with a product that is priced below the competition. Penetration pricing goes hand in hand with market penetration strategies (see Chapter 2) wherein the organization views price-sensitive markets as growth-opportunities. Penetration pricing is not just a market-entry strategy; it is also used to discourage new competition. Low competitive prices are an effective deterrent to all but the most efficient marketers.

Price signaling is a deliberate effort on the part of the seller to use price as an indicator of product quality. When consumers are unable or unwilling to make competent evaluations of quality, they sometimes rely on high price as a surrogate measure of quality. These price signals may or may not reflect the true worth of products. The marketplace is full of products whose prices are not justified by their quality. On the other hand, there are many high-priced products that live up to their quality image.

Reference pricing is the practice of marking products with the seller's price together with a competitor's higher price. Many drugstores and supermarkets often display their private labels next to higher priced national brands in order to assist customers in making price comparisons. The opportunity for customers to make price comparisons quickly and conveniently can be a strong selling tool provided the customer has confidence in the price comparison offered by the seller.[10] One variation of this strategy is to reference the seller's lower price to an average of the selling prices in a particular market.

Geographic Pricing

To accommodate the different physical distances between sellers and buyers, marketers sometimes engage in **geographic pricing**—the practice of including shipping and other related costs in the price of the product. A number of different pricing schemes have been devised to incorporate geographical adjustments. **F.O.B.(free-on-board) origin pricing** is a selling price that does not include shipping and handling charges. The buyer absorbs all of the freight costs and assumes responsibility for the shipment as soon as it leaves the seller's place of business. Each buyer pays the actual transportation cost of getting the shipment to its place of business. In **uniform delivery pricing,** the seller charges buyers the same price regardless of their location. Sometimes referred to as "postage stamp pricing," this pricing approach results in geographic price discrimination against buyers who are located closer to the point of origin. Closer customers subsidize the prices distant buyers pay.

A variation of uniform delivery pricing is **zone pricing**—a regional pricing scheme in which all buyers within a prescribed geographical region pay the same price.

In **freight absorption pricing,** the seller pays all or part of the transportation costs and does not pass them along to sellers in the form of higher prices. By absorbing freight costs the seller hopes to increase total sales enough to cover the additional costs and to generate extra profits. Sometimes sellers absorb freight charges to gain greater penetration of a market or to remain competitive in a contested market.

The last form of geographic pricing is **basing-point pricing**—a pricing strategy designed to increase a seller's geographic reach by designating a single basing-point location (such as St. Louis) or multiple basing-point locations (such as St. Louis, Atlanta, and Portland) and charging all buyers freight costs from a designated basing point to the buyers' locations regardless of where the shipment originated. For example, a buyer in Detroit would pay the shipping costs from St. Louis even if the shipment were sent from Cleveland. Under certain circumstances, these "phantom freight" charges are viewed as illegal.

Product-Line Pricing

Marketers have developed a number of different pricing strategies for dealing with an entire line of products or various product groups within a product line. **Price bundling** is the marketing of two or more goods or services in a single package for a special price.[11] By creating a package deal, the marketer hopes to generate additional profitable sales from current customers by offering them a price break. The Washington Bullets basketball team sells ten-packs—tickets for the ten most popular games of the season.[12] When fast-food retailers offer "value meals" by bundling a sandwich with french fries and a drink, they are practicing a product-plus-product bundling. The "weekend escape" offered by many hotels in which meals are part of the package deal is an example of a service-plus-product pricing bundle. **Captive pricing** is a variation on price bundling where the seller locks in the buyer by selling the basic product item at a reduced price, then selling essential consumables at highly profitable prices. The classic example is Gillette's practice of selling new-model razors at reasonable prices and charging a premium price for the razor blades.

Concept selling is the pricing strategy of charging a higher price for a good or service and justifying that price by convincing the customer that the total benefits package (the concept) is worth the extra cost. For example, a health club that packages several goods and services into a "total wellness" package of exercise, nutrition, and relaxation is selling the concept of health and well-being. In this case the whole is greater than its parts.

Price lining and bridge pricing deal with the problem of developing a logical pricing strategy for various product groupings within a product line. **Price lining** is the practice of grouping several product items into a "price zone" (a range of prices that appeals to a particular market segment such as low/economy, intermediate/family, or prestige/luxury) and offering several "price points" (high, middle, and low) within each price zone. In most apparel lines, department stores offer several price zones and multiple price points within each zone. In recent years, major consumer-products companies such as Procter & Gamble have used "price-tiering" in some product categories in order to create "fighting brands" (lower price lines and points) that are used to war against competitive brands and private labels.[13]

In implementing a **bridge pricing** strategy, the marketing manager establishes a price that spans or connects two distinctively different price lines or points. Fashion designers like Yves Saint-Laurent and Givenchy have developed lines that bridge the gap between their exclusive, high-fashion lines and the mass-fashion lines offered by national and store labels (such as Levi Strauss and The GAP). Anne Klein II, Calvin Klein Classification, and Donna Karan's DKNY are all excellent examples of product lines that are marketed using a bridge pricing strategy.

PSYCHOLOGICAL PRICING

Psychological pricing recognizes and adapts the organization's pricing practices in order to accommodate psychological influences (motivation, perception, learning, and attitudes) on consumer buying behavior. **Odd pricing** is the psychological ploy of setting prices that end in odd numbers (such as $39.95) in the belief that consumers perceive odd prices as being significantly below even-dollar prices. Some retailers use **even pricing** ($200) in the belief that it helps to project a prestigious image. **Multiple pricing,** a retail price reduction on a quantity purchase (three jars of pickles for $2.89), is a form of psychological pricing in that many consumers have been conditioned to expect a bargain price if they buy multiple quantities. **Customary pricing** involves charging customers the price that they have come to expect. While many stationary prices of the past (the five-cent candy bar and the ten-cent phone call) became almost traditional, the highly competitive market of today severely limits the use of this form of psychological pricing.

PROMOTIONAL PRICING

Promotional pricing entails several different pricing strategies whereby the seller uses lower prices to attract customers, build sales, and create value. Promotional pricing can be utilized as a temporary tactic or a long-term strategy.

Leader pricing offers high-demand products at attractive prices. Weekly newspaper specials offered by local supermarkets are one of the most common forms of leader pricing. Leader products contribute little if anything directly to profits. However, their indirect contribution to total dollar profit can be substantial if the supermarket makes anticipated additional sales on high-profit items. Leader pricing strategies differ depending on the extent of the markdown and the seller's purpose in attracting the potential shopper. **Low-leaders** is a leader pricing strategy in which prices are substantially marked down but are still high enough to cover the actual costs of the goods to the seller. **Loss-leaders** are prices reduced below the seller's costs of goods sold. Like low-leaders, loss-leaders are used to build customer traffic and to gain additional complementary and unplanned purchases. **Bait leaders** are extremely attractive advertised prices on products that the seller does not intend to sell. Rather, the highly attractive advertised price is the "bait" to attract the buyer to the seller's place of business where "switching" sales tactics can be applied to get the potential buyer to trade up to products that are more expensive and have a higher profit margin.

Everyday low pricing is the pricing strategy of maintaining price points at the same low level year-round. By avoiding the pricing yo-yo of markups and markdowns, the retailer establishes greater price creditability through a more consistent and understandable price program.[14] The success of this strategy lies in promoting a value image that the customer can trust. Wal-Mart is given credit for popularizing this form of pricing.

Toys 'R' Us, Circuit City, and Dillard's Department Stores have all initiated some form of the everyday low-price strategy.[15] In sharp contrast to everyday low pricing is the strategy of **high-low pricing**.

1. Buying and stocking up on large quantities of manufacturer's promotional items (known in the retail trade as forward buying) in order to take advantage of substantially lower prices

2. Using part of the order to support weekly, low-leader, promotional sales specials

3. Saving the other part of the order for normal selling periods when it can be sold at full markup

Concluding Remarks

Price represents the value of goods and services within a particular exchange process. Prices are expressed as fees, fares, dues, tolls, donations, and a host of other monetary terms. Prior to setting prices, the marketing manager must review such pricing determinants as demand characteristics, cost structures, customer expectations, competitive conditions, and legal constraints to ascertain their impact on the pricing decision. To guide and focus the price-setting process, the marketing manager establishes various competition-based, sales-oriented, and profit-directed objectives. A pricing method is selected in the third stage of the pricing process. The marketing manager can choose from one of five different approaches: cost-, profit-, customer-, competition-, or vendor-based methods. The various pricing strategies are implemented in the final stage of the price-setting process. Differential, competitive, geographic, product-line, psychological, and promotional pricing are all viable strategies the marketing manager can employ.

Endnotes

1. Michael Treacy and Fred Wiersema, "How Market Leaders Keep Their Edge," *Fortune* (February 6, 1995), 88.

2. Zachary Schiller, "From a Broom Closet in a Bar to 485 Pizza Restaurants," *Business Week* (May 23, 1994), 94.

3. Jim Carlton, "Price War Puts Powerful PCs Closer to Home," *Wall Street Journal* (April 3, 1995), B1, B3.

4. Mark Maremont, "The New Flash at Kodak," *Business Week* (May 16, 1994), 32.

5. George Anders, "Pharmacy Chain's Successful Sales Pitch Dismays Some Doctors and Drug Firms," *Wall Street Journal* (February 23, 1993), B1, B6.

6. David Woodruff, "Chrysler Is Burning up the Minivan Lane," *Business Week* (September 5, 1994), 31.

7. Chad Rubel, "Music Retailers in Battle; Prices Are Main Weapon," *Marketing News* (December 5, 1994), 2. Also see Nina Munk, "Shopping in Peace," *Forbes* (March 14, 1994), 94–96.

8. Joshua Levine, "A Dying Business?" *Forbes* (May 23, 1994), 208.

9. Robert Stowe England, "Piece of Cake," *Financial World* (March 28, 1995), 38.

10. See Anthony D. Cox and Dena Cox, "Competing on Price: The Role of Retail Price Advertising in Shaping Store Price Image," *Journal of Retailing* (Winter 1990), 428–45. Also see Tridib Mazumdar and Kent B. Monroe, "Effect of Inter-Store and In-Store Price Comparisons on Price Recall Accuracy and Confidence," *Journal of Retailing* (Spring 1992), 66–89.

11. Joseph P. Guiltinan, "The Price Bundling of Services: A Normative Framework," *Journal of Marketing* (April 1987), 74.

12. Amy Barrett, "Meet the Fastest Five-Footer in the NBA," *Business Week* (January 16, 1995), 91.

13. Jonathan Berry and Zachary Schiller, "Attack of the Fighting Brands," *Business Week* (May 2, 1994), 125.

14. See Gregory A. Patterson, "More Stores Switch from Sales to 'Everyday Low Prices,'" *Wall Street Journal* (November 12, 1992), B1.

15. See Stephanie Anderson Forest, "Dillard's has a Dilly of a Headache," *Business Week* (October 3, 1994), 85–86.

Marketing Actions

Chapter 14 **Implementing and Controlling the Marketing Effort**

IMPLEMENTING AND CONTROLLING THE MARKETING EFFORT

CHAPTER OUTLINE

- **INTRODUCTION**
- **MARKETING MANAGEMENT PROCESS REVISITED**
- **IMPLEMENTING**
    - ORGANIZING THE MARKETING EFFORT
    - EXECUTING THE MARKETING EFFORT
- **CONTROLLING**
    - MONITORING THE MARKETING EFFORT
    - MODIFYING THE MARKETING EFFORT
- **CONCLUDING REMARKS**

Introduction

The concern of marketing management is the effective and efficient attainment of the organization's aspirations and purposes. As discussed in Chapter 1, marketing managers achieve these aspirations and purposes through planning, implementing, and controlling marketing and facilitating activities. In this chapter, we will discuss the administrative tasks of implementing and controlling the organization's established strategic business and marketing plans, as well as its annual marketing plans. After a short review of the marketing management process, we will examine the tasks of implementation (organizing and executing the marketing effort) and control (monitoring and adapting the marketing effort).

Marketing Management Process Revisited

Planning, implementing, and controlling the marketing effort comprise the marketing management process. Figure 14-1 illustrates the more important tasks associated with each phase of the process.

Planning is concerned with defining what the marketing organization wants to be in the future and deciding how to get there. The tasks of identifying desired outcomes (in terms of the organizational mission or marketing goals and objectives), assessing current situations (using either a portfolio, SWOT, or situation analysis), and evaluating possible options (as in organizational opportunities or marketing strategies and programs) were discussed extensively with respect to the various levels and types of planning (the strategic business plan, the strategic marketing plan, and the annual marketing plan) in Chapters 2 through 4. Figure 14-2 summarizes and reviews the relationships between planning tasks and planning levels and types.

The focus of this chapter is the implementation and control phases of the marketing management process and the four tasks of organizing, executing, monitoring, and modifying the marketing effort.

Implementing

Marketing implementation is that part of the marketing management process concerned with translating business and marketing plans into action. In the recent restructuring at General Motors, the second stage of the turnaround strategy was to get the realigned organization to actually perform at world class levels. Previous to the restructuring, "a plethora of divisions, agendas, and egos made it extremely difficult to get things done."[1] GM simply did not implement new car rollouts well enough to remain competitive without a major reorganization. Successful implementation of business and marketing plans necessitates having the right organizational structure and the right set of policies and procedures for executing those plans (see Figure 14-1).

FIGURE 14-1

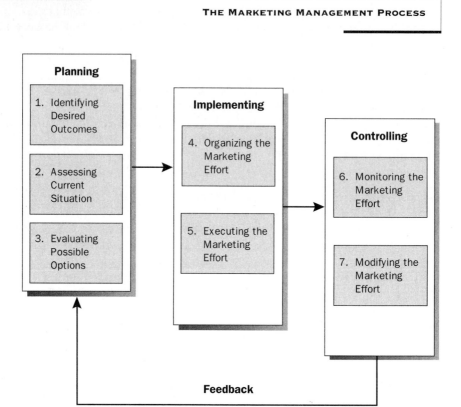

THE MARKETING MANAGEMENT PROCESS

ORGANIZING THE MARKETING EFFORT

The complexity and diversity of marketing strategies, tactics, and actions require an organizational structure, form, and culture that is conducive to the firm's marketing effort. Within a marketing context, **organizing** consists of designing the internal and external relationships and establishing the policies and procedures, as well as creating the means and methods by which various participants in the marketing function can carry out their responsibilities in an effective and efficient manner. Organization involves a coordinated effort, a resource allocation plan, and a system of checks and balances. Figure 14-3 outlines the three principal areas of concern when organizing the marketing effort.

ORGANIZATIONAL STRUCTURE Lines of authority and areas of responsibility need to be carefully identified within the marketing organization. To accomplish this task, the marketing manager creates an **organizational chart,** which shows the formal relationships among various parts of the marketing organization, defines the roles and responsibilities of each member of the marketing team, and spells out

FIGURE 14-2

PLANNING THE MARKETING EFFORT

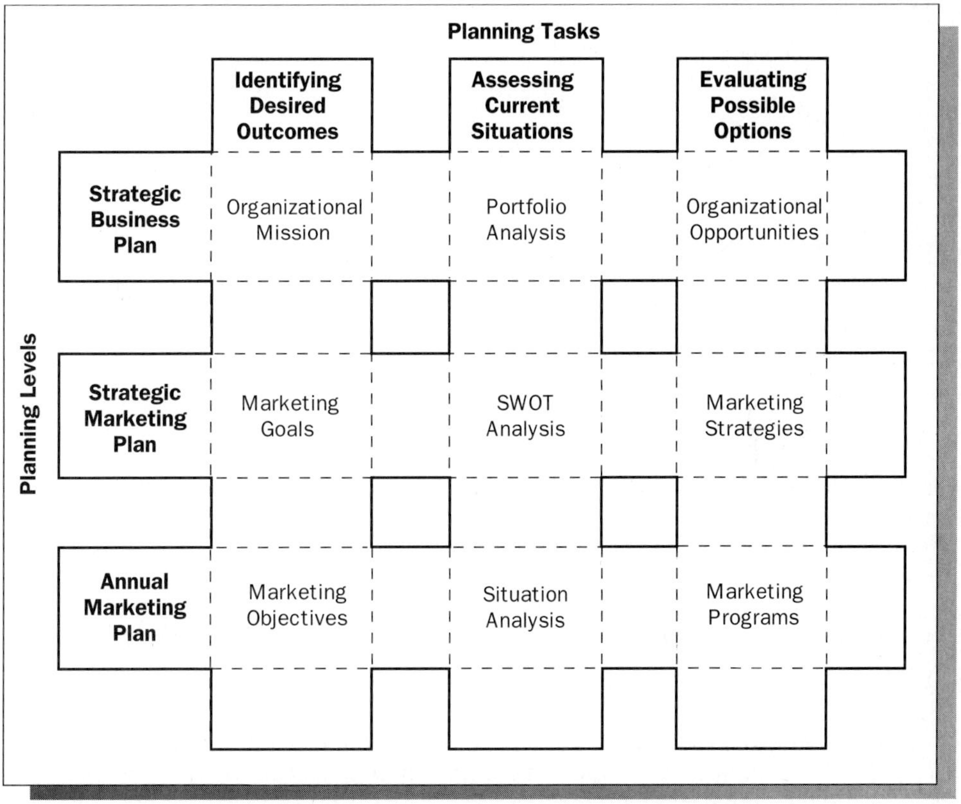

	Planning Tasks		
Planning Levels	Identifying Desired Outcomes	Assessing Current Situations	Evaluating Possible Options
Strategic Business Plan	Organizational Mission	Portfolio Analysis	Organizational Opportunities
Strategic Marketing Plan	Marketing Goals	SWOT Analysis	Marketing Strategies
Annual Marketing Plan	Marketing Objectives	Situation Analysis	Marketing Programs

the decision-making authority of each team member. As identified in Figure 14-3, organizational structure needs to answer three important questions:

1. Should the organization be vertical or horizontal?
2. Should the organization be centralized or decentralized?
3. Should the organization be bureaucratic or adaptive?

Vertical or Horizontal Organization? How many organizational levels are needed for the effective and efficient operation of the firm's marketing activities? The hierarchical structure of the marketing organization ranges from a **vertical organization** in which there are several levels separating the chief marketing officer from entry-level marketing employees to a **horizontal organization,** which restricts the number of line managers to one or two levels. The primary strength of the vertical organization is

FIGURE 14-3

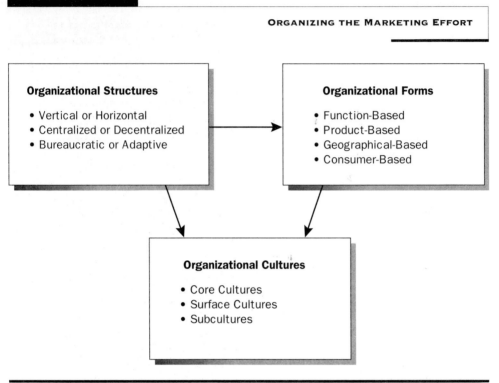

ORGANIZING THE MARKETING EFFORT

that lines of responsibility, areas of authority, and reporting relationships are more clearly defined and established. On the other hand, horizontal organizations promote closer relationships and more adaptive personal interactions and lend themselves to team efforts and project management.

Centralized or Decentralized Organization? What magnitude of managerial focus is needed to operate effectively and efficiently? In a **centralized organization,** decision-making authority is concentrated at the corporate or divisional level. Marketing managers who operate out of one centralized location are responsible for most of the important operational and marketing decisions.[2] Organizational structures in which the decision-making authority is delegated to marketing managers at the local operational level are classified as **decentralized organizations.** Greater control, better coordination, more consistency, and clearer direction are commonly cited strengths of the centralized marketing organization. A decentralized organization offers greater participation by all marketing personnel, which promotes higher morale, better understanding of customer needs (which results in closer relationships with the firm's customers), and quicker identification of operational and marketing problems (which allows faster response times to needed changes).

Bureaucratic or Adaptive Organization? What degree of structural rigidity is needed to control the organization? From the perspective of structural design, marketing organizations can be classified along a continuum ranging from bureaucratic to adaptive organizations.[3] **Bureaucratic organizations** are highly structured marketing organizations that tend to be characterized by high levels of centralized control, formal lines of authority, close supervision, and a less personal approach to work relationships. The bureaucratic marketing organization relies on rules and procedures for making decisions and solving problems. The **adaptive organization** is a loosely structured organizational design that features decentralized control, team problem solving, informal work relationships, and loose supervision. Employee participation and worker empowerment are two hallmarks of this form of organizational structure. In this type of learning organization, "people working together with integrity and authenticity and collective intelligence are profoundly more effective as a business than people living together based on politics, game playing, and narrow self-interest."[4] Whether management elects to go with a bureaucratic or adaptive organizational design or something in-between depends on the particular circumstances facing the organization at a given point in time. When circumstances dictate a high level of control, organizations tend to become more bureaucratic. On the other hand, dynamic environmental changes require highly adaptive organizations.

ORGANIZATIONAL FORMS The organizational structure of marketing activities takes on many different forms. Marketing departments can be loosely classified as functional-, product-, geographical-, or customer-based organizations (see Figure 14-3). Organizational form usually reflects the dominant nature of the marketing activity or problem. For example, product-based organizational structure is needed when product considerations dominate decision making or are at the core of customers' problems.

Function-Based Organizations The **function-based organization** is one founded on the basic marketing functions performed. Tasks are grouped and jobs are classified by such functional areas as marketing research, promotions, sales, and product and distribution management. Figure 14-4 illustrates one common function-based marketing organization. A high level of functional specialization, a more focused approach to task responsibilities, and a relatively simple administration are the most relevant advantages of this form of organization. Safeguards must be initiated to overcome resistance to cross-functional activities. The function-based organization tends to be more effective in small companies and loses some of its effectiveness as the firm becomes larger.

Product-Based Organizations In a **product-based organization,** many of the marketing functions are organized along product and brand lines. In this form of organization, each product line, product category, or brand

FIGURE 14-4

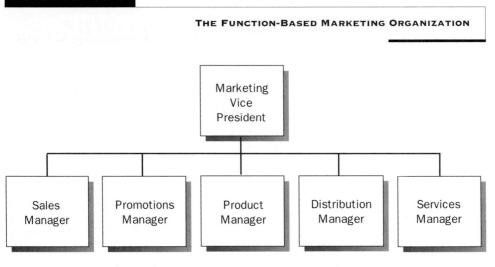

THE FUNCTION-BASED MARKETING ORGANIZATION

often has its own marketing organization. This organizational format is shown in Figure 14-5. For marketing organizations that must manage an extensive and complex set of product lines, this form of organization is both efficient and effective. An organization that focuses on product specialization offers considerable benefits in attempting to tailor specific marketing programs to targeted consumer groups. It is, however, an expensive approach to organizing the marketing effort.

Geographical-Based Organizations When the firm must market its products in diverse market areas under different market conditions, a **geographical-based organization** is appropriate. The vastly different demographic structures of market areas and the resulting differences in buying behavior sometimes require that the organization adapt its marketing programs from one region to another. These adaptive requirements are most pronounced when moving from domestic to international markets. Geographic diversity is an operational reality that must be accommodated in some fashion. Many firms have elected to meet these realities by assigning a marketing manager and creating a marketing organization on the basis of geographical considerations. Figure 14-6 demonstrates this form of organizational structure.

Customer-Based Organizations The **customer-based organization** recognizes that different customer segments have different needs; hence, the firm is organized around the type of customer being served. By structuring and tailoring the firm's marketing effort to take into account the specific needs of certain customer groups, the organization is better able to accommodate those differences and meet those needs. In reorganizing its international operations, IBM is "organizing its marketing and sales staffs

FIGURE 14-5

THE PRODUCT-BASED MARKETING ORGANIZATION

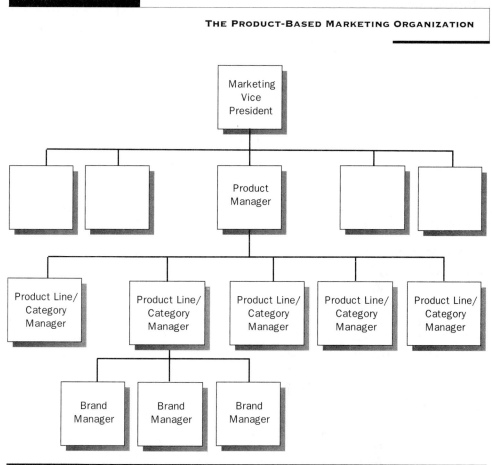

into fourteen industry groups, rather than by country."⁵ Perhaps the most common form of a customer-based marketing organization involves dividing the firm into two customer divisions—business-to-business marketing and consumer-products marketing.

ORGANIZATIONAL CULTURE All organizations have a culture, which strongly impacts how that organization implements its marketing programs. An **organizational culture** is created by accepting and sharing a set of values. When most or all of the members of an organization embrace a group of values, a prevailing set of traditions is created and passed on from older employees to new employees. The behavior of managers and employees toward one another often reflects the type of culture that prevails within an organization.

An organization's culture exists at two levels. As shown in Figure 14-7, the **core culture** is the basic value system (the deep beliefs and understanding that shape and guide attitudes and actions) that serves

FIGURE 14-6

THE GEOGRAPHICAL-BASED MARKETING ORGANIZATION

as an invisible foundation for the observable behavior within the surface culture. The **surface culture** manifests itself in the form of behavioral and personal relationships that can be observed or heard by walking around the organization. It is how members of the marketing organization relate. Given the high level of interpersonal relationships that surround most marketing activities, core and surface cultures are vital to the successful completion of the marketing mission. Pleasant working relationships, supportive working environments, amiable motivational pressure, and strong marketing traditions are all benefits that organizational members hope to find within a well-established and tested cultural environment.

Under the surface culture of an organization, a number of **subcultures** exist in which small groups of individuals hold to the core value system but have slightly different perspectives that usually reflect their particular set of circumstances. Subcultures are based on gender and racial differences, age and educational variations, and occupational and managerial positions. Creating the comfortable and productive organizational culture is one of the toughest challenges facing the marketing manager and crucial to effective execution of the marketing effort.

FIGURE 14-7

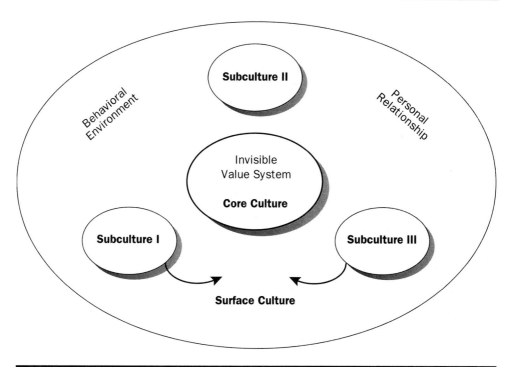

ORGANIZATIONAL CULTURE

EXECUTING THE MARKETING EFFORT

Execution requires action. It is in this part of the implementation phase that marketing strategies are translated into marketing actions. Successful execution of the organization's marketing plans requires an effective management style that encourages full participation by the marketing team and ensures complete coordination of the marketing effort. Along with a host of other concerns, effective managers are concerned with leadership, communication, motivation, and empowerment.

LEADERSHIP The marketing manager must provide leadership to gain the acceptance and support of all marketing team members for the organization's marketing plan and to get them to accept their roles and responsibilities for executing that plan. To accomplish this internal marketing goal, the marketing manager must possess certain leadership qualities. Good leaders are often quite different from one another. They can be extroverts or introverts, exuberant or reserved, articulate or inarticulate. Nevertheless, most true leaders possess certain common characteristics:

- *Love of the business*—It is easier to lead a business that you love. Love of business motivates leaders to teach the business, to pass its nuances, its secrets, and its craft on to others.
- *A clear vision*—Leaders have a clear vision of what they wish to accomplish. Leaders believe in their vision, inasmuch as they believe in values and strategy.
- *Students of change*—Exceptional leaders are students of change. They view continuous innovation as the lifeblood of the business. Leaders seek the new to strengthen the old.
- *High standards*—Leaders are implementers, not just strategists; doers, not just dreamers. And they are obsessed with doing things right.
- *High integrity*—Leaders do the right thing, even when it is inconvenient or expensive. They place a premium on being fair, consistent, and truthful with everyone. Great leaders have great character.[6]

COMMUNICATION Effective leadership requires effective communication. It is the marketing manager's responsibility to clearly communicate the organization's vision of the future, as well as its more immediate goals and objectives. Each member of the marketing team must have a clear understanding of, and an appreciation for, what the organization is trying to accomplish and what he or she is expected to contribute. Clarification of roles and responsibilities, coordination of plans and actions, and provision of information and intelligence, as well as delegation of tasks and duties, are all essential management responsibilities depending on effective communication. The same basic principles and processes that were introduced in Chapter 12 regarding marketing communication with consumers apply when describing effective communications within the marketing team.

MOTIVATION The successful execution of a marketing plan requires that the marketing team must be motivated. **Motivation** means to inspire individuals to act in a certain way. The effective marketing manager is capable of inspiring subordinates to act in such a fashion as to benefit the organization as well as themselves. There is no single process by which marketing managers can motivate their entire staff. Different employees are inspired for a variety of reasons at different times.

Quite often, the marketing manager utilizes both autocratic and democratic motivational techniques to encourage a particular behavioral response. Commonly employed autocratic techniques include the following:

- *Legitimate authority*—the ability to influence employees' actions as a result of the position the marketing manager holds within the organization's management hierarchy and the authority that is attributed to that position

❏ *Reward power*—the ability of the marketing manager to influence employee behavior by rewarding employees in terms of promotion, compensation, recognition, and better work conditions

❏ *Coercive power*—the ability to influence employee actions through the use of various types of punishment: undesirable work assignments, lower compensation rates, undesirable work schedules, and a lack of support

The more preferred means of motivation are those that tend to be more democratic. **Expert authority** is the marketing manager's ability to influence subordinate behavior based on the manager's special knowledge, expert skills, unique competencies, and extensive experience. **Referent power** is the ability of the marketing manager to guide employee actions based on the manager's strong and dynamic personality. These democratic motivational techniques are based more on respect and admiration of the individual marketing manager than on the authority of the manager's position.

EMPOWERMENT One of the most effective means of motivating employees to accomplish a certain goal is to empower them. Cadet Uniform Services of Toronto, Canada, allows its service representatives to act like mini-entrepreneurs by designing their own routes, managing their own accounts, and, to a large extent, determining the size of their paychecks.[7] With the right employees the best way to get something done is to let them do it. In contrast to monetary rewards and other forms of extrinsic incentives, empowerment is a form of intrinsic motivation that relies on the pride and self-esteem that comes with quality workmanship and superior performance.[8] For those marketing programs pursuing continuous improvement within total quality management (TQM), employee empowerment is both an essential and standard management practice.

Empowerment requires that the marketing manager clearly state the desired goals, provide adequate resources and support services, and extend the authority necessary for the successful completion of the goals. Empowerment draws on the ingenuity of the marketing team members, allowing them to make decisions and take actions typically reserved for management.[9]

CONTROLLING

Marketing control concerns itself with monitoring the marketing effort to ensure that the outcomes identified in the planning process are being achieved and that implementation policies and procedures are being followed. Marketing control also involves modifying business and marketing plans and adapting implementation strategies when desired outcomes are not being achieved.

Monitoring the Marketing Effort

Monitoring the marketing effort entails reviewing the organization's entire marketing effort and gaining a perspective on the effectiveness and efficiency of that effort. Marketing audits and performance evaluations are two monitoring processes that we will examine.

The Marketing Audit Auditing is a process by which managers assess their positions and monitor their progress toward meeting performance standards. The **marketing audit** is a comprehensive and systematic review of the organization's business philosophies and plans, marketing strategies and tactics, environmental opportunities and threats, market targets and positions, operating policies and practices, and decision-making and problem-solving processes, as well as its marketing programs and efforts. The marketing audit brings the planning process full circle (see Figures 14-1 and 14-2) because

1. It is an outcomes check on whether or not the organizational mission, marketing goals, and objectives have been achieved.

2. It is a situational assessment of all of the firm's businesses and their current internal and external environmental circumstances.

3. It is an options evaluation of how successful the organization is in taking advantage of its opportunities and implementing its marketing strategies and programs.

The marketing audit is a broad performance assessment that covers all or most of the organization's operations and activities. Marketing audits are conducted on a frequent and regular basis in order to closely monitor and immediately detect existing or potential problems. Prevention of unsatisfactory performance is an important goal of this continuous monitoring process. By gathering performance information on a systematic basis, the marketing manager is better able to control the implementation of business and marketing plans.

Marketing audits are complex undertakings that are expensive to conduct. Hence, experienced researchers and planners are needed to construct the set of detailed questions and inquiries that give the marketing audit structure. The marketing audit needs to be a marketing management tool tailored to the precise needs and unique characteristics of a particular organization. Although there is no single format for structuring a marketing audit, the most commonly used formats are a series of questions, or a checklist of factors, organized by topical areas that auditors should consider in making their assessment of the organization's performance.

Performance Evaluations The second step in monitoring the marketing effort is to conduct an evaluation of the firm's performance in key areas of the business. The two most widely used methods for accomplishing this evaluation are sales analysis and analysis of marketing costs.

Sales Analysis One of the most common methods for evaluating an organization's performance is a **sales analysis**—the use of sales figures to assess the firm's past and current performance. The sales analysis approach involves collecting, classifying, comparing, and interpreting sales records. These records are capable of providing a wealth of information on what was purchased, who made the purchases, when purchases were made, how much was purchased, and a host of other relevant facts. By comparing sales figures against stated sales objectives, past sales levels, or published industry norms, or by making benchmark comparisons with competitors, the marketing manager gains valuable measures of company performance.[10] The three traditional measures of sales volume are unit sales (the total numbers of units sold), dollar sales (the total amount of revenues generated), and market share (a measure of an organization's sales position relative to all other competitors within the same market).

To gain a better perspective on the organization's sales performances, the marketing manager develops a number of cross-tabulations and illustrative graphics that show the relationships between sales and the following characteristics:

1. *Product characteristics*—product line, category, item, brand style, model, color, size, grade, and package

2. *Customer characteristics*—types of customers and their buying behavior

3. *Transactional characteristics*—method of contact, reason for purchase, size of order, and method of payment and delivery

4. *Geographic characteristics*—local, regional, national, and international markets

5. *Marketing characteristics*—price structures, promotional programs, support services, and distribution networks

Sales records are also examined relative to persons and places to gain a measure of labor and physical plant productivity.

Marketing Cost Analysis A cost analysis of marketing activities is needed to gain an understanding of the organization's profitability. Marketing is an expensive group of activities, which management must control. Such costs as product development, marketing research, distribution systems, service supports, promotional campaigns, and selling activities require close monitoring in order to ensure that they are being accomplished in the most efficient and productive manner.

Marketing cost analysis is a study of the sources of marketing costs and an assessment of their appropriateness. Conducting a marketing cost analysis involves classifying costs by marketing activity and determining the relative efficiency of that activity. An efficient marketing program is one that generates high sales volume with fewer resources and lower costs. Regals Cinemas, Inc., generates net profit margins of 8 percent, almost double the margin of the larger, publicly held exhibitors because management knows exactly how much syrup should be in each soft drink, exactly how much popcorn oil goes into each batch, and how to operate several screens under one roof with minimum labor costs.[11] Compaq Computer Corp. was able to increase the productivity of its sales force by automating many of the routine sales tasks, thereby freeing salespeople to focus on developing new business and servicing accounts.[12] A high sales volume with high cost structures is not efficient, but it does provide the organization with an opportunity to increase profitability if costs can be contained. The primary difficulty associated with marketing cost analysis is the problem of accurately classifying costs and fairly allocating them to specific marketing activities.

Modifying the Marketing Effort

Rarely does the monitoring process fail to uncover areas in which improvement is needed. When performance levels fall short of expectations and performance standards are not met, the marketing manager can pursue one of the following courses of action:

- *Status quo acceptance*—acknowledgment of the failure to meet performance standards and acceptance of that fact with a pledge to try and meet standards next time

- *Resource enhancement*—allocation of additional resources in order to overcome the deficiency

- *Performance standard modification*—lowering performance standards in those cases in which the original standard is no longer appropriate

- *Marketing activity replacement*—deciding to replace or adjust how the marketing activity is performed in order to achieve greater effectiveness or efficiency in meeting stated performance standards

The regular and ongoing modification of the marketing effort is a natural reaction to the dynamic environments in which all organizations must operate. As stated earlier, the need for continuous improvement is a basic tenet of total quality management.

CONCLUDING REMARKS

Planning, implementing, and controlling the marketing effort are the three phases that comprise the marketing management process. Planning concerns itself with defining what directions the organization intends on taking in the future and determining by what means the organization will get there. Marketing implementation encompasses how to translate business plans and strategies into action. Organization is essential to implementation. Marketing activities are organized on the basis of function, product types, geographic areas, and customer types. Leadership, communication, motivation, and empowerment are among of the more important means by which marketing managers direct the actions of subordinates. Controlling, the third phase of the marketing management process, is where the marketing effort is monitored in order to ensure that the organization's desired outcomes are being achieved.

ENDNOTES

1. Alex Taylor III, "GM's $11,000,000,000 Turnaround," *Fortune* (October 17, 1994), 66.

2. See Hal Goetsch, "Centralized Marketing Is Still OK," *Marketing News* (September 26, 1994), 4.

3. This discussion is based on John R. Schermerhorn, *Management for Productivity* (New York: Wiley, 1992), 311–12. Also see Henry Mintzberg, "The Structuring of Organizations," in *The Strategy Process: Concepts, Contexts, and Cases* (Englewood Cliffs, NJ: Prentice Hall, 1988), 300–303.

4. Brian Dumaine, "Mr. Learning Organization," *Fortune* (October 17, 1994), 147.

5. John A. Byrne and Kathleen Kerwin, "Borderless Management," *Business Week* (May 23, 1994), 24.

6. This material was taken from Leonard L. Berry, "Qualities of Leadership," *Retailing Issues Letter* 4 (Center for Retailing Studies, Texas A&M University and Arthur Andersen & Co., January 1992), 1–4.

7. Ronald Henkoff, "Finding, Training, & Keeping the Best Service Workers," *Fortune* (October 3, 1994), 122.

8. See V. Daniel Hunt, *Quality in America* (Homewood, IL: Business One Irwin, 1992), 24–25.

9. See Chad Rubel, "Empower Employees So You Can Satisfy Customers," *Marketing News* (March 27, 1995), 14.

10. See Harvey K. Brelin, "Benchmarking: The Change Agent," *Marketing Management,* Vol. 2, No. 3 (1993), 33–48.

11. Matt Walsh, "Easy on the Popcorn," *Forbes* (September 26, 1994), 126–27.

12. R. Lee Sullivan, "The Office That Never Closes," *Forbes* (May 23, 1994), 212–13.

Marketing Issues

CHAPTER 15 SERVICE, NONPROFIT, AND
INTERNATIONAL MARKETING

SERVICE, NONPROFIT, AND INTERNATIONAL MARKETING*

CHAPTER OUTLINE

- INTRODUCTION
- SERVICE MARKETING
    - NATURE OF SERVICE MARKETING
    - STRATEGIES FOR SERVICE MARKETERS
- NONPROFIT MARKETING
    - NATURE OF NONPROFIT MARKETING
    - FORMS OF NONPROFIT MARKETING
- INTERNATIONAL MARKETING
    - MOTIVATION FOR MARKETING ABROAD
    - DETERRENTS TO INTERNATIONAL MARKETING
    - CULTURAL AND SOCIAL INFLUENCES
    - POLITICAL AND LEGAL INFLUENCES
    - ECONOMIC INTEGRATION
    - INTERNATIONAL MARKETING MIX
- CONCLUDING REMARKS

*This chapter was co-authored by Dr. Paulette Polley of the University of Akron.

Introduction

Having completed our overview of marketing management, we now turn our attention to several unique applications of marketing. Specialized marketing operations include services marketing, nonprofit marketing, and international marketing. In this chapter we will focus on what makes these applications different and how the marketing manager must adapt the marketing function in order to meet the needs of service, nonprofit, and international consumers.

Service Marketing

The new front line of the American economy is the service industry. The rapidly expanding service sector has profound implications for the way the organizations manage themselves. Unfortunately,

> the service economy, despite its size and growth, remains extraordinarily misunderstood, mismeasured, and mismanaged . . . American management practices . . . suffer from an acute Industrial Age hangover. Most people still view the world through manufacturing goggles.[1]

In this section, an overview of the key factors that make service marketing unique is presented.

A **service** is an intangible activity that typically involves the application of human skills within a problem-solving context. **Service marketing** includes any business enterprise in which the sale of a service or services represents the core business and the focus of the exchange process. The service enterprise can be an individual such as a medical doctor, a group of individuals such as a rock and roll band, or an organization such as a hospital or university. As opposed to goods marketers who emphasize the selling of goods, the focus of the service marketer is on the marketing of people, ideas, feelings, and information.

The distinction between goods and services marketing is rather blurred because most marketers include both goods and services as part of their market offering. While a cash-and-carry discount store is clearly a goods marketer and a management consultant is definitely a services marketer, many business operations, such as fine dining restaurants, are marketers whose success depends on offering an excellent combination of goods and services. Norwegian Cruise Lines is a service company whose primary product is recreational travel. However, a host of additional services (gambling, shows, tours, and exercise programs) and goods (food, personal care products, pillows, and mints) supplement the core service to arrive at the total product package.[2] To resolve this dilemma, the U.S. Census of Business delineates service marketers as those business establishments that derive more than one half of their revenue from the sale of services.

Nature of Service Marketing

The elusive nature of service marketing results from its multifaceted character. As described by the American Marketing Association (AMA), intangible services

> are exchanged directly from producer to user, cannot be transported or stored, and are almost instantly perishable. Service products are often difficult to identify, since they come into existence at the same time they are bought and consumed. They are composed of intangible elements that are inseparable, they usually involve customer participation in some important way, cannot be sold in the sense of ownership transfer, and have no title.[3]

In order to gain a clearer perspective of service marketing, we must first take a closer look at some of the unique characteristics of service marketers and then examine two different service classification schemes.

Characteristics of Services The AMA description of services identifies several characteristics that distinguish services marketing. Services are intangible, variable, inseparable, and perishable.

The major characteristic that distinguishes a service from a good is its **intangibility**—the inability of a service activity to directly appeal to the consumer's five senses. In most cases, it is hard to see, feel, smell, taste, or hear a service. Service consumers have a harder time understanding, appreciating, and judging a service activity because it is not distinguished by physical features created by tangible materials and workmanship. Feelings from a religious experience, memories from a concert, ideas from a lecture, enthusiasm for a political candidate, excitement from a sporting event, and energy from an aerobic workout are not tangible. Consumers have little or no physical evidence to show they have made a purchase or consumed a product.

Because service marketing is a people-intensive business, service providers have considerable latitude in structuring the service encounter and controlling the quality of the service offering. Both the service encounter (when, where, and how services are provided) and the service quality (the way customers are treated, assisted, and served) are totally dependent on who provide them. **Variability** is the lack of standardization in providing services. Creating a consistent and standardized service encounter that can satisfy the consumer can be extremely difficult because service providers vary considerably in terms of personal skills and abilities, as well as training and experience levels. Achieving service quality necessitates a highly motivated and trained workforce. As described by Leonard L. Berry in his book *On Great Service*,

> Most service jobs have high discretionary content. The maximum amount of energy and care an individual can bring to the service role and the minimum amount required to avoid penalty are quite different. Thus, the energy and care level of service are up to the service providers' discretion. Companies delivering great service have providers who live near the maximums; most companies do not. Service leadership is the difference.[4]

In an era of flattened organizational structures and heightened customer expectations, the service provider must be "resilient and resourceful, empathetic and enterprising, competent and creative—a set of skills, in short, that was once demanded only of managers."[5] For creating a successful service venture, the leadership role of the service manager is decisive.

Inseparability is the third distinctive characteristic of service offerings. The typical service exchange situation is one in which the service is produced and consumed simultaneously. **Inseparability** is the idea that service offerings cannot be separated from the service provider. Close customer-provider interaction is an inherent part of most service encounters; both parties need to be present in order for the exchange process to proceed in an effective and efficient manner. One of the biggest hurdles to building customer loyalty in the service business is the problem of employee turnover. To retain customers, the service organization must first retain productive employees.[6] With one of the lowest employee turnover rates in the airline industry, Southwest employees often go out of their way to amuse, surprise, or entertain passengers.[7]

The final distinguishing feature of a service is its **perishability**—the fact that services cannot be stored for use in the future. Services marketers carry no inventory. The revenue-producing capabilities of services are restricted to a specific time. Once that time has passed without the service being used, its value is lost forever. A doctor cannot go back and capture the revenue-producing capabilities of the previous hour if the scheduled patient does not show up. The airline cannot sell the empty seats on an airplane that left ten minutes ago. Service offerings have serious time constraints that must be accommodated.

CLASSIFICATION OF SERVICES A large variety of individuals, groups, and organizations market a wide range of services to many separate consumer markets. This multifaceted character of services has led to a number of different service classifications. Services can be classified on the bases of type of market (organizational versus final consumer markets), form of delivery (labor-based versus equipment-based activities), extent of customer contact (high- versus low-contact relationships), level of service provider's skills (high- versus low-skill levels), and nature of service provider's mission (profit versus nonprofit goals). For our purposes, we will examine two common service classification schemes developed by the U.S. Department of Commerce and the Harvard Business School.

Based on the nature or type of services offered, the Census of Business groups services into four major categories:

1. Transportation, communication, and public utilities

2. Finance, insurance, and real estate

3. Public administration

4. Services

While the makeup of the first three categories is self-explanatory, the composition of the fourth category requires further elaboration. Figure 15-1 identifies the fourteen subgroups that comprise the services category.

Writing in the Harvard Business Review, Dan R. E. Thomas presented a service classification based on the combination of service provider skill level and form of service delivery. Figure 15-2 illustrates this classification scheme where services are either *equipment-based services,* which range from fully automated machines (automatic teller machines) to mechanical operations that require the attention of a highly skilled operator (an airline pilot), or *people-based services,* which extend from the activities of relatively unskilled laborers (lawn mowing) to the sophisticated labors of professionals such as doctors, lawyers, and accountants.

STRATEGIES FOR SERVICE MARKETERS

Successful service marketing strategies must take into account the multifaceted and unique character of service activities and service providers. Like goods marketing, service marketing requires the development of a marketing mix consisting of product, distribution, promotion, and pricing strategies. Because most of these concepts have been discussed previously in the text and can be adapted to meet the requirements of services marketing, we will focus on some of the more unique concerns of the marketing service manager.

CONCEPT OF SERVICE QUALITY To ensure the reliability and accuracy of the service offering, the marketing service manager must control the variability of that offering.[8] **Service quality** is determined by comparing customer expectations against the performance of the service provider. When performance levels meet or exceed customer expectations, service quality is judged to be satisfactory or exceptional.[9] Quality control of a service involves watching a process unfold and evaluating it against the customer's judgment.[10] Judging service quality requires an understanding of how service quality is determined and the means by which service managers analyze the gaps between expected and perceived services.

Service Quality Determinants Many studies have been conducted in an attempt to identify the key determinants of service quality. One of the most widely accepted descriptions of service quality determinants identifies the following five factors: tangibles, reliability, responsiveness, assurance, and empathy.[11]

❑ *Tangibles*—providing physical evidence of the service. The physical atmospherics of the doctor's office, the personal appearance of the hostess, the professionalism of the organization's brochures, and the sophistication of the equipment used are all means by which the service provider can increase the tangibility of the service offering.

CHAPTER 15 ■ SERVICE, NONPROFIT, AND INTERNATIONAL MARKETING

FIGURE 15-1

CLASSIFICATION OF SERVICES BY THE BUREAU OF CENSUS

Service Categories
Transportation, Communication, and Public Utilities
Finance, Insurance, and Real Estate
Public Administration
Services
• Lodging places—hotels, motels, rooming and boarding houses, sporting and recreation camps, trailer parks, campsites
• Personal services—laundry and dry cleaners, linen and diaper service, carpet and upholstery cleaning, photographic studios, beauty and barber shops, shoe repair, funeral homes and crematoriums, reducing salons and health clubs, tax services, other personal services
• Business services—advertising, credit reporting and collections, blueprinting and photocopying, commercial photography, art and graphics, cleaning and maintenance services, employment agencies, computer services, data processing, research and development, management and administrative, public relations, security services, equipment rental or leasing, testing laboratories, other business services
• Automotive services—car, truck, trailer, and recreational vehicle rentals; auto and truck repairs; parking facilities; car washes
• Repair services—radio, television, appliance, and furniture repair; farm machinery; lawn and garden equipment; watch, clock, and jewelry repair
• Motion pictures—motion picture production and distribution
• Amusement and recreation services—dance group halls and studios, live theaters, radio and TV production, symphony orchestras, opera companies, music organizations and presentations, sporting establishments and clubs, golf courses and amusement parks, carnivals and circuses, museums and art galleries, other entertainment and attractions
• Health services—offices of health professionals, medical and dental labs, outpatient care facilities
• Legal services—offices of lawyers and other legal aid services
• Educational services—libraries, business and vocational schools, schools, other educational services
• Social services—job training and rehabilitation, child day care, residential care, individual and family social services
• Noncommercial institutions—noncommercial museums, art galleries, botanical and zoological gardens
• Membership organizations—business, professional, civic, social, and fraternal organizations
• Miscellaneous services—architectural, engineering, surveying, accounting, auditing, scientific, and research organizations

FIGURE 15-2

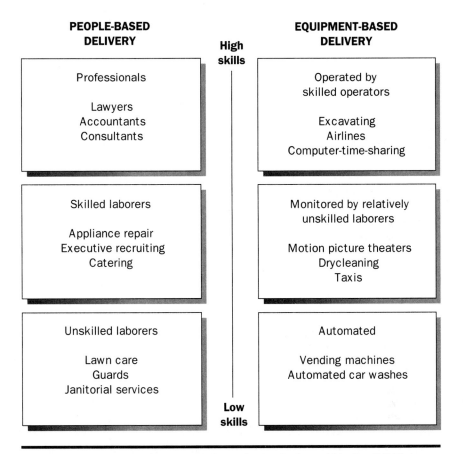

A CLASSIFICATION OF SERVICES BASED ON SERVICE PROVIDER SKILLS AND FORM OF SERVICE DELIVERY

SOURCE: From an exhibit in "Strategy in Different Service Businesses" by Dan R.E. Thomas, *Harvard Business Review*, July/August 1978. Reprinted by permission of *Harvard Business Review*. Copyright © 1978 by the President and Fellows of Harvard University. All rights reserved.

❑ *Reliability*—performing services in a consistent and dependable manner. Accuracy in billing, correctness in record keeping, completeness in task responsibilities, and timeliness in task completion are all examples of a reliable service offering.

❑ *Responsiveness*—providing services in a willing and ready fashion. Immediate handling of a customer request, quick reaction to a customer problem, prompt answer to a customer question, and timely return of a customer call are indicative of a responsive service organization.

❑ *Assurance*—communicating trust and confidence in the service offering. Using credible and knowledgeable employees, providing understandable and complete guarantees, and projecting a trustworthy and sincere image are all actions that offer quality assurance.

❑ *Empathy*—providing caring and individualized attention to customers. Learning and appreciating the specific needs of each customer, treating customers as individuals, and tailoring the service offering to the specific needs of the customer are all empathetic.

Service Quality Analysis Service gaps develop between *expected* service quality and *perceived* service quality. When the service experience exceeds what the customer expected, a positive service gap has been created. For example, the adventure movie turns out to be more exciting than previews suggested. Negative gaps result from services that do not meet expectations, such as a movie that does not live up to the two-thumbs-up reviews of the critics. To help service managers understand what, how, and where service gaps occur, marketing researchers have constructed a model that identifies a series of four gaps or miscues between the service provider and the customer. Figure 15-3 illustrates the expected-service/perceived-service gap model and describes the four different types of service gaps that require the service manager's attention. By eliminating the four service gaps described in Figure 15-3, the service manager ensures a closer match between services expected by the customer and what is actually received, in other words, better service quality.

CONCEPT OF MICROMARKETING Because of the variable nature of services and the fact that most services involve a simultaneous production and consumption exchange process, marketing service managers can seek to gain favor with customers by offering a customized service supported by a micromarketing effort carefully tailored to each buyer's expectations. **Micromarketing** is the process of planning, building, and delivering a highly focused marketing mix that is designed to be customer-specific. Micromarketing is often achieved through mass customization of a general service procedure at the point of sale. Although this immediate adaptation of the service procedure during the simultaneous production and consumption process does not lessen the need to provide quality work, it does reduce the need to completely control service variability. In applying a micromarketing strategy, the service manager creates the expectation that some differences in the service offering are part of a planned effort to provide individualized service and, by extension, better quality service.

CONCEPT OF CORE BENEFIT At the heart of most service offerings is the core benefit most desired by the consumer. A **core benefit** is the positive results the customer expects to realize from the service provider. Stated differently, a core benefit is a key value-creating attribute that the consumer derives from a service encounter; it is what the service does for the consumer. The first major responsibility of the service manager is to identify the core

FIGURE 15-3

THE EXPECTED-SERVICE/PERCEIVED-SERVICE GAP MODEL

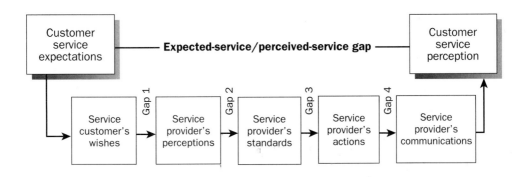

Gap 1: Service Customer's Wishes/Service Provider's Perceptions—the difference between what the service customer actually wants in terms of services and what the service provider thinks the customer wants. For example, a rental car agency may think that its customers want fast and friendly counter service supported by a choice of clean cars. The customer's wishes, on the other hand, are for a simple straightforward rental agreement without all of the complex rate structures and insurance options.

Gap 2: Service Provider's Perceptions/Service Provider's Standards—the difference between what the service provider perceives in terms of customer service expectations and the set of standards or specifications that are established by the provider to ensure adequate service performance. If studies conducted by our rental car agency showed that the expected transaction time at the service counter is five minutes or less and the agency, in a cost control effort, only staffs enough service stations to ensure transaction times of ten minutes, then a service gap is created.

Gap 3: Service Provider's Standards/Service Provider's Actions—the difference between standards set by the service provider and the actions taken by frontline personnel. Continuing the car rental scenario, if due to inadequate training, the ten-minute transaction time standard established by the firm's management is not achieved by those individuals who have face-to-face contact with the customer at the service counter, then the service provider's actual performance is short of its stated performance goal.

Gap 4: Service Provider's Actions/Service Provider's Communications—the difference between what the service provider promises to do in its advertising and promotion programs and what it actually delivers to the service customer. If a rental car agency promotes a promise of fast and efficient counter service but fails to staff service counters with well-trained service agents, then a false and unrealistic service expectation is created with the service customer.

SOURCE: Dale M. Lewison, *Retailing*, 5th ed. (New York: Macmillan Publishing, 1994), 792–93.

benefit or benefits that consumers feel are essential and useful. Different target markets expect to benefit in different ways. Some common core benefits of selected service industries include security (insurance), convenience (dry cleaning), acceptance (social club), prestige (credit card), practical advice (consultant), empathy (psychologist), efficiency (government official), friendliness (hotel clerk), and cleanliness (food server).

After the core benefit is identified for a particular service offering, the second major responsibility of the service manager is to "tangibilize" it so that the consumer realizes and appreciates that his or her primary concern is being met. Service offerings are made more tangible by one or more of the following marketing tactics:

- Create a *visual representation* of the service and its core benefits. For example, a scale model of a proposed golf course designed by Jack Nicklaus or a computer-generated visual diagram (planogram) of store shelf facings developed by a retail-store design consultant.

- Use of *physical or mental symbols* to show the real nature of a service and the benefits to be derived. The gold credit card (VISA or MasterCard) and the extra service features associated with it is a good example of using a physical symbol to convey the core service attributes. The extra protection offered under the Travelers' umbrella is an effective mental symbol of the security benefit.

- Exploit *name association* by linking the service and its core benefit to a descriptive brand name and image. Jiffy Lube auto-care centers, Dreyfus Strategic Aggressive mutual fund, and Overnite Transportation Company are all examples of brand names that help identify and differentiate an organization's service offering.

CONCEPT OF SYNCHRONIZATION The fluctuating demand for services together with the highly perishable nature of services require that service providers carefully balance their supply of services with the demand for their services. This synchronization of demand and supply is accomplished by adjusting one or both of these elements. Service providers use any of the following methods to accomplish this balance:

1. *Incentive systems,* such as lower prices, quantity discounts, and service extras that shift demand from peak times to off-peak periods

2. *Reservation systems,* that commit both the service provider and the service customer to a specific time and place

3. *Reminder systems,* that use the telephone and mail to confirm the time and place of the service encounter

4. *Punishment systems,* that charge customers for missed appointments or appointments that were canceled after a designated date

Roberts Express, a transportation services company that operates around the clock every day of the year, has thrived on solving emergency transportation and delivery problems. As described in Figure 15-4, Roberts Express provides an excellent example of an organization that has implemented many of the marketing service strategies identified in the previous discussion.

FIGURE 15-4

ROBERTS EXPRESS, INC.: FOCUS ON CUSTOMER SERVICE

Established in 1947, Roberts Express, Inc., an operating company of Roadway Services Inc., has grown to become the largest exclusive-use, expedited transportation carrier in the world. With more than 2,000 surface vehicles operating with on-line, two-way satellite communications that provide precise shipment tracking and control, Roberts utilizes the largest fleet of multisized vehicles and aircraft in North America.

The service mix consists of three special services: *Express* offers a faster and less expensive alternative to heavyweight air freight shipments; *White Glove* transports critical shipments that require special care in handling, special vehicles, or specially trained or equipped drivers; and *CharterAir* utilizes a multisized fleet of aircraft with companion surface operations.

At Roberts, customer satisfaction is not just a blurb in the mission statement; it is an attitude. It all starts from a simple philosophy: every piece of freight that Roberts handles is delivered *non-stop, door-to-door, anytime, and anywhere guaranteed*. This self-imposed standard of excellence gives the shipper the peace of mind that its freight will get where it is going, when it should be there, and at a reasonable price. It *means* that a customer's freight has exclusive right to the use of an entire vehicle. There is no consolidation or intermingling. The shipment will be picked up at any designated location and delivered within 15 minutes of the quoted delivery time. Services are available 24 hours a day, 365 days a year, no matter what day of the year. Any location in the United States and Canada is fair game and comes with a price and delivery-time guarantee. What's in the guarantee? It's up front, instant, and absolute! The cost of the shipment can be instantly quoted to the penny and will not change, regardless of future circumstances.

When a customer (Roberts includes its independent owner/operator driving teams as customers) calls in to central dispatch, the call is electronically routed to a specific Customer Assist Team (CAT) designated by geographic region. So, if one were to call from Little Rock, Arkansas, the call would be "vectored" automatically to the Little Rock CAT. Every time an emergency transportation need arises, the caller speaks to a member of the same seven- to nine- person CAT.

Roberts also uses state-of-the-art communications. Customer Link is a Roberts' developed freight tracking and shipment management program. With this system, Roberts is able to notify a shipper about delays, restrictions, and modified delivery times. This computer-monitored, two-way satellite communications system automatically alerts the customer to any delays. The Customer Link system can instantly pinpoint a truck's location within 300 yards by accessing the driver's onboard computer terminal. Because of the technology, Roberts wears a second hat, not just of a time-definite carrier, but also of a high-tech communications company.

Roberts is not just concerned with its shipping customers and drivers. The company has another classification of customer: its employees. Roberts employees are team members who ultimately strive to achieve the vision of the company. Team members reap the benefits of their dedication to total customer satisfaction. In addition to competitive salaries, Roberts team members also earn incentive pay by successfully accomplishing their Management By Objectives (MBO) goals and through the company gain-sharing program. Members are encouraged to be creative and to contribute innovative ideas. Cross training, the STAR program, a direct line to the president, and a relaxed yet professional work environment give team members stock in the company.

SOURCE: Kristopher Lewison, University of Akron.

NONPROFIT MARKETING

Nonprofit marketing is the marketing activity of individuals, groups, and organizations that directs their efforts at achieving social and public-interest goals. The social mission of most nonprofit marketing efforts tends to involve services (transportation of the disabled or elderly) or ideas (a conservative political agenda). While nonprofit marketers sell goods, this part of the marketing effort is usually in support of the social mission. The sale of cookies by the Girl Scouts is secondary to the organization's mission of building character and developing the abilities of young women. As the competition among various social, cultural, and political concerns for the hearts and minds of various consumer groups has intensified, the role of marketing within nonprofit organizations has increased tremendously.

NATURE OF NONPROFIT MARKETING

Because nonprofit marketing is largely concerned with the marketing of services and ideas, nonprofit marketing is similar to services marketing. Nonprofit marketers need to be concerned with the intangible, variable, inseparable, and perishable limitations of their product offering. One unique aspect of nonprofit marketing is that the marketer often acts as an intermediary between supporters/donors and recipients/clients. Both of these groups must be satisfied by the service or idea in order to successfully complete an exchange. For example, the manager of the local community food bank must convince supporters that the needs of the homeless are both real and worthy of their assistance. The indigent's need might be for a helping hand without undue strings attached.

A second interesting aspect of nonprofit marketing is the wide variety of mediums of exchange. Volunteer labor in exchange for a recognition dinner, political support in return for campaign funds, an "I voted" lapel pin in exchange for voter participation, a thank-you note in exchange for helping elderly residents fix up their homes, a drug-free lifestyle as a result of community supported counseling, and a free concert as payment in-kind for community backing are a few examples of the distinctive payoffs that can occur within the nonprofit sector.

Nonprofit marketing is carried out by either public or private nonprofit organizations.[12] **Public nonprofit organizations** include the following:

❑ Producers of public services, such as schools, libraries, and waste disposal

❑ Funds transfer agencies such as the Social Security Administration, Internal Revenue Service, and public assistance organizations

❑ Intervention-type agencies, such as regulatory agencies, court systems, and licensing bureaus

The primary categories of **private nonprofit organizations** are religious (churches and evangelical movements), social (fraternal and social clubs), cultural (museums, symphonies, and art leagues), knowledge (private schools and universities), protection (trade associations and unions), philanthropic (nursing homes, charity hospitals, and private foundations), and social cause (peace, consumerism, and environmental groups) organizations.

FORMS OF NONPROFIT MARKETING

Nonprofit marketing activities are most often directed at promoting and selling an idea, a person, a place, or an organization.

Idea marketing, or social marketing, is concerned with gaining the acceptance and support of a targeted group of individuals for a social issue or cause.[13] Gaining acceptance of a practice (recycling) or endorsement for a way of thinking (states' rights) are also common goals of the idea marketer. Convincing teenagers to "say no to drugs" is the focal point for many of the marketing activities of the Partnership for a Drug Free America. In idea marketing, the idea is the benefit that the consumer receives as part of the exchange process.[14] Commonly referred to as "green marketing," environmental concerns and issues have been a popular cause of the idea marketer.[15]

Person marketing is directed at marketing an individual or a group of individuals, such as President Clinton and the Democratic Party. In person marketing, the nonprofit marketer might be responsible for creating awareness and acceptance of the person or for creating an impression or image for that individual. In seeking employment, individuals market themselves using a variety of self-marketing practices.

Place marketing is used to attract people or organizations to a particular geographical area. Local and state governments have agencies whose sole responsibility is to attract business on a permanent (new industrial plant) or temporary (convention) basis. Additional agencies are charged to market state and local areas as desirable vacation destinations. Myrtle Beach, South Carolina, aggressively markets its beaches, golf courses, and country-music theaters.[16] Marketing the benefits (climate, tax abatements, centrality, workforce, support facilities, and so on) of a location is paramount to creating a favorable image acceptable to the targeted audience.

Organization marketing is an attempt to build the membership of an organization and to gain support for the organization's goals and activities. Churches, schools, museums, political parties, fraternal societies, professional associations, service leagues, and unions are some of the more common nonprofit organizations that market themselves. The U.S. Army markets its junior officership program as an alternative to a Master of Business Administration degree by promising "training in leadership and responsibility that can be useful in business." [17] Institutional advertising and public-relations events are popular marketing activities employed to create and maintain an organization's image.

International Marketing

Markets around the world have progressed beyond being collections of local, regional, or national entities. National markets are now interrelated and interdependent to the point that they make up global and international markets. Organizations taking part in **global marketing** develop basic marketing strategy and use a standardized business format to reach similar customers in each of the foreign markets targeted by the organization. Global marketers take the worldview that the world is a stateless market without national boundaries. An integral part of a successful global strategy is the ability to adapt business formats and strategies to the nuances of each local culture. Companies that practice **international marketing** usually develop entirely new business formats and strategies for each national market they target. In some cases, these multinational organizations adapt existing formats and strategies to the individual needs of each national or perhaps regional market. The international marketer develops a portfolio of business formats that serve individual domestic markets.

Many firms with a strong presence in the United States are foreign owned. Goldstar, the South Korean electrical appliances and consumer electronics maker,[18] Michelin, the French tire producer,[19] and Delhaize "Le Lion" SA, the Belgian conglomerate that operates Food Lion supermarkets throughout the southern portion of the United States are all examples of foreign-owned corporations that have successfully penetrated the U.S. market. Many American corporations earn significant amounts of their revenue outside the United States. Anheuser-Busch earned $13 billion in net revenues from its overseas operations in 1993[20]; American Express has more than 30 percent of its issued credit cards in circulation in foreign markets. The total business done with the American Express card internationally is even greater when one considers that card users are inclined to be global consumers whose cards are not only registered in one country but also used abroad for both business and pleasure.[21] Ford Motor Company set up its initial overseas branch in France in 1908, just six years after its original founding. Today, Ford continues to expand its international interests throughout the world.[22]

Motivation for Marketing Abroad

Organizations get involved with global and international marketing for a variety of reasons. Firms going international often cite both proactive and reactive reasons.

Proactive Reasons Proactive reasons are offensive actions wherein the organization attempts to exploit external international opportunities and internal operational advantages. Operating economies, managerial preferences, diversification strategies, and risk management are four commonly cited reasons for pursuing international business objectives.

The potential for greater **operating economies** can be substantial for the organization that successfully penetrates new international markets. Economies of scale in production are achieved because the firm can maintain long production runs and fully utilize existing production capacity. Supply economies are realized by buying in large quantities at reduced unit prices. Ford, for example, estimates that by globalizing its product development, purchasing and supply, and other activities, it could save up to $3 billion a year.[23] Also, international sourcing expands the available market for raw resources and component parts, which can lead to lower procurement costs. Marketers also go abroad in search of goods and services that can be used to expand their product offering and reduce their selling cost by creating more and better sales opportunities. Tambrands, the inventor of the tampon, went to Europe to come up with Tampets, a nonapplicator tampon being sold in the United Kingdom. They are currently assessing the opportunities to expand the distribution into China and Latin America where women have serious misgivings concerning the safety of such products.[24] The net result of greater operating economies is larger profit margins. In Europe, General Motors' "Vauxhall and Opel lines have established themselves as the most reliable and robust source of profits in the GM group."[25]

Managerial preferences for entering the international marketing arena are strong motivating factors in many firms' decisions to look beyond their national boundaries. There is an element of prestige associated with an organization functioning as a multinational. Corporate officers take pride in proclaiming that their firms are international in scope. Having status as an international player can be a strong motivating force for overseas expansion. The social and recreational advantages for company executives of having international operations are positive factors influencing the decision to go international.

Organizational diversification can be a powerful motivator for expanding internationally. The international marketer who develops different businesses for different markets is able to pursue a wide range of business opportunities. By using an international business portfolio approach, the organization employing a diversification strategy is able to spread its risks among different businesses in different industries and among different markets in different countries.

Risk management requires the organization to reduce both the type and the degree of risk exposure. While international operations are new ventures that carry considerable risk, they can also help the organization reduce risks by spreading these dangers over different economic and financial conditions and separate social and cultural environments, as well as various political and legal systems. For example, an economic downturn in the country where a firm has sole operations can lead to serious financial difficulties for the organization.

In a similar vein, organizations that operate on an international scale can reduce their financial risks. No one country's monetary or fiscal policy can devastate a multinational firm. Even the expropriation or confiscation of the firm's assets means the loss is confined to one nation while the firm continues to operate in other national markets. **Expropriation** occurs when the host country's government seizes the assets of a foreign-owned firm. Such a seizure is allowed by international law because the government, acting as a sovereign entity, makes compensation to the foreign organization's headquarters. (The amount of financial compensation by the government has traditionally been below the value that the firm places on its loss.) On the other hand, **confiscation** is the impoundment of foreign-owned assets by a host country and is not recognized by international organizations as legal because the multinational is not compensated for its lost land, capital equipment, processes, or potential sales.

REACTIVE REASONS Reactive reasons are responses to changing market conditions in order to maintain market share, preserve profit margins, or implement some other defensive objective. Defensive reasons for going international are equally varied.

Developed countries such as the United States, Japan, and Great Britain often represent **mature markets** for many product lines. Because of market saturation, domestic business organizations in such countries are being forced to look overseas for new markets and revenue growth. Refrigerators provide a good example of this phenomenon. Practically all existing homes in developed nations contain one or more refrigerators. Additional refrigerator sales are limited to new housing construction or replacement sales. By contrast, less-developed countries (LDCs) may be able to offer vast market potential. With the expanding distribution of electrical power and improving income levels, practically every household represents a potential refrigerator or other electrical appliance sale.

Host country activities can also generate defensive reasons for domestic firms to react. For example, in cases where a country has a **shortage of foreign exchange** to pay for imported goods, the national central bank may limit or abolish the importation of foreign goods and services. Nations may also restrict imports to **protect local jobs.** Such motivation caused the United States to request that Japan institute voluntary restraints on its exports of automobiles to the United States. Japan responded by acquiring production facilities within the United States so that market share could be maintained despite import controls. **Following the customer** is another reason for international ventures. For example, a component parts supplier follows a producer by opening an offshore operation that services the needs of that producer. Coca-Cola got a jump start on international business by following American soldiers abroad during World War II. Today, Coca-Cola earns almost 80 percent of its soft-drink profits abroad. By comparison, less than 6 percent of PepsiCo's profits are derived from international sales.[26]

DETERRENTS TO INTERNATIONAL MARKETING

Despite the multitude of good reasons for undertaking international operations, many American firms refuse to take the plunge. A number of deterrents to international expansions exist that limit the need and desire for global involvement. First, there is little need in most industries to look offshore for sales growth. The United States provides a large, wealthy population that represents an expanding market for nationally produced goods and services.

Second, the uncertainty of international operations can be unsettling. Differences in language, customs, business practices, and legal requirements all conspire to make the newcomer to international activities feel uneasy. Both organizations and individuals prefer to restrict business dealings to the familiar where they have an acceptable comfort level and where interactions are more predictable. Chrysler sees continued opportunities at home. Having experienced unsuccessful overseas ventures, Chrysler's management views international opportunities with caution. According to its CEO, Robert Eaton, overseas expansion will develop slowly and be directed at sensible opportunities.[27]

Third, organizations avoid foreign markets because they do not want to adapt current products or develop new products that are more suited to the needs of the host country. The willingness of organizations and individuals to adapt to new market conditions and business environments depends on their view of the world. Worldviews can be ethnocentric, polycentric, or geocentric. **Ethnocentrism** is the belief that one's native culture is superior to other cultures. This attitude makes the marketer resistant to instituting the changes necessary for successful operations abroad.

Approaches more suitable to successful foreign operations are polycentric and geocentric. **Polycentrism** is the belief that each market is a separate and distinct entity that must be recognized and accepted. **Geocentrism** is the view of the world as a global marketplace that requires adaptation and change in some cases and the carryover of national methods across cultures and markets in other situations. The lack of desire to move beyond home-country centeredness is a strong motivator in avoiding international business.

CULTURAL AND SOCIAL INFLUENCES

Cultural universals are those beliefs, attitudes, and behaviors that anthropologists have found to exist across groups of people and across the span of human existence. All cultures have demonstrated the use of personal names, etiquette, hygiene, joke making, courtship, music, trade customs, and more. How culture is manifested around the world poses both opportunities and as obstacles to marketers. While complete coverage of these influences is beyond the scope of this discussion, a brief summary of such influences as language, aesthetics, religion, attitudes, customs, education, and social organizations will provide an adequate sample of how cultural and social influences impact international marketing operations.

LANGUAGE Language is often the most obvious difference among cultures. Firms going abroad find that existing forms of communication need to be changed. An American firm setting up a distribution center and sales office in Brazil will have to change its communications to employees, suppliers, and customers to Portuguese. The same firm entering Belgium will be compelled to communicate in both French and Dutch. Even marketing in Great Britain poses a language hurdle. Americans and the British may both speak English, but they do not speak the same language. Winston Churchill is said to have described the United States and Great Britain as "two nations divided by a common language."[28] In Great Britain, the elevator is called the lift, cookies are referred to as biscuits, and a sweater is termed a jumper. Furthermore, the English, as do many other nationalities, describe themselves and their market offering in modest terms, while Americans are inclined to overstate their assets by describing them as the "best," "greatest," and "superior to all others." These different approaches make for markedly different advertising strategies.

Language also consists of **nonverbal cues** and messages. Does one show up for a meeting five minutes early or twenty minutes late? Should a gift be presented upon arrival at an initial business meeting? How close does one stand to a business associate? Will the other person be offended if handed documents with the left hand? The answers to these and a host of other questions is that it depends upon the culture. The unspoken messages can make or break the marketing experience.

CULTURAL AESTHETICS How a people perceives beauty and good taste is the **aesthetics** of a culture. The marketing manager needs to be acutely aware of the cultural aesthetics in developing the marketing mix. Black symbolizes mourning in Europe while white holds that distinction in the Far East; purple is the mourning color of choice in Latin America. Sexual appeals are effective in the United States while Islamic countries view the display of scantily clad women to be in poor taste and in some cases even sacrilegious. The Japanese are beginning to use sexual imagery, but they are careful to use models who exhibit the features (blue-eyed blonds) of Western women.

RELIGIOUS BELIEFS Religion has a major impact on what products and services are acceptable in a culture. Pork products are unacceptable to Jewish people; Muslims are prohibited from drinking alcoholic beverages. Buddhism discourages the acquisition of any material goods. By contrast, Christmas precipitates major sales opportunities for Christians, and Hanukkah has the same influence for those practicing Judaism. The Islamic month-long celebration of Ramadan includes fasting during sunlight hours—a factor that significantly reduces productivity. These are but a few of the factors that international marketers must take into account as they move from one culturally dominant area to another.

ATTITUDES AND CUSTOMS Attitudes toward work vary from culture to culture. Americans and western Europeans subscribe to what is termed the **Protestant Work Ethic.** It advocates hard work over leisure. The Japanese follow a similar philosophy termed the **Shinto Work Ethic.** Latin Americans "work to live, not live to work." In Mexico, this laid-back work ethic (referred to as the *mañana syndrome*) limits the amount of discretionary income that consumers have to spend on nonessential goods and services. Marketers have sometimes been able to motivate consumers by using the **demonstration effect**— the practice of ensuring the use of their product by opinion leaders so that others can see its application and benefits. The result is not only increased demand for the product but also better worker participation as employees seek to earn the money required to pay for the item. The demonstration effect is also valuable in introducing new products in cultures that revere traditional products and are resistant to change.

International marketing managers are agents of change. When introducing new products and services into an international market, international marketers must be mindful of respecting traditional customs while effectively gaining acceptance of new marketing programs. Knowledge and respect for customs and manners help marketers to avoid falling into the pitfall of making decisions based on their **self-reference criterion**—the tendency to think and react in a fashion that is consistent with the norms of their home-country culture rather than the accepted behavioral norms appropriate to the host country's cultural heritage. For example, business transactions proceed more smoothly when the Western executive knows that the Chinese place the family surname first followed by the given name or that Arabs are insulted by crossed legs because it shows them the bottom of the foot. In Mexico and many other countries it is customary for men to greet each other with a hug.

EDUCATION AND EMPLOYMENT Education is an important indicator of the skill levels of a nation's workforce and, in turn, has a significant impact on the employment opportunities that a nation's citizenry has in both domestic and foreign markets. Historically, the lack of employment opportunities has created a **brain drain** of bright, young, educated people leaving LDCs for developed countries. Multinational firms entering LDCs frequently find a shortage of skilled and educated employees. In recent years, a **reverse brain drain** has emerged in which natives of countries such as South Korea and Taiwan are returning to their homeland in order to participate in these emerging economies. While the reverse brain drain has created a dilemma for the developed nations of the West, it represents both a talent and a market boom for these newly emerging economies and multinationals who participate in these economies. Indians returning to their native land are bringing back "not only money but technology, marketing know-how, and financial expertise. Their return could emerge as a powerful tool in the reshaping of India's economy."[29]

FAMILY AND REFERENCE GROUPS   The role of the family and other reference groups changes across cultures. Marketers need to be mindful that people with strong family ties, such as the Chinese, will be influenced by kinship more than by peer or nationality groups. The relevant family unit also varies from culture to culture. In some countries, the term *family* denotes mother, father, and dependent children. Other countries have extended family units that also include grandparents, grandchildren, aunts, uncles, and cousins. Each family member often has an influential role in a wide variety of purchasing decisions.

Reference groups that impact consumer behavior consist, in part, of gender-based groups and like-age groups. Adults who desire status provide marketing opportunities for the sale of certain brands of automobiles, designer clothing, and banking and investment services. All around the world the teen market likes denim jeans, athletic shoes, and Western popular music. Reference groups also expand to include other groups to which consumers compare themselves in identifying their status within the larger society.

POLITICAL AND LEGAL INFLUENCES

Individual nations are **sovereign states** that maintain control and power over activities that take place within their respective borders. Motivation for maintaining control begins with the basic desire for the country to exercise self-preservation. The objective of protecting and enhancing national security causes governments to buy homegrown defense materials even when foreign-produced goods are more readily available or even less expensive.

Stimulating the national economy is another factor prompting a country's political and legal actions. Multinationals that add productivity and increase a nation's GNP by creating goods and services in that host country are generally nurtured; whereas, in global firms that merely export items to, and siphon financial resources from, the host country may find their actions discouraged both officially and unofficially.

Actions taken by countries to foster internal business growth and stimulate national employment are termed **protectionist** because they protect local firms from foreign competition. International marketers must plan for these business impediments in selecting target markets, planning product offerings, implementing promotion campaigns, and devising pricing strategies.

TRADE BARRIERS   Protectionism can take the form of tariff barriers and nontariff barriers. **Tariffs** are federal taxes that are assessed on imported goods and services. The added cost drives up the price of imports, thereby making foreign items more expensive. Tariffs encourage price-sensitive consumers to buy domestically produced goods and services. When imported products are purchased, the tariff generates additional government revenue.

Nontariff barriers also restrict the marketer's ability to conduct business internationally. This form of protectionism functions by posing obstacles to trade without adding directly to the cost of the product. Examples of nontariff barriers include quotas, voluntary export restraints, subsidies, standards, and customs procedures.

❏ *Quotas*—government limits on the quantity of items that may be imported into a country. This form of trade barrier is used when higher tariffs have no effect on the quantity bought and consumed.

❏ *Voluntary export restraint agreements*—places the responsibility on the exporter to set limits on the quantity of items it imports into a given country. Japan agreed to implement voluntary restraints on the number of cars exported to the United States.

❏ *Subsidies*—support allowances or payments given to domestic producers and distributors to enable them to compete successfully with foreign imports. Governments can also distort trade flows by subsidizing domestic products both for local consumption and for export. Subsidies keep the cost of goods and services artificially low, making it easier for the marketer to increase or sustain market share.

❏ *Standards*—legal requirements established by nations determining what constitutes acceptable and legal design, materials, workmanship, and construction for various goods and services. Sovereignty gives the nation the right to impose specific standards to protect the life and health of its people (such as approval of pharmaceuticals by the Food and Drug Administration), to preserve the nation's environment (emission controls), or to keep out foreign-produced goods (a North Carolina furniture manufacturer has the added cost of labeling its furniture in ancient Gaelic if it wishes to export to Ireland).

❏ *Customs*—procedures that can be used to obstruct international trade. A country wishing to limit imports can have customs officials reclassify items to categories with higher tariffs, look for errors in documentation as an excuse to reject shipments, or simply delay the processing of paperwork to stall product entry into the country. France sought to stem the tide of foreign-made video cassette recorders (VCRs) flowing into the country using a stalling procedure that required all imported VCRs to enter the country through an out-of-the-way port staffed by a skeleton crew of customs agents.

Marketing actions can also be thwarted when governments and international organizations, such as the United Nations impose embargoes and sanctions to achieve political and economic goals. **Embargoes** are complete trade bans that prohibit all business dealings with a specific country. **Sanctions** are more narrow in focus. They interrupt international trade with specifically defined prohibitions, such as disallowing the sales to third-world countries of materials that can be used in building nuclear weapons.

LEGISLATIVE ACTIONS The government of India used its legislative prerogatives to pass legislation that pressured Coca-Cola to either reveal its syrup formula or withdraw from a potentially lucrative market. An incoming Indian government administration saw the application of the law as a win-win situation. Either they would gain knowledge of arguably the world's most desirable formula, or they would force the withdrawal from their country of a multinational that had supported the previous opposing administration. Coca-Cola departed from India, and PepsiCo immediately took advantage of the void created.

Laws governing the use of bribery differ from country to country. The enforcement of these laws can be even more variable. Authorities may overlook bribery or even expect the multinational to pay bribes to obtain contracts and licenses and receive tax breaks. Bribes can provide the primary source of revenue for workers in LDCs, surpassing their income from salaries and wages. Countries such as the United Kingdom and Germany recognize that their multinational firms incur such costs as a business expense overseas, and they allow bribes to be tax deductible. American marketers operate in a different environment. The Foreign Corrupt Practices Act was passed in 1977 to put a halt to American firms bribing foreign nationals. Not only was bribery made illegal but also the accounting gimmicks used to conceal the payment of bribes. The act did allow for the payment of **grease,** which is a nondiscretionary, facilitating payment. An example of grease would be paying customs officials to process—in a timely manner documentation that was part of their assigned job.

Other countries disapprove of the U.S. Foreign Corrupt Practices Act or the application of other laws to business operations within their national boundaries. The enforcement of U.S. laws on the foreign operations of American firms is termed **extraterritoriality.** Foreign governments actively resent U.S. extraterritoriality incursions into their sovereign authority to set rules of commerce.

France and Canada are two countries that have passed laws making it illegal for U.S. branches and subsidiaries operating in their countries to adhere to American laws that are in conflict with French and Canadian trade practices. International marketers operating in multiple environments with opposing laws and customs find themselves in a precarious position as they attempt to navigate through this legal minefield. It is a common practice for multinational firms to contract with lobbyists who work to mediate such conflicts.

ECONOMIC INTEGRATION

Nations that allow goods, services, and factors of production to move freely across national borders enjoy the benefits associated with the efficient use of resources and the advantages that accrue to a competitive marketplace, such as a usually higher standard of living at a lower cost.

Despite the known benefits of free trade, numerous interest groups oppose this practice because of the potential dangers to specific industries or labor groups if markets were left unprotected. Although the world has yet to see all countries eliminate barriers to trade, an increasing number of nations are joining together in regional groups with varying levels of economic integration. Figure 15-5 identifies several of these economic unions.

Because it represents the simplest organizational structure and the least restrictive type of economic cooperation, economic integration usually begins with the establishment of a **free trade area.** A free trade area eliminates trade barriers such as tariffs and quotas among member nations on goods and services. Participating countries continue to enjoy the sovereign right to set independent policies on trade with nongroup nations.

FIGURE 15-5

FORMS OF INTERNATIONAL INTEGRATION

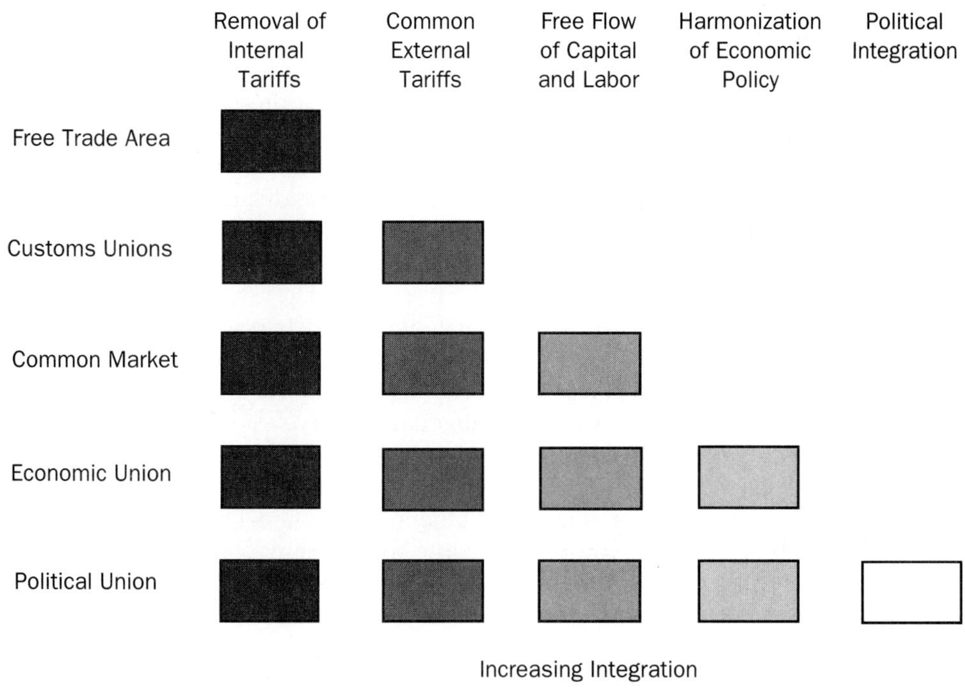

	Removal of Internal Tariffs	Common External Tariffs	Free Flow of Capital and Labor	Harmonization of Economic Policy	Political Integration
Free Trade Area	■				
Customs Unions	■	■			
Common Market	■	■	■		
Economic Union	■	■	■	■	
Political Union	■	■	■	■	■

Increasing Integration →

SOURCE: Ruel K. Kahler, *International Marketing*, 5th ed., 343. Reprinted by permission of South-Western Publishing Company.

The North American Free Trade Agreement (NAFTA) unites Canada, Mexico, and the United States, forming a market of 360 million consumers and creating a $6-trillion economy, "more than one and a half times the size of the European economy."[30] NAFTA is the newest and largest existing free trade area. Other significant free trade areas are the European Free Trade Association, the Casablanca Group, the Latin American Integration Association, and the Association of South East Asian Nations.

Next, in terms of advanced integration, is the **customs union.** A customs union has not only reduced internal trade barriers but also common external tariff and nontariff barriers with nations outside of the union. Examples of this form of economic alliance are the East African Customs Union and the Economic Community of Western African States.

The **common market** incorporates all of the elements of a customs union plus the free movement of factors of production such as capital, labor, and technology. Workers are permitted to freely relocate to another country within the common market where employment opportunities are more inviting. Investors and technology owners are equally allowed to invest where the return is the most attractive within the common market. The West African Economic Community, the Central American Common Market, the Caribbean Community and Common Market, and the Arab Common Market utilize this level of economic integration.

Finally there is the **economic union (EU),** which is the most developed form of economic alliance. An economic union has all of the components of a common market. Additionally, member nations coordinate their economic policies so that their monetary and fiscal policies are in harmony. Much national sovereignty is relinquished with the formation of this type of integration. The requirement for this surrendering of control causes many individuals, institutions, and political systems to oppose the economic union. Only one example of the EU currently exists, the Afro-Malagasy Economic Union.

The twelve-member European Community is presently in the initial stages of forming an EU. Most European Community countries have linked their currencies and monetary and fiscal policies through an **exchange rate mechanism**. Member nations have also created a **European Currency Unit (ECU)** to serve as an international currency. The ECU presently has limited use in business dealings. While some countries are promoting the usage of the ECU, others, such as Great Britain, are opposed to any action that would lead to one central bank controlling monetary policy for a united Europe. The issues of sovereignty and control of national destiny and well-being will no doubt continue to influence the marketers' ability to do business internationally.

Many international organizations have been established to facilitate world trade as well as negotiate and arbitrate dealings between firms and governments of trading countries. These organizations are summarized in Figure 15-6.

FIGURE 15-6

INTERNATIONAL ORGANIZATIONS

International Monetary Fund (IMF)	Established to stabilize currency exchange rates. Also assists nations in meeting Balance of Payments deficit obligations. The IMF created Special Drawing Rights, a basket of currencies (composed of the Japanese yen, U.S. dollar, British pound, German mark, and French franc) that are credited to the central banks of member countries.
International Bank for Reconstruction and Development (IBRD)	Also known as the World Bank, this institution was originally intended for reconstruction and development of countries that were devastated as the result of World War II. Its current emphasis is assisting the developing countries of Africa, Asia, Eastern Europe, the Middle East, and South America.
International Finance Corporation (IFC)	Assists member countries of the World Bank in developing private enterprise by both making direct loans and facilitating loans from commercial international financial markets.
International Development Association (IDA)	Loans funds to the poorest member nations of the World Bank for long-term projects. It has the most lenient repayment provisions of any component of the World Bank.
United Nations (UN)	The largest of the international organizations, this institution had as its original goal maintaining world peace. The UN now increasingly focuses on promoting socio-economic development, humanitarian concerns, and strengthening cooperation among nations.
United Nations Conference on Trade and Development (UNCTAD)	A subset of the UN dedicated to highlighting the problems that developing countries face in international trade and proposing solutions to those problems.
Organization for Economic Cooperation and Development (OECD)	A research center that focuses on the development of LDCs. It also directs discussion and cooperation between the LDCs and developed countries. An excellent source of quarterly and annual statistics on its member nations.
General Agreement on Tariffs and Trade (GATT)	Created in 1947 as a temporary agreement to facilitate world trade until a more inclusive and formal organization could be approved by member nations, GATT has survived as a mechanism to reduce tariff and nontariff barriers for many goods. It also serves as a mediator for international trade disputes.
World Trade Organization (WTO)	Additional rounds of negotiations of the GATT have led to the formation of the WTO, which expands GATT's authority and effectiveness. The WTO further reduces trade barriers for goods to previously uncovered areas such as textiles and agricultural products; services, including legal representation, accounting, and software; and intellectual property, for example, patents, trademarks, and copyrights.

International Marketing Mix

International marketing offers the organization opportunities that are sufficiently inviting to offset the risk and expense of developing international operations. These opportunities can be an expansion of new and existing domestic operations or the development of new uncharted areas of operations. In this discussion, we examine some of the relevant issues surrounding the development and implementation of a marketing mix for international markets.

Product Life Cycle First, consider the concept of the product life cycle. Often products and services are introduced in developed countries where consumers are both eager to embrace the latest innovations and have the financial resources to purchase the items. The demonstration effect encourages others to mimic the consumption behavior of early adopters, so sales grow at an increasing rate. Eventually, the market matures as most consumers who are receptive to the product have already acquired it, and, finally, there is an inevitable decline in sales.

At the very time when sales of the product are peaking in the developed country, the product may have just been introduced or have acquired acceptance in less-developed countries. This late recognition might be the result of traditional lifestyles that resist the introduction of any new ways and pose an obstacle to new consumption patterns. Another reason may be the need for the price of the product to come down, as it inevitably will once research and development costs are recouped and mass production begins. A lower price tag makes the item a potential purchase in countries where citizens have lower discretionary incomes. The end result is that increased sales in the later adopting country offset decreased sales in the early adopting country.

Product Standardization Businesses have several options available to them in terms of the products they will offer in the host country. These include marketing the same product sold in the home country, modifying the firm's existing product to better meet the needs of consumers in the new market, or creating an entirely new product better suited to the host country's consumers.

Industrial goods that are sold to organizations are generally standardized globally. Machinery and technology necessary for production and business operations tend to be the same regardless of geographic location. This phenomenon allows industrial-goods marketers to use a standardized marketing approach for both domestic and foreign products. Goods and services are sold worldwide with no, or minimal, adaption.

Consumer goods are more sensitive to regional tastes and desires. The clothes people wear, the automobiles they drive, and the banking services they expect are all influenced by the local economy, climate, laws, customs, and sense of propriety. Given the need for consumer products to respond to local demands, goods and services in this category need to be adapted to regional requirements. Before introducing its Opel Astra into the Indian market, General Motors had to strengthen the car's suspension so that it could withstand the harsh road conditions.[31] In other situations, a totally new product must be created if local consumption is to be successfully achieved.

PRODUCT POSITIONING Sometimes the need to modify the product is minimized or eliminated by simply positioning the product differently. Positioning can be used to target varying markets based on the applicable economic and cultural forces. For example, Dunkin Donuts is a breakfast food and anytime snack in the United States. Latin Americans consider donuts a special treat to be brought home by family members making excursions into the city, and the local Dunkin Donuts store is considered an impressive place to take a date. The Buick Motor Company markets its LeSabre model as a good-value family car in the United States. Without modifying the automobile, the company sells the same vehicle in Nigeria as a luxury car for the country's elite, who enjoy being road hogs on the nation's narrow roadways.

TOTAL PRODUCT CONCEPT The total product concept is an important consideration in international marketing because it not only covers the product itself, it also includes the packaging, labeling, use instructions, and brand name. Because of their extremely important communication function, these components of the total product must be reviewed carefully for their appropriateness in international markets.

Detergent is sold in the United States and Canada in cardboard boxes and plastic bottles, but in Mexico consumers expect to find it in plastic bags. Package size will also vary because of income and local custom. Cigarettes and razor blades are sold one at a time in countries where income levels are too low to allow them to be bought by the carton or pack. American consumers buy grocery products in large-sized containers, carry the items home in their autos, and store them in spacious cupboards. Europeans prefer to shop daily for fresh foodstuffs. They either walk or bicycle to and from the market, then store the groceries in small kitchens. All of these factors encourage Europeans to purchase groceries in smaller package sizes than their American counterparts.

Labeling and use instructions must consider language requirements and the literacy level of the population. At times the language of the home producer may generate the most favorable marketing image, such as the labeling in French of wine produced in the Burgundy region of France. However, in most cases, the local language will generally produce the greatest sales.

Some countries have citizens who speak different languages, thus requiring multilingual labeling. Goods sold in Canada must be labeled in both English and French or the government can legally pull the items from the shelves. Products in Switzerland require both German and French labeling.

Multinational enterprises would prefer to use an established brand name in every nation in which they operate. Brand recognition facilitates acceptance and purchase by consumers. McDonald's believes that its brand name transcends national boundaries and cultures. McDonald's operates on the premise that "People are more the same than different." [32] As International chief James Cantalupo said, "I don't think our food is seen as American. It's seen as McDonald's."[33] Sometimes, though, that is not practical.

PRICE STRATEGIES Just as the most desirable product for each market may be different, so may be the appropriate price. It is not uncommon for a firm to set prices consistent with the competition in a given market. This tactic is used most frequently by small firms in industries where a few large firms dominate the market.

A high price in foreign markets may be set to reflect the additional costs of doing business internationally. These include transportation, insurance, customs and license documentation, international financing, foreign-exchange conversions, and translations. Some organizations elect to engage in **price skimming** by setting higher prices in order to turn a fast profit on a limited number of sales. Price skimming may also be used simply because there is less competition in the new market and consumers are willing to pay a premium for the good or service.

A firm entering a new market may decide to set a lower price than that charged in the home country in order to entice skeptical consumers into trying the new product. This **price penetration** strategy is used when the company is willing to price low to gain market share. Moderately priced new wines from South Africa and Australia have entered the U.S. market and are winning favor with American imbibers. The tasty varietals are capturing market share to the point that California and Chilean vintners are being forced to rethink their long-standing pricing systems.[34] In some cases, firms set low price points because that is the only way consumers can afford the goods. Competitive conditions necessitate a low price. Selling goods below production costs or below the price charged in the home market is often viewed as **dumping**. Dumping is seriously contested by firms in similar industries in the host country. The affected companies will usually seek legislative protection to institute quotas or tariffs in retaliation. Firms and nations will also approach the World Trade Organization to resolve the pricing issue.

Price standardization is the strategy of setting prices in all markets based on appropriate fixed and variable costs as well as those expenses related to exports. Export costs include transportation and tariffs.

Whether **transportation costs** influence sales depends on the nature of the product and the percentage of the price attributed to transportation expenses. Magnetic-resonance imaging scanners are available from only a handful of manufacturers worldwide; therefore, few options for purchasing such medical equipment and little opportunity for negotiating transportation charges exist. However, although all suppliers will charge high transportation fees, the cost will be a small percentage of the total cost. These factors cause transportation cost to be of negligible importance. In contrast, most agricultural products are available from a number of sources. Grocery stores can opt to purchase produce from distributors whose low transportation costs allow them to keep their lettuce and apple prices low. Food stores know that grocery shoppers will, in many cases, compare prices and shop accordingly.

Not only must the exports be transported abroad, but also they are often assessed a **tariff** or **duty** before they are allowed to enter the foreign market. Tariffs and duties are government taxes imposed on imported goods and services for the purpose of discouraging trade or to raise revenue for the government. An **ad valorem tariff** is a percentage of the invoice price of the import. For example, an engineering bill for $5,000 may have a 20-percent tariff of $1,000, making the actual costs $6,000. **Specific duties** are assessed according to the quantity of the physical unit. Each kilogram of cocoa beans imported might have a duty of $.50. Therefore, an 80-kilogram shipment of cocoa beans imported into the country is charged $40 by the government, regardless of the invoice price.

The price charged to other branches and subsidiaries of the same corporate entity is termed an **intracompany** or **transfer price.** Both the buyer and the seller want the highest profit margin available. This goal encourages the supplying member to charge the same price that it imposes on nonrelated firms, an **arm's length price.** Corporate headquarters, however, may have other objectives to meet through the firm's transfer pricing. The pricing mechanism can be used to achieve high corporate profits in countries with low tax rates. Transfer pricing also allows the firm to repatriate earnings from countries that may otherwise have legal barriers to other means of returning profits to the home country.

PROMOTIONAL STRATEGIES A variety of promotion alternatives exist for the marketer in international markets. These range from advertising to sales promotion to personal selling. Here again, the firm must weigh the advantages and disadvantages of standardization and adaptation. Standardized promotional campaigns create economies but may not be practical because of language differences, cultural differences in symbolism, and the availability of promotional media.

American advertising often uses sexual imagery to sell everything from beer to toothpaste. Traditional cultures, such as those found in China and Iraq, find such imagery offensive and unacceptable.

Commercial radio and television are commonly used in the United States to sell consumer goods. Other media, such as cinema advertising, are an alternative worth considering in poorer countries where few households possess radios or televisions or in countries where the government operates the broadcast media and commercials are not allowed.

Firms that rely on the print media and education levels of Western countries are faced with a hurdle when they attempt to advertise in countries with low literacy rates. Such countries also generally have few newspapers and magazines.

Sales promotions in the form of contests are well received in both rich and poor nations. However, cents-off coupons have more appeal in wealthier countries where consumers are pleased to get a bargain. In underdeveloped countries, the same coupons are avoided because they reflect a lack of resources. Americans also enjoy the bargain of obtaining free gifts such as the airline tickets and upgrades accorded frequent fliers and the tableware and cookware that can be acquired by saving the coupons from boxes of Betty Crocker products. Promotional gifts cannot be used universally. Some governments regulate such activities to the point where it becomes burdensome to the firm. Countries with a shortage of consumer goods often see a black market develop for such promotional items. It is not uncommon for the free conditioner being given away with shampoo or the prize inside the box of cereal to disappear before the consumer makes his or her purchase. Companies need to become creative and look for promotional alternatives such as sponsoring local events, both cultural and sporting, and performing in-store demonstrations.

Personal selling is an excellent means of demonstrating a new product to wary or unfamiliar consumers. The personal contact allows for two-way communication where questions can be answered and consumers can even have hands-on opportunities. This type of promotion also negates illiteracy because the product and its uses are explained verbally. Avon Products, Inc., has enjoyed considerable success in China, Mexico, Argentina, Brazil, and Poland with its army of sales representatives selling door-to-door. [35] Obstacles to personal selling are the high costs in high-wage countries and the fact that sales is a low-status occupation in some countries, making it difficult to recruit personnel.

DISTRIBUTION STRATEGIES Successful international marketers know that sales occur when goods and services are readily available to consumers. Firms initiating business outside of the United States are often surprised to learn of the longer and more complex distribution channels in other countries. Physical distribution consists of three basic components:

1. The product
2. Available transportation modes
3. Sales and delivery outlets

Some relevant questions to ask regarding international distribution include the following inquiries:

Does the product require technical sales and support?

Is the product perishable, or does it have a long shelf life?

Is the service time-and-place dependent?

Is the product or service sold in small or large quantities?

Is the product or service high in cost, therefore limiting the channel members who can participate in its distribution?

The existing infrastructure of the home company needs to be examined to see if roads, railroads, airports, and waterways are conducive to transporting the product. The United States has a railway system that crisscrosses the nation. England, by contrast, has a transportation system that converges on London. In many cases, goods must first be shipped into London, transferred, then shipped out to their final destination. The Rhine Waterway carries substantial amounts of goods across Europe. Australia, however, has no inland waterway of commercial importance.

The outlets used to market a product can pose a significant challenge to international firms. Whether the product being introduced is something new and different or similar to existing products on the market, distributors and retailers may be resistant to relinquishing valuable storage and shelf space to an untried item. Creativity is required to encourage adopting the firm's product. Some companies, such as L.L. Bean, have been able to gain inroads into the Japanese consumer market through the use of catalog sales.[36]

Distribution options may also be a matter of making contact with the right subculture, a fact that will not be documented anywhere, but require discreet inquiries to reveal their existence. Having connections with the right tribe pays off in Nigeria. It is the appropriate political party in India that carries weight. In Japan one must establish a business relationship with the proper **Sogo Shosha,** or trading company. Kodak alleges that Fuji Photo Film Company has maintained its hold on the Japanese market by controlling the largest distribution channels. As a result, in Japan, Fuji has a 70-percent market share as compared to 9 percent for Kodak.[37] In trying to make a success of its Tatra truck plant, Chrysler found out that having connections with the right government officials is what carries weight in the Czech Republic.[38]

International marketers find that personal contact is the key to successful ongoing business activities. It is important to get a feel for the host country, its people, and its culture. Doing preliminary research is good, but going there is better. Latin American, Asian, African, and Middle Eastern retailers and distributors want to personally know and size up the individuals with whom they are doing business. Contracts should spell out all duties, responsibilities, and rights, but often eye contact, a handshake, and a shared meal are necessary prerequisites to completing a transaction.

Concluding Remarks

Service marketing, nonprofit marketing, and international marketing all have unique marketing circumstances and requirements that necessitate special examination. Service marketing requires that service providers take into account the nature of service activities and their special characteristics. Services are intangible, variable, inseparable, and perishable. Each of these characteristics has a profound effect on developing an appropriate marketing mix for services. Nonprofit marketing is distinguished by the fact that the primary goals are social and public interest in nature. Nonprofit marketing activities include the marketing of ideas, people, places, and organizations. Organizations can approach international markets from the perspective of a global marketer who uses a standardized business format to reach similar customers in each foreign market it targets or of an international marketer who develops an entirely new business format for each market served by the organization. The decision to enter the international marketplace requires that the organization carefully consider the unique cultural, social, political, and legal circumstances of each national and subregional market it enters.

Endnotes

1. Ronald Henkoff, "Service Is Everybody's Business," *Fortune* (June 27, 1994), 49–50.

2. Matt Walsh, "You Gotta Believe," *Forbes* (November 21, 1994), 68, 70.

3. *Dictionary of Marketing Terms,* ed. Peter Bennett, (Chicago: American Marketing Association, 1988), 184.

4. Leonard L. Berry, *On Great Service* (New York: The Free Press, 1995), 8.

5. Ronald Henkoff, "Finding, Training, and Keeping the Best Service Workers," *Fortune* (October 3, 1994), 110.

6. Rahul Jacob, "Why Some Customers Are More Equal Than Others," *Fortune* (September 19, 1994), 222.

7. Kenneth Labich, "Is Herb Kelleher America's Best CEO?" *Fortune* (May 2, 1994), 46.

8. See Leonard L. Berry and A. Parasuraman, *Marketing Services—Competing through Quality* (New York: Free Press, 1991), 15–33.

9. See *Service Quality, New Directions in Theory and Practice*, ed. Roland T. Rust and Richard L. Oliver (London: Sage Publications, 1994). Also see Karl Albrecht, "Total Quality Service," *Quality Digest* (January 1993), 18.

10. Ron Zwmke and Dick Schaaf, *The Service Edge* (New York: NAL Books, 1989), 14.

11. This discussion is based on A. Parasuraman, Valarie A. Zeithamal, and Leonard L. Barry, "A Conceptual Model of Service Quality and Its Implications for Future Research," *Journal of Marketing* (Fall 1985), 47; Valarie A. Zeithamal, Leonard L. Barry, and A. Parasuraman, "Communication and Control Processes in the Delivery of Service Quality," *Journal of Marketing* (April 1988), 46.

12. This discussion and classification is adapted from Philip Kotler, *Marketing for Nonprofit Organizations*, Second Edition (Englewood Cliffs, NJ: Prentice-Hall, 1982), 13–14.

13. See Nora Ganim Barnes, "Cause-Related Marketing Revisted: The Effects of the United Way Scandal," *American Business Review* (May 1994), 95–99.

14. See Lisa Gubernick and Robert La Franco, "Charity as a Commodity," *Forbes* (September 26, 1994), 118–21.

15. See Ann Reilly Dowd, "Environmentalists Are on the Run," *Fortune* (September 19, 1994), 91; John Carey, "A Green Industrial Policy Takes Root," *Business Week* (July 25, 1994), 83–84; Kevin Goldman, "Green Campaigns Don't Always Pay Off, Survey Finds," *Wall Street Journal* (April 11, 1994), B8; Cheryl Powell, "The Green Movement Sows Demand for Ecofurniture," *Wall Street Journal* (September 2, 1994), B1; Suzanne Oliver, "Eco-Profitable," *Forbes* (June 20, 1994), 110; and Dan Cordtz, "Green Hell," *Financial World* (January 18, 1994), 38–42.

16. Emory Thomas, Jr., "How Does a Quiet City Become a Tourist Spot? Ask Myrtle Beach, S.C.," *Wall Street Journal* (April 18, 1995), A1, A8.

17. Dyan Machan, "We're Not Authoritarian Goons," *Forbes* (October 24, 1994), 246.

18. See Laxmi Nakarmi, "Goldstar Is Burning Bright," *Business Week* (September 26, 1994), 129–30.

19. See Roula Khalaf, "Le Tire, C'est Moi," *Forbes* (August 1, 1994), 48–49.

20. Julia Flynn, "Heineken's Battle to Stay Top Bottle," *Business Week* (August 1, 1994), 61.

21. Jon Berry, "Don't Leave Home without It, Wherever You Live," *Business Week* (February 21, 1994), 76–77.

22. See Jerry Flint, "One World, One Ford," *Forbes* (June 20, 1994), 40–41. Also see Jerry Flint, "You Know What's in My Heart," *Forbes* (February 13, 1995), 42–44.

23. John A. Byrne and Kathleen Kerwin, "Borderless Management," *Business Week* (May 23, 1994), 25.

24. Dyan Machan, "Will the Chinese Use Tampons?" *Forbes* (January 16, 1995), 87.

25. Peter Fuhrman, "Meanwhile, in Europe … ," *Forbes* (October 24, 1994), 44.

26. Patricia Sellers, "Pepsi Opens a Second Front," *Fortune* (August 8, 1994), 72.

27. Jerry Flint, "Old Stay-at-Home," *Forbes* (November 7, 1994), 66.

28. Christopher H. Lovelock, "What Language Shall We Put It In?" *Marketing Management*, Vol. 3, No. 3 (1994), 38.

29. Joyce Barnathan, Sharon Moshavi, Heidi Dawley, Sunita Wadekar, and Helen Chang, "Passage Back to India," *Business Week* (July 17, 1995), 44. Also see Peter Fuhrman and Michael Schuman, "Now We Are Our Own Masters," *Forbes* (May 23, 1994), 128–38.

30. Blayne Cutler, "North American Demographics," *American Demographics* (March 1992), 38.

31. Peter Fuhrman, "Meanwhile, in Europe … ," 44.

32. Andrew E. Serwer, "McDonald's Conquers the World," *Fortune* (October, 17, 1994), 106.

33. Ibid.

34. Nina Munk, "More Bucks from the Same Grapes," *Forbes* (December 19, 1994), 134, 138.

35. Veronica Bryd, "The Avon Lady of the Amazon," *Business Week* (October 24, 1994), 93–94, 96.

36. Edith Hill Updike and Mary Kuntz, "Japan Is Dialing 1 800 Buyamerica," *Business Week* (June 12, 1995), 64.

37. Mark Maremont, Brian Bremner, and Edith Updike, "Next, A Flap over Film," *Business Week* (July 10, 1995), 34.

38. Richard C. Morais, "Hong Kong of Europe," *Forbes* (June 20, 1994), 70.

APPENDIX A

A Business Student's Guide to Library Resources

Gary White
Dale M. Lewison

Introduction

College and university libraries contain a wealth of information pertinent to the needs of both businesspeople and students of business administration. Although libraries differ according to the size of the institution, the number of students, and the type of programs offered, they usually contain the same types of materials: books, journals and magazines, indexes and other reference sources, audiovisual materials, and, in some cases, government documents. This appendix serves as a guide for finding these types of materials in a typical college or university library.

Good library skills are necessary to conduct research properly and in a timely manner. Technology has made a major impact on libraries. Most libraries now have computerized card catalogs and offer many indexes and other materials in electronic formats. While technological improvements are designed to make library research easier and faster, they may cause apprehension and uncertainty in people who have not used the library for a few years. This guide will explain many of the technological improvements and electronic resources that students may encounter in a typical college or university library.

People conducting library research spend much of their time in the reference department. Usually the on-line catalog, indexes, and reference sources, such as directories, encyclopedias, and statistical works, are located here. Most reference departments have service desks staffed by reference librarians. Students unfamiliar with materials in the library should consult a reference librarian for instruction on how to use the on-line catalog and how to select and search appropriate indexes or for assistance in finding specific materials or information. While reference librarians have a master's degree in library science, some larger libraries also have librarians who are subject specialists, such as business librarians or engineering librarians. These specialists usually have a master's or doctoral degree in a specific subject area.

Finding Books

Most college and university libraries use either the Library of Congress or the Dewey Decimal classification systems when assigning call numbers to books. A call number is a code, usually typed on the spine of the book, which is used to find books on the shelf. Call numbers are assigned to books on the basis of the book's subject matter. With this arrangement, books on similar topics will be shelved together. Examples of the two types of classification systems are

Library of Congress	Dewey Decimal
HF	650.873
223	
.W57	
1993	

The Library of Congress classification system is an alphabetical arrangement. Different letters of the alphabet indicate different subject areas. For example, the letter "H" is for social sciences materials. These are further classified by additional subjects, such as "HB" for materials in economics and "HG" for finance materials. The numbers and letters on the second and third lines of the call number are additional breakdowns within the specified subject area.

The Dewey Decimal classification system is a numerical classification system based on the progressive use of numbers 0 through 9. For example, numbers beginning with 0 are general works, numbers beginning with 5 are materials in the pure sciences, and 6 are useful arts. The example above is a further breakdown under the category "useful arts." Books with a "650" classification deal with communications or business.

In order to find the call number of a particular book, or books on a specific subject, it is necessary to use the card catalog or the on-line catalog. Most people are familiar with the traditional card catalog. This system usually consists of two different sections, one with author/title listings and one with subject listings, both arranged in alphabetical order. When a particular title or author is known, a search in the author/title catalog will tell you whether the library owns the book. Most researchers will be conducting subject searches and will need to look in the subject section of the card catalog. Once an appropriate subject is found, all of the books with this subject classification will be located together. The call number is in the upper left corner. Author, title, publisher, year of publication, and notes are located in the center of the card. The numbered sections at the bottom of the card indicate the different subjects that have been assigned to the particular book. In the subject catalog, the subject of the book or other type of library holding is also typed across the top of the card.

On-line catalogs are also designed to allow searches by author, title, or subject. Someone using the on-line catalog usually must specify the type of search they wish to perform. Usually this requires typing in a letter and a command, such as "T=Romeo and Juliet" to search for this title, "A=Shakespeare" for this author, or "S=Advertising" for this subject. Exact commands vary with different computer systems. Most systems offer some kind of "help" screen that explains the various commands. Many on-line catalogs also allow for key-word searches in which the computer will search for any records containing a certain word or words. Some systems allow patrons to limit searches by particular years, languages, or other criteria. Once the appropriate items are located, the call numbers and the locations of those items will appear on the screen. Most on-line catalogs also display information such as the publisher, place and year of publication, and subject headings that have been assigned to the work. Subject headings are useful to note since these same subjects can be entered back into the computer to obtain a list of all of the materials on the same subject. Many on-line catalogs also state whether the book is currently available or is checked out to another person. On-line catalogs are typically faster to search than card catalogs, are updated more frequently, and allow for searches that are not feasible with a card catalog. People with computers and a modem in their homes or offices can often log onto the on-line catalog and perform searches without visiting the library.

Once a call number for a desired book is found, the next step is to locate the book on the shelf. Most libraries have a circulating collection, which consists of books that patrons can check out, and a reference collection, which consists of materials that cannot be checked out and must be used in the library. Reference materials almost always have some designation on the call number, such as the abbreviation "Ref." at the top of the call number.

The process for locating dissertations or master's theses varies depending on whether the library classifies these materials as it does other books or whether it holds them in separate collections. Often materials written by students at the institution are held separately from the library's other materials. Some researchers like to browse through theses or dissertations of an institution to note format, length, or other stylistic features. Because theses and dissertations are expected to cover new or unexplored topics, some researchers may require a comprehensive search in order to ensure that their subject has not already been investigated by other researchers. Generally, libraries classify dissertations and theses as books. They will therefore be searchable on the on-line or card catalogs by author, title, and subject if the library catalogers have assigned subjects to the works. Most libraries routinely add to their collections those dissertations and theses that are written by students of the same institution. Dissertations from other institutions are also available for purchase through University Microforms International (UMI). Many libraries purchase some dissertations that support their collections, which are also searchable by author, title, and possibly subject.

A more thorough search of published dissertations is accomplished by using *Dissertation Abstracts International* (DAI), a publication listing dissertations by both subject and author. This source provides the author name, the institution, and an abstract or summary of the dissertation. DAI is available in print, on CD-ROM, and through on-line databases. See a reference librarian for assistance in locating and using *Dissertation Abstracts International*.

FINDING JOURNAL ARTICLES

Definitions of some commonly used, and often misused, words relating to periodical literature will help clear up uncertainties and misunderstandings that occur when performing searches. An **index** is a listing, usually alphabetical, of sources on a particular subject area. The list may include books, but the primary focus is on journal articles. Subject areas are usually listed alphabetically. Indexes can be either in printed volumes, usually published monthly, quarterly, or annually, or in CD-ROM or other computerized formats. Researchers consult indexes to search for materials on a given subject area. Specific subject areas have their own indexes. Some examples of business indexes are *Business Periodicals Index, Accounting and Tax Index,* and *ABI/Inform,* a popular computerized business index. Indexes in libraries should not be confused with indexes at the back of books, which list the page numbers on which various terms are mentioned or discussed.

A **bibliography** is a list of sources on a given subject area and may include books, journal articles, reports, or other materials. It is a compilation of materials on a particular subject matter. Bibliographies may be published at the end of books or chapters of books, in journal articles, or as stand-alone publications. Bibliographies are compiled by consulting indexes.

The words *serial, journal, periodical, magazine,* and *standing orders* are often used interchangeably, but there are differences in the meanings of these terms. **Serials** are materials that are published at regular time intervals. **Periodicals, magazines, journals,** and **standing orders** are all serials. **Periodicals** are a type of serial published at regular time intervals and in which there is no future ending date planned for the publication, such as *Business Week* or *The Journal of Marketing*. **Standing orders** are serials published at regular intervals in which there is a planned ending, though the exact date may not always be known. The difference in the definitions of magazines and journals is of a qualitative nature. The term **magazine** most often refers to serial publications that are popular titles or are available in newsstands or stores. **Journals** usually are scholarly publications typically published by professional bodies or associations, or by academics. The term *refereed journal* refers to journals that will only publish articles that have been reviewed by some expert panel in order to ensure that the articles are of an appropriate nature and scholarly level for the publication.

The first step in conducting a search of the periodical literature is to identify and select the appropriate indexes to use. As previously mentioned, different indexes are available for particular subject areas. Most libraries have a combination of indexes in both print and electronic formats. Electronic formats may include CD-ROM versions of indexes or indexes that are accessible through the on-line catalog. Users unfamiliar with a library should consult with a reference librarian to find out which indexes are available for a particular subject matter and in what format.

Once an index is identified, the search can proceed. Most users are searching for a particular subject. Most print indexes are published in volumes that cumulate by either year of publication or volume number. Updates are available as they are published. Searching a print index by subject requires that the user first find the appropriate subject term and then search in all of the years or volume numbers pertinent to the researcher's needs. For example, *Business Periodicals Index* began publication in 1958, comes out in either monthly or quarterly supplements, and is cumulated into annual volumes. Users may have to search under the same subject in several different volumes to gather a complete search on a particular subject. Many indexes also permit searches by author name. Entries in indexes usually include the name of the article; the author(s); title, volume number, and year of the journal; and page numbers. This information is called a **citation.** Some indexes include **abstracts,** or short summaries of the articles.

Computerized indexes provide the same type of information but are typically easier to use and more flexible in the types of searches that can be done. They usually combine a number of years' worth of indexed materials into one database, so that a single search can yield a complete set of results. Computerized indexes more often contain abstracts than do printed indexes. Most computerized indexes allow for many different types of searches. For example, users can type in a word or set of words, and the computer will search for them anywhere in the record. Many databases allow searchers to specify particular journal titles, author names, years of publication, or combinations of these searches. Many libraries allow users to print or download their search results.

Once a list of relevant citations is found, the next step is to see whether the library owns, or subscribes to, the journals that contain the desired articles. Remember, indexes are produced by companies or organizations, not the library itself. They are either purchased or leased by the library. Indexes, therefore, do not necessarily reflect the journal titles actually available in a particular library. In order to check whether a journal title is available, users should check the name of the journal as it appears in the citation from the index and search a listing of the library's journal holdings to see if the title *and* the desired year or volume number is available. Many libraries produce print copies of the journal titles they own, usually listing the titles and the years or volume numbers that are available. Some libraries also enter this information into their on-line catalogs. In this case a researcher can determine if the library owns the title by performing a title search on the on-line catalog using the journal title.

Arrangement of journals or periodicals differs from library to library. Many libraries have a separate periodicals department. Journal or periodical titles are sometimes arranged alphabetically, while some libraries will assign call numbers using the Library of Congress or Dewey Decimal classification systems. Most libraries also have a microforms area or department. Microforms are photographically reduced copies of materials, usually journals or newspapers. Microforms are used both to save library space and to preserve a copy of items that may eventually be damaged, destroyed, or lost. For example, many libraries receive the *New York Times* on microform. This newspaper is published daily during the week and has been in publication since 1851. Most libraries could not afford the space required to store all of these issues, much less preserve the quality for future users. A microform copy ensures that the title is available for users. Microforms generally include three types of materials: microfilm, microfiche, or microcard. Each type of material requires special machines to read and to make photocopies. Types of microform materials and equipment vary from library to library. Students should check with the reference or periodicals section of their library to identify and use microforms.

Many libraries also have a current periodicals section or room. Periodicals are kept here when they first arrive at the library. When there are enough issues to create a single volume or a complete year's run, they may be bound together. When searching for a journal title, researchers should be aware that recent dates may be in the current periodicals section, while older dates may be in the bound periodicals section or in the microforms area.

Many libraries are able to obtain copies of journal articles or may borrow books or other items from other libraries. The process of obtaining materials from another library or institution is called **interlibrary loan.** Researchers who need materials not available in one library should inquire about obtaining materials from other libraries through an interlibrary loan. Some libraries place certain restrictions on this type of loaning or may charge fees for this service.

THE REFERENCE DEPARTMENT

Researchers conduct most of their research activities in the reference department or area, which usually has a reference desk staffed by reference librarians. The card catalog or terminals for the on-line catalog are usually in the reference area. Many reference departments also have a special section for their indexes. If there are computerized indexes, these will be located in the reference area also.

The reference collection consists of library materials that usually cannot be checked out by library patrons, such as encyclopedias, directories, statistical sources, and bibliographies. Materials in reference collections are likely to be needed by a variety of people; therefore, most libraries do not allow reference materials to circulate outside of the library. The call-number classification for reference materials should be the same as for the circulating collection, but it will usually contain some designation that specifies that it is shelved in the reference area.

In addition to print and computerized indexes and reference sources, reference librarians have access to hundreds of on-line databases containing information on many different subject areas. These databases are sometimes similar to other resources available in the library but are usually more current. Many libraries charge fees for these types of searches because they use staff time and because libraries themselves are charged for the use of these databases. Consult a reference librarian for information about on-line databases.

Government Documents

The federal government, through its various departments, agencies, bureaus, and divisions, produces an enormous amount of information. Many government publications are available to the public through libraries that have been designated **depository libraries.** Depository libraries receive documents from the government free of charge but must classify and organize them to make them available to the public. Depository libraries differ from each other in the percentage of documents that each receives. Full depository libraries receive all government documents that are produced for the public. Usually only a few full depository libraries exist in each state. Most depository libraries receive only a portion of the documents produced, usually based on the size and staffing of the library. These libraries also choose some of the materials that they will receive. Most larger university libraries receive government documents and may have separate government documents departments.

Both libraries not designated as depository libraries and individuals can purchase government documents through the **Government Printing Office (GPO),** or through regional GPO bookstores, which are located throughout the country. The GPO is the agency of the federal government responsible for producing and disseminating all government information to the public.

Government documents are classified by a unique call-number system called the **SuDoc** system. Each SuDoc number begins with a letter that designates which department or bureau of the government produced the document. For example, government documents with a call number beginning with the letter "A" are produced by the Department of Agriculture, those with the letter "L" by the Department of Labor, and those beginning with "C" are from the Department of Commerce.

The *Monthly Catalog of U. S. Government Publications* is a comprehensive listing of the publications produced by the U.S. government. Several commercial sources also exist that index these publications. These indexes are searchable by subject and provide the prices, catalog numbers, and SuDoc numbers of each publication. Once a document is found in one of these listings, it is necessary to check with the library's holdings to see if the document is owned by the library. Many libraries' government documents will appear on their on-line or card catalogs.

Government documents are important sources of business information. The Securities and Exchange Commission (SEC) compiles and disseminates information and filings about public corporations, including their annual reports. The Bureau of the Census produces not only the Census of Population and Housing but also publications from the Economic Census. These publications come out every year ending in "2" and "7," meaning economic census publications were produced in 1982 and 1987. These publications include the *Census of Manufacturers, Census of Retail Trade, Census of Service Industries,* and *Census of Wholesale Trade,* as well as several others. These publications provide vital statistical data. Other important publications include the *Survey of Current Business, Current Business Reports,* and the *Monthly Labor Report.* These publications provide significant sources of information on business and economic trends. The *U.S. Industrial Outlook,* a standard reference work available in most libraries, describes the current situation and future outlook for many U.S. industries.

The *Standard Industrial Classification Manual* is a standard reference source used not only with government documents but also with most other reference sources related to business. This manual classifies businesses by assigning a **Standard Industrial Classification,** or **SIC,** number to each type of business. SIC numbers vary in length depending on the specificity of the type of business, but the four-digit SIC number is used most often. The arrangement is hierarchical. For example, numbers beginning with "30" refer to rubber and miscellaneous plastics products manufacturers, "308" are manufacturers of miscellaneous plastics products, and "3084" are plastics pipe manufacturers. Students researching a particular industry or business will likely need to consult this manual to determine the appropriate SIC number. Companies that produce more than one product or service are assigned multiple SIC numbers.

Some other government documents important to business students include the *Federal Register,* which is published five days a week and lists rules, proposed rules, notices, new regulations, and proposed changes in regulations for each government agency. Regulation changes are then published in the *Code of Federal Regulations* (CFR), which is the official source of current federal government regulations. The major source for finding statistical information is the *American Statistics Index,* a subject index to U.S. government statistics.

These are just a few examples of the many government information sources that are of use to the business student. The GPO has recently started releasing many of its publications on CD-ROM and in other electronic formats. Many libraries have government-documents librarians who are available to assist students in searching for, locating, and using sources of government information.

Audiovisual Materials

Many libraries collect nonprint materials generally called audiovisual materials. Examples of audiovisual materials include videocassettes, filmstrips, cassette tape recordings, records, CD-ROMs, computer files, slides, photographs, laser disks, or other visual aids such as maps, globes, charts, or models. Audiovisual departments also have the necessary equipment to run or use these materials, including televisions, VCRs, tape and CD-ROM players, computers, slide and overhead projectors, record players, and laser disk players. The purpose of audiovisual departments are two-fold. First, they support classroom instruction. Instructors use these materials as part of the course curriculum in their classes. Second, these materials are available to students for their personal use or as aids in their studies.

The size and scope of audiovisual departments depend on the size of the library and the institution as well as the curriculum offered. Business students should find many audiovisual materials supporting their curriculum. Examples may include videocassettes illustrating personnel issues, how to make business presentations, or examples of selling techniques. Many libraries catalog their audiovisual materials in the on-line or card catalogs.

Business Information Sources

This section covers many of the major business information sources available in many college and university libraries offering business programs. Since thousands of sources of business information are available, only the major ones will be listed here. Consult a reference librarian for help in locating and using these materials in your library. Since some of these products are similar in scope, many libraries select only certain ones for their collections.

Indexes

ABI/Inform. This index, probably the most popular and comprehensive business index, is available on CD-ROM or through on-line databases. *ABI/Inform* indexes about 900 business and trade publications and includes abstracts for each entry. The database began in 1971, though the exact time coverage available in libraries varies depending on whether they have purchased or have access to the back files.

Accounting and Tax Index This index includes articles, books, and reports in all areas of accounting and taxation. Formerly entitled *Accountants' Index,* this index dates back to 1912.

Business Index This index, available on microfilm, CD-ROM, or on-line, covers more than 350 business periodicals and trade publications. It also indexes the *Wall Street Journal* and the business section of the *New York Times.* Indexing began in 1979.

Business Periodicals Index Dating back to 1958, this is the most popular paper index for business publications. The arrangement is by subject and author listings. BPI comes out in both monthly and quarterly updates, which cumulate into annual volumes. BPI covers about 350 publications.

F&S Index of Corporations and Industries This index is published in two sections, one arranged by products and industry type and the other by company name. This source, dating back to 1960, is a major index of trade publications. It also includes major newspapers, such as the *Wall Street Journal* and the *New York Times.*

Journal of Economic Literature This publication is a combination of both scholarly articles and an indexing source to economic literature. The indexing is broken down by a numerical classification scheme. This publication began in 1963 under a slightly different title.

New York Times Index This index, which began in 1851, is published semimonthly, with quarterly and annual updates. Subjects are arranged alphabetically, and entries are arranged beneath subjects in chronological order. Each entry includes the title of the article, a brief summary, and the date, section, page, and column number where the article appears.

Public Affairs Information Service Also known as *PAIS,* this index covers publications in political science and government, and includes coverage of materials from around the world. Many subjects are covered that will be of interest to business students, especially the coverage of international issues. Publication began in 1915.

Readers' Guide to Periodical Literature The first major indexing source, the *Readers' Guide* began publication in 1890. The coverage is primarily general-interest periodicals but includes such business publications as *Fortune, Forbes, Business Week,* and *Money.* While this source provides good coverage of these "popular" titles, researchers and students seeking more scholarly sources should also consult other indexes.

Social Sciences Index Published by the H.W. Wilson Co., the same company that produces the *Readers' Guide to Periodical Literature* and the *Business Periodicals Index,* the *Social Sciences Index* is also available in monthly, quarterly, and cumulative yearly volumes. While this index covers all areas in the social sciences, it will be of value to the business researcher because of its coverage of both economics and international business topics. This title began in 1974.

Wall Street Journal Index This index began publication in 1958 and is divided into two sections, a subject or general news section and a company name section. Each entry includes the title of the article, a brief summary, and the date, section, page, and column number where the article appears.

Please note that many indexes are available in multiple formats: print, CD-ROM, on-line sources, or through on-line catalogs. University Microforms International (UMI), publisher of the *ABI/Inform* database, also produces the *Periodical Abstracts* and *Newspaper Abstracts* databases. *Periodical Abstracts* is an index covering general-interest periodicals, and *Newspaper Abstracts* indexes major U.S. newspapers, including the *Wall Street Journal* and the *New York Times.*

MARKETING INFORMATION SOURCES Here, described briefly, are some sources of marketing information.

American Public Opinion Index Annual publication indexing thousands of public opinion surveys. Includes information on the size of the poll, the survey method, and the source and date of the poll.

Brands and Their Companies Annual publication listing brand names and their owners. Contains alphabetical and company name sections.

Broadcasting Yearbook Annual publication listing television and radio stations and cable television services and information on other businesses related to the broadcasting industry.

Consumer Expenditure Survey Annual publication listing survey data gathered by the U. S. Bureau of Labor Statistics.

Donnelly Demographics On-line database offering demographic statistics on population, household characteristics, age, employment, race, sex, income, and marital status.

Gallup Poll Monthly Monthly publication listing results from Gallup Polls. Gallup conducts more than 100 polls on a variety of topics each year.

Lifestyle Market Analyst Annual publication providing marketing data based on demographics and on consumer buying patterns. Includes sections arranged by geographic location, lifestyle interests, and household characteristics.

LNA/Arbitron Multi-Media Service Provides advertising expenditures by media type.

Market Profile Analysis Annual series of reports covering household characteristics, business statistics, new construction, and bank deposits by branch for each Metropolitan Statistical Area (MSA) in the country.

Market Share Reporter Annual publication providing market share information by SIC code, company name, and geographical region.

Public Opinion On-line On-line database of opinion polls gathered by the Roper Center for Public Opinion Research.

Simmons Study of Media and Markets Annual publication based on a survey of more than 20,000 U.S. households. This multivolume set includes information on usage of products by type and brand name and by demographic characteristics of the respondents; and media reports on television, radio, newspaper, and magazine characteristics, advertising data, and demographic characteristics of the viewers or readers.

Sourcebook of ZIP Code Demographics Annual publication providing demographic information by ZIP Code. Includes information on population, household income, age, and race and indexes of "market potential."

Standard Directory of Advertisers Directory of large companies' advertising information, including their advertising agencies, budgets, and names of executives. Available in either a classified or a geographic edition. The classified edition is arranged by product type and includes indexes by company and brand names. The geographic volume provides information arranged by city and state.

Standard Directory of Advertising Agencies Annual directory listing advertising agencies. Includes rankings by gross billings.

Standard Rate and Data Service Directories Publications providing advertising rates and policies for different media. Also provides information on submission requirements/deadlines, information on the frequency, editorial policy, and circulation of print media, and ratings and broadcast formats of television or radio programs. Major titles include *Business Publications Rates and Data, Newspaper Rates and Data, Network Television and Radio Rates and Data, Consumer Magazine and Agri-Media Rates and Data, Spot Radio Rates and Data,* and *Spot Television Rates and Data.*

Survey of Buying Power Data Service Annual publication providing statistics on consumer market data. Data of population, retail sales, and income are broken down by state, county, Metropolitan Statistical Area, and major cities.

Television and Cable Factbook Annual publication listing information on television stations and cable systems, including profiles and market share data.

COMPANY, INDUSTRY, AND INVESTMENT INFORMATION There are hundreds of sources available covering company, industry, or investment information. This section lists only the most popular sources found in many business libraries. Many of these sources are available in different formats, including print, CD-ROM, or on-line databases.

Annual Reports Many libraries maintain a file of annual reports or other filings of public companies with the Securities and Exchange Commission.

Barron's National Business and Financial Weekly Business periodical containing investment information.

Best's Insurance Reports Insurance company information and ratings.

Compact Disclosure CD-ROM product containing company information derived from filings with the Securities and Exchange Commission. Also available on-line.

Daily Stock Price Record Daily stock prices and numbers of shares traded. Published in three sections: The New York Stock Exchange, the American Stock Exchange, and the Over-the-Counter markets. Published quarterly.

Investor's Daily Articles, financial tables, and statistics providing investment advice and information. Published five times per week.

Manufacturing USA Guide to manufacturing industries in the United States. Published annually.

Moody's Bond Record Information on bond prices, dates issued, interest rates, and ratings. Published monthly.

Moody's Bond Survey News and advisory information for bonds. Published weekly.

Moody's Dividend Record Dividend information. Published semi-weekly.

Moody's Handbook of Common Stocks Summary descriptions and investment advice for common stocks. Published quarterly.

Moody's Manuals and News Reports Public company information including personnel, operations, and financial information. Published in eight sections according to type of company: Bank and Finance, Industrial, International, Municipal and Government, OTC Industrial, OTC Unlisted, Public Utility, and Transportation.

Morningstar Mutual Funds Weekly or monthly mutual funds information services.

Service Industries USA Guide to service industries in the United States. Published annually.

Standard and Poor's Bond Guide Monthly publication containing information on bonds.

Standard and Poors' Corporation Records Current company information and news reports.

Standard and Poor's Creditweek Covers bond and money markets.

Standard and Poor's Dividend Record Current dividend information.

Standard and Poor's Industry Surveys Quarterly publication that provides statistical data and forecasts for major industries.

Standard and Poor's Outlook Weekly newsletter containing articles and recommendations on the stock market.

Standard and Poor's Security Owner's Stock Guide Monthly publication providing summary stock information including price ranges, dividend information, corporate earnings, and summary balance sheets.

Standard and Poor's Stock Reports Quarterly publication summarizing the activities of companies. Published in three sections covering the New York Stock Exchange, the American Stock Exchange, and stocks traded Over-the-Counter.

U.S. Industrial Outlook Annual publication providing statistical and narrative information on more than 350 industries. Includes the current situation and the future outlook.

Value Line Investment Survey Weekly publication providing stock ratings, reports, and investment advice.

Weisenberger Investment Companies Investment guide to mutual funds, closed-end funds, and money market funds.

DIRECTORIES AND MANUALS Many business publications provide information about business organizations and the industries within which they operate. Some of these publications are listed here.

Directory of Corporate Affiliations Directory of corporations and their divisions, subsidiaries, and affiliates. Includes a volume on international corporate affiliations and a volume on private companies.

Dun's Business Rankings Rankings of public and private companies by state, SIC code, sales volume, and number of employees.

Dun's Principal International Businesses Guide to international companies by country name and SIC code.

Encyclopedia of Associations Guide to trade, labor, and professional organizations.

Million Dollar Directory Dun and Bradstreet's publication listing U.S. businesses by name, location, and SIC code.

Standard and Poor's Register of Corporations, Directors, and Executives Directory of American corporations that includes the name, address, executives, and SIC codes for each company.

State/Regional Manufacturing and Industrial Manuals There are several publishers producing manufacturing and industrial manuals by state or region.

Thomas Register of American Manufacturers Annual publication listing industrial products, services, company profiles, and catalogs.

Ward's Business Directory of U.S. Private and Public Companies Annual directory listing companies by name, geographic region, and sales figures.

STATISTICS SOURCES Numerous publications provide sources of statistical information. Some of the more important sources of statistical information related to business and economics are listed here.

Almanac of Business and Industrial Financial Ratios By Leo Troy. Annual compilation of business and financial ratios for 180 SIC codes.

American Statistics Index Subject index to government statistics.

Annual Statement Studies Published by Robert Morris Associates. Provides financial norms for more than 375 industry groups.

Census of Population and Housing Decennial publications summarizing statistics compiled by the U.S. Bureau of the Census.

County Business Patterns Annual source of detailed industry data at county and local levels. Data are arranged by SIC code. Published by the U.S. Bureau of the Census.

CRB Commodity Yearbook Annual publication providing statistics and narrative information on more than 100 commodities.

Current Business Reports Government publications covering wholesale and retail trade statistics.

Current Industrial Reports A series of about 100 reports on specific industries published monthly, quarterly, or annually by the U.S. Bureau of the Census.

Economic Census Publications Publications covering construction, manufacturing, retail trade, services, wholesale trade, transportation, and mineral industries. Contain statistics gathered by the U.S. Bureau of the Census. Published every five years.

Financial Studies of the Small Business Assets, liabilities, ratios, and sales analysis by type of business.

Industry Norms and Key Business Ratios Financial ratios for more than 800 industry groups.

Predicasts Basebook Annual publication providing current and historical industry statistics. Each volume contains fourteen years of historical statistics.

Standard and Poor's Statistical Service Current and historical information of industries, economic indicators, and securities.

Statistical Abstract of the United States Annual publication providing a wide array of statistical data gathered primarily from government sources.

Statistical Reference Index Guide to American statistical publications from private organizations and state government sources.

Statistics Sources Annual subject guide to publications, databases, and sources of unpublished statistical information.

Survey of Current Business Monthly publication listing many business statistics.

Locating Materials outside of the College or University Library

OCLC Researchers are often interested in finding materials that may not be available in their own library. One method of obtaining such materials is through interlibrary loan. Another method is to go directly to another library that owns the materials. Many libraries have areas of specialty, or areas in which they concentrate or try to acquire a comprehensive collection of materials on a given subject. Many libraries also have special collections, which can include rare materials, older works, autographed copies, or any other works or materials that are distinguished in some way from the rest of the collection and are considered valuable. One method of finding the holdings of other libraries is through the On-line Computer Library Center (OCLC), which is based in Columbus, Ohio.

OCLC maintains and operates a computer database that lists the holdings of thousands of libraries both in the United States and in other countries. The database consists of entries input by the member libraries. Each member library enters a holding on OCLC each time it acquires an additional work. Most reference departments have OCLC terminals in which reference librarians can look up the title of specific works and can determine which libraries own the materials. Recent developments allow both subject and key-word searches on the OCLC database. Consult with a reference librarian to learn more about using OCLC.

CONSORTIUMS Many libraries, in an effort to offer a broader range of materials to their users, form consortiums with other libraries, usually within the same geographical region. With these arrangements, patrons are able to use library resources or check out materials from member libraries if they are affiliated with one of the libraries. Some libraries form collection development policies with libraries in their consortium. For example, they may agree not to purchase the same periodicals. If libraries in a consortium all purchase different periodicals, the number of titles available for all users will increase.

Some libraries have sources for checking the holdings of libraries in their consortium, such as databases listing book holdings or printed lists of periodical holdings. See a reference librarian for more information on library consortiums.

INTERNET RESOURCES The Internet, the "information superhighway," is an interconnection of thousands of different computer systems in the United States and other countries. Information is stored at various sites and is accessible over the Internet, either by going directly to the source or through a "gopher," which entails getting to the information through menus or other search options. Information on the Internet can be downloaded or transferred through various commands to the user's own computer system. Among the thousands of sources of information available on the Internet, some of the more useful and popular sources related to business include the Economic Bulletin Board based at the University of Michigan; LC MARVEL, the Library of Congress gopher, which contains information on governmental agencies, Congress, current legislation, and a variety of other governmental information sources; and EDGAR, a site containing, among other things, information on public corporations from the Securities and Exchange Commission.

Many colleges and universities are connected to the Internet. Some offer their students access either through a computer center or through the library's on-line catalog. Students interested in accessing the Internet should consult with their computer center personnel or with a reference librarian. Many reference books are available that describe how to access and use the Internet. Beginners should consult one of these books to learn more about the Internet, how to conduct searches, and how to find information.

PUBLIC LIBRARIES Public libraries can be good sources of business information. Many large public libraries, such as the New York, Chicago, or Los Angeles public library systems, have collections that rival those of the major universities. Public libraries in medium-sized and smaller cities with substantial industrial and business economic bases usually have good business research collections. Many larger public libraries have separate business divisions that contain business information sources and other resources to aid the business researcher. Some public libraries also have departments to meet specific business-related needs, such as small-business development centers or patent/copyright information offices.

Appendix B

A Business Student's Guide to Professional and Trade Associations

ADVERTISING

Advertising and Marketing International Network
Sullivan, Higdon & Sink, Inc.
P.O. Box 11009
Wichita, KS 67202
(316) 263-0124

Advertising Research Foundation
641 Lexington Ave.
New York, NY 10022
(212) 751-5656

Affiliated Advertising Agencies International
2280 South Xanadu Way
Suite 300
Aurora, CO 80014
(303) 671-8551

American Advertising Federation
1101 Vermont Ave. NW
Suite 500
Washington, DC 20005
(202) 898-0089

American Association of Advertising Agencies
666 Third Ave., 13th Fl.
New York, NY 10017
(212) 682-2500

Association of National Advertisers
155 E. 44th St.
New York, NY 10017-4270
(212) 697-5950

Business/Professional Advertising Association
Metroplex Corporate Center
100 Metroplex Dr.
Edison, NJ 08817
(201) 985-4441

International Advertising Association
342 Madison, 20th Fl.
Suite 2000
New York, NY 10017
(212) 557-1133

International Federation of Advertising Agencies
1450 E. American Ln.
Suite 1400
Schaumburg, IL 60173-4973
(708) 330-6344

Newspaper Advertising Sales Association
405 Lexington Ave.
New York, NY 10174
(212) 661-6262

Outdoor Advertising Association of America
1850 M St.,
Suite 1040
Washington, DC 20036
(202) 833-5566

Point-of-Purchase Advertising Institute
66 N. Van Brunt St.
Englewood, NJ 07631
(201) 894-8899

Retail Advertising and Marketing Association, International
500 N. Michigan Ave.,
Suite 600
Chicago, IL 60601
(312) 245-9011

Society of Publication Designers
60 E. 42nd St.
Suite 721
New York, NY 10165
(212) 983-8585

Women in Advertising and Marketing
4200 Wisconsin Ave. NW
Suite 106-238
Washington, DC 20016
(310) 369-7400

Graphic Arts

American Institute of Graphic Arts
1059 Third Ave.
New York, NY 10021
(212) 752-0813

National Association of Schools of Art and Design
11250 Roger Bacon Dr.
Suite 21
Reston, VA 22090
(703) 437-0700

Insurance

Alliance of American Insurers
1501 Woodfield Rd.
Suite 400W
Schaumburg, IL 60173-4980
(708) 330-8500

American Association of Insurance Services
1035 S. York Rd.
Bensenville, IL 60106
(708) 595-3225

American Council of Life Insurance
1001 Pennsylvania Ave. NW
Washington, DC 20004-2599
(202) 624-2000
(800) 942-4242

American Insurance Association
1130 Connecticut Ave. NW
Suite 1000
Washington, DC 20036
(202) 828-7100

Council of Insurance Agents and Brokers
316 Pennsylvania Ave. SE
Suite 400
Washington, DC 20003
(202) 547-6616

General Agents and Managers Association
1922 F. St. NW
Washington, DC 20006
(202) 331-6088
(800) 345-2687

Independent Insurance Agents of America
127 S. Peyton
Alexandria, VA 22314
(703) 683-4422

Insurance Information Institute
110 William St.
New York, NY 10038
(212) 669-9200

Insurance Institute of America
720 Providence Rd.
Malvern, PA 19355-0716
(215) 644-2100

Life Insurance Marketing and Research Association
Box 208
Hartford, CT 06141
(203) 677-0033
(800) 235-4672

Mass Marketing Insurance Institute
3101 Broadway St.,
Suite 585
Kansas City, MO 64111
(816) 561-1920

National Association of Independent Insurers
2600 River Rd.
Des Plaines, IL 60018
(708) 297-7800

National Association of Insurance Brokers
1401 New York Ave. NW
Suite 720
Washington, DC 20005
(202) 628-6700

National Association of Insurance Women (International)
P.O. Box 4410
1847 East 15th St.
Tulsa, OK 74159
(918) 744-5195

National Association of Professional Insurance Agents
400 N. Washington St.
Alexandria, VA 22314
(703) 836-9340

Professional Insurance Mass-Marketing Association
4733 Bethesda Ave.
Suite 330
Bethesda, MD 20814-5228
(301) 951-1260

Logistics/Transportation

American Society of Transportation and Logistics
216 E. Church St.
Lock Haven, PA 17745

Council of Logistics Management
2803 Butterfield Rd.
Suite 380
Oak Brook, IL 60521
(312) 574-0985

National Institute of Packaging, Handling, and Logistics Engineers
6902 Lyle St.
Lanham, MD 20706-3454
(301) 459-9105

Marketing/Management

American Management Association
135 W. 50th St.
New York, NY 10020-1201
(212) 586-8100

American Marketing Association
250 S. Wacker Dr.
Suite 200
Chicago, IL 60606
(312) 648-0536

Bank Marketing Association
1120 Connecticut Ave. NW
Washington, DC 20036
(202) 663-5268
(800) 433-9013

Direct Marketing Association
11 W. 42nd St.
New York, NY 10036-8096
(212) 768-7277

Direct Marketing Creative Guild
516 Fifth Ave.
New York, NY 10036
(212) 213-0320

Financial Marketers Association
P.O. Box 14167
Madison, WI 53714
(608) 271-2664

Marketing Research Association
2189 Silas Deane Hwy.
Suite 5
Rocky Hill, CT 06067
(203) 257-4008

Marketing Science Institute
1000 Massachusetts Ave.
Cambridge, MA 02138
(617) 491-2060

National Association of Display Industries
133 W. 25th St., 4th Fl.
New York, NY 10001
(212) 989-7331

Promotional Marketing Association of America
257 Park Ave. S., 11th Fl.
New York, NY 10001
(212) 206-1100

Promotional Products Association International
3125 Skyway Circle N
Irving, TX 75038-3526
(214) 252-0404

Sales and Marketing Executives International
Statler Office Tower, No. 458
Cleveland, OH 44115
(216) 771-6650

Society for Marketing Professional Services
99 Canal Center Plaza
Suite 250
Alexandria, VA 22314
(703) 549-6117

Women in Advertising and Marketing
4200 Wisconsin Ave. NW
Suite 106-238
Washington, DC 20016
(301) 369-7400

MERCHANDISING/MANUFACTURING

General Merchandise Distributors Council
1275 Lake Plaza Dr.
Colorado Springs, CO 80906
(719) 576-4260

National Association of Manufacturers
1331 Pennsylvania Ave. NW
Suite 1500
Washington, DC 20004
(202) 637-3000

National Association of Service Merchandising
118 S. Clinton St.
Suite 300
Chicago, IL 60661-3628
(312) 876-9494

National Automatic Merchandising Association
20 N. Wacker Dr.
Chicago, IL 60606
(312) 346-0370

PURCHASING

American Purchasing Society
11910 Oak Trail Way
Port Richey, FL 34668
(813) 862-7998

National Association of Purchasing Management
2005 E. Centennial Circle
P.O. Box 22160
Tempe, AZ 85285-2160
(602) 752-6276
(800) 888-6276

National Purchasing Institute
7910 Woodmont Ave.
Suite 1430
Bethesda, MD 20814-3015
(301) 951-0108

PUBLIC RELATIONS

Public Relations Society of America
33 Irving Place, 3rd Fl.
New York, NY 10003-2376
(212) 995-2230

REAL ESTATE

National Association of Real Estate Brokers
1629 K St. NW
Suite 306
Washington, DC 20006
(202) 785-4477

National Association of Realtors
430 North Michigan Ave.
Chicago, IL 60611-4087
(312) 329-8200

Real Estate Brokerage Management Council
430 N. Michigan Ave.
Chicago, IL 60611-4092
(312) 670-3780

Real Estate Educators Association
1 Illinois Ctr., No. 200
111 E. Wacker Dr.
Chicago, IL 60601
(312) 616-8088

RETAILING

American Collegiate Retailing Association
Florida State University
318-C Sandels, R-86B
Tallahassee, FL 32306-2033
(904) 644-9883

ARMS—The Association of Retail Marketing Services
3 Caro Ct.
Red Bank, NJ 07701-2315
(908) 842-5070

International Mass Retail Association
1901 Pennsylvania Ave. NW, 10th Floor
Washington, DC 20006
(202) 861-0774

National Association of Retail Dealers of America
10 E. 22nd St.
Lombard, IL 60148
(708) 953-8950

National Retail Federation
701 Pennsylvania Ave. NW
Suite 710
Washington, DC 20004
(202) 783-7971

Retail Advertising and Marketing Association, International
500 N. Michigan Ave.
Suite 600
Chicago, IL 60601
(312) 245-9011

SALES

Association of Sales Administration Managers
Box 1356
Laurence Harbor, NJ 08879
(908) 264-7722

Council of Sales Promotion Agencies
750 Summer St.
Stanford, CT 06901
(203) 325-3911

Direct Selling Association
1776 K St. NW
Suite 600
Washington, DC 20006
(202) 293-5760

International Association of Sales Professionals
13 E. 37th St., 8th Fl.
New York, NY 10016-2821
(212) 683-9755

National Association of Display Industries
133 W. 25th St., 4th Fl.
New York, NY 10001
(212) 989-7331

National Association for Professional Saleswomen
1730 N. Lynn St.
Suite 502
Arlington, VA 22209
(800) 823-6277

National Association of Sales Training Executives
203 East Third St.
Sanford, FL 32771-1803
(407) 322-3364
(800) 752-7613

Sales and Marketing Executives International
Statler Office Tower, No. 458
Cleveland, OH 44115
(216) 771-6650

Women in Sales Association
8 Madison Ave.
P.O. Box M
Valhalla, NY 10595
(914) 946-3802

SECURITIES

Financial Marketers Association
P.O. Box 14167
Madison, WI 53714
(608) 271-2664

National Association of Securities Dealers (NASD)
345 Madison Ave.
New York, NY 10017
(212) 972-2010

National Association of Securities Professionals
1100 Peachtree St. NE
Suite 1660
Atlanta, GA 30309
(404) 875-2161

Securities Industry Association
120 Broadway
New York, NY 10271
(212) 608-1500

Security Traders Association
1 World Trade Center
Suite 4511
New York, NY 10048
(212) 524-0484

TRAVEL

American Society of Travel Agents
1101 King St.
Alexandria, VA 22314
(703) 739-2782

Association of Retail Travel Agents
1745 Jefferson Davis Hwy.
Suite 300
Arlington, VA 22202-3402
(703) 413-2222

Association of Travel Marketing Executives
P.O. Box 43563
Washington, DC 20010
(202) 232-7107

Institute of Certified Travel Agents
148 Lindon St.
P.O. Box 812059
Wellesley, MA 02181-0012
(617) 237-0280
(800) 542-4282

Travel Industry Association of America
2 Lafayette Center
1133 21st. St. NW
Suite 800
Washington, DC 20036
(202) 293-1433

WHOLESALING/DISTRIBUTION

American Warehousemens Association
1300 W. Higgins
Suite 111
Park Ridge, IL 60069
(708) 292-1891

American Wholesale Marketers Association
1128 16th St.
Washington, DC 20036
(202) 463-2124

General Merchandise Distributors Council
1275 Lake Plaza Dr.
Colorado Springs, CO 80906
(719) 576-4260

National Association of Wholesaler-Distributors
1725 K. St. NW
Washington, DC 20006
(202) 872-0885

Appendix C

A Business Student's Guide to Case Analysis

Gary White
Dale M. Lewison

Introduction

What is the best method for learning about marketing strategies, tactics, and techniques? Although the lecture is probably the most frequently used teaching method, other methods often prove more effective in providing useful insights into analyzing and handling actual business situations. The **case analysis method** is an excellent tool for learning about real business situations and gaining experience in problem solving and decision making. In a case analysis, students are presented with actual business problems and are asked to assume the role of the marketing manager or some other decision maker. The case analysis method requires that students analyze the facts of the case, consider possible alternative courses of action, choose the most appropriate course of action, and justify the decision.

The case analysis method gives students the opportunity to think critically, to apply the principles and analytical techniques they have learned, and make judgments when formulating opinions and making final decisions. In addition, the case analysis method improves communication skills and gives students practice in making decisions when there is less-than-perfect information available. This reality-based learning process is directed at better preparing students for the problems they will face as marketing managers.

A **case** or **case study** can be thought of as a business story problem or a description of a specific company's situation. A more complete definition is

> A case is typically a record of a business issue which actually has been faced by business executives, together with surrounding facts, opinions, and prejudices upon which the executives had to depend. These real and particularized cases are presented to students for considered analysis, open discussion, and final decision as to the type of action which should be taken.[1]

Cases were first used in higher education by the Harvard Business School in the 1920s.

Business cases are drawn from problems experienced by managers during the everyday operation of their companies. The information presented in cases are the circumstances managers had to work with at the time. In order to simulate reality, case information typically is flawed and limited because actual case information was imperfect and incomplete.

Studying cases allows students to put their knowledge of business and marketing into practice. Students are able to take the facts and concepts they have learned from the classroom and textbooks and apply them to real situations. It also allows students to use their individual practical experiences by applying them to different problem-solving situations. Students thus learn to solve problems on their own rather than relying on the professor or the textbook to give them the solutions. The case method also allows students to develop their skills in analyzing facts and assumptions, organizing and developing their ideas into structured concepts, and formulating opinions that can be supported and justified. Cases also further develop reasoning and logic skills as well as strengthen communication skills.

Discussing cases in the classroom setting provides students with an opportunity to develop skills in exchanging ideas and to interact with others who may have differing opinions. Classroom discussions are often led by the students rather than the professor. Students are thus able to analyze and constructively criticize other opinions and to learn from other students in the class. They also learn that there is not usually just one "right" answer and will instead learn to focus on the analysis of the problem in order to determine one or more appropriate courses of action.

In summary, the case method of teaching requires students to take an active role in the learning process. Students are asked to evaluate the facts given in the case and to come to a decision. This method gives students the opportunity to handle the problems and decisions that business managers face in the business world.

Case Analysis

Case analysis is a process. As such, analyzing a case problem is best accomplished by following a set of procedural approaches and by using a proven organizational structure.

Case Analysis Procedures

One possible approach to the logical consideration of a case problem involves the following procedural steps:

- *First Reading*—A quick reading of the entire case in order to gain a total perspective of the case and to get a general idea of the issues that are addressed in the case.

- *Second Reading*—A careful reading of the case with the goal of gaining a more detailed understanding of the facts of the case and a better grasp of specific concerns.

- *Note Taking*—Record impressions of central problems and related issues. Also register the facts and data relevant to each problem and issue.

- *Interpreting*—Decipher the meaning of all facts and data, and verify their relevance to the case problem.

- *Analyzing*—Identify the nature of the relationships that exist between case facts/data and case problems/issues. Describe the implications of these relationships, and draw conclusions as to their actual and potential impact.

- *Supporting*—Discover and integrate any relevant information from sources outside the case (library searches, field investigations, and personal experiences). Use appropriate outside information in support of interpretations and the analytical results.

- *Identifying*—Distinguish various alternative solutions to the case problem(s), and describe the pros/cons, strengths/weaknesses, advantages/disadvantages, or costs/benefits of each viable alternative.

- *Recommending*—Select an alternative solution, and defend recommendations by developing a list of justifications for the chosen action.

- *Implementing*—Describe how case recommendations might be implemented, and provide some prediction of likely outcomes.

- *Reporting*—Develop the appropriate written or oral presentations. Carefully proof the written report and rehearse the oral presentation.

CASE ANALYSIS STRUCTURE

Many different ways to organize and present a case analysis exist. Students should therefore seek the guidance of their professor regarding any specific requirements, expectations, or preferences in preparing and presenting their cases. The following format represents a traditional structure for case organization:

- *Part I* The Situation: Review and Analysis
- *Part II* The Problem: Identification and Description
- *Part III* The Alternatives: Recognition and Evaluation

❏ *Part IV* The Recommendation: Decision and Justification

❏ *Part V* The Implementation: Application and Assessment

THE SITUATION: REVIEW AND ANALYSIS The first section of a case report is comprised of a review and analysis of the situational circumstances that form the background for the case problem. A review and analysis of the situation typically involves the consideration and examination of some or all of the following factors:

I. Marketing Plans

    A. Strategic Marketing Plans

        1. Organizational Mission

        2. Market Share and Industry Growth Rate of Strategic Business Unit(s)

        3. Industry Attractiveness and Business Strengths of Strategic Business Unit(s)

        4. Organizational Opportunities for Growth and Restructuring

    B. Strategic Marketing Plans

        1. Marketing Goals and Objectives

        2. Marketing Strengths and Weaknesses of Strategic Business Unit(s)

        3. Marketing Opportunities and Threats of Strategic Business Unit(s)

        4. Marketing Strategies for Differentiation and Positioning

II. Marketing Situations

    A. Environmental Analysis

        1. Population and Demographic Trends

        2. Economic and Competitive Forces

        3. Social and Cultural Influences

        4. Political and Legal Issues

        5. Scientific and Technological Advances

    B. Consumer Analysis

        1. Psychological Influences

        2. Personal Influences

3. Social Influences

4. Situational Influences

C. Competitor Analysis

1. Competitive Levels

2. Competitive Forms

3. Competitive Relations

4. Competitive Advantages

5. Competitive Strategies

D. Market Analysis

1. Market Segments

2. Market Targets

3. Market Positions

III. Marketing Decisions

A. Product Decisions

1. Product-Mix Management

2. Product Life Cycle Management

3. New Product Development

B. Distribution Decisions

1. Marketing Channel Design

2. Marketing Channel Conflict

3. Marketing Channel Control

4. Marketing Channel Cooperation

C. Promotion Decisions

1. Communication Mix

2. Advertising Program

3. Personal Selling Effort

4. Direct Marketing Effort

5. Sales Promotion Incentives

6. Public Relations Effort

D. Price Decisions

1. Price Determinants

        2. Pricing Methods

        3. Pricing Strategies

IV. Marketing Actions

    A. Marketing Program Implementation

        1. Marketing Organization

        2. Marketing Execution

    B. Marketing Program Control

        1. Program Monitoring

        2. Program Modification

A careful analysis of the situation will provide the proper context for identifying and describing the case problem. Reviewing the case situation should provide the case analyst with a sufficient understanding of the organization, its operating environments, and its marketing programs. Students must be careful not to simply rehash or summarize the facts in the case. Students need to *analyze* the facts and relate what they mean to the company and to the situation that the company faces.

THE PROBLEM: IDENTIFICATION AND DESCRIPTION The second part of the case report deals with the question "What are the major issues and concerns to be addressed in the case analysis?" A clear and precise problem statement for each issue must be formulated, and the relative importance of each problem must be determined and expressed. The old adage "a problem well defined is a problem half solved" is quite true when conducting case studies. A case that is either poorly or incorrectly defined will result in an analysis that is weak or wrong.

The number of case problems and their importance vary considerably from one case study to another. A case may have one major problem and several minor ones or several problems that are equally important. Case problems occur in many different forms. A case problem may be

1. A threat that requires attention

2. An opportunity that needs to be explored

3. A negative situation that needs to be corrected

Students should use this section of the case analysis to describe the nature of each problem and to relate it to the organization and its operating environment. This will provide the analyst with the appropriate background information and the context for analyzing the alternative solutions or courses of action.

The problem or problems may be easily identified or they can be disguised. When problems are not explicitly stated, they must be identified or derived from problem symptoms. For example, the student may be inclined to identify declining sales and customer loyalty as the problem when in fact they are only symptoms of a much larger problem—an inappropriate pricing strategy or an ineffective distribution system. Distinguishing problems from symptoms can be a difficult task.

Some case studies present questions or situational statements at the end of the case. These questions and statements may or may not be an appropriate guide to the case problem. Sometimes they represent an adequate description of the problem, while at other time they are simply presented as "food for thought" that represents additional information to be used in discovering the case problem. It may be advisable to discuss with the class instructor how these questions and statements are to be used.

THE ALTERNATIVES: RECOGNITION AND EVALUATION With a correct and complete description of the problem, the next step is to recognize the range of possible solutions or courses of action that might be appropriate for each problem. These alternatives should be realistic choices that the organization could make to effectively handle the problem or situation. Once again, students must be aware that there is rarely one "right" answer, but there may be a best alternative for a company's particular situation. Identifying the alternative solutions requires both a thorough understanding of the company and its situation and the ability to think creatively. Some suggestions for identifying possible courses of action include brainstorming with classmates, conducting a literature search to discover how other firms have handled similar situations, or speaking with experts or businesspeople who may have encountered a similar problem.

Many possible alternative solutions to a given problem or situation usually exist. The case analyst usually lists the major alternative solutions to each problem. Depending on the number of problems and their importance, one rule of thumb is that the analyst should consider three to five alternatives for each problem. One of the most common methodologies for evaluating alternative solutions is to organize and compare each alternative by constructing a list of the pros and cons, strengths and weaknesses, advantages and disadvantages, or costs and benefits of each solution. Another common method of alternative evaluation is the weighted-rating score, determined by the following:

1. Constructing a list of factors important to the solution of the problem

2. Developing a weighing system that indicates the relative importance of each factor—such as 3 = major importance, 2 = important, 1 = minor importance

3. Creating a rating scale by which each alternative solution can be evaluated on each evaluation factor—4 = excellent, 3 = good, 2 = fair, 1 = poor

4. Calculating a weighted-rating score for each alternative solution on each factor by multiplying the factor weight times the factor rating

5. Summing all weighted-rating scores

6. Rank-ordering each alternative solution on the basis of its total weighted-rating score

THE RECOMMENDATION: DECISION AND JUSTIFICATION   Every case analysis must include a recommendation as to the course of action to be taken. Even taking no action is a course of action. Given the available information and the student's analysis of that information, decide which alternative(s) can be recommended as an appropriate solution to the identified problem? Students must choose the course of action that they think is most appropriate and should describe clearly and persuasively why their choice is the best alternative. The choice should be explained logically by justifying the decision with supporting facts from the case or from the outside reference sources. Although there is no one "right" answer, students must be able to convince the reader that they made the appropriate choice.

THE IMPLEMENTATION: APPLICATION AND ASSESSMENT   Choosing the most appropriate course of action is only half of the solution. Students must also present a plan to implement the solution. The process of thinking through the implementation of the solution will alert students to any pitfalls of the plan, such as lack of funds, time constraints, or other obstacles to implementation. The final section of the written case analysis should include a discussion of the implementation plan for the chosen solution. A cost estimate should be included, and the plan should answer questions concerning *what* and *when* it will occur. A forecast of the outcome of the implementation might also be appropriate. Sometimes a cost/benefit analysis of implementing the solution will aid in convincing the reader that the choice is an appropriate solution. A checklist for preparing a written case analysis is given in Figure C-1.

CASE ANAYLSIS PITFALLS

Analyzing cases is a time-consuming activity requiring a lot of thinking and preparation. Students encounter some common problems when doing a case analysis. An awareness and understanding of these problems helps students avoid them when studying a case.

Probably the most common mistake is to try to recommend a solution without first thoroughly analyzing the problem or situation. Students should have knowledge of all of the relevant facts and circumstances affecting the company, as well as a good understanding of the problem, before identifying possible solutions. Some students tend to choose their solution before thoroughly thinking through the problem or thinking about all of the possible alternative solutions.

FIGURE C-1

GUIDELINES FOR PREPARING A WRITTEN REPORT

1. Start with a good outline that will force you to organize your thoughts.
2. Review your notes from your classes in written business communication and become familiar with the use of the various levels of headings in writing your report.
3. Do not write your report in a first-person format.
4. Double-space your report, and use lists where appropriate to emphasize your points.
5. Watch your margins, especially when you have to bind your report for submission to your instructor.
6. Buy a good style manual and follow it. Consistency in style is a "must."
7. Avoid unnecessary footnotes, and don't use content footnotes. If the material is important enough to be a part of the paper, include it in the body.
8. Start each paragraph with a good topic sentence that captures the essence of the paragraph.
9. Use tables and charts to communicate your materials.
10. Make sure you include an explanation for each chart and table. An explanation in the report should precede each table or chart.
11. Avoid overoutlining your material. Keep in mind, also, that you should have at least two subheadings for each major heading.
12. Remember that tables and charts alone do not provide analysis. Rather, write your report so you establish the significance of the tables and charts you use. Finally, don't make your tables or charts the subject of a sentence. Rather, introduce them incidentally. Whenever possible, use action verbs and the active voice as well as simple, short words.
13. Indicate the source of your information when you use someone else's material.
14. Clearly state your assumptions whenever you have to make them.
15. Strive for objectivity throughout.
16. Include a bibliography of source material.
17. Avoid plagiarism. If you are quoting or closely paraphrasing someone else's material, indicate your source in a footnote. Be sure to place quotation marks around all materials that you are quoting directly.
18. Remember to include a summary and recommendation section. Consider itemizing your points here, but do not go into too much detail. Also, combine your points whenever it is appropriate to do so.
19. Stick to the length limitations established by your instructor. You may find, for example, that your report can be no longer than one single-spaced page. Such a restriction will force you to organize your thoughts very carefully.

SOURCE: J. Barry Mason, Morris L. Mayer, and Hazel F. Ezell, *Cases and Problems in Contemporary Retailing* (Dame Publications, Inc., 1992), 22.

Many students complain that there is not enough information to choose a solution. Students should be aware, however, that the information that they have is the same information that the marketer had in the real situation. One goal of the case analysis is to provide students with an opportunity to study and handle real-world problems. They should be aware that there is rarely complete or perfect information available in the real world.

Students often think that there is one "right" answer and sometimes tend to either spend too much time searching for this one answer or too much time trying to justify what they think is the correct answer. Remember that there are usually several alternatives that might be considered reasonable solutions. Students need to analyze all of these alternatives and logically choose the one that they think is *most* appropriate.

Another common pitfall is to underanalyze the case. Many students simply rehash the facts from the case without providing any analysis or insight into how those facts impact the case problem or its potential solutions. The goal of the case analysis is to analyze and interpret the information given in an effort to identify an appropriate course of action. Students must be able to relate the facts in the case to these possible solutions. Simply rehashing the facts, without any analysis, will usually not be adequate to support the chosen solution.

Many students also make the mistake of spending too much time analyzing the case as if the facts or the situation were different. For example, they may recommend a solution based on something that does not exist, such as "I'd do this, if the firm had spent more on advertising." Students must analyze the facts of the case as they exist and should recommend a course of action based on these facts. The facts in the case have already happened, and they cannot be changed in order to make the case analysis easier.

The tendency to overgeneralize case solutions must be avoided. The course of action to be taken must be clear and specific. Do not use a statement such as "I'd spend more on advertising." Instead, use a specific statement, such as "I would increase advertising expenditures by $650,000 per year." Remember to provide information to support these recommendations. Sometimes, solutions are offered that are not realistic given the circumstances. Students must make sure that their recommendations are realistic and utilize the facts provided in the case.

CONCLUDING REMARKS

Good case analyses require much time and effort. Students are required to take an active approach to learning when studying cases and should be adequately prepared for each class session so that they are ready to contribute to the classroom discussion. Case analyses provide students with an opportunity to study situations that have occurred in the real business world. They also provide students with an opportunity to develop creative thinking and logic skills. Devoting a proper amount of time and effort to studying these cases will provide students with a valuable learning experience that is not usually available in the traditional lecture course.

ENDNOTE

1. Charles I. Gragg, "Because Wisdom Can't Be Told," *Harvard Alumni Bulletin* (October 19, 1940).

Credit List

	Figure Number	
Chapter 1	Figure 1–4	Adapted from Walter Van Wareshoot and Christophe Van den Bulte, "The 4P Classification of the Marketing Mix Revisited," *Journal of Marketing*, Vol. 56, No. 4, October 1992, 90. Reprinted with permission of the American Marketing Association.
	Figure 1–6	"The Four Categories of Relational Exchanges", Adapted from Shelby D. Hunt and Robert M. Morgan, "Relationship Marketing in the Era of Network Competitions," *Marketing Management*, Vol, 3, No. 1, 1994, p. 22. Reprinted with the permission of the American Marketing Association.
Chapter 2	Figure 2–5	"PIMS Databank Items," Strategic Planning Institute, Cambridge, Massachusetts.
Chapter 3	Figure 3–4	"The Right Service," from Dale M. Lewison, *Retailing*, 5th edition, p. 29. Copyright © 1994. Reprinted by permission of Prentice Hall, Upper Saddle River, New Jersey.
Chapter 5	Figure 5–5	"Selected Examples of Syndicated Marketing Intelligence Sources," Reprinted by permission from Chales D. Schewe, *Marketing: Principles and Strategies*, p. 107. Random House, 1987.
	Figure 5–6	"Selected Marketing Intelligence Offerings of the Most Popular On-Line Vendors". Reprinted by permission from Charles W. Lamb, Jr., Joseph F. Heiser, Jr. and Carl McDaniel, *Principles of Marketing*, p. 185. Cincinnati: South-Western Publishing Co., 1992.
	Figure 5–8	"Comparison od Surveys," from William F. Schoell and Joseph P. Guiltinan, *Marketing*, 6/e, p. 116. Copyright © 1995. Adapted by permission of Prentice Hall, Upper Saddle River, New Jersey.
	Figure 5–9	"Types of Probability and Nonprobability Samples," Dale M. Lewison, *Retailing*, 5th Edition, p. 680. Copyright © 1994. Reprinted by permission of Prentice Hall, Upper Saddle River, New Jersey.
	Figure 5–10	"Using the Observation Method," Dale M. Lewison, *Retailing*, 5th Edition, p. 675. Copyright © 1994. Reprinted by permission of Prentice Hall, Upper Saddle River, New Jersey.
	Figure 5–11	"Internal Records", Donald S. Tull and Lynn R. Kahle, *Marketing Management*, p. 234. Copyright © 1990. Reprinted by permission of Prentice Hall, Upper Saddle River, New Jersey.
Chapter 6	Figure 6–4	American Marketing Association, Code of Ethics. Courtesy of the American Marketing Association.
	Figure 6–7	William Lazer, Priscilla La Barbera, James M. MacLachlan, and Allen E. Smith, "Marketing 2000 and Beyond," p. 16. Chicago: American Marketing Association, 1990. Reprinted by permission.
Chapter 7	Figure 7–9	"Characteristics of Organizational Markets," from Charles W. Lamb, Jr., Joseph F. Heiser, Jr. and Carl McDaniel, *Principles of Marketing*, p. 115. Cincinnati: South-Western Publishing Co., 1992. Reprinted by permission.

CREDIT LIST

	Figure 7–10	Richard Lancioni and Terence H. Oliva, "Penetrating Purchaser Personality," *Marketing Management,* Vol 3, No. 4, p. 24. Reprinted with permission of the American Marketing Association.
CHAPTER 8	Figure 8–4	"A Competitor Analysis Template," reprinted by permission from Peter R. Dickson, *Marketing Management,* (Fort Worth, TX: The Dryden Press, 1994), pp. 140–141.
	Figure 8–5	David B. Montgomery and Charles B. Weinberg, "Toward Strategic Intelligence Systems," *Journal of Marketing,* Vol. 43, No. 3, (Fall 1979), p. 46. Reprinted with permission of the American Marketing Association.
	Figure 8–7	Adapted from Michael E. Porter, *Competitive Advantage: Creating and Sustaining Superior Performance,* (New York: The Free Press 1985). Reprinted with permission of Simon & Schuster, Inc.
	Figure 8–8	Adapted from Phillip Kotler and Ravi Singh, "Marketing Warfare in the 1980s," *Journal of Business Strategy,* Winter 1981, pp. 31–40.
	Figure 8–9	Adapted from Phillip Kotler and Ravi Singh, "Marketing Warfare in the 1980s," *Journal of Business Strategy,* Winter 1981, pp. 31–40.
CHAPTER 9	Figure 9–6	"Geodemography: Tracking Where Customers Live," *STORES ,* November 1989, pp. 42–43. Reprinted with permission from *STORES Magazine.* Copyright © 1989 by NRF Enterprises, Inc.
	Figure 9–7	"Using ZIP Codes to Segement Customers," *STORES* November 1989, pp. 42–43. Reprinted by permission of *STORES Magazine.* Copyright © 1989 by NRF Enterprises, Inc.
	Figure 9–8	Adapted from Penny Gill, "New VALS 2 Values and Lifestyles Segmentation," Stores , November 1989, p. 35. Reprinted by Permission of *STORES Magazine.* Copyright © 1989 by NRF Enterprises, Inc.
	Figure 9–12	"A Perceptual Map of Department Store Industry," adapted from Dale M. Lewison, *Retailing,* Fifth Edition p. 52. Copyright © 1994. Reprinted by permission of Prentice Hall, Upper Saddle River, New Jersey.
CHAPTER 10	Figure 10–11	"Sources of Innovation," reprinted by permission from Peter R. Dickson, *Marketing Management,* p. 299. The Dryden Press, Fort Worth, TX 1994.
	Figure 10–13	"New Product Failures," from Glen L. Urban, John R. Hauser, and Nikhilesh Dholakia, *Essentials of New Product Management,* pp. 37–38, Prentice Hall. Copyright © 1987. Adapted by permission of Prentice Hall, Upper Saddle River, New Jersey.
CHAPTER 12	Figure 12–10	"Advantages and Disadvantages of Selected Media Alternatives," reprinted by permission of the author from William H. Bolen, *Advertising,* 2nd Edition, pp. 601–602. John Wiley & Sons, 1984.
	Figure 12–12	"Closing Techniques," from Dale M. Lewison, *Retailing,* 5th edition, p. 565. Copyright © 1994. Reprinted by permission of Prentice Hall, Upper Saddle River, New Jersey.
CHAPTER 15	Figure 15–2	From an exhibit in "Strategy in Different Service Businesses," by Dan R.E. Thomas, *Harvard Business Review,* July/August 1978. Reprinted by permission of *Harvard Business Review.* Copyright © 1978 by the President of Fellows of Harvard University. All rights reserved.
	Figure 15–3	"The Expected Service/Perceived GAP Model," from Dale M. Lewison, *Retailing,* 5th Edition, pp. 792–793. Copyright © 1994. Reprinted by permission of Prentice Hall, Upper Saddle River, New Jersey.
	Figure 15–5	Ruel K. Kahler, *International Marketing,* 5th ed., p. 343. Reprinted by permission of South-Western Publishing Company.
APPENDIX A	Figure A–1	J. Barry Mason, Morris L. Mayer, Hazel F. Ezell, *Cases and Problems in Contemporary Retailing,* Dame Publications, Inc., 1992, p. 22.

INDEX

ABCs of positioning, 59
Abell, Derek F., 61
ABI/Inform, 412, 417
Ability to buy, 11
Above-market pricing, 345
Absolut bottle, 312
Absolute standards, 120
Abstracts, 413
"Accelerator principle," 156
Acclaim Entertainment, 251
Accounting and Tax Index, 412
Action stage, 298
Activities, 145–146
Adaptive organization, 361
Administered vertical
    marketing system, 290–291
Adolph Coors, 308
Adoption, 253
Adoption control, 287–288
Adoption process, 251
Ad valorem tariff, 403
Advertising
  creative campaign, 308–316
  described, 299–300
  management of, 316–317
  types of, 305–308
Advertising agency, 317
Advertising associations,
    427–428
Advocacy advertising, 308
Aesthetic features, 57, 221–222
Aesthetics, 392
Affective component, 144
African-Americans, 121, 123
Age profiles, 111–114
Agins, Teri, 22, 162, 256
AIDA model, 297–298
Aided recall test, 316
Alamo, 193
Alday, Ramon J., 54
Alexander, Keith L., 215, 293
Allowances, 346–347
Alternative evaluation stage, 138
American Airlines, 179

American Brands, 32
American Express, 308, 388
American Greetings, 280
American Marketing
    Association (AMA), 89,
    120, 122–123, 377
American Statistics Index, 416
Anacin, 168
Analytical models, 84, 102
Analytical research, 100
Anders, George, 353
Anderson, Stephanie, 44
Anheuser-Busch, 388
Anne Klein II, 351
Annual marketing plan, 64–67
Antecedent states, 153
Antitrust legislation, 127
Apple Computer Inc., 69
Approaching, 320
Arbitration control, 287
Armani, George, 38
Arm's length price, 403
Aroused tensions, 139
Art, 312
Asian culture, 123
Aspirational group, 150
Assessing planning stage, 21
Association information
    sources, 87–88
Assurance, 382
A. T. Cross Co., 11
At-market pricing, 345
Attack strategies, 181–182
Attention stage, 298
Attitudes, 143–144, 392–393
Attributes (identifying), 60
Audi-visual materials, 417
Augmented product, 222
Autonomic, 152
Average total cost, 339
Avis, 193, 239
Avon Products, Inc., 404
Awareness, 298
A/X, 38

Babej, Marc E., 257
Baby boomers, 113
Baby boomlets, 111–112
Bacardi, 238
Backward integration, 39, 292
Bait leaders, 352
Baker, Stephen, 293
Ballon, Marc, 189
Banks, Howard, 179, 188
Barnathan, Joyce, 407
Barnes & Noble, 243
Barnes, Nora Ganim, 407
Barrett, Amy, 354
Barter transactions, 10, 336
Basic communication model,
    296–297
Basing-point pricing, 350
"Battle of the brands," 240
Bayer Select lines, 168
BCG industry-growth/market-
    share matrix, 31–33
Beck, Melinda, 131
Behavioral component, 144
**Behavioristic segmentation,
    199, 203**
Beliefs, 119, 144, 392
Belk, Russell W., 153, 162
Below-market pricing, 345–346
Ben & Jerry's, 52–53
Benefits,
  described, 12
  delineating, 60
Benefit segmentation, 203
Bennett, Amanda, 131
Bennett, Peter, 406
Berman, Phyllis, 79, 215, 256, 332
Bernstein, Aaron, 131
Berry, Jonathan, 45, 132, 214, 332,
    354, 407
Berry, Leonard L., 371, 377,
    378, 406
Berss, Marcia, 61
Best Buy, 52, 346
B.F. Goodrich, 43

451

Bibliography, 412
Bird, Laura, 162
Blimps (advertising), 313
Bloomingdale's, 169, 213, 214
Bolton, Ruth N., 104
Books-A-Million, 243
Boone, Louis E., 61
Borders Books and Music, 167, 243
Boroughs, Don L., 132
Boston Consulting Group (BCG), 31
Boyd, Harper W., Jr., 188
Bradford's Directory, 89
Brain drain, 393
Brand, 235–236
Brand acceptance, 237
Brand equity, 238
Brand image, 237
Brand licensing, 239
Brand loyalty, 237
Brand mark, 236
Brand name, 236
Brand preference, 237
Brand recognition, 237
Brandt, Richard, 188
Break-even analysis, 344
Break-even point, 344
Break-even point return of investment, 344–345
Brelin, Harvey K., 371
Bremner, Brian, 408
Bridge pricing, 351
Brimelow, Peter, 215
Brinker International, 40
Bristol-Meyers Squibb, 180
Bristol-Myers, 273
British Petroleum, 154
Broadcast media, 313
Bryd, Veronica, 407
Budiansky, Stephen, 131
Budweiser, 151, 238
Buffett, Jimmy, 220
Building option, 41–42
Bulkeley, William M., 61
Bureaucratic organizations, 361
Burns, Greg, 44, 214, 292, 293, 333
Burrows, Peter, 44, 333
Business analysis, 249–250
Business cycle, 116–117
Business directories/manuals, 422–423
Business Index, 418

Business information sources, 417–424
Business opportunities, 37–43
Business Periodicals Index, 86, 412, 418
Business planning, 19
Business strengths, 33–35
Business-to-business marketing, 152
Buy classes, 158
Buyer, 151
Buyer's market, 15
Buying behavior, 134
Buying center, 157–158
Buy or no-buy decision, 138
Bypass attack strategy, 183–184
Byrne, John A., 371, 407
Byrnes, Nanette, 132, 162, 333

Cable and Wireless, 30
Cadet Uniform Services, 367
Callaway Golf, 193
Call number systems, 410–412, 414
Calvin Klein Classification, 351
Caminiti, Susan, 131, 215, 257
Campbell's, 238
Canon, 53
Cantalupo, James, 402
Capital goods, 231
Captive pricing, 351
Carbone, Lewis P., 162
Carey, John, 407
Carey, Susan, 44
Carlton, Jim, 255, 353
Cartier, 272
Case analysis method
described, 438–439
pitfalls of, 445, 447
procedures of, 439–440
structure of, 440–445
written report guidelines for, 446
Case/case study, 438–439
Cash cows, 31
"Cash traps," 32
Catalogs, 328
Category competition, 167
Category killer, 167
Causal research, 93–94
CD-ROM, 412–413, 416, 419, 421
Census of Manufactures, 416
Census of Retail Trade, 416
Census of Service Industries, 416
Census of Wholesale Trade, 416

Centralized organization, 360
Century 21, 239
Chakravarty, Subrata N., 188
Chandler, Susan, 162, 256
Chang, Helen, 407
Channel captain, 285–288
Channel complexity, 273
Channel conflict, 282-285
Channel flows, 262–264
Channel integration, 288
Channel length, 274–278
Channel multiplicity, 273
Channel power, 286
Channel scope, 28
Channels partners, commitment to, 29
Channel structure, 268
Channel width, 270–273, 278
Chevrolet, 56
Chevy, 179
Chinni, Dante, 131
Christian Dior, 226
Chrysler Corp., 29, 68, 235, 241, 342, 391, 405
Churbuck, David C., 132
Circuit City, 167, 187
Citation, 413
Classical conditioning, 142
"Clienteling," 137
Closed-end question, 97–98
Closing the sale, 322–323
Closing signals, 322–323
Cobra Golf, 12, 193, 300
Coca-Cola, 53, 184–185, 301, 390, 396
Code of ethics, 119–121
Code of Federal Regulations (CFR), 416
Coercive power, 286
Coexistence, 176
Cognitive component, 144
Cognitive dissonance, 139
Cognitive learning, 142–143
Cohen, Nancy, 255
Coleman, Richard P., 162
Colgate-Palmolive, 71, 181
Collins, Michael P., 162
Collusion, 177
Combination branding, 239
Combination strategy, 304
Command economies, 116
Commercial information sources, 88–89
Commercialization, 246, 251

Index

Common Market, 398
Communicate claims, 60
Communication difficulties, 285
  See also Marketing communications
Communities commitment to, 29
Company directories/manuals, 422–423
Company information sources, 421–423
Compaq Computer Corp., 370
Comparative advertising, 307–308
Competencies scope, 29
Competing for the Future (Hamel and Prahalad), 164
Competition
  advantages in, 177–181
  conditions for, 339–340
  forms of, 168–171
  gathering information for, 171–176
  levels of, 166–168
  relations within, 176–177
  strategies used within, 181–187
Competition-based pricing, 345–346
Competitive advantage, 177–181
Competitive advertising, 307
Competitive environment, 115
Competitive position objectives, 68–70
Competitive price comparisons, 341
Competitive pricing, 349–350
Competitive scope, 28
Competitive strategies, 181–186
Competitor analysis, 74
Competitor analysis model, 164–165
Competitor audit, 74, 171–172
Competitor identification, 165–171
Competitor intelligence system, 171–176
Completely open questions, 97
Compuserve, 91
Computer City Superstore, 31
Computerized indexes, 413
Concentrated marketing, 211–212
Concentric diversification, 40
Concept development, 246, 248

Concept selling, 351
Concept test, 248
Conditioning financing agreements, 263
Conformity, 150
Conglomerate diversification, 41
Cooperation, 176–177
Constraint, 54–55
Consumer analysis, 74
Consumer buying behavior, 134
Consumer buying decision process, 135–152
Consumer channel, 261
Consumer image, 69
Consumerism movement, 124
Consumer markets, 75
Consumer patronage objectives, 68
Consumer population, 191-192
Consumer products, 228–231
Consumer promotions, 330
Consumer rights, 124
Consumers
  buying decision process of, 135–139
  individual vs. organizational, 14
  information search by, 137–138
  learning process of, 142–143
  life cycle of, 147
  needs/wants/demands of, 10–12
  perception process of, 140–142
  personal influences on, 144–147
  problem recognition by, 136–137
  psychological influences on, 139–144
  situational influences on, 152
  social influences on, 147–152
  See also Customers
Consuming purpose, 191
Consumption potential, 191
Consumption process, 13–14
Contemporary marketing concept, 16–17
Continental Airlines, 179
Continuous media schedule, 315
Contraction defense, 187
Contractual vertical marketing system, 291
Controlling process, 7–8
Convenience products, 229

Conventional marketing channel (CMCs), 288–289
Cooperative advertising, 308
Copy, 311–312
Cordtz, Dan, 22, 407
Core benefit, 382–384
Core culture, 363–364
Corporate review, 73
Corporate vertical marketing system, 291–292
Cost efficiency, 49
Cost justification, 340
Cost leadership, 178–180
Cost-plus pricing, 343–344
Counteroffensive strategy, 186–187
Cox, Anthony D., 354
Cox, Dena, 354
Coy, Peter, 215
Crawford, C. Merle, 248, 257
Creative advertising campaign, 308–316
Creative elements, 311–312
Crocker, Richard A., 333
Crosby, Philip B., 256
Crown Books, 243
Crystal Pepsi, 57
Cultural aesthetics, 392
Cultural agenda, 121, 123–124, 147
Cultural diversity, 121
Cultural universals, 391
Culver, Alberto, 39
Current Business Reports, 416
Customary pricing, 352
Customer-based organization, 362–363
Customer-based pricing, 345
Customer-driven, 16-17
Customer intimacy, 30
Customer loyalty, 68
Customer postpurchase satisfaction, 139
Customers
  "bundle of benefits" to, 75–76
  commitment to, 29
  competitive advantage with, 177–181
  desire for value by, 337
  following the, 391
  new market segments of, 38
  personality types of industrial, 158

Customers *(continued)*
  prices and expectations of, 339
  See also Consumers
Customer satisfaction, 16
Customer scope, 28
Customer service actions, 59
Customer service features, 58–59
Customer traffic, 68
Customer type, 325
Customer value disciplines, 30
Custom marketing, 212
Custom marketing-intellgence services, 89
Customs, 121, 392–393
Customs Union, 398
Cutler, Blayne, 407
Czepiel, John A., 188

Dalrymple, Douglas J., 188
d'Amico, Michael, 132
Darlin, Damon, 22, 188, 214, 332
Databases, 85
Data collection, 94–101
David, Gregory E., 44
Davidow, William H., 62
Davidson, D. Kirk, 79
Davis, 152
Dawley, Heidi, 407
Dayton-Hudson, 137
Dreyfus Strategic Aggressive mutual fund, 384
Dean, Joel, 332
Decentralized organizations, 360
Deceptive pricing, 340
Decider, 151, 158
Decision domain disagreements, 284–285
Declarative sentence, 92
Decoding messages, 297
Defense strategies, 184
Delhaize "Le Lion" SA, 388
Delineate benefits, 60
Dell Computer, 30, 38, 212
Delta, 179
Demand-backward pricing, 345
Demand curve, 338
Demands
  characteristics of, 338
  consumer, 11
  synchronization of, 384
Demarketing, 118
Demographic profile, 112
Demographics, 145–146

Demographic segmentation, 195–198
Demography, 111
Demonstration effect, 393
Dentzer, Susan, 131
Depository libraries, 415
Depression, 117
Derived demand, 156
DeRose, Rodger L., 249
Description buying, 159
Descriptive research, 93
Desires (consumer), 11–12
Desire stage, 298
Dewey Decimal system, 410, 414
Dholakia, Nikhilesh, 252
Dialog, 91
Dichotomous questions, 97
Dickson, Peter R., 174, 247
Differential advantage, 56
Differential pricing, 346–349
Differentiated marketing, 210–211
Differentiating Strategies, 56–59
Differentiation, 56, 180
Diffusion process, 253–255
Dillard's, 169, 213, 214
Diplomacy control, 286–287
Direct-action appeals, 310
Direct mail marketing, 327–328
Direct marketing, 300, 327–330
Direct Marketing, 300
Directory of On-line Databases, 89
Direct response, 313
Direct response marketing, 329–330
Discounts, 346
Discount Tires, 169
Disney World, 167
Dissertation Abstracts International (DAI), 411–412
Dissociative groups, 150
Distribution
  decisions on, 76–77
  establishing objectives of, 266–268
  evaluating alternatives of, 273–278
  identifying alternatives for, 268–273
  intensive/exclusive/selective, 270–273
  international market, 404–405

  recognizing needs of, 265
  selecting alternatives for, 266, 279–280
Distribution/wholesaling associations, 437
Diversified growth opportunities, 40–41
Divesting, 45
Divisional planning, 19–20
Dixon, Carolyn K., 333
DKNY, 38, 351
Dodge, 239
Doebele, Justin, 132
Dogs, 32
Dollar markup, 344
Domino's, 38
Donath, Bob, 333
Dowd, Ann Reilly, 407
Dow Jones (on-line), 91
Downward stretch, 241
D.R. Horton, Inc., 212
Dr. Scholl's, 230
Drucker, Peter, 49
Dubashi, Jagannath, 132
Dumaine, Brian, 371
Dumping, 341, 402
Durability, 228–229
Durable goods, 228
Duty, 403
Dwyer, Paula, 44

Early adopters, 254
Early majority, 254
Earnings per share, 70
Eaton, Robert, 391
Echikson, William, 292
Economic Census, 416
Economic conditions, 116–117
Economic environment, 115
Economic issues, 117–118
Economic systems, 115–116
Economic Union (EU), 398
Ecotrin, 168
Eddie Bauer, 169
Education, 393
Effectiveness, 6–7
Efficiency, 6–7
80/20 rule, 203
Eisenstodt, Gale, 61
El-Ansary, Adel I., 293
Elastic demand, 338
Embargoes, 395
Emergency products, 229
Emotional appeals, 311
Empathy, 382

Employees
  commitment to, 29
Employee search, 325
Empowerment, 367
Encirclement strategy, 183
Encoded (messages), 297
Encyclopedia of Associations, 88
England, Robert Stowe, 62, 332, 354
Eng, Paul M., 188
Environment, 108
Environmental analysis, 73, 109
Environmental forecast, 109
Environmental management, 109
Environmental monitoring, 109–110
Environmental scan, 109
Environmental scope, 28
Equipment-based service delivery, 381
Equipment-based services, 379
Establishing rapport, 320
Ethan Allen, 57
Ethical business practices, 72
Ethics, 119–120
Ethnocentrism, 391
European Currency Unit (ECU), 398
Evaluating planning stage, 21
Evaluation, 253
Even pricing, 352
Everyday low pricing, 352–353
Evoked set, 138
Excedrin, 168
Exchange, 10
Exchange process, 10–13
Exchange Rate Mechanism, 398
Exclusive distribution, 271–272
Exclusively distributed products, 278
Execution style, 311
Executive summary, 65
Expectational miscalculations, 284
Expected-service/perceived-service gap, 382, 383
Expense goods, 231
Experimentation method, 99–100
Expert authority, 367
Expert power, 286

Exploratory research, 93
Exposure, 150
Expropriation, 390
Extending decisions, 39
Extensive decision making, 136
External environmental scan, 52–53
External information, 82–83
External information search, 137–138
Extraterritoriality, 396
Ezop, Phyllis, 104

Facilitating activities, 8–10
Facilitating agents, 261
Fahey, Liam, 188
Fair profit, 16
Family branding, 238
Family influences, 151–152
Family life cycle, 147
Family reference groups, 394
Farquhar, Peter H., 256
Farrell, Christopher, 131
Federal Express, 239
Federal Register, 416
Federal Trade Commission (FTC), 340–341
Feedback, 297
Feldman, Amy, 22, 44, 215, 292, 293
Ferrell, O. C., 132
F&S Index of Corporations and Industries, 418
Field experiments, 100
"Fighting brands," 42
Fighting media schedule, 315
Financial objectives, 70–71
Financial resources, 49
Financing (inventory), 9
Finkelman, Daniel P., 22
Five-level channels, 270
Fixed costs, 338
Flank attacks, 183
Flanking defense strategy, 186
Flexible pricing, 347, 349
Flint, Jerry, 407
Flynn, Julia, 333, 407
F.O.B. (free-on-board) origin pricing, 350
Focus group interviews, 95
Focus strategy, 180
Following the customers, 390
Fondiller, David S., 189
Food Lion, 182

Ford Motor Company, 204, 241, 388
Forecasting methods, 239, 207
Foreign Corrupt Practices Act, 396
Forest, Stephanie Anderson, 215, 354
Former price comparisons, 340–341
Formula selling, 321
Form utility, 13
Forward integration, 39, 292
Foster, Robert, 292
Four-level channel, 269–270
Four P's of marketing, 8
Franklin Mint, 273
Franklin Quest Co., 12–13
Free Trade Area, 397
Freight absorption pricing, 350
Frito-Lay, 31, 52
Frontal attack strategy, 182
Fuhrman, Peter, 188, 407
Fuji Photo Film Company, 405
Full-member institution, 261
Functional attributes, 221
Functional features, 56–57
Functional planning, 20–21
Functional training, 326
Function-based organization, 361

GAP, The 142, 169, 239, 351
Garvin, David A., 256
Gatekeeper, 158
Gateway, 38
Gatorade, 39, 265
Gender relationships, 114
General Electric, 31, 120, 169
General Electric's business screen, 33–35
General Mills Total Corn Flakes, 167
General Motors, 27, 56, 273, 357, 389, 401
General Nutrition Company, 283
General-purpose advertising, 306–307
Generation X, 113
Generic competition, 168, 178
Generic product, 222
Generics, 239
Geocentrism, 391
Geodemographic segmentation, 199

Geographically-based organization, 362, 364
Geographic pricing, 350
Geographic segmentation, 195
Geographic territory, 323, 325
Gibson, 280
Gilbert, Nick, 132
Gillette Co., 238, 245, 351
Gill, Penny, 202, 215
Girl Scout cookies, 386
Givenchy, 351
Global marketing, 388
  See also **International marketing**
Gloria Jean's Coffee Bean, 230
Goal, 48
Goal-directed behavior, 139
Goal incompatibilities, 285
Goetsch, Hal, 371
Gold credit card, 384
Goldman, Kevin, 407
Goldstar, 19, 388
Good-faith justification, 340
Good Guys, Inc., 187
Goods
  described, 12
  differentiation, 56–57
  durable and nondurable, 228–229
  expense and capital, 231
  homogeneous/heterogeneous shopping, 230
  See also **Products**
Goodyear Tire & Rubber Co., 15, 169, 239, 292
Government documents, 415–416
Government information sources, 86–87
Government markets, 154
Government Printing Office (GPO), 415, 416
GPO bookstores, 415
Grading, 10
Gragg, Charles I., 448
Grand Metropolitan PLC, 41
Graphic arts associations, 429
Grease, 396
Green Giant, 154
Green marketing, 124, 387
Green zone, growth and primary investment, 34
Greising, David, 22, 62, 215
Gross domestic product (GDP), 116

Gross national product (GNP), 116
Gross, Neil, 188, 215
Grover, Ronald, 79
Growth opportunities, 37–41
Gubernick, Lisa, 62, 131, 215, 407
Gucci, 239, 272
Guerrilla warfare, 184
Guiltinan, Joseph P., 354
Gymboree, 69

Haeckel, Stephan H., 162
Hager, Bruce, 132
Haggar Apparel, 38, 138
Hallmark, 280
Hamel, Gary, 187
Hanes, 170
Harley-Davidson Motor Company, 145
Harvesting, 42
Hauser, Jorn R., 252
Hayes, John R., 79
Heinz, 238
Heiser, Joseph F., Jr., 91
Henkoff, Ronald, 188, 371, 406
Herman's Sporting Goods, 187
Herndon, Neil, 44
Hertz, 193
Heterogeneous shopping goods, 230
Hewlett-Packard, 53, 245
Hierarchy of Effects Model, 298–299
High-low pricing, 353
"High margin-low turnover" strategy, 264
Hispanic Americans, 123
Hof, Robert D., 189, 257
Home Depot, 186, 259
Home interviews, 95
Homelife Store (Sears), 307
Home shopping, 329
Homogeneous shopping goods, 230
Honda, 151
Horizontal conflict, 283
Horizontal diversification, 40–41
Horizontal integration, 39–40
Horizontal organization, 359–360
Horizontal price fixing, 340
Human resources, 49
Hunt, Shelby D., 22
Hunt, V. Daniel, 371
Husband dominant, 152
Hwang, Suein L., 131

Hypothesis formulation, 93

IBM, 187, 239, 259, 362–363
Idea generation stage, 245–248
Ideal self, 145
Idea marketing, 387
Ideas, 12
Idea screening, 246, 248
Identification planning stage, 21
Image, 69
Image extras, 222
Implementing (management process), 7–8
Impulse items, 229
Incentive systems, 384
Income inequalities, 114–115
Incredible Universe, 31
Indexes (computerized), 413
Indirect-action appeals, 310
Individual branding, 238
Individual consumer, 14
Individual values (VA), 199
Industrial channel, 259
Industrial customer personality types, 159
Industrial market, 154
Industry attractiveness, 33
Industry competition, 168–169
Industry information sources, 420–421
Industry scope, 28
Inelastic demand, 156, 338
Inflation, 117
Influencer, 151, 158
Infomercials, 329
Information
  competitor audit to gather, 171
  consumer search for, 137–138
  gathering, 83–84
  internal records on, 102
  locating, 81–83
  processing, 84–85
  sources of competitive, 175–176
  sources of, 86–89
  through analytical research, 102
  through marketing research, 89–102
  through records research, 102
  utilizing, 85–86
  See also Library resources
Information dissemination, 85
Information flow, 264
Information presentation, 85
Information utilization, 85–86
Informing, 9–10

Informs, 295
In-house advertising department, 316–317
Initial contact, 320
Initiator, 151, 157
Innovation, 49
Innovators, 254
Inquiry test, 316
Inseparability, 378
Inspection buying, 159–160
Institutional advertising, 307
Institutional market, 154
Insurance associations, 429–431
Intangibility, 377
Integrated growth opportunities, 39–40
Integrated marketing communication (IMC), 301
Integration, 39–40
Intel, 186
Intensive distribution, 270–271
Intensive growth opportunities, 37
Intensively distributed products, 278
Interactive television, 329–330
Interests, 145–146, 253
Interest stage, 298
Interlibrary loan, 414
Internal information, 82
Internal information search, 137
Internal organizational scan, 50–52
Internal records, 103–104
International legislation, 396
International marketing
  cultural/social influences in, 391–394
  described, 388
  deterrents to, 390–391
  economic integration within, 396–398
  marketing mix within, 400–405
  motivation for, 388–390
  political/legal influences on, 394–396
International organizations, 400
Internet information resources, 425–426
Interpersonal message channels, 297
Intertype competition, 169
Intracompany price, 403
Intratype competition, 169
Inventory productivity, 71

Investment information sources, 421–422
Involvement control, 287
Item addition, 241
Item competition, 167

Jacob, Rahul, 406
Jatusripitak, Somkid, 188
JCPenney, 214, 239
Jell-O, 238
Jennings, Suzanne L., 214
Jenny Craig International, 203
Jiffy Lube, 384
Joan & David, 235
Job description, 325
Joe Camel advertising campaign, 301
Johnson, Richard M., 215
Johnson Wax, 248–249
Joint demand, 156
Jones, Geoffrey, 22
Josephson, Edna, 132
Josephson, Joseph, 132
Josephson, Michael, 132
Journal articles, 412–414
Journal of Economic Literature, 418
Journals, 412

Karan, Donna, 38
Kellogg's Corn Flakes, 167, 238, 239
Kelly, Kevin, 162
Kelly, Michael, 333
Kenderdine, James M., 293
Kenmore, 238
Kennedy, John F., 124
Kentucky Fried Chicken (KFC), 31
Kerwin, Kathleen, 371, 407
Khalaf, Roula, 256, 407
Kids 'R' Us, 167
"Killer instinct," 167
Kimelman, John, 44, 45
Kim, Junu Bryan, 333
Kirkland, Richard I., Jr., 131
Kmart, 43, 169, 292
Knight, Robin, 131
Kodak, 238, 239, 405
Koselka, Rita, 257, 332
Kotler, Philip, 62, 181–182, 185, 188, 407
Kraft General Foods, 308, 325
Kroger, 182, 239
Kuntz, Mary, 408
Kurtz, David L., 61

LaBarbera, Priscilla, 130, 132, 162
Labatt, 40
Labich, Kenneth, 406
Laboratory experiments, 100
Labor productivity, 71
La Franco, Robert, 215, 255, 407
Laggards, 254
Lamb, Charles W., Jr., 91
Lancioni, Richard, 158, 159, 162
Landler, Mark, 79
Lane, Randall, 215, 255
Language, 391–392
Lantos, Geoffrey P., 132
Larson, Erik, 332
Late majority, 254
Laura Ashley, 60–61
Lautman, Martin R., 62
Lavin, Douglas, 162
Law of demand, 338
Lazer, William, 130, 132, 162
Leader pricing, 352
Leadership, 365–366
Lead (sales), 318–320
Leapfrogging, 183–184
Learning, 142–143
Leasing arrangements, 160
Legal environment
  of company operations, 127
  competitive actions within, 126–127
  defined, 125
  described, 126–128
  of marketing activities, 127
Legitimate power, 286
Legitmate authority, 366
Lehmann, Donald R., 166, 187
Lele, Milind M., 162
Lenox, 179
Lerreche, Jean-Claude, 188
Less-developed countries (LDCs), 390, 393, 396
Leverage, 53–54
Levine, Joshua, 22, 62, 131, 256, 332, 333, 354
Levi Strauss, 29, 72, 154, 170, 193, 351
Levy, Sidney J., 104
Lewison, Dale M., 100, 101, 132, 214, 324, 383
Lewison, Kristopher, 385
Library of Congress system, 410, 414
Library consortiums, 425
Library information sources, 86

Library resources
  audio-visual materials as, 417
  business information sources in, 417–424
  call number systems, 410–412
  importance of, 409
  information materials outside of, 424–426
  locating government documents, 415–417
  locating journal articles, 412–414
  public libraries as, 426
  reference department as, 414–415
  See also Information
Life cycle, 147
Life-styles, 145–146, 199
Likert scale, 98
Limited decision making, 136
Limited-member institutions, 261
Limited, The, 169
Linden, Dana Wechsler, 255
Liz Claiborne, 170, 273
L. L. Bean, 405
Logical appeal, 311
Logistics/transportation associations, 431
Long channels, 268
Looking-glass self, 145
Loss-leaders, 352
Louis Vuitton, 273
Lovelock, Christopher H., 407
Lower-lower class, 150
Lower-upper class, 149
Lowe's Construction, 186
Low-leaders, 352
"Low margin-high turnover" philosophy, 264
Loyalty status, 204
Lucky Strike, 32
Lublin, JoAnn S., 61
Lubove, Seth, 22, 188, 215, 256
Lusch, Robert F., 292–293

McCammon, Bert C., Jr., 293
McDaniel, Carl, 91
MacDonald, Douglas, 256
McDonald's, 69–70, 171, 179, 402
MacFarquhar, Emily, 131
McGinn, Daniel, 132
Machan, Dyan, 407
MacLachlan, James M., 130, 132, 162

McMenamin, Brigid, 256
Macroenvironment, 109
Macy's, 169, 239
Magrath, Allan J., 256
Mail order marketing, 328–329
Mail survey, 95
Maintaining, 42
Make-up Art Cosmetics, Ltd., 138
Mall intercept interviews, 94
Mallory, Maria, 188, 189, 332
Maloney, John C., 332
Management/marketing associations, 431–432
Management process, 6–7
Managerial preferences, 389
Managerial scope, 29
Mañana syndrome, 393
Mandel, Michael J., 79
Manners, 121
Manufacturer brands, 239
Manufacturing/merchandising associations, 433
Maremont, Mark, 353, 408
Margaritaville Records, 220
Marginal costs, 339
Market, 191
Market analysis, 74–75, 191–194
"Market challenger" strategies, 181
Market development opportunities, 38
Market-driven, 16–17
Market economies, 116
Marketing
  cost analysis of, 369–370
  described, 6
  global/international, 388–405
  legal aspects of, 126–127
  regulatory forces in, 127–128
  scientific/technological advances in, 128–130
Marketing actions, 66
Marketing activities, 8–9
Marketing audit, 368
Marketing-channel design, 265
Marketing channel of distribution, 259
Marketing channels
  described, 76–77
  design of, 265–280
  flows of, 262–264
  interactions within, 261–262
  management of, 281–292
  marketing team of, 261

  subsystems of, 259
  See also **Products**
Marketing communication
  advertising component of, 305–317
  by leadership, 365–366
  described, 295
  direct marketing component of, 327–330
  elements of, 295
  personal selling component of, 317–327
  process of, 296–299
  promotion management process in, 302–305
  promotion mix of, 299–301
Marketing communications mix, 299–301
Marketing concept, 15–16
Marketing control, 367
Marketing cost analysis, 369–370
Marketing effort, 365–370
Marketing environments, 108
Marketing eras, 14–15
Marketing goals, 48–49
Marketing implementation, 357
Marketing Information Guide, 86
Marketing information sources, 419–421
Marketing information system (MIS), 81–86
Marketing intelligence, 83–84, 86–89
Marketing issues, 66
Marketing management, 6
Marketing/management associations, 431–432
Marketing mix
  described, 8
  international, 399, 400–405
  tailoring, 213
Marketing networks, 17
Marketing objectives, 66, 67–70
Marketing philosophies, 15–19
Marketing programs, 66, 75
Marketing research, 84, 89–102
Marketing strategies, 55–61
"Marketing Warfare" (Kotler and Singh), 181
Market niches, 193

Market organizations
  effort executed by, 365–367
  forms of, 361–363
  international, 400
  modifying effort of, 370
  monitoring effort of, 368–370
  types of, 358–361
Market penetration, 38
Market position, 213
Market positioning, 59–60, 212–213
Market positioning strategy, 59, 212–213
Market repositioning, 60–61
Markets
  analyzing, 194
  characteristics of organizational, 156–157
  competitor relations within, 176, 177
  defining, 191–194
  organizational, 154–157
  segmenting, 193
  targeting, 207, 210
Market scope, 28
Market segmentation
  described, 75, 195
  evaluating, 206–207
  identifying, 195–204
  profiling, 204–205
  selecting specific, 207–209
  targeting specific, 209–212
Market segments, 193
Market share, 68–69, 342
Market standing, 49
Market structures, 118
Market survival, 341
Market type, 325
Markup pricing, 344
Marlboro, 238
Marshall Fields, 138
Maslow's Hierarchy of Needs, 140
Mass customization, 212
Mass market, 193
Mass message channels, 297
MasterCard, 384
Mathematical programming, 102
Mathur, Anil, 131
Mattel Inc., 238
Mature consumers, 113–114
Mature markets, 390
Matzer, Marla, 131

May Co., 213, 214
Mayflower, 183
Mazumdar, Tridib, 354
Media alternatives, 313
Media schedules, 315
Media selection, 313–315
Media strategy, 312–315
Mediation control, 287
Membership group, 150
Merchandise cost, 339
Merchandising/manufacturing associations, 433
Merredith, Geoffrey E., 131
Message appeal, 310
Messages, 297
Meyerowitz, Steven A., 256
Michaels, 167
Michelin, 388
Microenvironment, 108–109
Microforms, 414
Micro market, 193–194
Micromarketing, 382
Microsoft, 238
Middle class, 149
Mikasa, 179
Miller, 240
Miller, Annetta, 214
Miller, Cyndee, 44, 61, 131, 132, 162, 255, 256, 257
Miller, Karen Lowry, 162
Miller, Nicole, 238
Mintzberg, Henry, 371
Missionary salespeople, 318
Mission statement, 27
Mitchell, Russell, 44, 79
Mixed economies, 116
Mobile defense, 185–186
Models, 85
Modified rebuy, 158
Monetary transactions, 10
Monopolistic competition, 118, 340
Monopoly, 118, 340
Monroe, Kent B., 354
Montgomery, David B., 176
Montgomery Ward, 213, 214
Monthly Catalog of U.S. Government Publications, 87, 415–416
Monthly Labor Report, 416
Morais, Richard C., 256, 408
Morgan, Robert M., 22
Mortal Kombat, 251
Morton, John, 256

Moschis, George P., 131
Moshavi, Sharon, 407
Motivation
  for global marketing, 388–390
  for marketing plan, 366–367
  as psychological influence, 139–140
Motorola, 238
Moukheiber, Zina, 189, 255
Multiple-choice questions, 97
Multiple pricing, 352
Multiple sourcing strategy, 161
Multiple variable segmentation, 204–206
"Multiplier effect," 156
Munk, Nina, 215, 354, 407
Murphy, Ian, 257

Nakarmi, Laxmi, 22, 407
NASCAR sponsorship, 313
National Football League, 38
Nayyar, Seema, 214
Needs
  consumer, 10–12
  recognition/specification of, 160
Need-satisfaction selling, 321
Neiman Marcus, 137
Néscafe, 238
New Belgium Brewing Co., 193
Newcomb, Peter, 131
New geographic markets, 38
New market levels, 38
New market segments, 38
New product management, 245
New task buy, 158
New York Times Index, 418
Niching, 42–43
Nicklaus, Jack, 239
Nike, 30, 151, 193, 282–283
Nine geodemographic nations, 200–201
Nintendo, 238
Noise (communication), 297
Nondurable goods, 228–229
Nonprice competition, 341
Nonprobability samples, 99, 100
Nonprofit marketing, 386–387
Non-tariff barriers, 395
Nonverbal cues, 392
Nonverbal feedback channels, 297
Nordstrom, 137, 213, 214
Noritake, 179
Norman, James R., 45

North American Free Trade
  Agreement (NAFTA), 398
Norwegian Cruise Lines, 376
Now or later decision, 139
Nuprin, 168
Nutri/Systems Inc., 202

Obermayer, James W., 333
Objective, 48
Observation method, 99, 101
OCLC, 424–425
Odd pricing, 352
Office Depot, 186
Office interviews, 95
OfficeMax, 167
Ogilvy & Mather Worldwide, 317
Oldsmobile, 193, 349
Oligopolistic market, 340
Oligopoly, 118
Oliva, Terence A., 158, 159, 162
Oliver, Richard L., 406
Oliver, Suzanne, 188, 407
Oneal, Michael, 293
On Great Service (Berry), 377
On-line catalogs, 410–411, 416
On-line Computer Library
  Center (OCLC), 424–425
On-line databases, 415, 419, 421
On-line database vendors, 89, 91
Ono, Yumiko, 162
Open-ended questions, 97
Operant conditioning, 142
Operating economies, 389
Operational excellence, 30
Operational product benefits, 223
Opinion leaders, 151
Opinions, 145
Opportunities, 52
Order getters, 318
Order takers, 318
Organizational buying, 157–161
**Organizational buying
  behavior, 134, 152–161**
Organizational buying model, 154–155
Organizational chart, 358–359
Organizational consumers, 14
Organizational culture, 363–364
Organizational diversification, 389
Organizational markets, 75
  demand characteristics of, 156
Organizational mission, 26–30

Organizational products, 231
Organizational sales, 318
Organization marketing, 387
Organization portfolio, 30–31
Organization training, 326
Organizing marketing, 358, 360
Ourusoff, Alexandra, 44, 255, 256
Out-of-home media, 313
Overnite Transportation
  Company, 384
Ownership flow, 263

Pacific Island culture, 123
Package, 240
PAIS, 418
Pall Mall, 32
Palmeri, Christopher, 44, 257
Pancho's Mexican Buffet, Inc., 308
Papa John's pizza restaurants, 337–338
Papiernik, Richard L., 188
Parasuraman, A., 406
Parker-Pope, Tara, 44
Parsons, Leonard J., 188
Participation, 143
Partnership for a Drug Free
  America, 387
Patagonia, 171
Patronage reasons, 203–204
Patterson, Gregory A., 354
Payment flow, 263–264
Penetration pricing, 349
Pentium chip, 186
People-based service delivery, 381
People-based services, 379
PepsiCo, 31, 53, 186, 273, 390, 396
Perceived-value pricing, 345
Percentage markups, 344
Perception, 140–142
Perceptual differences, 284
Perceptual maps, 213
Periodical, 412
Periodic discounting, 349
Perishability, 378
Perry Ellis International, 239
Personal influences, 144–147
Personal interview, 94–95
Personality, 144
Personal selling, 300, 404
Personal selling component, 317–327
**Personal selling process,
  defined, 318**

described, 318–323
Person marketing, 387
Personnel selection, 326
Persuades, 295
Peters, Tom, 256
Phalon, Richard, 257
Philip Morris, 286
Physical flow, 262
Physical resources, 49
Pioneering advertising, 307
Pizza Hut, 31, 38
Place marketing, 387
Place utility, 13
Planning, 7–8, 357
Planning model, 19–21
Planning process
  three stages, 21
Plans, 85
Playtex Apparel, 140
Point-of-purchase (P-O-P), 138
Political environment, 125
Political system, 126
Politz, Alfred, 332
Pollard, C. William, 120
Polley, Paulette, 375
Polycentrism, 391
Pontiac, 56
Population, 98–99
Porter, Michael E., 177–178, 188
Porter's model of generic
  strategies, 178
Portfolio analysis, 31
**Position defense strategy,
  184–185**
Positioning strategies, 59–61, 401
Possession utility, 13
Post, 239
Postpurchase evaluation, 139
Posttest, 316
Potential rating index for ZIP
  markets (PRIZM), 199, 201
Powell, Cheryl, 407
Prahalad, C. K., 187
Preapproach preparations, 320
Predatory pricing, 340
Preemptive defense strategy, 186
Presenting, 320–321
Pretest, 316
Price
  described, 12
  determinants of, 338–341
  exchange process and, 336
  objectives of setting, 341–342

Price *(continued)*
  strategies for, 346–353, 402–403
  value concept and, 336–338
Price bundling, 351
Price decisions, 78
Price discrimination, 340
Price elasticity of demand, 338
Price fixing, 340
Price leadership, 341
Price lining, 351
Price matching, 346
Price penetration, 402
Price signaling, 349
Price skimming, 402
Price standardization, 402
Pricing methods, 342–343
Pricing process, 335
Pride, William M., 132
Primary information, 82
Print media, 313
Private brands, 239–240
Private nonprofit organizations, 387
Proactive reasons, 388
Probability samples, 99, 100
Problem definition, 92
Problem recognition, 136–137
Problem (SWOT matrix), 55
Procter & Gamble, 239, 242, 351
Product adoption process, 251, 253
Product advertising, 306–307
Product-based organization, 361–362
Product branding, 235
Product concept, 248
Product decision, 75–76
Product design, 235
Product development, 38–39
Product guarantees, 235
Production era, 14
Product item, 223–224
Product-item management, 231–240
Productivity, 71
Product leadership, 30
Product life cycle, 225–228, 400
Product line, 325
Product-line consistency, 242
Product-line contraction, 241–242
Product-line extensions, 240–241
Product-line filling, 241
Product-line management, 240–242

Product-line pricing, 350–351
Product lines, 223
Product-line stretching, 241
Product-management decisions, 233
Product mix, 223
Product-mix depth, 242–243
Product-mix management, 242–243
Product-mix width, 242
Product packaging, 240
Product quality, 13, 231–235
Products
  consumer, 228–231
  convenience, 229
  described, 8, 220
  failure of new, 252
  inspection/evaluation of, 161
  intensively/exclusively distributed, 278
  item management of, 231–240
  life cycle of, 225–228
  line management of, 240–242
  management of new, 245
  mix management of, 242–243
  organizational, 231
  positioning, 59–60, 401
  product-mix concept of, 223–224
  shopping, 229–230
  specialty, 230
  total-product concept for, 220–223, 401–402
  unsought, 230–231
  See also **Goods; Marketing channels; Value**
Product scope, 28
Product standardization, 400–401
Product units, 224
Product utility, 12–13
Product warranty, 235
Professional and trade associations, 427–437
Profitability, 49, 70–71
Profit-based pricing, 344–345
Profit-impact-of-market strategy (PIMS), 35–37
Profit maximization, 342
Profits (fair), 16
Promotion, 295
Promotional pricing, 352–353
Promotional strategies, 403–404
Promotion budget, 305
Promotion campaign, 303–305

Promotion decisions, 77–78
Promotion flow, 264
Promotion management process, 302–305
Promotion mix, 299–301
Promotion objectives, 303–305
Proposal solicitation/evaluation, 160–161
Prospecting, 318–320
Prosperity, 117
Protectionism legislation, 125
Protectionist countries, 394
Protect local jobs, 390
Protestant Work Ethic, 393
Prototype development, 246, 250–251
Pruning decisions, 39
Psychographics, 146
Psychographic segmentation, 199
Psychological influences, 139–144
Psychological pricing, 351–352
Psychological benefits, 57, 222–223
Public Affairs Information Service (PAIS), 418
Publicity, 301
Public libraries, 426
  See also Library sources
Public nonprofit organizations, 386–387
Public relations, 300–301
Public relations associations, 433
Publix Super Markets, 182
Pull strategy, 304
Pulsing media schedule, 315
Punishment systems, 384
Purchase decisions, 138–139
Purchasing associations, 433
Pure competition, 118, 340
Push strategy, 304

Quaker Oats Co., 39, 265
Quality, 49, 231–234
Quality level, 234
Quality of life, 124
Quelch, John A., 256
Question marks, 32
Questionnaire, 95, 97–98

Radio Shack, 31
Randell, Geoffrey, 22
Random discounting, 349
Rank-ordered questions, 97

Raw resource producers, 76
Reactive reasons, 390
Readers' Guide to Periodical Literature, 418
Readiness stage, 204
Real estate associations, 434
Real-self, 145
Rebello, Kathy, 79
Receivers, 297
Recession, 117
Recognition, 151
Records search, 84, 104
Recovery, 117
Recruiting, 325
Red Wolf, 240–241
Red zone, harvest management and limited divestiture, 35
Reebok, 193
Reference department (library), 414–415
Reference groups, 150–151
Reference pricing, 349–350
Reference sources, 66–67
Reference strategies, 55–56
Referent power, 367
Regals Cinemas, Inc., 370
Reibstein, Larry, 131
Reich, Robert B., 115
Reichheld, Frederick F., 22
Reinforcement, 143
Relationship marketing, 17–18
"Relationship retailing," 124
Relative standards, 120
Reliability, 381
Religious beliefs, 392
Remind, 295
Reminder advertising, 308
Reminder systems, 384
Renaissance Cosmetics, 71
Repetition, 143
Reports, 85
Republic Steel, 154
Research design, 93–94
Research hypothesis, 93
Reseller markets, 154
Reservation systems, 384
Resource scarcities, 283–284
Response coupons, 329
Responsiveness, 381
Restructuring opportunities, 41–43
Retailing associations, 434–435

Retention marketing, 17–18, 124
Return on investments (ROI), 342
Return on net sales (ROS), 70, 342
Reverse brain drain, 393
Reward power, 286, 367
Riemer, Blanca, 215
Rifkin, Glenn, 215
Rigaux, 152
Risk management, 389
Risk taking, 10
R.J. Reynold's Tobacco Company, 301
Roadway Services Inc., 385
Roberts Express, Inc., 384–385
Role, 283
Role incongruities, 283
Roman, Monica, 131
Rosenbloom, Bert, 292, 293
Rossant, John, 293
Roush, Chris, 62, 333
Routinized response behavior, 136
Rubel, Chad, 44, 188, 256, 333, 354, 371
Rudnitsky, Howard, 61, 79, 215
Rule of Reciprocity (Golden Rule), 120
Rust, Roland T., 406
Rutherford, Andrea, 255
Ryder, 183

Safeway, 292
Sales analysis, 369
Sales associations, 435–436
Sales era, 15
Sales force development, 325–327
Sales forecasting, 206–207
Sales forecasts, 207
Sales incentives, 326
Sales lead, 318–320
Sales management, 323–327
Sales objections, 321–322
Sales objectives, 68
Sales-oriented objectives, 342
Sales potential, 206–207
Sales presentation, 320–321
Sales promotions, 300, 330–331, 404
Sales quotas, 326
Sales volume, 342
Sally Beauty Supply, 39
Sampathkurmaran, Sreekanth, 22

Sample, 99
Sample frame, 99
Sample item, 99
Sample size, 99
Sampling, 159
Sam's Club, 38
Samuel, Peter, 61
Sanctions, 395–396
Sasseen, Jane A., 188
Schaaf, Dick, 406
Schermerhorn, John R., 371
Schewe, Charles D., 90, 131
Schifrin, Matthew, 44
Schiller, Zachary, 45, 257, 353, 354
Schlossberg, Howard, 256
Schultz, Don E., 22, 332
Schuman, Michael, 22, 407
Science, 128
Scope statement, 27–29
Seagrams, 40
Sears, 61, 169, 213, 214, 228, 292, 307, 311
Seasonal media schedule, 315
Secondary information, 81–82
Second-market discounting, 349
Securities associations, 436
Sega Enterprises, Ltd., 167–168, 238
Selective distortion, 142
Selective distribution, 272–273
Selective exposure, 142
Selective perception, 141–142
Selective retention, 142
Self-concept, 145
Self-image, 145
Self-reference criterion, 393
Sellers, Patricia, 407
Semantic differential scale, 98
Sentence completion tests, 97
Serials, 412
Service delivery, 381
Service differentiation, 57–59
Service extras, 222
Service marketing
 described, 376
 nature of, 377–379
 strategies for, 379–384
Service Master, 120
Service quality, 379
Service quality analysis, 382
Services, 12, 376–379
Serwer, Andrew E., 79, 407
Shapiro, Benson P., 22
Shareholders
 commitment to, 31

Index

Shermach, Kelly, 162, 256
Sherwin-Williams, 273, 292
Sheth, Jagdish N., 162
Shinto Work Ethic, 393
Shopping products, 229–230
Shortage of foreign exchange, 390
Shortages, 117–118
Short channels, 268
SIC numbers, 416
Sims, J. Taylor, 292
Simulation models, 102
Singh, Ravi, 181–182, 185, 188
Single sourcing strategy, 161
Single variable segmentation, 204
Situational influences, 152–153
Situation analysis, 66
Situation analysis, 72–75
Six-level channels, 270
Slogans, 311
Smith, Allen E., 130, 132, 162
Smith, Emily T., 130
Smith, Geoffrey, 44, 332
Smith, Jack, 27
Snapple, 39
Social agenda, 119–121
Social class, 147–150
Social influences, 119, 147–152
Social relationships, 120–121
Social responsibility, 49, 72
Social Sciences Index, 418–419
Societal marketing concept, 18–19
Societal objectives, 72
Sogo Shosha (Japan), 405
Solomon, Jolie, 132
The Source, 91
Source (communication), 297
Southwest, 179, 182
Sovereign states, 394
Space productivity, 71
Sparks, Debra, 45, 293
Specialty media, 313
Specialty products, 230
Specification buying, 160
Specific duties, 403
Spiro, Leah Nathans, 62
Sports Authority, 167
Standard Industrial Classification Manual, 416
Standard Industrial Classification (SIC), 154, 416
Standard of living, 124

Standing orders, 412
Staples, 229
Starbucks Coffee Co., 230
Stars, 31
Stated question, 92–93
Statistical Abstracts of the United States, 87
Statistical hypothesis, 93
Statistical inferences, 102
Statistical information, 423–424
Stearns, Timothy M., 54
Steere, John, 132
Stern, Gabriella, 44
Stern, Louis W., 293
Stern, William M., 257, 293
Stimulated needs, 139
Stimulus interpretation, 141
Stimulus organization, 141
Stimulus reception, 141
Stimulus-response selling, 321
Stockholder dividends, 71
Stock-keeping units (SKUs), 224
Stodghill, Ron, II, 44, 332
Story completion tests, 97
Straight commission plan, 327
Straight rebuy, 158
Straight salary plans, 327
Strategic business plan
  described, 19, 26
Strategic business units (SBUs)
  BCG's matrix for, 331–33
  business opportunities of, 37–43
  divisional planning for, 19–20
  marketing goals of, 48–49
  marketing strategies of, 55–61
  organization portfolio of, 30–31
  SWOT analysis of, 49–55
  using GE's business screen, 33–35
Strategic marketing plan
  described, **47–49**
  marketing goals of, 48–49
  SWOT analysis of, 49–55
Strategic planning, 21
Strategic Planning Institute, 35
Strategic windows, 50
Strategy, 21
Strength, 50–52
Strengths, weaknesses, opportunities, and threats (SWOT), 20
Subcultures, 147, 364
Substitute competition, 167–168
SuDoc system, 415

Sullivan, R. Lee, 79, 215, 332, 371
Summarization procedures, 102
Supervalu, 39
Supervising, 326
Surface culture, 364
Suris, Oscar, 162
Survey of Current Business, 416
Survey method, 94
Survey research, 94
Survey sampling procedures, 98–99
Sviokla, John J., 22
SWOT analysis, 49–55
SWOT matrix, 53–55
Symonds, William C., 189
Synchronization of demand/supply, 384
Syncratic, 152
Syndicated marketing-intelligence services, 89
Systems competition, 171

Table of contents, 65
Taco Bell, 31, 171
Tactic, 21
Tactical planning, 21
TAG Heuer, 57, 272
Takeuchi, Hirotaka, 256
Talbots, 273
Tales from Margaritaville (Buffett), 220
Tambrands, 389
Tandy, 31
Tangible product, 221
Tangibles, 379
Targeted returns, 70
Target market, 207
Target marketing, 59, 207, 210
Target return, 342
Target return pricing, 344
Tariffs, 394, 403
Task definition, 153
Taylor, Alex, III, 44, 61, 371
Technical specialists, 318
Technology, 128–129
Tedlow, Richard S., 22
Teens, 112–113
Telephone interviews, 95
Temporal perspective, 153
Test marketing, 246, 251
Thematic apperception tests, 97
Thomas, Dan R. E., 379, 381
Thomas, Emory, Jr., 407
Thomas, Paulette, 162
Threats, 52–53

Three-level channel, 269
Timberland, 308
Time utility, 13
Time Warner, 40
Title page, 64
Total costs, 338
Total population, 111
**Total-product concept,
220–223, 401–402**
**Total quality management
(TQM), 234, 367**
Total Research Corp., 238
Toy, Stewart, 62
Toys 'R' Us, 167
Trademark, 236
Trade promotions, 330
Training, 326
Transactions, 10–13
Transfer price, 403
Transportation costs, 402–403
Transportation/logistics
associations, 431
Travel associations, 436–437
Treacy, Michael, 44, 256, 353
Treece, James B., 44
Trial close, 323
Tropicana, 38, 40
Troy, Leo, 423
Tully, Shawn, 61, 131
Two-level channel, 268
Two-way stretch, 241

U-Haul, 183
Unaided recall test, 316
Underemployment, 117
**Undifferentiated marketing,
209–210**
Unemployment, 117
Uniform Commercial Code, 263
Uniform delivery pricing, 350
Unique selling proposition, 311
United Airlines, 179, 182
University Microforms
International (UMI), 411
Unsought products, 230–231
Updike, Edith Hill, 408
Upper-lower class, 150
Upper-middle class, 149
Upper-upper class, 149
UPS, 13
Upward stretch strategy, 241
Urban, Glen L., 252
Usage occasion, 203
Usage rate, 203
Usage regularity, 203

USAir, 179
User, 151, 158
User status, 203
U.S. Industrial Outlook, 416
Uttal, Bro, 62

VALS 2 System, 199, 203
Value
  actual/perceived, 177
  described, 12–13, 119
  payment flow remuneration
  of, 263–338
  price and, 336–338
  See also **Products**
Value analysis, 160
Values (personal), 119
Value statement, 29
Vanguard, 243, 244
Variability, 377
Variable costs, 338–339
Vendor-based pricing, 346
Vendor identification, 160
Vendor relations, 69–70
Ventritex, 129
Verbal feedback channels, 297
Verbal hypothesis, 93
Vertical competition, 170–171
Vertical conflict, 282
Vertical integration, 39
**Vertical Marketing Systems
(VMSs), 289–292**
Vertical organization, 359–360
Vertical price fixing, 340
VF Corp., 259
Videologs, 328
Videotex, 329
Virgin Atlantic Airways, 177
VISA, 384
Vision statement, 29–30
Volatile demand, 156
Vulnerability, 54

Wadekar, Sunita, 407
Waldman, Peter, 130
Walker, Orville C., Jr., 188
Wall Street Journal Index, 419
Wal-Mart, 30, 38, 169, 179, 259
Walsh, Matt, 44, 188, 371, 406
Walt Disney Studio, 239
Ward, Judy, 132, 257
Warner, Fara, 332
Warner, Joan, 131
"Warranty of title," 263
Washington Bullets, 351
Weakness, 52

Weber, Joseph, 188, 292
Webster, Frederick E., Jr., 16–17,
22, 215
Weight Watchers International,
203
Weinberg, Charles B., 176
Wendy's, 171
Wetterau, 39
Whalen, Jeanne, 332
Where and how decision, 139
Where is Joe Merchant? (Buffett),
220
Whirlpool Corporation, 52
Wholesaling/distribution
associations, 437
Wiersema, Fred, 44, 256, 353
Wife dominant, 152
Williamson, Debra Aho, 333
Willingness to buy, 11
Windstar minivan version, 68
Winer, Russell S., 166, 187
Winett, Ruth, 104
Winn Dixie, 182, 239
Woodruff, David, 79, 188, 353
Woodside, Arch G., 292
Word association tests, 97
Working class, 149
Working women, 114
W.R. Grace & Co., 52

Xerox, 185

Yang, Dori Jones, 132, 293
Yellow zone, earnings management and selective investment, 34–35
Young & Rubicam, 317
Young, David, 131
Yves-Saint Laurent, 351

Zegna, Ermenegildo, 13
Zeithamal, Valarie A., 406
Zellner, Wendy, 44, 188, 292
"Zero defections" goal, 18
Zikmund, William G., 132
Zinn, Laura, 44, 61, 131, 215
Zizzo, Deborah, 293
Zone pricing, 350
Zwmke, Ron, 406